Reading Putnam

B

Reading Putnam

Edited by Peter Clark and Bob Hale

BLACKWELL
Oxford UK & Cambridge USA

Copyright © Basil Blackwell Ltd 1994, 1995

First published 1994
Reprinted 1995
First published in paperback 1995

Blackwell Publishers Inc.
238 Main Street
Cambridge, Massachusetts 02142
USA

Blackwell Publishers Ltd
108 Cowley Road
Oxford OX4 1JF
UK

Library of Congress Cataloging-in-Publication Data
Reading Putnam / edited by Peter Clark and Bob Hale.
    Includes bibliographical references and index.
        ISBN 0–631–17907–0 (hbk) — ISBN 0–631–19995–0 (pbk)
        1. Putnam, Hilary.   I. Clark, Peter, Ph.D.   II. Hale, Bob.
    III. Series.
    B945.P87R43   1994
    191—dc20   93–37348
                                                    CIP

British Library Cataloguing in Publication Data
A CIP catalogue record for this book is available from the British Library

Typeset in 10½ on 12 pt Ehrhardt
by Graphicraft Typesetters Ltd., Hong Kong
Printed and bound in Great Britain by
Hartnolls Limited, Bodmin, Cornwall

This book is printed on acid-free paper

Jacket photograph of Hilary Putnam by Toby Bornstein.

Contents

Contributors

SIMON BLACKBURN is Edna J. Koury Distinguished Professor of Philosophy at the University of North Carolina, Chapel Hill, and Adjunct Professor at the Australian National University. He is the author of *Spreading the Word* (Oxford University Press, 1984) and the collection *Essays in Quasi-Realism*. (Oxford University Press, 1993).

GEORGE BOOLOS is Professor of Philosophy at the Massachusetts Institute of Technology. He is currently Vice-President of the Association for Symbolic Logic and an editor of the Journal of Symbolic Logic. His books include *The Unprovability of Consistency* (Cambridge University Press, 1979), *The Logic of Provability* (Cambridge University Press, 1993), and *Computability and Logic*, with Richard C. Jeffrey (Cambridge University Press, 1974, 1980, 1989). He edited *Meaning and Method: Essays in Honor of Hilary Putnam* (Cambridge University Press, 1992).

MICHAEL DUMMETT is Wykeham Professor of Logic Emeritus in the University of Oxford. His major publications include *Frege Philosophy of Language* (Duckworth, 1973, 1981, 1986, 1990), *Truth and Other Enigmas* (Duckworth, 1978), *The Interpretations of Frege's Philosophy* (Duckworth, 1981), *The Logical Basis of Metaphysics* (Duckworth, 1991), *The Principles of Intuitionism* (Oxford University Press, 1977), *Frege and Other Philosophers* (Oxford University Press, 1991) and *Frege Philosophy of Mathematics* (Duckworth, 1991).

CLARK GLYMOUR is Alumni Professor of Philosophy at Carnegie Mellon University and Adjunct Professor of History and Philosophy of Science at the University of Pittsburgh. He is the author of *Theory and Evidence*

(Princeton University Press, 1980), *Discovering Causal Structure*, with R. Scheines, P. Spirtes, and K. Kelly (Academic Press, 1987), *Thinking Things Through* (MIT Press, 1992), *Causation, Prediction and Search*, with P. Spirtes and R. Scheines (Springer Lecture Notes in Statistics, 1993), and is the co-editor of volumes on foundations of physics, holistic medicine, and, with K. Kelly, of *Logic, Computation, and Discovery* (Cambridge University Press, forthcoming).

MICHAEL HALLETT is Associate Professor of Philosophy at McGill University, Montreal. He is the author of *Cantorian Set Theory and Limitation of Size* (Clarendon Press, 1984), and is currently writing a book on the foundational work of David Hilbert.

CORY JUHL is Assistant Professor of Philosophy at the University of Texas, Austin.

KEVIN KELLY is Associate Professor of Philosophy at Carnegie Mellon University. He is the author, with C. Glymour, R. Scheines, and P. Spirtes, of *Discovering Causal Structure* (Academic Press, 1987), and of a number of papers on learning theory and philosophy of science. His forthcoming book, *The Logic of Reliable Inquiry*, presents a systematic investigation of implications of learning theoretic frameworks. He is the editor, with C. Glymour, of *Logic, Computation, and Discovery* (Cambridge University Press, forthcoming).

HILARY PUTNAM is Walter Beverly Pearson Professor of Mathematical Logic and Professor in Philosophy in Harvard University. Among his major publications in philosophy are *Philosophy of Logic* (Harper and Row, 1971), *Philosophy of Mathematics*, edited with Paul Benacerraf (Cambridge University Press, 1983), *Mathematics, Matter and Method* (Cambridge University Press, 1975), *Mind, Language and Reality* (Cambridge University Press, 1975), *Realism and Reason* (Cambridge University Press, 1983), *Meaning and the Moral Sciences* (Routledge and Kegan Paul, 1978), *Reason, Truth and History* (Cambridge University Press, 1981), *The Many Faces of Realism* (Open Court, 1987), *Representation and Reality* (MIT Press, 1988), *Realism with a Human Face* (Harvard University Press, 1990), and *Renewing Philosophy* (Harvard University Press, 1992).

MICHAEL REDHEAD is Professor of History and Philosophy of Science in the University of Cambridge. His book *Incompleteness, Nonlocality, and Realism* (Oxford University Press, 1987) was the winner of the 1988 Lakatos Award for an outstanding contribution to the philosophy of science.

THOMAS RICKETTS is Associate Professor of Philosophy at the University of Pennsylvania. He is the author of essays on Frege, early Wittgenstein, Carnap, and Quine.

DAVID WIGGINS is Professor of Philosophy at Birkbeck College, London. His published writings include *Identity and Spatio-temporal Continuity* (Blackwell, 1967), *Sameness and Substance* (Blackwell, 1980), and *Needs, Values and Truth* (Blackwell, 1987).

CRISPIN WRIGHT is Professor of Logic and Metaphysics at the University of St Andrews and James B. and Grace J. Nelson Professor of Philosophy at the University of Michigan. His books include *Wittgenstein on the Foundations of Mathematics* (Duckworth and Harvard University Press, 1980), *Frege's Conception of Numbers as Objects* (Aberdeen University Press, 1983) *Realism, Meaning and Truth* (Blackwell, 1987, 1993), and *Truth and Objectivity* (Harvard University Press, 1992).

Introduction

Peter Clark and Bob Hale

In the Martinmas term of 1990, Hilary Putnam delivered at the invitation of the Special Lectureship Committee of the University of St Andrews a series of ten Gifford Lectures under the title "Renewing Philosophy." To packed audiences, many of the members of which had travelled considerable distances to hear him, Putnam spoke, with characteristic forcefulness, clarity, and a remarkable combination of accessibility and depth, on an impressive range of issues of philosophical – indeed, general intellectual – concerns, ranging from quantum physics and its bearing upon the problems of free will and determinism, through technical issues in the philosophy of language, to fundamental questions concerning rationality, values, and religious belief. These lectures have since been published with the title *Renewing Philosophy* by Harvard University Press in 1991. There was never any question but that the opportunity afforded by Putnam's presence in St Andrews for the greater part of that term was far too good to be missed. Accordingly, an international conference devoted to his philosophy was arranged to coincide with the conclusion of his Gifford Lectures. The conference took place in the Old Union Diner, St Andrews, on 23–6 November 1990, with papers presented by Simon Blackburn, George Boolos, Michael Dummett, Michael Hallett, Kevin Kelly, Michael Redhead, Thomas Ricketts, David Wiggins, and Crispin Wright. Hilary Putnam was present at all the sessions and made extensive impromptu comments.

The present volume includes all nine papers presented at that conference. They are included here, not in the order they were delivered at the conference, but in alphabetic order by contributor's name. Between them, they cover a good range of major philosophical issues to which Putnam has made, over the years, substantial and highly influential contributions. Perhaps the most conspicuous omission – which we regret but could not, in the event, avoid – is any systematic discussion of his work in the philosophy of mind. Putnam subsequently prepared a series of written replies of varying length to most but not all of the papers, based on his contributions made at the time to the sessions in which the papers were delivered and later reflection on the final versions of the papers. These, besides speaking to the specific issues raised in the conference papers, constitute a valuable new source of illumination not only of his own current position on the various issues but of the issues themselves. These replies and comments are included in the last chapter of this volume. We have made no attempt to summarize Putnam's contributions here, as we feel it best to leave Putnam to speak for himself.

If there has been a dominant theme in Putnam's work over the last decade or so, it must surely be his advocacy of internal realism. Getting to grips with this position is, Simon Blackburn argues in his 'Enchanting Views', no straightforward task. Arguably, our understanding of it can be no better than our understanding of what it is intended to be contrasted with – facile versions of relativism on the one side, and external or metaphysical realism on the other. Blackburn explores these contrasts and finds them less palpable than Putnam's explanations of them might encourage us to suppose. What characterizes the metaphysical realist, according to Putnam, is commitment to a traditional realist notion of truth, the marks of which are "Correspondence, Independence, Bivalence, and Uniqueness." Taking it, Blackburn argues, that the first three of these features can be given "hygienic, non-metaphysical" explanations of a kind with which Putnam should have no quarrel, Blackburn largely concentrates attention on the last – uniqueness, or the idea that the metaphysical realist position involves a distinctive commitment to there being "one true theory."

At first sight, argues Blackburn, such a view might appear to be incompatible with the idea of a determinate ontology and a conventional identity relation and as such exclude one possible form of internal realism. However, he sees this as illusory, for the realist, of whatever sort, can always draw the distinction so that nothing which is genuinely conventional by his or her lights is determined by the ontology. Thus, Blackburn argues, this commitment to uniqueness too is one which a realist of any sort – even an internal realist – ought to acknowledge. Similarly he argues that internal realism is no better placed than metaphysical realism over the issues of semantic determinacy and the model theoretic arguments. If they work against the latter view then they work equally well against the former. Finally he contrasts Putnam's internal realism with his own quasi-realist thesis, which he asserts is not a perspectival view, but one which seeks to resolve the inconsistency between the natural and the normative by showing how the latter can be explained and justified in terms acceptable within the former.

In his chapter entitled "1879?" George Boolos takes up two characteristic themes of Putnam's writings on logic and mathematics (to which of course he made so salient a contribution in the resolution, along with Martin Davis, Julia Robinson and Yuri Matiyasevich, of Hilbert's tenth problem). The first theme is where to draw the line between logic and set theory or mathematics proper, and the second, which is intimately connected with the first, is just how important the year 1879 (the year of the publication of Frege's *Begriffs-schrift*) was in the history of logic, for what logical achievements, Boolos asks, in the work of Boole, Peirce, Dedekind, and Hamilton had preceded it?

Famously, Quine argued that second-order logic is really set theory in disguise and that logic is exhausted by first-order quantification theory. In his *Philosophy of Logic* Putnam challenged this view and has returned to the issue often, most recently in his paper "Peirce the Logician." He now holds that we should count second-order universal quantifications of valid first-order schemata, but only those as, logical truths. But this, Boolos argues, will let in as logical truth either too much or too little. It will let in too much if we want to regard as logically valid statements to the effect that certain inferences are logically valid, in particular ones involving the ancestral relation. For then, as Boolos shows, we will have to regard certain Π_2 sentences as logically valid and thus violate Putnam's constraint. It will, however, let in too little if we accept the constraint, for then – Boolos argues – certain plainly logical modes of reasoning will fail to count as such.

The second part of Boolos's paper is devoted to what he sees as the central claim of Putnam's "Peirce the Logician" (this paper is reprinted in Putnam's (1990) *Realism with a Human Face*, ed. James Conant, Cambridge, MA: Harvard University Press) that great achievements were made in logic before 1879. This claim Boolos strongly endorses. He provides a highly informative discussion of an axiomatization of arithmetic due to Peirce and a near-equivalent of the ancestral relation due to Dedekind produced a few years before 1879. However, it is the year 1858 that Boolos regards as most plausibly the year in which logic became a great subject, for it was then that Dedekind discovered, using the method of cuts of the rationals, a rigorous proof of the theorem that every bounded increasing function on the reals approaches a limit. He draws out a close comparison between Dedekind's proof of the completeness of the real numbers introduced by cuts in the rationals (every real number corresponding to a cut where completeness holds in the sense that every cut in the reals is produced by a real) and the failure of what Boolos regards as a similar attempt at a completeness proof by Frege, this time for extensions – these latter being the unique correspondents of concepts introduced using Basic Law (V) of the *Grundgesetze*. Whereas repeating Dedekind's construction over the reals as opposed to the rationals produces no new reals, repeating

Frege's construction over a domain automatically produces a new extended domain, since no domain can contain all of the objects corresponding to the concepts definable over it. Boolos ends his chapter with a speculation based on the comparison he has elicited between the methods of Dedekind and Frege as to why the latter accepted the deadly Basic Law (V).

Michael Dummett's chapter, "Wittgenstein on Necessity: Some Reflections," like Blackburn's, bears upon Putnam's internalism, and concludes in qualified agreement with it. Dummett returns to issues he discussed some thirty years ago, in "Wittgenstein's Philosophy of Mathematics" (*Philosophical Review*, LXVIII, 1959, 324–48). In that paper, Dummett interpreted Wittgenstein as maintaining an extreme form of conventionalism about necessity – "radical conventionalism" – according to which, in effect, each necessary statement is so simply because we decide to treat it as such. He offers a new defence of this interpretation, the central component of which is focused on Wittgenstein's key thesis that a proof supplies a new criterion for the concept(s) involved in its conclusion. In seeking to interpret this thesis, we seem to confront an insuperable dilemma. We may easily give what Dummett calls a banal interpretation, compatible with the assumption that the new criterion will always agree with the old criteria: whenever we apply the new criterion correctly, we should have been justified by the old criteria in making the assertion that we do, even if we had failed to notice this. But this merely reinstates modified conventionalism by making the validity of the new criterion a consequence of the old. To get a non-platitudinous interpretation, it appears we must somehow construe it as claiming it to be possible that there be an apparent counter-example to the theorem proved which could not be recognized as merely apparent on the basis of the old criteria – but it appears impossible to do so without lapsing into incoherence. But the dilemma, Dummett now suggests, is – on Wittgenstein's view at least – a false one: both horns assume, in effect, that there is a fact of the matter about e.g. which plane figures are elliptical, quite independently of what we treat ourselves as having reason to say. Wittgenstein's view, according to Dummett, is that we can and should reject this assumption. We may then agree that what a proof does is to secure acceptance of a new criterion as being justified by the old criterion – but without thinking that, independently of our acceptance of the proof, it is a fact that the new criterion agrees with the old one, and so without reinstating modified conventionalism.

Going on to the offensive, Dummett argues that this resolution of the dilemma comes at too high a price, namely "full-blown internalism." This contrasts with more moderate internalism of the kind advocated by Hilary Putnam, which identifies truth with what we should eventually arrive at were we to commit nothing that was a mistake by our lights. Dummett takes this to involve a substantial concession to externalism, because it assumes there to be a fact of the matter about what we should believe, were we to make no mistakes, and this is something which, in the nature of the case, we cannot always know. Wittgenstein's commitment to extreme internalism comes out, Dummett claims, in his saying, of a calculation that we have not made and never will make, that it is wrong to say that God knows what its result would have been, had we carried it out – because there is nothing for God to know. This is because, on Wittgenstein's view, it is only our doing the calculation and "putting it in the archives" that constitutes its result as being what is obtained by doing it correctly. In the case where the calculation is an ordinary addition, this involves maintaining either that it is not determinate, until someone actually does it, what would count as performing one of the ingredient steps correctly – such as adding 7 and 8 – or that, while it is determinate what would count as performing each ingredient step correctly, it is not determinate what the outcome of some sequence of such steps should be. So much, Dummett claims, is what comes from "an un-flinching application of Wittgenstein's ideas about rules." Since he finds the conclusion incredible, he concludes that "the 'rule-following considerations' embody a huge mistake." The mistake, he suggests, lies with the general in-ternalist premise that there is nothing to truth beyond our acknowledgement of it. This premise is required, he contends, to get us from Wittgenstein's correct claim that in the fundamental case there is nothing by which we judge something to be a correct application of a rule, to the conclusion that, if we never in fact apply the rule in a particular case, there is nothing which would have been a correct application. The principal conclusions of this rich and wide-ranging discussion are that the validity of deductive inferences is indeed something which we discern, rather than impose (as on a conven-tionalist account), and that while an extreme externalism is no more defensible that full-blown internalism, some concession to externalism is required, if our practice of deductive inference is have any point or justification.

Michael Hallett's contribution is devoted to a critical analysis of two model-theoretic arguments which Putnam has deployed to great effect in many of his recent arguments against metaphysical realism and for internal realism. They are the permutation argument and the Skolem argument, or more accurately the Downward Löwenheim–Skolem Theorem. Hallett sees both these arguments as presenting something of an epistemological circle. They purport to show that there is an ineliminable circle in the way language is tied to the world if the metaphysical realist's view of how that tie is made is true. Since there is no such circle the metaphysical realist's account must be false.

According to Hallett the circle arises because metaphysical realism involves three claims: first that there is a unique, language-independent world, second that there is a unique reference function which takes terms of our language into objects or kinds of objects in the world, and third that given the unique reference function there is a set of truths about the world expressible in our language determined by that reference function. But, argues Hallett, the purpose of the model theoretic arguments is to show that no *one* component can be determined without first determining the other two. Hallett provides a very careful account of the necessary model theory which lies behind Putnam's use of the permutation and Löwenheim–Skolem arguments to establish the existence of the circle. However, Hallett argues that the model theoretic arguments are to some extent misplaced, because models are really set theoretic structures and the most that the model-theoretic arguments could show is that the notion of set cannot be entirely separated from set *theory*. The metaphysical realist begins with the idea that the world is an entirely theory–language-independent entity or collection, so the model-theoretic arguments do no more than exhibit a relativism about truth and reference for theory-dependent entities; so they do not satisfy the key assumption of the metaphysical realist that the world is *theory*-independent.

Nevertheless, as Hallett sees it, this cannot diffuse the core thrust of Putnam's argument, for his target was the moderate version of realism which asserts that the axioms of set theory have a privileged status, that of characterizing the conceptual core of the notion of set. These constitutive principles embodied in the axioms need not be exhaustive, in the sense that new principles might be found which, for example, might refine our concept of set sufficiently to naturally decide the continuum hypothesis. This view is certainly a realist one for facts about sets are precisely given by the consequences of the axioms. However, the consequence relation is entirely determinate and given by logic. It is utterly unaffected by matters of accessibility, decidability, or any other form of epistemic constraint. This form of moderate or conceptual realism about sets is certainly distinct from the metaphysical realist's account but it must be deeply vulnerable to the issue of the relativity of set theoretic notions, that is, the argument to the effect that axioms cannot characterize the concept of set in its intended interpretation. But if they cannot, to ask Putnam's question, what can?

This raises the important question of the real significance of the Skolem "paradox" in the history and philosophy of set theory, and it is to this issue that the remaining part of Hallett's chapter is devoted. There he gives a careful analysis of the history and conceptual evolution of the problem that the Skolem "paradox" raises in the philosophy of set theory, in particular the crucial but often overlooked connection between that result and the notions of absoluteness and impredicativity. Finally he identifies two theses in the treatment of the relativity of set theoretic notions. The first is the thesis of individual specification – that is to say the claim that a set cannot be said to exist unless there is a predicative specification of all of its potential members. This thesis – which he attributes to Poincaré and which is clearly an extreme form of theory dependence for sets – is not satisfied by classical set theory (ZF). The second is the weaker thesis that a set cannot be said to exist unless there is a specification of it. The profound question which is raised by Hallett's analysis is: to what extent does classical set theory's rejection of the individual specification thesis commit us to a metaphysical realist view of set theory? To what extent would we then be committed to the view that there is a universe of sets which set theory attempts to describe, a view which would run immediately up against the Skolem paradox in an unequivocal form, as Putnam rightly saw?

At the Gifford Conference Kevin Kelly presented a paper examining very important work undertaken in the early sixties by Putnam and Mark Gold on the logical foundations of learning theory and its connection with reliabilist theories of knowledge. This volume contains an expanded version of this paper by Kelly, Cory Juhl, and Clark Glymour. This contribution examines the relation between Putnam's earlier views on limiting reliabilism and the theses of Putnam's later work on internal realism. The fundamental idea which the authors exploit in a systematic way is Putnam's foundational insight on the strong link between inductive methods and computation.

The first part of their chapter, which as a whole is certainly a methodological tour de force, develops in modern computational terms Putnam and Gold's early insights into the mathematical structure of inductive methods (in particular Putnam's diagonalization argument) and his criticism of Carnap's probabilistic inductive logic, and they show that such methods are embeddable in the well-known structure of the arithmetical hierarchy. The second and third parts of the paper examine the consistency of Putnam's analysis of the computational structure of inductive inference with his later claims concerning the conception of truth as idealized acceptability and his espousal of a moderate relativism, to the effect that truth is dependent upon conceptual framework. They find, by deploying a Putnam-type diagonal argument, that any reasonable methodological substitute for truth cannot be both consistent and complete; some form of incompleteness or "gappiness" is *bound* to arise. Once again they are able to embed various notions of reliable hypothesis assessment within the structure of the arithmetic hierarchy by establishing a representation theorem. In the concluding sections of their chapter the authors discuss how reliabilism survives relativism in varying degrees of severity. Surprisingly they are able to show that even with very strong notions of theory-ladenness and incommensurability, a form of convergent reliabilism survives and, in particular, that a number of often-vaunted claims to the effect that methodological nihilism follows immediately from relativism and incommensurability simply do not hold.

Two central concerns characterize Putnam's work in the philosophy of physics, upon which he, like his teacher Hans Reichenbach, has had a seminal influence. They are understanding the scientific revolutions produced by the theory of relativity, and quantum mechanics. Michael Redhead's paper is devoted to the evolution and development of Putnam's views on quantum mechanics and in particular on the foundational programme called "quantum logic." Redhead examines the radical changes in Putnam's analyses of the two–slit experiment from his view in the late 1950s that three-valued logic was needed to interpret the two–slit experiment, as Reichenbach had argued, to his key idea some ten years later that it would be possible to remove the air of paradox associated with realist interpretations of quantum mechanics by employing a bivalent but non–distributive logic, this latter being a natural reading of the underlying Hilbert space representation of quantum theory. He then considers the evolution through the 1970s of Putnam's account of exactly how, using a non–distributive lattice, the two–slit experiment is to be understood.

Redhead argues that this evolution was guided by Putnam's rejection of the view that knowing simultaneous values for incompatible observables would be impossible because it would amount to knowing a contradiction. Redhead then analyses Putnam's positive argument, based on a thought experiment discussed in his 1981 paper "Quantum Mechanics and the Obsever," for the claim that one can simultaneously know the values of incompatible observables, and suggests that this argument is successful only if one has already agreed to deploy quantum logic in deriving the conclusion. This result – that no reason, independently of the prior acceptance of quantum logic, has been given by Putnam for his conclusion about knowing simultaneous values for non–commuting observables – Redhead regards not as a flaw in Putnam's reasoning, but as an exhibition of the implicit consistency of Putnam's whole approach to the problem of interpreting the two–slit experiment and the foundational program of quantum logic.

Thomas Ricketts's essay is a sustained analysis of Rudolph Carnap's *The Logical Syntax of Language* and in particular of the role that the principle of tolerance plays in that work. Central to Ricketts's essay is the claim that *Logical Syntax* cannot be understood as a combination of conventionalism for logic and mathematics and radical empiricism for the language of science.

He argues that the basic core of the work is immune from the criticisms leveled against it by Gödel and subsequently by Putnam and Friedman. Gödel, Ricketts claims, misunderstands Carnap's philosophy of mathematics. He does so by regarding Carnap as taking the analytic sentences of a language adequate for science to be conventionally stipulated syntactic rules, which are contentless, and allow for inference, mathematics, and meaning postulates within the language while the truth values of synthetic sentences are fixed by the facts. Gödel, given this view of Carnap's programme in *Logical Syntax*, then argues that the justification in terms of conservativeness and consistency of such a set of syntactic conventions (for example, a proof that the consequences of analytic sentences are themselves always analytic) would require, by virtue of his own second theorem, the deployment of mathematics comparable in strength to the mathematics the conventions are intended to introduce. Clearly no such a justificatory procedure could be other than viciously circular. However, Ricketts argues that this ignores the role of the principle of tolerance.

Now Putnam had already pointed out that, on one reading at least, the principle of tolerance could not possibly be used to rescue the distinction between the analytic and synthetic, a distinction fundamental to empiricist epistemology. The reason he adduces is that the argument that there can be no question of fact concerning the representational adequacy of a language, which is the essence of the principle of tolerance, itself hinges upon an empiricist claim, namely the verification principle. Thus it seems that Carnap's radical empiricist programme is riddled with circularity. These charges Ricketts seeks to rebut.

He argues against the Gödel–Friedman objection that they misunderstand the principle of tolerance as a principle rather than as a proposal. Understood in the latter fashion, the only questions that can be asked legitimately concerning a formal language are questions concerning the purposes for which the language was introduced. It may well be that matters of consistency are important for such purposes and it may well be that the mathematics needed to answer such questions is more powerful than the system of syntactic rules being studied, but this, Ricketts argues, would only be an objection to Carnap if we believed that the rules were meant to be responsible to some language-independent truth. But that there is no language-independent distinction between convention and fact is precisely the core idea behind Carnap's proposal. Similarly, Ricketts argues, in the case of Putnam's objection that the principle of tolerance requires the verification principle, the argument only works against Carnap if we think of the principle of tolerance as a thesis in the market for truth, rather than as a proposal as to what philosophical characterization and elucidation can, at best, consist in.

We very easily suppose that Putnam's well-known treatment of natural kind words is in head-on collision with any account of the meaning or understanding of such words in terms of Fregean conceptions of sense and reference. Putnam himself does little to discourage us from such a view – quite the reverse: by presenting his positive view as sharply contrasted with the orthodoxy that meaning or intension determines reference or extension, he leaves us with the impression that we have no option but to jettison the Fregean framework. The principal thesis of David Wiggins's illuminating contribution, "Putnam's Doctrine of Natural Kind Words and Frege's Doctrines of Sense, Reference, and Extension: Can They Cohere?," is that Putnam's insight into the functioning of natural kind words is, some appearance to the contrary notwithstanding, quite consistent with Frege's doctrine. The Fregean claim that sense determines reference need not, he suggests, be understood as implying the priority of sense; it can be construed so as to cohere with the idea that the sense of a proper name is object-invoking, and that of a natural kind word extension-invoking. On Wiggins's preferred account, a name has sense "by somehow presenting its object," this way in which the name presents its object – what he dubs a "conception" of the object – being a body of information in which the object itself plays a special role. And in an analogous way, a predicate has sense by presenting the (Fregean) concept it stands for in a certain way – by being linked to a certain conception of that concept. In general, coming to understand a predicate is a matter of coming to know what it takes for something to be what that predicate stands for (e.g. what it takes for a thing to be blue, or a pencil). Natural kind terms are then to be seen as a special case, where coming to know what it takes for something to be e.g. a lemon requires exposure to the extension of the term.

The notorious "brain-in-a-vat" hypothesis has by now a well-established place in contemporary epistemologists' discussions of skepticism about the external world, where it standardly appears as a modern-dress variation on Descartes's malicious-Demon hypothesis. The thought, familiarly enough, has been that, if we are to have the knowledge, or justified belief, about the external world of which we normally take ourselves to be capable, we must somehow show either that the possibility the hypothesis apparently expresses can justifiably be discounted, or that we need no assurance that the skeptical possibility goes unrealized, if our ordinary claims to knowledge or justified belief are to be upheld. The primary focus of Putnam's discussion of the hypothesis, in the early pages of *Reason, Truth and History*, is, however, ontological or metaphysical, rather than epistemological: on a metaphysical realist view, he contends, the hypothesis (or more precisely, a certain generalized version of it) ought to express a live possibility –

his argument to the conclusion that it is necessarily false, because thinkable only if false, is thus an argument against metaphysical realism. Crispin Wright's contribution provides a searching study of Putnam's purported proof that we cannot be brains in a vat, arguing that, several plausible counter-moves notwithstanding, it does indeed constitute "a transcendental argument which works." He differs from Putnam, however, over just how much the argument can be taken to establish: first as regards epistemological skepticism and second – coming closer to Putnam's central concern – over its capacity to undermine metaphysical realism.

There is no doubt at all that, like the Gifford Lectures themselves, the Gifford Conference was a great success. This was due not only to the efforts of the conference speakers, the chairmen of session, and participants, but also to the delightful attitude both personal and intellectual of Putnam himself. It might have been thought that the experience of delivering ten public lectures over five weeks to packed houses with extra speaking and seminar engagements on the side would have left the Gifford lecturer exhausted. This, however, was clearly not the case, for Putnam contributed vigorously to every session. The only matter of regret as far as the organizers were concerned was that Ruth Anna Putnam, who had visited St Andrews earlier in the term, was not free to attend the conference, because of teaching duties.

The Gifford Conference on "The Philosophy of Hilary Putnam," which attracted some seventy visiting scholars to St Andrews, was made possible by financial grants from our publisher Blackwell Publishers, the Mind Association, the British Academy, and the University of St Andrews. We gratefully acknowledge their support, which was essential in bringing the conference about. We should also like to thank explicitly our chairmen of sessions. Given that the conference took place in term time, we should especially thank our colleagues in both our philosophy departments and our graduate students who helped so much in ensuring the smooth running of the conference. Our thanks should also be extended to the administrative and catering staff of the university, who took on the awkward task of servicing a large academic conference amid their other demanding term-time duties. Finally we should express our thanks to the Special Lectureship Committee of the University, whose enlightened stewardship of the bequest of Lord Gifford provided us with the opportunity of inviting to St Andrews one of the great philosophers of our time.

Peter Clark
Bob Hale

1 Enchanting Views

Simon Blackburn

1 An Orthodoxy

Doctrines combining something called "realism" with what then seems like a qualification – internal, perspectival, modest, immanent, anthropocentric, minimal – have been in the air for a long time. Kant is their forefather, although Descartes might also be mentioned. For although the project of pure enquiry, as Williams calls it, seems aimed at an absolute conception of knowledge, under pressure the ambitions seem to change. When Mersenne queries the connection between an idea being clear and distinct and its being true, Descartes replies, on behalf of "perceptions so transparently clear and at the same time so simple that we cannot ever think of them without believing them to be true:"

> What is it to us that someone may make out that the perception whose truth we are so firmly convinced of may appear false to God or an angel, so that it is, absolutely speaking false? Why should this alleged "absolute falsity" bother us, since we neither believe in it nor have even the smallest suspicion of it?[1]

And a little later he simply says that the evident clarity of our perceptions does not allow us to listen to anyone who makes up this kind of story. The problem, of course, is to present a view of the world that vindicates this bare confidence, and it is here that the combination of realism and a suitable modesty, a view acknowledging that the real world is "our world" or the "human" world, or a world-as-it-is for us, is such an attractive one. On the one hand we have the real world – the world of physics, or of maths, or of colour, beauty, and goodness – and on the other a frank awareness that any such reality is like a scene or a view: partly constituted by the lens of the viewer. Putnam is not alone, and not to be criticized, for being drawn to such a combination. In fact, some kind of perspectival realism is almost orthodox. A philosopher like Peter Strawson can counsel us to approach the free-will problem by reflecting that the perspective of physics is just one perspective; that of human agency another. A philosopher as different as Carnap could allow us the frank ontological assertions of set theory or physics, while reminding us of the not so frank and ontological, external, decision to adopt these languages or perspectives in the first place. Quine constantly counsels us to "work from within," and he and many others warn against the folly of trying to step outside our own skins, or adopt the position of cosmic exiles, or look for Archimedean points or dry docks giving us an external view of our conceptual boats. Quine also tell us to   s approach the problems of semantics by reflecting that while within the perspective of physics semantic facts are invisible, if we "acquiesce in a home language," truth, and perhaps meaning, become visible again. The response Kripke offers on behalf of Wittgenstein to the rule-following paradox has the same structure. But Quine and the Kripkean are half-hearted perspectivists, for they stay reluctant to attribute truth to the determinate intepretations of ourselves and others that we make. From a proper perspectivist's standpoint this reluctance is unnecessary – a false modesty, covering up the wrong place. The determinate attributions give us assertions, and the assertions are often true. They are true of the semantic world that we view through the practice of making them. A similar interpretation of Wittgenstein is possible. Many other philosophers, including Putnam, make the Berkeleyan move of restoring color, goodness, and beauty to the world by insisting that what is perspectival or relative to us about them is equally perspectival or relative to us in any alleged set of objective or primary properties with which they might have been contrasted.

So we are dealing with a central theme of modern philosophy, one to set alongside the post-Galilean scientific world view as the orthodox escape route from the problems of that view.[2] In what follows I shall not at all try to upset the orthodoxy, but I shall raise a number of questions about its exact effects. Putnam's handling of the orthodoxy includes a number strands   of that I shall not discuss, most notably the attack on old dichotomies (subjective vs. objective, projected vs. real). But by raising doubts about other elements of the view, I hope at least to make us pause when we reach for the Kantian solution to problems of reality and our access to it.

2   Identifying the Doctrine

The main problem with any kind of internal realism will be identifying the doctrine without falsifying the dependencies that, as a kind of realism, it will want to respect. In other words, two thoughts need balancing. The one is that many aspects of our world are independent of us; the other is that the world is somehow constituted by or dependent upon our conceptual scheme or point of view. It is extremely hard to do justice to both sides: perhaps the clearest example of this difficulty is attempting to frame Wittgenstein's anthropocentric view of mathematics without representing it as involving false or at best incredible views about the way in which procedures count as proofs only because of our choice and decision, We may want to go silent at this point, if we are where realism and idealism coincide, so far inside our boat that we can only show and not say that it is a boat at all. But Putnam presents internal realism as a distinct doctrine, or direction in which to find a doctrine, and it is this doctrine, and the work it can allegedly do, that I want to explore.

Perhaps then we ought to be able to locate it with the help of two bearings, a negative one and a positive one. Negatively, I want to highlight what it is not. It is not, in particular, to be vulnerable to the famous "model theoretic" argument that defeats "metaphysical realism." It is not involved with a "traditional metaphysical realist" notion of truth, with its associated ideas of "Correspondence, Independence, Bivalence, and Uniqueness."[3] On the other hand it is not a "facile" relativism.[4] In *Reason, Truth and History* it is not either a "cultural relativism," since there Putnam tells us that the dichotomy "either unchanging canons of rationality *or* cultural relativism" is one that he regards as outdated.

The *via negativa* will work only if we have a clear sense of the things that internal realism is not. Primarily this means being sure of what metaphysical realism is, on the one hand, and cultural relativism or facile relativism on the other. But this is not always easy. Consider the bearing from cultural relativism. I have mentioned Putnam's conviction that his doctrine stands apart from that. But in the later *Representation and Reality* this is not so clear, for although he still casts aspersions on cultural relativity, he does associate internal realism with what he calls "conceptual relativity," and since concepts are cultural objects – indeed the only means by which a culture can exercise its view of things – it is not clear why cultural relativity is such a bad thing.[5] Of course, it had better not be "facile," but there is no particular reason why it should be.

Far the most important point of contrast is metaphysical realism, which comes primarily, I believe, as an attempt to understand truth in a certain way. Putnam lists "Correspondence, Independence, Bivalence, and Uniqueness" as his set of diagnostics for a metaphysical realist understanding of truth. We could read whether a thinker believes truth has these properties; if it does, then he or she is saddled with a metaphysical realist understanding of it, and if it does not, then he or she is not. This would assimilate the situation to that conceived by Michael Dummett, in which adherence to a bivalent logic is a mark of a particular conception of truth, and one that is fairly straightforwardly detectable and might in principle be replaced by another. But for Putnam the issue is not so straightforward. Consider, for instance, his handling of the issue of the independence of truth and assertibility. Internal realism allows the independence we all like to claim. It allows that "whether a sentence is true is logically independent of whether a majority of the members of the culture *believe* it to be true."[6] This is allowed because it is not a philosophically weighted doctrine, but "simply a feature of our notion of truth." But now the ground begins to slip. For if this much independence is allowed for this reason, perhaps a similarly hygienic version of the other diagnostics might be allowed too. Correspondence? Well, there is nothing harmful about noticing that corresponding with the facts is a suitable synonym for "true;" it does not raise the theoretical temperature to acknowledge it as a dictionary definition (as William James, for one, insisted). Nor is it harmful to set up "trivial" disquotational T sentences, at least within a language. It can only be if correspondence is thought of in some particular way that the association is harmful – but then we need to know what the particular way is, and it will not help to be told that it is the metaphysically realist way, for that is what we were hoping to learn to identify. (I discuss in detail later the alleged model theoretic infirmities of correspondence.) Bivalence? Perhaps it is not a philosophically weighted doctrine, but simply "a feature of our notion of truth" that we practice as though a determinate proposition is either true or false.

I do not say that such a Wittgensteinian reminder of the actual features of our practice with the concept of truth is particularly attractive. A theorist might attempt not just to cite these features of our notion of true, but to explain them. And an explanation might present itself as genuinely, metaphysically, realistic, and be genuinely flawed because of that. Typically the trap will be attempting to step outside our own skins, and believing that we can mount an explanation of logic from a standpoint that cannot be occupied. The natural response is to retreat within, and that will mean sitting tight on the salient features themselves. Correspondence, independence, bivalence, and uniqueness then lose their status as diagnostics of one way or another of understanding truth, and become instead labels for aspects of our practice. In this chapter I am going to take it that bivalence, correspondence, and independence can be given hygienic, non-metaphysical explanations, of the kind Putnam himself provides for independence. If that is so, the only diagnostic for a metaphysical realist understanding of truth is uniqueness, and that is the feature I shall discuss.

Putnam is prone to characterize metaphysical realism as the view that there is one true theory: "there cannot be more than one complete and true description of Reality."[7] By comparison internal realism, while retaining various apparently realist trappings (independence, perhaps bivalence, perhaps trivialized correspondence) fully acknowledges that there can indeed be more than one complete and true description of reality. This accords with the metaphor of perspective with which I started: the main point of the metaphor must be that there can be more than one perspective on a particular state of affairs. Is this an opposition of which we can make good sense?

I suppose anything worth calling metaphysical realism might demand that there is one reality. Its constituents are debatable: a space–time continuum, physical inhabitants, perhaps more: possibilities or possible worlds, minds, classes, numbers, universals, and other disputed candidates. But why should realism demand that there is one true description? At first blush it might be like this: there is the one reality, and among its denizens are minds capable of representing the reality to themselves. There are, however, different ways of representing it: different minds may select different features, and some may select features which are either invisible or outrageously gerrymandered to others. So one reality can admit a plurality of descriptions. But this is no departure from metaphysical realism – just the addition of a sensible view about representation, according to which the way it is done will be partly a function of properties of the representing medium. Here the metaphysical realist turns the metaphor of perspective on its head. It is, surely, no departure from the idea of one spatial configuration of objects that the same configuration can be "represented" in an indefinite variety of reflecting media – represented not only it can be from different points, but also in mirrors of different curvature or through lenses of different focal length. It would be bizarre to demand of a realist about spatial configuration that he or she should admire "one true" perspective. Why is it any more sensible in the general case?

If it is more sensible I take it that the reason must be *concatenation*: if we learn that there is a true description of reality from one point of view, and another true description from another, then we must in principle be able to conjoin them, and enjoy the fact that reality can truly be described in way A, and truly be described in way B. There is no problem, provided, of course, that A and B are consistent. To stay with the spatial analogy, we can shift perspectives at will, adopting one position or one medium and then another position or another medium, and we rightly see no inconsistency between the one position and the other. From one position the chimney looks larger than the spire, and from the other the spire looks larger than the chimney.

The implication is that the realist can distinguish between insisting on "one true" perspective, which he or she has no motive to do, and insisting that the results of different perspectives need to be rendered consistent, and that when they are they can be concatenated. If, *per impossibile*, we could survey or accommodate all of them, then, like God, we would have a complete picture of reality. However, a realist, on this understanding, might even tread delicately when thinking about the possibility of concatenation. In the spatial case we cannot *simultaneously* enjoy the view in which the chimney is closer and looms larger, and the view in which the spire is closer and looms larger. It might be that there are different perspectives on the world for which the parallel obstacle is not merely temporal; where there is a principled difficulty about coupling their results even in an intellectual synthesis. First-person perspectives and temporal perspectives are clear candidates. If that were so, not all truth could be knowable by any one mind.

Again, however, it is difficult to be sure that this is a problem peculiar to realism. It amounts to maintaining that there are propositions that can be apprehended only from a point that it is not open to others to take up: local propositions, we could call them. On the face of it a realist can accommodate this: he or she just needs to point out that a fortiori there can be no inconsistency in the concatenation of local propositions, even if there is no single mind that can perform the concatenation.

Things would be different if the results of different perspectives were essentially incompatible, as they are not in the spatial case, at least from the standpoint of common sense. If, like Berkeley, we denied ourselves the resources to reconcile different perspectives, and to synthesize one reality upon which we have different points of view, then indeed we lose the one reality. But we also lose the notion of different perspectives, leaving ourselves only with a train of ideas with no shared content, and between which no questions of compatibility or incompatibility can arise.

There are puzzling features in Putnam's discussion of internal realism and the problem of inconsistent perspectives. In both *Representation and Reality* and *The Many Faces of Realism* he takes as his main example the different actual and possible ways in which a mereologist and a more orthodox subject might count the "objects" in a room. But he draws from this two rather extraordinary consequences. The first is that "so long as the meaning of 'object in the logical sense' is unspecified, the meaning of the quantifier is unspecified. So it looks as if *the logical connectives themselves have a variety of possible uses*" (Putnam's italics).[8] The second is that since this is so, "different statements – in some cases, even statements that are 'incompatible' from the standpoint of classical logic and classical semantics – can be true in the same situation because the words – in some cases the logical words themselves – are used differently."[9] But classically we do not draw the conclusion that quantifications using different predicates involve a different use of the logical connective. One who says there are seven thousand words in the book is not using a logical connective differently from one who says that there are two hundred pages. But if some bizarre view insisted on the opposite, perhaps as someone might insist that an indexical has different meaning when used for one thing or another, then in any case we do not get statements that are inconsistent from the standpoint of classical logic and semantics. A classical formalization of a language which allows shifting interpretations of one term will simply insist on associating different items from its lexicon with the different uses, precisely in order to avoid a gratuitous appearance of inconsistency. If we associate "Fa" with "this is a book" said of the book, we do not associate "−Fa" with "this is not a book" said of something else.

Of course, taken strictly, any classical philosophy can allow what Putnam says he wants: different and apparently incompatible statements can be true in the same situation because the words − in some cases, the logical words themselves − are used differently. That is, while "there are several philosophers in St Andrews" is true in English, there are possible languages in which the same sentence is false because "there are" is used to mean something else − "there are not," for example. Nobody ever denied that, surely, although we may insist that a better way of putting it is not in terms of statements, but in terms of the difference between uninterpreted and interpreted sentences, thereby avoiding the appearance that some difficulty for classical semantics has been produced.

The apparent inconsistency between the mereologist and the other is not very troubling if one is saying that there are seven "objects" in the room, and other that there are three. It may appear more troubling if one says that there is an object which is partly blue and partly red in the room, and the other says that there is no such object. Insisting that they use the word "object" differently is one way of reconciling the apparent dispute and saving the thought that they are both within their rights, or that (apart from any other difficulties) we can adopt either way of speaking. But that means precisely that we are finding the opinions consistent, so that we can have both. And the question of consistency is paramount, because it is the only reason a realist of any kind must allow to stand in the way of a concatenation of the results of different perspectives. If Putnam cannot make us see that we must allow genuinely inconsistent but "internally" true descriptions of things, then we have no reason to deny the uniqueness of truth, the last hallmark of metaphysical versus internal realism.

If the actual example puts no pressure on a classical explanation of the situation, we must dig deeper. One way of attacking metaphysical realism would be to find an internal inconsistency in it. A combination giving rise to such an inconsistency might be that of a determinate ontology, and an indeterminate or conventional identity relation. Thus we cannot both believe in a determinate, unique, mathematical ontology, containing numbers and sets, and also hold that whether we identify numbers and sets is a matter of convention. For either the ontology, which is not "up to us," has numbers as well as sets, in which case it would be a mistake to identify them, or it has only sets, in which case it would be a mistake to separate them. A determinate ontology takes away our freedom with identity; conversely, freedom with identity undermines the view that there is a determinate ontology.[10] Similarly, if we think it is up to us whether we identify everyday objects with mereological sums of their parts, we should not also think that ontologically it is determinate whether there are objects as well as parts.

The point is undeniable, but it is very unclear why a realist of any kind should be troubled by it. The contradiction of holding both that the identity of As and Bs is "up to us" and that it is not, because it is metaphysically determinate whether there are As as well as (i.e. not identical with) Bs, must indeed be avoided. But the means of avoidance are to hand: one draws the ontology so that nothing genuinely "up to us" is determined by it (for example, in the numerical case, by sticking with sets and construing arithmetic not as concerned with objects at all).

Now it is true that a typical conundrum about identity will ask how we identify one kind of thing (ships, persons through time, numbers) *given* the identity of others (parts, states, sets). Putnam can try insisting that *all* questions of identity are up to us. Metaphysical realism can either deny this, or retreat to the image of one dough and many "cookie cutters." Putnam wants the internal realist suggestion to be quite different; but his own explanation of the difference is not reassuring. Continuing the example of different choices of sortals under which to count things, he insists that the cookie-cutter metaphor *denies* rather than explains the phenomenon of conceptual relativity:

> The internal realist suggestion is quite different. The suggestion, applied to this very elementary example, is that what is (by commonsense standards) the same situation can be described in many different ways, depending on how we use the words.[11]

If this is the internal realist suggestion then surely we can all agree with it. But its distance from the metaphysical realist reading is not identified. For the point is that the example is precisely one where "by commonsense standards" we have the same situation, described in different ways. What we are not given is any help in understanding how much of the commonsense standard we are being asked to abandon, or why we should do so.

I conclude, then, that the excursus through identity has not actually enabled us to see why we should be prepared to abandon uniqueness as a desideratum of truth. I want to press this difficulty by highlighting a tension between the *image* behind internal or perspectival realism, and its supposed *consequences*, or the work it is actually intended to do in philosophy (the positive bearing). What I have in mind is this: the work intended is often, as in my examples at the beginning of the chapter, one of reconciliation. It is to make us content with each of two apparently conflicting points of view: the point of view of physics, and that of interpretation, for example, or that of determinism and that of freedom. Now reconciliation can certainly take the form of pointing out that an apparent conflict is only apparent because of different points of view. But such reconciliation does indeed imply seeing the inconsistency as only apparent. It requires that we take up a point of view whereby the original verdicts can be seen in their partiality. I can reconcile the view in which the spire is larger and the view in which the chimney is larger precisely because I can understand them for what they are: views from different places on one located object. But if I cannot do this, an apparent inconsistency remains a genuine inconsistency, and relativizing to points of view is an evasion. To see this, imagine an extended deception or conjuring trick. Suppose someone contrives two vessels, A and B, such that one prolonged and proper test – pouring liquid from one to the other, say – proves that A has greater volume than B, and another – measuring their displacement and the width of their walls – proves that B has greater volume than A. It would be utterly inadequate to rest content with the thought that from one point of view, or in the terms of one language or theory (that of amount held), A is larger than B, whereas from the other point of view (that of measurement) B is larger than A. What we would want is a story reconciling those points of view, and that means precisely showing how they *could* be just different perspectives on the one reality. To use Kant's words, unity is here set us as a task.

So I present a puzzle. Perspectival realism offers a framework within which to reconcile apparent conflict. But the reconciliation only takes place if inconsistency can be shown to be apparent, and that means obtaining a background, different conception of how things are, whereby the initial conflicting views can be seen as only apparently in conflict. If we lack this we are simply left with conflict, and unable to think how the different views can be related at all, or even count as views. But if we get it, then we have a third conception, and as far as that goes, having the further doctrine that this background conception is itself only a perspective plays no part at all. The reconciliation goes just as well if we stop at thinking just "This is how things are."

If it denies the imperative towards unity, "internal" realism may be a yet more radical doctrine than any that employs the image of different perspectives, precisely for this reason. Different perspectives need reconciling if they are to maintain their status as different views of the one reality. Suppose that internal realism does not see unity as set us as a task, and does not demand a reconciliation if what is given in one view is left genuinely inconsistent with what is given in another. In this it would be going far beyond, for example, the Copernican revolution or even the lesson of relativity theory, which is precisely that when different views appear to give different verdicts we are under an obligation to find a theory, or third view, explaining how the appearance of inconsistency came about, and how it can be transcended.

My own view is that we cannot be cavalier about unification without ending up treating our commitments not as beliefs at all, but as instrumental acceptances of a different kind. That is, I think it is plausible to hold that *the* criterion for treating acceptance of a theory as something other than belief would be a preparedness to ignore its conflict with other theories. Thus if I am an instrumentalist about theories of particles I can happily treat them as waves in one context and as particles in another, and if each instrument works in its own sphere, I need acknowledge no imperative of unity. But if I believe my descriptions to be worth believing, I incur the obligation. This need not be because of a prior metaphysical vision, but rather because beliefs gain their identity through what they exclude. To hold a belief at all is to incur an obligation to reject whatever falls in its exclusion zone. To show the force of that obligation I shall work through the central example: the model theoretic case for the indeterminacy of reference.

3 Quine: A Worked Example

We can sketch the doctrines, ultimately due to Quine, that give rise to the problem like this. We allow ourselves to think in terms of a certain totality. This is a base totality of physical facts, and of facts about a person's dispositions to assent or dissent, or other behavioral dispositions. We can include in the base totality the dispositions of others in the person's home community. We can include actual histories of nerve hits and sound productions. We can include anything non-intentional that we like: a total choreography of places and movements of all the things that there are in space. But we now find that reference is underdetermined by the base totality. That is, for any hypothesis that a term "rabbit" that the person uses refers to something (rabbits), there is a different hypothesis that the term refers to a proxy (rabbit parts, rabbit stages). So the first claim is that:

A The base totality does not determine whether (1) "rabbits" refers
to rabbits, or (2) "rabbits" refers to stages of rabbits. That is, each
of (1) and (2) is compatible with the same base totality.

The second claim is that:

B There is nothing else to make true either (1) or (2).

But the third claim is that:

C Relative to a translation manual or home language, we can assert
(1) as opposed to (2).

This final doctrine is supposed to alleviate the eliminativism, or loss
of meaning altogether, that seems to be a consequence of (A) and (B) by
themselves.

This structure is mirrored in Putnam, and with a little tailoring in Kripke's
Wittgenstein. Putnam's model theoretic argument generalizes the point
about rabbits: almost any set of sentences can be interpreted in almost any
domain, where the "almost" simply points to requirements of consistency
and size. The base totality does not determine which domain the subject's
sayings are to be interpreted in, so, again, it is only "within" a particular
scheme that we can see him or her as referring to rabbits and not almost
anything else we like. Kripke's argument takes the case of predicates and
functions rather than kind terms. But it wisely allows into the base totality
anything purely conscious that we care to add, where purely conscious
means non-intentional. We can add anything in the way of images, or
flashes of confidence, provided these are not supposed to be in any way self-
interpreting. The solution Kripke provides (but does not himself necessarily endorse) is that it is only in the verdict of others that "plus" means plus
and not quus. And just as Quine characterizes what goes on relative to a
scheme of translation as use of an "essentially dramatic" idiom, so in Kripke's
story the verdicts of the public, while assertible, lack strict truth or falsity.
Putnam's more thoroughgoing perspectivism enables him to insist that what
is generated within the internal perspective is indeed true or false.

The problem is this: how does relativization to a "translation manual" or
acquiescence in a "home language" help? How do we recover even a limp-
ing substitute for the truth of (1) or (2) by invoking such things? The
crucial question is whether anything they provide is to be found within the
base totality or not. Think of it like this: here are two possible worlds each
of which shares the base totality. In each of them, after consulting all the
relevant facts given by that totality, someone issues a verdict: "rabbits"

means rabbits. Each of them "acquiesces in this saying." But there is nothing to stop us from thinking that in the one possible world, the acquiescence was in a language or relative to a manual in which "rabbits" means rabbits, while in the other, it is acquiescence to a language or manual in which "rabbits" means rabbit parts. In fact, if the original argument was good, we *have* to think of it like that. The original thesis (A) is precisely the thesis that there could be two such extensionally identical, but intensionally inequivalent, possible worlds. The fact that the dispositions mentioned in the totality include dispositions to look up manuals, or acquiesce in the production of one mapping of words on to other words rather than another, makes no difference.

On the other hand, if the base totality included a manual, or "home language," with a determinate semantics, it could indeed mean (1) rather than (2). But we must ask exactly how it managed to acquire this determinate role: why is mention of it not just mention of an extra and mysterious intentional fact, a semantic determinacy galloping in from nowhere to effect a rescue? If the base totality includes so much, the argument for (A) simply could not have got started in the first place.

Stroud has detailed the way in which Quine struggles to avoid this dilemma.[12] In "Ontological Relativity" Quine raises the threatened *reductio*, that reference becomes nonsense not just in radical translation but at home, and attacks the problem by reminding us that we can only ask whether "rabbits" refers to rabbits "relative to some background language."[13] But then, obviously, we seem poised to raise the question of the determinacy of the background language: it is no good trying to anchor one free-floating term by attaching it to another equally free-floating term.[14] What stops the regress is described in a variety of ways: acquiescing in the mother tongue; staying aboard a home language and not rocking the boat; choosing as our manual of translation (for the home language) the identity transformation. But none of this solves the problem. Either we take talk of translation seriously, in which case we are on one horn of the dilemma: a manual linking words to words is something that is extensionally acceptable, is visible in the base totality, but leaves indeterminate any question of the reference of any of the words. Or we fall onto the other horn, as we do if we allow that there is such a thing as taking the words of the home language at face value, which means taking them determinately to do one thing rather than another. For that is a success that, according to the original thesis, cannot exist. It is a success described in an intensional idiom, and either it can exist or it cannot. We might reflect wryly that what is needed at this point is a good helping of use/mention indeterminacy, and this is exactly what Quine is giving us.

And what of Putnam? At first sight he seems to be in the same predicament. The crucial passage is this:

For an internalist like myself, the situation is quite different. In an internalist view also, signs do not intrinsically correspond to objects, independently of how those signs are employed and by whom. But a sign that is actually employed in a particular way by a particular community of users can correspond to particular object *within the conceptual scheme* of those users. "Objects" do not exist independently of conceptual schemes. We cut up the world into objects when we introduce one or another scheme of description. Since the objects *and* the signs are alike *internal* to the scheme of description, it is possible to say what matches what.[15]

The ingredient this adds to Quine's ineffective retreat to the home language is a dash of idealism. But how exactly does the idealism help? We should start by reflecting that if an object is within the conceptual scheme of a subject, its image under the proxy function will be so too. Quine's problem arose within his conceptual scheme, and that of his readers. Both rabbits and rabbit stages, plus and quus, are within my conceptual scheme. And then, Putnam's claim is only that signs can be employed in particular ways in communities so as to correspond to particular objects – that is, so as to refer determinately; which, if true, amounts to a simple denial of the indeterminacy thesis.

Perhaps this mistakes the intended effect of internal realism on the argument. One way of making reference determinate would be to reject the thought experiments altogether. Quine originally lured us into the problem by telling us to treat the "home" case exactly as we treat the problem of translation of a foreign tongue, where "we are always ready to wonder about the meaning of a foreigner's remarks."[16] The home case cannot be like this, not merely because a subject will as a matter of fact be unable to treat the meaning of "rabbits" as anything other than rabbits, but because he or she will inevitably be relying on an indefinite number of such determinacies in order to think at all. Here we come up against a limit to the possibility of stepping outside our own skins or adopting the position of the cosmic exile. The idea will be that only metaphysical realism encourages the fantasy that this position is even possible; by contenting ourselves with internal realism we avoid the fantasy. The idea will be to "divide the spoils": Quine's point remains that reference construed "transcendentally" vanishes into indeterminacy, but we can console ourselves by construing it "internally," according to trivial disquotations.[17]

I think this is a popular way of reading Quine and Putnam, and of allowing some plausibility in their position. But I find it inadequate. The crucial difficulty is that the base totality is insufficient *even to fix a perspective* in which a determinate interpretation exists. This is because *everything is the same* in the possible world in which the internal reading is one thing, and that in which it is another – or at least, everything extensional is the same, and the suggestion is not supposed to be that we invoke extra, non-supervening intensional determinacies. That is, a determinate perspective within which "rabbits" means rabbits is simply not a legitimate notion at this stage of the game. It is exactly as if some set of considerations made us lose our grasp of how such a thing as a determinate visual point of view is possible, and met the reply that within one determinate visual point of view we can identify others as possessing determinate visual points of view as well.

It may help in understanding this objection if I briefly rehearse some other reactions to the problem. One possibility is to qualify my remark above that rabbit stages or the quus function are as much within my conceptual scheme as rabbits or the plus function. While this is strictly true, it is also true that they have a highly derivative place within that scheme, only introducible as functions of the more primitive concepts.[18] There is a choice about our reaction to this point. One direction urges that we should attempt to see this as a parochial point about us and our actual priorities, easily imagined otherwise in different kinds of mind. This was the line that Goodman originally took about his bent color classifications, but it met strenuous, and I think proper, resistance on the grounds that we cannot intelligibly do the required imagining.[19] A different direction accepts that to us the asymmetries are absolute, but at the same time tries to insist that that is "Just as." It is sometimes thought that this is the true reaction of the later Wittgenstein to his own examples of bent rules: a kind of "transcendental internalism." If so, he is certainly at the point where realism and idealism coincide: the difficulty is that what is promised by the internalism (it is just us, just one perspective) is taken away by the absolutism (the "us" is transcendental: we cannot make sense of any other perspective).

In this chapter I do not want to assess the complex issue of whether the "straight" interpretations are ineliminably more primitive than the bent ones. If they are not then Putnam's passage misfires and the problem returns, for both bent and straight interpretations exist in our scheme. If they are, then that fact can play a part in a straight solution. We can find that one term is primitive relative to another, and this debars us from a translation or interpretation in which the complexity is reversed. This is an example of the general problem I posed for "perspectival" realism in the last section. That problem was that a reminder of separate perspectives could play no role in a reconciling project. For either we can adopt a view according to which the original conflict was only apparent, or we cannot, and in either case the thought that our view is only our view, our boat, or whatever plays no role. In the case of (A), (B), and (C) this means that we have three options. One is to bite the bullet, and say that it is not determinately true that by "rabbits" I refer to rabbits. This is semantic eliminativism, which

I shall not explore. The second is to stay within the framework Quine sets, but to find more constraints, so that if we take causal factors, or semantic complexities and asymmetries, into account, one mapping of words on to things stands out as the reference relation. A cognate line is to expand our conception of what can go into the base totality, but still within the Quinean framework. This is what McGinn attempts to do, for example, when in opposition to Kripke he urges that adding capacities instead of just dispositions dissolves the rule-following problem. We can then deny (A). I shall not here explore this either.

An increasingly popular third approach simply denies (B) by insisting that in addition to the extensional, base totality, we must acknowledge self-standing or additional facts of semantics. If skepticism about meaning is the alternative, then we must refuse to give the requisite authority to the base totality, and refuse to respect the problem of relating semantics to it. In various ways Stroud, McDowell, Boghossian, and Searle all take this line.[20] One could see Putnam as poised to adopt it, since the drift of his work is to refuse to grant especial ontological privilege to any particular kind of fact, and that would include facts from the base totality. But there is a cost.

The problem is not epistemological. Searle, for example, insists both that the first-person case is a rock on which Quine (and Davidson) founder, and that it illustrates knowledge of an intentional content which is not "conclusively testable" by objective or third-person means. He is quite right that for me the fact that I mean rabbits by "rabbits" is a Cartesian point, a sufficiently clear and distinct perception that if someone points out that it may be false to God or an angel I am entitled simply to shrug my shoulders. Not only is this true, but in a strange way it is a presupposition of the whole problem that it is true. The reason is that I have to be standing upon my own understanding of the different interpretations offered even to understand the possibility of indeterminacy, and no sound argument that requires me to do this can conclude that it is actually something I cannot do. This is doubtless correct, but a reminder that our epistemology must be liberal enough to accommodate it is idle. For the real difficulty is not epistemological, but ontological. For Quine appears to put into the base totality everything we could possibly want in order to determine reference and meaning. If we say he did not, then we are making an ontological claim. We are denying that semantics supervenes on the extensional facts about things – any things, including occurrent conscious states, and words, and fits, and starts – and their relations and dispositions and behaviors classified extensionally. This means, for instance, that there could be two possible worlds in which all the particles and their mereological sums are the same, and all the relations of force and position and movement through time, and all the occurrent conscious happenings that supervene on all that, but in one of which "rabbits" refers to rabbits, and in the other of which it does not. That is, we are denying the supervenience of the semantic on the extensional.

This is a cost. The cost is the denial that meaning is use, except in the trivial sense that to mean rabbits by "rabbits" is to use "rabbits" to mean rabbits. It is the insistence that there may be a difference that makes no difference: a semantic difference that has no manifestation or exercise in the happenings in the world and the dispositions of its inhabitants. This is a cost we should be prepared to pay only in despair, and it is not a cost we should be prepared to pay, if, like Putnam, we insist that meaning is use. Once we pay the cost we have a straightforward reconciliation of the point of view of semantics and that of physics. We can acquire one true theory, by conjoining all the descriptions from each without strain, for we have abandoned the principles that generated the strain in the first place.

My claim in this section has simply been that this cost is neither avoided nor lessened by saying "We are only taking up a different perspective, working with a different scheme from that of the extensional." For the problem is that of seeing how any such different perspective is *possible*. A perspective within which we determinately mean plus or rabbits, and by means of which we interpret others as doing so as well, is on the forbidden side of the fence, and mentioning it does nothing to alleviate the problem.

The consequence, then, is that internal realism is no better placed than any other, "metaphysical" realism when it comes to deflecting the model theoretic arguments. If they refute "metaphysical realism" they refute the internal version just as effectively; conversely, a "straight" solution enabling us genuinely to understand semantic determinacy and its relation to the rest of the world has to be found by anyone.

4   More General Considerations

The net result is that uniqueness, along with correspondence, bivalence, and independence, emerges not as a hallmark of metaphysical realism, but as a necessary constraint on any reconciliation of apparently inconsistent perspectives. Being unable to obtain it simply means that our understanding has been baffled. It does not mean that we have two theories rather than one, and no need to concern ourselves about their relations. But with that point in place, the enterprise of actually distinguishing a tenable internal realism from the opposing metaphysical kind comes to a full stop. We could say, if we wished, that metaphysical realism is a consequence of the way we have to think: if we like to remain Kantian, bivalence, independence, correspondence, and uniqueness will be regulative principles, governing our theory building. If we gain consolation by stressing that they are *our* principles, so be it, but that does not lessen their hold. It is not as if we well see how to conduct ourselves without them, as I have urged in this chapter for the particular case of uniqueness.

Some readers may be surprised by my reservations about internal realism. They may have thought of it as not far removed from a project with which I have been much concerned, the development of a "quasi-realism" about such things as morals and modals. Each philosophy promises something like a realism, but with a qualification. Each might be described, as they are by Lewis, as realism feigned. Each of us might seem equally to be a target for Lewis's further description:

> The plan is to speak exactly as the realists do (except in the philosophy room – I have no idea how that lapse can be justified); and to do so in good conscience, in the hope that one's words are destined to join the ideal theory, and so are "epistemically true;" but to do so without any intention of describing the world by saying something that will be true only if the world is one way rather than another.

Although, as Lewis then admits, "the Internalist will *say* that he intends to be 'describing the world . . .' his plan is to speak *exactly* as the realists do!"[21] Similarly the quasi-realist will say, if he or she feels it helps, that he or she is describing the moral or modal facts. He or she thus splits apart two ideas that Putnam always associates: the idea that we have in some area a "projection" of a non-representative state of mind, and the idea that there is no truth or falsity in our eventual commitments. Putnam might insist, with others, that in so far as the enterprise is successful it tends to undermine the initial metaphor of projection, and indeed the bifurcation between the treated commitments and others, but this is not a very severe point of difference. One might, on that score, be grateful to quasi-realism for making blanket internalism feel more comfortable.

The real difference is this: the quasi-realist does not merely compare a naturalistic perspective in which moral or modal facts become invisible, and a frame of thought in which they are highly visible. The point is to reconcile the two perspectives, by giving a reconstruction of the practice of making modal or ethical discriminations in a way that is entirely acceptable to the naturalist. That reconstruction intends to act as a *defense* of the practice against the error theorist or eliminativist, and enable us to understand the use we make of notions of moral or modal truth. So, whether or not he or she is successful, at least the quasi-realist takes seriously the threat of eliminativism. He or she does not rest content with two perspectives, but seeks to show how the one can be explained and justified in terms acceptable within the other. And, again, the upshot is that there is no inconsistency left: we can have both our naturalistic view of the world and our moral commitments, in one breath. Lewis's jibe about the lapse from realism only in the philosophy room misses this target, for it is only in the philosophy room that we are concerned to give the theory that reconciles the different views we wish to hold.

But a quasi-realist approach is not magical. It cannot by itself enable us to see how we can have determinate semantic truths which do not supervene upon extensional reality, nor can it enable us to turn our back, without cost, on the view that meaning must be exercised in use. In semantics it must work with everyone else to find a way of blocking indeterminacy doctrines, enabling us to rest content with semantics as determinately fixed by the base totality that our naturalistic understanding of the world give us. The role of quasi-realism here would be to explore the existence of the *normative* element in meaning, and to bring to bear success in understanding normative judgements in other areas.

I cited Putnam as an example of an almost universal trend in philosophy. And although I have been critical of his use of internal realism as a response to the indeterminacy of reference, I do not suppose the vision of a qualified realism will cease to possess us. Yet the problem I have identified seems set to reappear in other cases as well. Suppose we puzzle about the relation between the colorless world of physics and the colored human world. How, out of these colorless forces, can anything *colored* be made? We do not advance much by insisting that we have a visual perspective within which the world is indeed colored ("colored-for-us"), for the problem was just as much one of how such a perspective could arise at all. How do our gray brains produce colored sensations? Or suppose we attack the problem of the physical world versus free will by self-consciously supposing a shift in perspective, from that of science to that of agency. A reconciling project has not got far if we cannot understand how what is given in each perspective could be true; that is, if we cannot conjoin them. If we cannot say, for example, that while this bunch of molecules is determined, and the man is the bunch of molecules, the man is free, counselling us that the verdicts come from different perspectives is simply counselling us to stay away from the area where our understanding sinks without trace.

In this chapter I have been constantly nudging against the threat that realism and idealism coincide. If what I have said is right, at least they coincide this far: when we find an inconsistency in what we want to say about the world, it does not help to drop the last three words, leaving it just an inconsistency in what we want to say. Nor does it help to italicize the "we." An inconsistency in what *we* want to say is just as bad, and takes just as much effort to resolve.

30   *Simon Blackburn*

Notes

1 Descartes (1984): *Meditations (The Second Set of Replies)*, ed. J. Cottingham, R. Stoothoff, and D. Murdoch. Cambridge: Cambridge University Press, p. 103.
2 Hilary Putnam (1987) places his internal realism in this context in *The Many Faces of Realism*, La Salle, Illinois: Open Court, p. 16ff.
3 Hilary Putnam (1988), *Representation and Reality*. Bradford Books, ch. 7, p. 110.
4 Hilary Putnam (1981), *Reason, Truth and History*. Cambridge: Cambridge University Press, p. 54.
5 See Putnam (1987), p. 17.
6 Ibid., p. 109.
7 Putnam (1988), p. 107.
8 Putnam (1988), p. 112.
9 Putnam (1987), pp. 18–20.
10 I was encouraged to believe that this is the essence of the argument by remarks made by Professor Putnam at the Gifford Conference. The classic use of this argument against a determinate ontology of numbers is Paul Benacerraf (1965), "What Numbers Could not Possibly Be," *Philosophical Review*, 75, 47–73; reprinted in P. Benacerraf and H. Putnam (eds) (1983), *Philosophy of Mathematics* (2nd edn), Cambridge: Cambridge University Press.
11 Putnam (1988), p. 114.
12 Barry Stroud (1989), "Quine on Exile and Acquiescence," *Proceedings of the San Marino Conference*.
13 W.V. Quine (1969), *Ontological Relativity and Other Essays*. New York and London: Columbia University Press, p. 48.
14 Stroud (1989), p. 11. See also J.R. Searle (1987), "Indeterminacy, Empiricism, and the First Person," *Journal of Philosophy*, 84, 123–46, esp. p. 132.
15 Putnam (1981), p. 52.
16 W.V. Quine (1960), *Word and Object*. Cambridge, MA: MIT Press, p. 76.
17 I owe this way of putting it to Michael Resnik.
18 This point was urged upon me at the Gifford Conference by Michael Dummett, who also pointed out that the same structure arises when we contemplate the possibility of non-standard models for the number series.
19 I still stand by most of the discussion in *Reason and Prediction* (1973), Cambridge: Cambridge University Press, ch. 4.
20 Lewis is difficult to characterize. He adds additional facts – relations of relative privilege among universals. There are neither immediately facts that Quine or Kripke are likely to welcome, nor simply semantic facts. But they work towards a straight solution, by providing a broad category of real facts of which semantic facts are a consequence. Some of the following remarks are relevant to this theory and its costs as well.
21 David Lewis (1984), "Putnam's Paradox," *Australasian Journal of Philosophy*, 6, 221–36, esp. p. 231.

2 1879?

George Boolos

In "Peirce the Logician," a paper in his collection of articles called *Realism with a Human Face*,[1] Hilary Putnam takes exception to a remark of Quine's, "Logic is an old subject, and since 1879 it has been a great one," the first sentence of the preface to each of the first two editions (1950, 1959) of Quine's textbook *Methods of Logic*.[2] (Putnam used *Methods of Logic* as a textbook in his logic courses in the late 1950s.) Putnam justifiably considers the statement a slight to Boole. But the remark is dropped from the prefaces to the third and fourth editions and I have not been able to find it anywhere else in either later edition.[3]

In any case, I am grateful to Putnam for recalling the excised remark and thereby prompting me to rethink a view about the history of logic that I had held for a long time: that 1879 was a *watershed* year for logic. 1879 was, of course, the year in which Frege's *Begriffsschrift* was published. There is no question that with its publication logic took a gigantic step forward. I want to suggest here that there is a respect in which the advance represented by the *Begriffsschrift* may not have been so great as some (myself certainly included) have supposed. Not that the advance wasn't great; just not *so* great.

Harvard University Press publishes an anthology entitled *From Frege to Gödel: A Source Book in Mathematical Logic 1879–1931*.[4] Among those whose help the editor, Jean van Heijenoort, acknowledges are Dreben, Parsons, Quine, and Wang, all of whom have at one time been on the faculty of the university whose press publishes that work. It is interesting to see the Putnam of "Peirce the Logician" standing in opposition to the Fregecentrism that has hitherto prevailed in his home university. Much of this paper consists of ruminations on the history of logic which support the iconoclastic tendency of Putnam's article.

The historical note to chapter 46 of the fourth edition of *Methods of Logic*, called "Classes," reads, "The construction illustrated in the definition of ancestor was introduced by Frege in 1879 for application to number. It was rediscovered independently a few years later by Peirce, and again by Dedekind, who propounded it in 1887 under the name of the method of *chains*."[5] In his *Mathematical Logic*, Quine writes, "The line of reasoning used in D30 was first set forth by Frege in 1879 (*Begriffsschrift*, p. 60) in defining what I have called the proper ancestral."[6] Later we shall later take a look at this historical commonplace.

It is well known that Quine's later, post-*Mathematical Logic* view is that the discovery of the ancestral was not an advance in logic at all, but only an advance in the theory of classes, a portion of "mathematics." Although the ancestral is described in his textbook on logic, Quine's account of it is contained in part IV, "Glimpses Beyond" – beyond logic, as the term, according to the later Quine, is properly used, of course. Putnam has views about the scope of logic that differ interestingly from Quine's and from my own; before discussing the year 1879, I want to lay out Putnam's views about the scope of logic and what I take to be our differences on this question.

In *Philosophy of Logic*, Putnam argues that "(a) it is rather arbitrary to say that 'second-order' logic is not 'logic'; and (b) even if we do say this, the natural understanding of first-order logic is that in writing down first-order schemata we are implicitly asserting their validity, that is, making second-order assertions."[7]

He suggests that it is one quite natural choice to take statements like "For all classes, S, M, P, if all S are M and all M are P, then all S are P," which refer explicitly to classes, as statements of logic. He holds that this statement expresses the validity of the inference: $\forall x(Sx \rightarrow Mx)$, $\forall x(Mx \rightarrow Px)$ $\therefore \forall x(Sx \rightarrow Px)$. At least some statements expressing the validity of certain valid inferences should thus be counted as logical truths.

He writes, "The decision of the great founders of modern logic . . . was unhesitatingly to count such expressions as $\exists F$ as part of logic, and even to allow such expressions as $\exists F^2$, with the meaning *for every class of classes*."[8] He continues, "Suppose, however, we decide to draw the line at 'first-order' logic ('quantification theory') and to count such expressions as '$\exists F$', '$\exists F^2$', etc. as belonging to mathematics."[9] But, one might wonder, if one draws the line here, what happens to expressions like '$\forall F$' and '$\forall F^2$'? Are these still expressions of logic? Putnam here seems to be hinting at a position on which truths of the form $\forall F_1 \forall \ldots \forall F_n \phi$, ϕ a valid first-order formula, should be counted as logical truths, while truths $\exists F \phi$, which on his view assert the existence of classes with certain properties, should not.

To object that $\exists$ is definable in terms of $\forall$ and negation is to miss the point of this view, which is that those "Π_1" statements obtained from valid formulae of first-order logic by prefixing strings either of universal second-order quantifiers ∀F or of their definitional equivalents ¬∃F¬ are more justifiably counted as logical truths than class-existence assertions and other true "Σ_1" statements.

In "Peirce the Logician," Putnam writes:

> (1) Where to draw the line between logic and set theory . . . is not an easy question. The statement that a syllogism is valid, for example is a statement of second-order logic. (Barbara is valid just in case
>
> ∀F∀G∀H(∀x(Fx → Gx) ∧ ∀x(Gx → Hx) → ∀x(Fx → Hx)),
>
> for example). If second-order logic is "set theory," then most of traditional logic becomes set theory. (2) The full intuitive principle of mathematical induction is definitely second-order in anybody's view. Thus there is a higher-order element in arithmetic whether or not one chooses to "identify numbers with sets" just as Frege realized.[10]

And at the Quine conference in San Marino, Putnam explicitly said he wanted to "split the difference" between Quine and me, and to count second-order universal quantifications of valid first-order schemata, but only those, as logical truths. Some fretting over a few uncomfortable aspects of this position is called for.

First of all, Putnam writes, "Barbara is valid just in case

∀F∀G∀H(∀x(Fx → Gx) ∧ ∀x(Gx → Hx) → ∀x(Fx → Hx))."

This is what R.C. Jeffrey calls Loglish. What's not perfectly clear to me is what the formula "∀F . . ." is supposed to mean. What does the first-order variable x range over? One naturally supposes over (absolutely) all the things there are. Otherwise, the second-order statement would not give the full force of the validity; one can, one supposes, make a Barbara syllogism about any things whatsoever. But if so, then what do the second-order variables range over? Classes? Well, O.K.; but then it had better not be that all classes are things. But then can one or can't one speak about everything – and by everything, I mean everything including all classes there might be – with one's first-order variables? Putnam would be the last person to want to say that one could use the word "everything" to quantify over everything but one could not use a universal quantifier to do so.

But if it means "If F, G, and H are classes, everything that belongs to F belongs to G, and everything that belongs to G belongs to H, then everything that belongs to F belongs to H," how is one to symbolize:

> If each thing that is a class containing all ordinals is a class that is not a member of anything and each thing that is a class that is not a

member of anything is a class that is the same size as the universal class, then each thing that is a class containing all ordinals is a class that is the same size as the universal class

a valid, indeed syllogistically valid, statement, each of whose propositional constituents is true, according to the currently standard theory of classes? If one symbolizes it as

$$(\forall x(Fx \rightarrow Gx) \land \forall x(Gx \rightarrow Hx) \rightarrow \forall x(Fx \rightarrow Hx)),$$

with "x" ranging over all classes, and "Fx" abbreviating "x is a class containing all ordinals," etc., then how is this statement supposed to be a consequence of the second-order assertion about classes? The problem, of course, is that according to the standard theory of classes, there aren't any classes that contain all classes that contain all ordinals, etc.

I don't wish to suggest that these difficulties can't somehow be overcome. In a pair of articles published some years ago,[11] I suggested that the plural number can be used in explaining what validity of Barbara comes to. It is admittedly rather taxing to pronounce the explanation, and to do so risks the Hilarious response: "*That's* clearer than introducing classes?" But here goes:

> No matter what certain things – call them F things – may be, no matter what certain things – call them G things – may be, and no matter what certain things – call them H things – may be, if everything that is an F thing is a G thing, and everything that is a G thing is an H thing, then everything that is an F thing is an H thing.

Not so bad after all, and even if appreciably more awkward, certainly less involved with classes and the serious theoretical difficulties that attend their introduction than the formulation offered by Putnam. Whether use of the plural number frees one from these worries or not, it remains the case that talk about classes won't get one out of the sorts of difficulty that prompted their introduction in the first place.

Other possible responses, of course, are to admit a hierarchy of classes, superclasses, superduperclasses, etc., to claim that, actually, we can't talk about everything at once, to invoke some doctrine of typical or systematic ambiguity, or to mutter something about a ladder. I prefer the tongue-twisting to the mystical or the nonsensical, and particularly to the nonsensical that advertises itself as such, "strictly speaking."

Putnam's remark that mathematical induction is second-order and that there is a higher-order element in arithmetic is perplexing. The position of the remark in Putnam's paper makes it seem as if he were arguing *against* a Quinean. But the remark is one that Quine could happily accept.

I suspect – hope – that the view Putnam wanted to put forth is that just as statements like the second-order statement expressing the validity of Barbara should be regarded as logical truths, so the ancestral should be counted as a logical notion. The (weak) ancestral R_* of a relation R may be defined by a formula that is a universal second-order quantification of a first-order formula: $xR_* y$ iff

$$\forall F(Fy \wedge \forall w \forall z(Fz \wedge wRz \rightarrow Fw) \rightarrow Fx).$$

Thus a good deal of the content of arithmetic, expressible with the aid of the ancestral, would count as logic.

If Putnam wishes to count the ancestral as a notion of logic, then one wants to know about inferences involving the ancestral. Are any of them to be counted as logically valid? What about inferences in which a statement to the effect that one person is an ancestor of another is a premise? Here's a favorite example of mine, a near-relative of an inference made by Frege in deriving (83) of the *Begriffsschrift*:

Xavier is an ancestor of Yolanda.	$xP_* y$
Yolanda is blue.	By
Any parent of anyone blue is red.	$\forall w \forall z(Bw \wedge zPw \rightarrow Rz)$
Any parent of anyone red is blue.	$\forall w \forall z(Rw \wedge zPw \rightarrow Bz)$
∴ Xavier is either red or blue.	$\therefore Rx \vee Bx$

Of course "$xP_* y$" here abbreviates its second-order definition.

There is a way to express, in English, an argument that shows the validity of this inference without explicitly introducing the notion of a class. By the first premise, no matter who certain people may be, if Yolanda is one of them and every parent of any one of them is also one of them, then Xavier is one of them too. Now consider the people who are either red or blue. By the second premise, Yolanda is one of them. By the third and fourth premises, every parent of any one of them is also one of them. Thus Xavier is one of them, and is therefore either red or blue.

I find it an uncomfortable position to want to admit the ancestral as a logical notion, but not to admit as (logically) valid inferences such as the one just given which involve the ancestral in at least a moderately interesting way. Does one want to accept a doctrine on which the foregoing argument is not a piece of logic, in the fullest sense of the word?

But then if the inference is logically valid, then either the statement that it is valid is not itself valid or some true Π_2 statements are logical truths.

The reason is that the statement that the inference is valid will be a universal quantification (with respect to P, R, B) of a formula in which a universal second-order quantifier occurs in the *antecedent* of a conditional; its prenex equivalent will thus begin: $\forall P \forall R \forall B \; \exists F$. . . . I would have supposed that the desire to count the statement that Barbara is valid as itself valid would have arisen from a more general, and perfectly reasonable, wish: to count a true statement to the effect that any given inference is valid as itself valid.

Thus Putnam's position on the scope of logic strikes me as unstable: either certain plainly logical modes of reasoning fail to count as such or more than just the valid Π_1 sentences are going to have to come out as logical truths.

In the articles I mentioned, I offered a scheme of translation from the notation of second-order logic into natural language augmented with devices for cross-reference. (Such devices are a necessary addition to natural language if one wishes to translate sentences in *first*-order notation with even a moderately complicated quantificational structure into natural language.) The key feature of the scheme was the clause for the translation of the second-order existential quantifier "$\exists X$," which was to be rendered roughly as "There are some things that$_X$ are such that . . . ."[12] Under the assumption that the first-order variables range over all the things there are, the translation of $\exists X \forall x (Xx \leftrightarrow \neg x \in x)$ into English is equivalent, not to a contradiction, but to the trivial truth: if there is at least one thing that is not a member of itself, then there are some things that are such that each thing is one of them if and only if it is not a member of itself.

As was mentioned in Boolos (1984), Charles Parsons claimed that there appeared to be no non-artificial way to translate "$\forall X$" into natural language, and that any translation would seem to have to proceed via the equivalence of "$\forall X$" with "$\neg \exists X \neg$". David Lewis later suggested, however, that the construction "No matter what some (or certain) things X may be . . ." is a perfectly adequate way to render second-order monadic universal quantifiers into familiar English.

Lewis's suggestion was particularly striking to one who had been taught[13] that it was not perfectly correct to read "$\forall x (Fx \rightarrow Gx)$" as "for every x, if x is an F, x is a G", since "every" cannot be followed by a linguistic item that also functions as a pronoun, and that the proper way to read it was: "No matter what a thing may be, if it is an F, then it is a G." Pluralizing "a" to "some" (and pronounced: [sm], not [sum], as Helen Cartwright points out), or to "certain," yields the desired correct and natural version of "$\forall X$."

A more serious drawback, first pointed out to me by Hartry Field, is that the scheme provides no way to translate into natural language second-order dyadic or, more generally, polyadic quantification. In favorable cases, of course, pairing functions will be definable in the language and higher-degree second-order quantification reducible to monadic. But the availability of pairing functions cannot be considered to be guaranteed by logic: any domain closed under an ordered pair function contains (Dedekind) infinitely many objects if it contains at least two. Field's observation appears to be unassailable.

In the absence of a way to translate sentences of second-order logic containing second-order polyadic quantifiers into natural language, must we regard second-order polyadic logic as capable of being made intelligible only via quantification over polyadic relations, and thus as legitimate only when first-order quantifiers range over a set?

I am not sure, but I don't see that we must. We need not regard translatability of a notation into language we already understand as a necessary condition of the intelligibility of that notation. To be sure, our ability to translate second-order monadic statements into English enables us to take them as having a sense – the one given by the translation. (The issue, of course, is whether they have a sense when the first-order variables range over objects that do not together constitute a set.) But the provision of a translation scheme into an antecedently understood language need not be the only way to confer sense upon statements in some notation; we didn't learn our mother tongue that way, for sure. And after all, we understand the basic formal machinery of second-order logic rather well; the syntax (including the devices of quantification and predication, as well as elementary proof theory) of polyadic second-order notation can be understood by one who understands that of polyadic first-order logic and monadic second-order logic. Moreover, we can imagine sufficiently well how enough additional resources – "pro-verbs" – might have been present in natural language for us to be able to translate into it the entire formalism of polyadic second-order logic. Thus I incline to think that our understanding of both the syntax of polyadic second-order logic and the semantics of polyadic first-order and monadic second-order logic has combined with our ability to envisage an extension (possibly a quite radical one) of the language we speak to afford us an understanding of the semantics of polyadic second-order logic, even though we cannot express that understanding in the language we presently speak.

I shall not speculate on the question whether we can imagine extensions of English that would make possible a translation scheme for such third-order statements as "$\exists\alpha\exists F\exists x(\alpha F \wedge Fx)$", "$x$" again being understood to range over all objects. Instead, hoping that I have opened the way for Putnam to move closer to my position, and aware that I have sufficiently nudged him in that direction, I shall now turn to one of the historical issues raised by Putnam's paper, the extent to which 1879 was an "epochal"[14] year in the history of logic.

The main point of "Peirce the Logician" seems to me entirely correct: great accomplishments in logic *were* made before 1879. I want to begin to sharpen the point by describing an observation about propositional logic that Boole made towards the end of his 82-page monograph *The Mathematical Analysis of Logic,*[15] which was published in 1847.

In the next-to-last section, called "Properties of Elective Functions" (elective functions are truth functions, or in current parlance, Boolean functions), Boole notes that, as we would now put the matter, any formula $\phi(x)$ of propositional logic containing the propositional variable x is equivalent to the formula $(\phi(1) \wedge x) \vee (\phi(0) \wedge \neg x)$. Here 1 and 0 are constants of propositional logic for truth and falsity. The disjuncts are incompatible, and nothing is lost by replacing the Boolean exclusive disjunction with the inclusive $\vee$.

What Boole realized was that iterating this operation shows that an arbitrary propositional formula $\phi(x_1, \ldots, x_m)$ is equivalent to the disjunction of the 2^m formulas $(\phi(i_1, \ldots, i_m) \wedge \pm x_1 \wedge \ldots \wedge \pm x_m)$, where each i_j is either 1 or 0 and $\pm x_j$ is x_j or $\neg x_j$ according as i_j is 1 or 0. Boole termed the equivalence the law of development, and called (his analogues of) the constant formulae $\phi(i_1, \ldots, i_n)$ the moduli of $\phi(x_1, \ldots, x_m)$. Since each modulus is equal to 1 or 0 (and it can be easily calculated which), every propositional formula $\phi(x_1, \ldots, x_m)$ is, as Boole saw, equivalent to the disjunction of those formulae $\pm x_1 \wedge \ldots \wedge \pm x_m$ for which the moduli $\phi(i_1, \ldots, i_m)$ do not vanish (are not = 0). Thus Boole know that every formula of propositional logic is equivalent to one in what we now call perfect disjunctive normal form.

Boole clearly had the idea of all possible distributions of truth-values: "It is evident that if the number of elective symbols is m, the number of different moduli will be 2^m, and that their separate values will be obtained by interchanging in every possible way the values 1 and 0 in the places of the elective symbols of the given function." Thus one main feature of the method of truth-tables, usually credited to Post and Wittgenstein, was on prominent display in Boole's early monograph.[16] Another feature was not: the now familiar manner in which the truth-values of compound sentences are inherited from those of their components; for that reason, it would be injudicious, I think, to try to credit Boole with the discovery of truth-tables.

No edition of *Methods of Logic* provides a natural deduction system for Boolean notions. It may be that Quine was inclined to minimize the significance of the propositional calculus simply because truth-functional validity is decidable. Although quantifiers are important in logic – very important – it is not strictly true that "their importance cannot be overemphasized." It may have taken the rise of the computer for us to see the interest and importance of the propositional calculus, but it is not now possible to forget that a problem about the propositional calculus, the P=NP problem (which Putnam worked on with Martin Davis in the 1950s, by the way), is generally considered to be one of the ten most important unsolved problems in the whole of mathematics. We now see the decidable as a realm with an interesting structure in which Boolean notions are anything but trivial. Truth-functional validity is certainly decidable, but it is also, in the apt technical term, hard. *Logic is an old subject, and since 1847 it has been a hard one.* Quine himself has of course made important contributions to propositional logic, which, he has noted with apparent pride, contributors to engineering journals have frequently cited. The offending sentence having been removed from later editions of *Methods* and with "Boolean" a term now known to every student of programming, amends should be thought made.

Along with the publication of the *Begriffsschrift*, another event of logical note occurred in 1879. A passage in the introduction to volume 4 of the *Writings of Charles S. Peirce*[17] relates that according to lecture notes taken by a student of Peirce's, Allan Marquand, Peirce gave a lecture in December of 1879 in which he presented the following axiomatization of arithmetic:

1 Every number by process of increase by 1 produces a number.
2 The number 1 is not so produced.
3 Every other number is so produced.
4 The producing and produced numbers are different.
5 In whatever transitive relation every number so produced stands to that which produces it, in that relation every number other than 1 stands to 1.
6 What is so produced from any individual number is an individual number.
7 What so produces any individual number is an individual number.

Letting "Pxy" mean "x by process of increase by 1 produces y," we may symbolize these:

1 $\forall x(Nx \rightarrow \exists y(Pxy \wedge Ny))$
2 $N1; \forall x(Nx \rightarrow \neg Px1)$
3 $\forall y(Ny \wedge y \neq 1 \rightarrow \exists x Pxy)$
4 $\forall x \forall y(Nx \wedge Ny \wedge Pxy \rightarrow x \neq y)$
5 $\forall R(\text{Trans}(R) \wedge \forall x \forall y(Nx \wedge Ny \wedge Pxy \rightarrow Ryx) \rightarrow \forall x(Nx \wedge x \neq 1 \rightarrow Rx1))$
6 $\forall x \forall y(Nx \wedge Pxy \rightarrow Ny)$
7 $\forall x \forall y(Ny \wedge Pxy \rightarrow Nx)$

"Trans(R)" abbreviates: $\forall x \forall y \forall z(Rxy \wedge Ryz \rightarrow Rxz)$, of course.

The editors write that Peirce went on to define the relation "greater than." Not having seen Marquand's notes, I can only guess that the definition ran, more or less: a number is greater than another if it stands to that other in every transitive relation in which every number so produced stands to that which produces it. If so, then axiom (5) would be equivalent to the statement that every number other than 1 is greater than one.

There are at least one and possibly two serious omissions from Peirce's axiomatization. It is not clear from Peirce's language that at most one number is produced by process of increase by 1 from any number. What he says allows, I think, that some number produces two distinct numbers, and that the tree of finite sequences of zeros and ones or even the full infinitary tree of finite sequences of objects in any one set whatsoever might be a model of his axioms. Perhaps, though, the phrase "the producing and the produced numbers" in axiom (4) is meant to imply uniqueness of the produced number; we might then adjoin the conjunct $\forall x \forall y \forall z (Nx \wedge Pxy \wedge Pxz \rightarrow y = z)$ to the symbolization of (4).

The second omission is that Peirce's axioms, even with the emendation of axiom (4) just given, do not guarantee that production is one–one, that is, that different numbers produce different numbers. Dedekind's condition δ in *The Nature and Meaning of Numbers* [*Was sind und was sollen die Zahlen?*] explicitly provided just such a guarantee. The omission from Peirce's list is serious: Peirce's axioms are true in the three-element model in which 1 produces 2, 2 produces 3, and 3 produces 2:

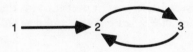

But we can easily supply Peirce with the necessary axiom: $\forall x \forall y \forall z \forall w (Pxy \wedge Pzw \rightarrow (x = z \leftrightarrow y = w))$. What is worth dwelling on in Peirce's list of axioms is not what it leaves out, but what it contains. The fifth axiom, which says that whenever R is a transitive relation which includes the relation on numbers *is produced by*, then every number other than 1 bears R to 1, is remarkable. It is, audibly, a second-order axiom, universally quantifying over all relations of a certain sort: "in whatever transitive relation . . . in that relation . . . ." What the axiom says, and how it is supposed to work, though, may not be immediately apparent.

However, translating "is produced (by process of increase by 1) by" as "succeeds" enables us see that it implies the principle of mathematical induction. For suppose that 1 has a certain property F and that every number that succeeds a number with property F also has property F. [F1 $\wedge \forall x (Nx \wedge Ny \wedge Fx \wedge Pxy \rightarrow Fy)$.] We are to show that every number has

F. Let R be the relation that holds between w and z if and only if w and z are numbers and if z has F then w has F. [Rwz iff $Nw \wedge Nz \wedge (Fz \rightarrow Fw)$).] R is transitive, by the transitivity of material implication. Moreover, every number produced by a number stands in R to that number, for if y is produced by x, i.e. y succeeds x, then by our supposition, if x has F, y has F, that is to say, y stands in R to x. [$Pxy \rightarrow (Fx \rightarrow Fy)$, and so $Pxy \rightarrow Ryx$.] By axiom (5), every number other than 1 stands in R to 1. That is, if x is a number other than 1, if 1 has F, then x has F; since 1 does have F, x has F. Thus every number x has F.

In the presence of the other axioms, mathematical induction implies Peirce's axiom (5); we may safely leave this derivation to the reader.

It is at least moderately plausible to conjecture that Peirce recognized that mathematical induction thus followed from axiom (5) and conversely. But whether or not he did, it is certain that the idea of applying the logic of relations to the "primitive" relation of one number's succeeding another in order to characterize the natural number series was in the air over Baltimore, far from that over Jena, the year the *Begriffsschrift* was published.

The date of the preface of the *Begriffsschrift* is 18 December 1878, and there is absolutely no question that Frege's achievements were thus much in advance of those of Peirce, even if one ignores Peirce's omissions. The opening paragraph of van Heijenoort's (1967) introduction to the *Begriffsschrift* enumerates several of the excellencies of Frege's book. I note with pleasure, by the way, that van Heijenoort refers to the definition of the ancestral as "a *logical* [my italics] definition of sequence."[18] I am not now concerned with the excellencies of Frege's work but want instead to raise the question of whether Frege was actually the first to define the ancestral. Peirce came close, we have seen, but whatever he may be thought to have done, Frege had him beat by at least a year.

x bears the (strong) ancestral of the relation R to y if y belongs to every class containing all objects to which x or some member of the class bears R: xR^*y iff $\forall K(\forall z(xRz \vee \exists w(Kw \wedge wRz)) \rightarrow Kz) \rightarrow Ky)$, i.e. $\forall K(\forall z(xRz \rightarrow Kz) \wedge \forall w \forall z(Kw \wedge wRz \rightarrow Kz) \rightarrow Ky)$. The class of all objects to which x bears the ancestral of R is itself a class containing all objects to which x or some member bears R. Was Frege the first person to define a class in this manner, as the class of objects belonging to all classes satisfying a certain condition, where that class is itself one of the classes that satisfy the condition? Frege gives the definition of the ancestral of a relation in section 26 of the *Begriffsschrift*. His "elucidation" of his (symbolic) definition is:

> If from the two propositions that every result of an application of the procedure f to x has property F and that property F is hereditary in the f-sequence it can be inferred, whatever F may be, that y has

property F, then I say: "*y* follows *x* in the *f*-sequence", or "*x* precedes *y* in the *f*-sequence."

Did anyone give such a definition before Frege? Of course it must be somewhat vague what "such" denotes here.

The preface to the second edition of Richard Dedekind's monograph, *The Nature and Meaning of Numbers*, dated 24 August 1893, contains the statement,

> About a year after the publication of my memoir I became acquainted with G. Frege's *Grundlagen der Arithmetik*, which had already appeared in the year 1884. However different the view of the essence of number adopted in that work is from my own, yet it contains, particularly from §79 on, points of very close contact with my paper, especially with my definition (44).[19]

Definition 44 runs: "If A is an arbitrary part [subset] of S, then we will denote by A_0 the intersection of all those chains (e.g. S) of which A is a part; this intersection A_0 exists (cf. 17) because A itself is a common subset of all these chains. Since by 43, A_0 is moreover a chain, we will call A_0 the chain of the system A, or for short the chain of A."[20] K is a *chain* with respect to a function ϕ, it may be recalled, if every image of a member of K is a member of K, if as we would say, K is closed under ϕ. Thus according to Dedekind's definition, $y \in A_0$ iff $\forall K(\forall z(z \in A \rightarrow z \in K) \wedge \forall w(w \in K \rightarrow \phi(w) \in K) \rightarrow y \in K)$. It is clear that Dedekind's definition of A_0 is strikingly like Frege's of "*y* follows *x* in the *f*-sequence*," and is "such" a definition.

Was sind was first published in 1888, nine years after the *Begriffsschrift*. In the preface to the first edition, dated 5 October 1887, Dedekind wrote,

> The design of such a presentation I had formed before the publication of my paper on *Continuity*, but only after its appearance and with many interruptions occasioned by increased official duties and other necessary labors, was I able in the years 1872 to 1878 to write out a first draft on a few sheets of paper, which several mathematicians examined and in part discussed with me.[21]

The question thus arises whether those few sheets of paper contained anything like the definition of A_0 Dedekind would later give in section 44 of his published monograph.

The answer may have come to light only as recently as 1976, with the publication of Pierre Dugac's *Richard Dedekind et les Fondements des Mathématiques*,[22] which contains a large number of unedited texts, including the first draft of *Was sind* mentioned by Dedekind. It turns out that the draft contains most of the ideas and proofs found in the later version, including the definition of a chain, that of a principal element (*Hauptelement*), which is an element of the given set S that is contained in *all* chains (Dedekind emphasizes "all"), and the argument that the system of principal elements is itself a chain. These all appear near the beginning of the draft. Dedekind's first definition of "chain" reads: "A part K of S shall be called a *chain* (or any other name) if K' is a part of K."[23] It strongly appears that different parts of the draft were composed at different times, for Dedekind later defines a group in the same way: "(with respect to this mapping) G is called a group if G' is a part of G."[24] B is then called dependent on A "if B is a part of every group of which A is a part."[25] A theorem immediately follows: "The system of all things dependent on A is a group, which shall be designated A_0."[26] Dedekind was evidently dithering over which term to use. Later in the manuscript he settles on "chain," defines it as before, defines a thing, *b*, in S to be dependent on a thing, *a*, in S if "every chain that contains *a* contains *b*", introduces the notation: (*a*) to denote the system of all things dependent on that thing *a*, and proves that (*a*) is a chain.[27] Towards the end of the draft there is even a fourth series of similar definitions and theorems.

Dedekind and Dugac give only the span of years 1872–8 as the period during which the draft was written. But since it appears that different parts of the draft were composed at different times (for it seems rather unlikely that Dedekind would have written down much the same thing four times over within the space of a year or two), it is quite possible that Dedekind formulated the definition of A_0 for the first time several years before 1878, possibly towards 1872, and quite possibly before Frege arrived at the definition of "*y* follows *x* in the *f*-sequence." It may be that we shall never know who came first, and perhaps that is all to the good. Reading the draft convinces me, however, that it is at least as probable that Dedekind had the definition of A_0 before Frege had that of the ancestral as that he had it after.

The draft contains much else that is familiar from the monograph: definitions of one–one mapping, (Dedekind!) infinity, the connection between the principle of complete induction[28] and the notion of a principal element, the recursion equations for addition (not multiplication), and the assertion that numbers are creations of the human mind (*Geist*). Notable is the elaborateness of the development of the theory of chains that Dedekind gives towards the end of the draft, after the fourth definition of "chain" (counting that of "group" as the second). Another remarkable feature, as Dugac notes, is the *absence* of an analogue of Theorem 66 of *Was sind*, "There are infinite systems," and hence of any dubious or non-mathematical proof of that theorem.

Dedekind, of course, did not quite define the ancestral of a relation. But the difference between his definition of A_0 (with respect to a mapping φ) and

Frege's of the ancestral is small. y is an element of A_0 iff $\forall K(\forall z(z \in A \rightarrow z \in K) \wedge \forall w(w \in K \rightarrow \phi w \in K) \rightarrow y \in K)$; xR^*y iff $\forall K(\forall z(xRz \rightarrow Kz) \wedge \forall w \forall z(Kw \wedge Rwz \rightarrow Kz) \rightarrow Ky)$. Dedekind's notion is less general than Frege's in what is perhaps a significant respect: it covers only functional, rather than arbitrary, relations. For Dedekind to have had a notion fully as general as Frege's, however, he need only have changed the definition of K' from: $\{\phi w: Kw\}$, i.e. $\{z: \exists w(Kw \wedge \phi w = z)\}$, to: $\{z: \exists w(Kw \wedge Rwz)\}$. The difference between the definitions of A_0 and R^* is insignificant in comparison with the idea of making definitions in this manner at all.

Whether or not Dedekind anticipated by a few years one of Frege's greatest discoveries, there is another year before 1879, namely 1858, which it would not be implausible to take as the one in which logic became a "great" subject. Indeed, logic as we now know it might be said to have arisen precisely on 24 November 1858. For on that date, according to the preface to *Continuity and Irrational Numbers*, Dedekind succeeded in discovering the "true origin in the elements of arithmetic" of the theorem that every bounded increasing function on the reals approaches a limit.[29] The key idea needed to prove the theorem rigorously was one of the most celebrated of all logical constructions, Dedekind's definition of the real numbers via cuts in the rational numbers. Although exceedingly familiar, the construction seems to me to be of possible philosophical interest in a way that has not been much remarked upon. Let me review it and describe the aspect I find noteworthy.

Take as given the set Q of rationals and the less-than relation on them. In section 4 of *Continuity*, called "Creation of the Irrational Numbers [*Schöpfung der irrationalen Zahlen*]", Dedekind defines a cut as a pair (A_1, B_1) of non-empty classes of rationals such that every element of A_1 is less than every element of B_1. Every rational number r produces two cuts, viz. $([q: q \leq r], [q: q > r])$ and $([q: q < r], [q: q \geq r])$, which are identified, regarded as "inessentially different." Some cuts, however, e.g. $([q: q < \sqrt{2}], [q \geq \sqrt{2}])$, are not produced by any rational number.

"Now anytime a cut (A_1, A_2) occurs that is produced by no rational number, we then *create* [*erschaffen*,[30] emphasis in the original] a new, irrational number α, which we regard as completely defined by this cut (A_1, A_2); we shall say that the number α corresponds to this cut, or that it produces this cut."[31] If α is produced by (A_1, A_2) and β by the essentially different cut (B_1, B_2), then α is said to be less than β if and only if A_1 is properly included in B_1 (in which case B_2 is also properly included in A_2).

In *The Nature and Meaning of Numbers* Dedekind argues that the term "free creation [*freie Schöpfung*]" is an appropriate one to apply to the natural numbers. His thought is that one may come to recognize the numbers by considering an arbitrary system satisfying the "Dedekind–Peano" axioms while "disregarding" all non-structural aspects of that system. Despite Dedekind's use of "*erschaffen*" in *Continuity*, it is plausible that he regarded the creation of the irrationals and that of the natural numbers as two instances of the same phenomenon. On Frege's view, of course, nothing at all is created by inattention or postulation: one merely recognizes what there is. Frege, though, would certainly have accepted the mathematical part of Dedekind's claim, which can be symbolized:

$$\forall X[X \subseteq Q \wedge \Lambda \ne X \ne Q \wedge \forall q(Xq \to \forall r(r < q \to Xr) \wedge$$
$$\exists r(q < r \wedge Xr)]) \to \exists! \alpha(\forall r(Xr \to r < \alpha) \wedge \forall r(\neg Xr \to \alpha \le r))].^{32}$$

From our point of view, the crucial aspect of Dedekind's construction is that iterating it produces nothing new, as he proves in section 5 of *Continuity*. Unlike the rationals, every cut in the reals (a well-defined notion, since less-than on the reals has been defined) is produced by a real. (Indeed the cut (A_1, A_2) in the reals is produced by the real corresponding to the cut $(\{r\colon \exists \alpha(A_1\alpha \wedge r < \alpha)\}, \{r\colon \exists \alpha(A_2\alpha \wedge \alpha \le r\})$ in the rationals.) Thus after taking the rationals, making all possible cuts in them, and then introducing in Dedekind's manner numbers corresponding to these cuts, one obtains no *new* numbers by taking the numbers one has so far gotten, making all possible cuts in them, and then introducing new numbers corresponding to the cuts made the second time around.

Cuts are two-sided. Dedekind defined them as pairs (A_1, A_2) of sets of certain sorts of numbers in which A_2 is the set of all numbers of the relevant sort not in A_1. Cuts, however, are not numbers; instead, they "are produced by" numbers, "correspond to" them, or "define" them. It is thus natural to think of a cut not as a first-order object, but either as a pair of second-order entities (A_1, A_2), as *two* second-order entities, A_1 and A_2, or, perhaps most naturally, as a second-order entity A together with another one N, a "sort of number," such that $\forall x(Ax \to Nx)$, $\exists x Ax$ and $\exists x \neg Ax$. It is equally natural to formalize Dedekind's account of the reals in second-order logic with the second-order variables ranging over cuts (or their left-hand halves), and relativized first-order variables ranging over the numbers, which are the objects Dedekind is primarily interested in.

Like cuts, Fregean concepts are also two-sided; they are functions from objects to the two truth-values. There is a striking analogy between Dedekind's definition of the reals as objects to which cuts in the rationals correspond uniquely (if one ignores inessentially different cuts) and Frege's ill-fated attempt in Basic Law (V) of *Grundgesetze* to introduce extensions as objects corresponding uniquely to concepts. Both begin with a domain of objects, take all possible second-order two-sided entities of an appropriate sort over that domain, and then introduce (recognize, Frege would say) certain objects in the domain in one–one correspondence with those second-order entities. Repeating the operation yields (or in the case of Frege, is supposed to yield) no objects not obtained (or recognized) after the operation has been performed only once.

Frege, as is well known, was not altogether confident about Basic Law (V). "I have never concealed from myself its lack of the self-evidence which the others possess, and which must properly be demanded of a law of logic" he wrote in the Appendix to *Grundgesetze*; earlier, as he notes there, he had said, "A dispute can arise, so far as I can see, only with regard to my Basic Law concerning courses-of-values (V)." Saul Kripke once wondered aloud why Frege did not make the experiment of seeing whether or not Cantor's paradox could be derived in the formal system of *Grundgesetze*. It is of course conceivable that he simply did not know of it; it is not conceivable that he did not know of Cantor's proof that the power class of a class is not equinumerous with it, for section 164 of Volume II of *Grundgesetze* contains the following noteworthy paragraph:

> We thus require a class of objects, which stand to one another in the relations of our domain of quantities, and this class must certainly contain infinitely many objects. Now to the concept *finite number* there belongs an infinite number, which we have called "endless" [*endlos*]; but this infinity still does not suffice. If we call the extension of a concept that is subordinate to the concept *finite number*, a CLASS OF FINITE NUMBERS, then to the concept *class of finite numbers* there belongs an infinite number, which is bigger than endless; i.e. the concept *finite number* can be mapped into the concept *class of finite numbers*, but the latter cannot be mapped into the former.[33]

Frege cites Dedekind's work in his own. It strikes me as a quite plausible speculation that the success of Dedekind's well-known construction may have given Frege confidence that a similar procedure could be used to introduce extensions in the manner he wanted and needed.

Dedekind's construction, of entities of one sort out of entities of another sort, is certainly not the first "logical construction" in mathematics. Hamilton's definition of the complex numbers as ordered pairs of reals, as good a logical construction as any ever made, antedates it by twenty-five years.[34] I shall not attempt to say whether I think Hamilton's philosophically brilliant construction counts as a contribution to *logic*, however.[35] Of special interest in Dedekind's work, as opposed to Hamilton's, is the use of what Quine would regard as set theory and what I, and I hope Putnam, would call logic. I wonder whether any piece of mathematics remotely comparable in logical sophistication antedates it.

In thus speculating upon the causes of Gottlob Frege's acceptance of *Grundgesetze*'s deadly Basic Law (V), I have strayed rather far from the theme of this volume, the philosophy of Hilary Putnam. But I recall from undergraduate days a certain professor of mine who once remarked that the way to seduce good students into philosophy was to teach them the Frege–Russell definition of number. I had been thus led astray, and if I am now to be faulted for dallying still in the early history of logic, I simply propose to transfer the blame to the author of that remark, Hilary Putnam.

Notes

1 Hilary Putnam (1990), *Realism with a Human Face*. Cambridge, MA: Harvard University Press, pp. 252–60.
2 W.V. Quine (1950, 1959), *Methods of Logic*, 1st and 2nd edns. New York: Henry Holt & Company. The quoted sentence is on p. vii of both editions.
3 W.V. Quine, *Methods of Logic* (1972, 1982). 3rd edn, New York: Holt, Rinehart and Winston, Inc.; 4th edn, Cambridge, MA: Harvard University Press.
4 Jean van Heijenoort (ed.) (1967), *From Frege to Gödel: A Source Book in Mathematical Logic 1879–1931*. Cambridge, MA: Harvard University Press.
5 Quine (1982), p. 294.
6 W.V. Quine (1955), *Mathematical Logic*, revised edition. Cambridge, MA: Harvard University Press, p. 221.
7 Hilary Putnam (1971), *Philosophy of Logic*. New York: Harper Torchbooks, p. 32.
8 Ibid., p. 30.
9 Ibid., p. 31.
10 Putnam (1990), p. 259. There are some first-order quantifiers missing from the text, which I have here restored.
11 George Boolos (1984), "To Be is To Be a Value of a Variable (or To Be Some Values of Some Variables)," *The Journal of Philosophy*, 81, 430–49; and Boolos (1985), "Nominalist Platonism," *The Philosophical Review*, 94, 327–44.
12 A small qualification must be made to provide for the "null class."
13 As I had been, by C.G. Hempel.
14 Thus van Heijenoort (1967): "A great epoch in the history of logic did open in 1879 when Gottlob Frege's *Begriffsschrift* was published" (p. vi).
15 Reprinted by Basil Blackwell, Oxford, 1951. The monograph is much less well known than Boole's *Laws of Thought* (1854), probably because it is too short for a proper book and too long to be included in a collection of articles.
16 William and Mathea Kneale (1962, 1984), *The Development of Logic*, Oxford: Oxford University Press, contains an extensive and very useful account of Boole's *Mathematical Analysis of Logic* and *Laws of Thought*.
17 The passage, to which Joe Ullian called my attention, is in (1982–), *Writings of Charles S. Peirce: A Chronological Edition*, ed. Max H. Frisch et al., Bloomington: Indiana University Press, vol. 4, p. xliv.
18 van Heijenoort (1967), p. 1.

19   Richard Dedekind (1963), *Essays on the Theory of Numbers*, trans. Wooster Woodruff Beman, New York: Dover Books, p. 42.
20   Ibid., pp. 57–8.
21   Ibid., p. 32.
22   Pierre Dugac, *Richard Dedekind et les Fondements des Mathématiques* (1976). Paris: Vrin. I am extremely grateful to Jan Sebestik, of the Institut d'Histoire des Sciences, Université de Paris I, for calling my attention to Dugac's book and its appendix LVI, which contains Dedekind's 1872–8 draft of *Was sind und was sollen die Zahlen?*
23   Ibid., p. 295.
24   Ibid., p. 296.
25   Ibid.
26   Ibid.
27   Ibid., p. 298.
28   Early on in the draft one finds the parenthetical phrase "(*Schluss von* n *auf* n+*1*)"; in the *Grundlagen* Frege refers to induction as "*die Schlussweise von* n *auf* n+*1*."
29   Dedekind, *Essays on the Theory of Numbers*, p. 2.
30   My colleague Irene Heim informs me that the etymologies of "*erschaffen*" and "*Schöpfung*" converge, but only at a rather remote date.
31   Ibid., p. 15.
32   Q is the set of rationals, "*q*" and "*r*" are variables ranging over the rationals, and "*α*" a variable ranging over the reals. In words, "for every downward closed concept X under which only rational numbers fall, under which some but not all rational numbers fall, and under which no greatest rational number falls – cuts determined by rationals necessitate this proviso – there is a unique real number greater than every rational falling under X and less than or equal to under every rational number not falling under X."
33   G. Frege (1903), *Grundgesetze der Arithmetik*, vol. II. Jena: Hermann Pohle, p. 161 (reprinted 1962, Hildesheim: Georg Olms).
34   Thirty-nine, if one considers publication dates.
35   Hamilton's treatment is a piece of philosophy if ever there was one. The insight was not merely to recognize that a problematic sum of a real and a product of a real with the square root of −1 could be explicated as an unproblematic pair of reals, but also to understand that the new problem the explication seems to give rise to – whether one can really *add* and *multiply pairs* of reals – is irrelevant to mathematics, since it is obvious which definitions of the various operations on pairs of reals have to be given.

3 Wittgenstein on Necessity: Some Reflections

Michael Dummett

A realist believes that there are, or at any rate may be, true statements that it is beyond our capacity to recognize as true: for instance, statements about the remote past, or number-theoretic statements no proof of which is possible by means of any resources we have or ever will have. A moderate constructivist will deny that there are any true statements whose truth we *could not* have recognized, had we been suitably placed; and a more radical constructivist will deny that there are any true statements whose truth we *can never come* to recognize. But constructivists of both persuasions are likely to agree that there are true statements whose truth we do not at present recognize and *shall not in fact ever* recognize; to deny this would appear to be to espouse a constructivism altogether too extreme. One surely cannot crudely equate truth with being recognized, or with being treated, as true.

It is otherwise with necessity; or, at least, it appears that necessity and truth differ in this regard. A long time ago, I attributed to Wittgenstein the thesis that for a statement to be necessarily true is simply for it to be *treated* as being necessarily true, that is, as being unassailable or as providing a standard by means of which other statements, at best contingently true, may be judged. The effect of a mathematical proof, on this account, is to induce us to treat the theorem as unassailable – to "put it in the archives." Having done so, we have a new criterion for the application of some mathematical concept. For instance, when we first encounter the proof that a cylinder intersects a plane in an ellipse, we acquire, provided that we accept the proof, a new criterion for the application of the term "ellipse"; we might, for example, appeal to the theorem in a particular case to establish that a certain figure, which, perhaps, did not look quite like an ellipse, *must be* one.

It can be objected that we do not, in fact, treat as unassailable whatever has been accepted as having been proved. There are actual cases of putative theorems having been acknowledged as such over many years, from which other putative theorems have been derived, only to be eventually confronted by a counter-example, leading to the detection of an error in the original proof; whereas, if our behavior matched the account of it Wittgenstein frequently gives, we should have ruled out the apparent counter-example a priori, declaring that there must be a mistake in the characterization of it as one. This may lead one to suspect that Wittgenstein confused necessity with certainty; whether we reject the counter-example or the theorem, in advance of locating a specific mistake in the description of the former or the proof of the latter, depends upon which we are more certain of. The thesis can, however, be formulated so as to allow for revisions in what we take as having been proved, by admitting proofs, in general, to be only *provisionally* compelling. A counter-proof of the same general character, or even an apparent empirical counter-example, will threaten the status of the theorem, although a failure then to locate a mistake either in its proof or in its purported refutation will provoke a crisis demanding resolution. What is necessary is what we treat as such and will continue to do so. But the Wittgensteinian account will not tolerate the introduction of the *ideal*. We must not say that the necessary is what the ideally competent mathematician *would* treat as such, for that invokes the conception of an external standard of correct judgement – one perhaps formulated by us, but certainly not applied by us – and there is none on this account. According to it, there is not in general any truth of the matter concerning what the ideally competent mathematician would and would not do or acknowledge, or even concerning what should count as ideal competence.

Hilary Putnam and I are agreed that the radical conventionalism about necessary truth which I attributed to Wittgenstein evades a fatal objection to the more restrained conventionalism advocated by the logical positivists and their fellow travellers. According to restrained conventionalism, all necessary truth derives, immediately or remotely, from linguistic stipulations we have tacitly made, linguistic conventions we are trained to observe. Some necessarily true statements, such as "There are seven days in a week" or "April comes after March," are the direct subjects of such stipulations; learning to treat them as true is expressly required for learning the use of the word "week" or the names "March" and "April." Other necessarily true statements, however, do not directly reflect conventions we consciously follow, but are *consequences* of more basic conventions. This prompts the objection that it leaves the necessity of the consequences unaccounted for: what makes it the case that, if we observe such-and-such conventions, which require us to treat such-and-such statements as true, we *must* accept such-and-such other statements as true? Radical conventionalism escapes this objection by treating *every* necessary truth as the direct expression of a linguistic convention. It does not, indeed, obliterate the distinction between basic necessary truths, in defence of which we can say no more than "That's what the word *means*," or something of that order, and consequences of those basic truths, for which we can offer a proof: but the latter are consequences solely because we count them as being consequences, which is to say that we accept their proofs as compelling; there is no sense in which they would be consequences whether we recognized them as such or not.

Hilary Putnam's comment on my proposed interpretation of Wittgenstein runs as follows:

> Michael Dummett (1959)[1] suggested a daring possibility: namely, that Wittgenstein was a *radical conventionalist*. That is, Wittgenstein was a conventionalist who held not just that some finite set of meaning postulates is true by convention, but that whenever we accept what we call a "proof" in logic or mathematics, an *act of decision* is involved: a decision to *accept* the proof. This decision, on Dummett's reading, is never *forced* on us by some prior thing called the "concepts" or "the meaning of the words"; even given these *as they have previously been specified*, it is still *up to us* whether we shall accept the proof as a valid deployment of those concepts or not. The decision to accept the proof is a *further* meaning stipulation: the "theorems of mathematics and logic" that we actually prove and accept are not just *consequences* of conventions, but *individually* conventional. Such a "radical" conventionalism, Dummett pointed out, would be immune to the Quine–Wittgenstein objection to the Ayer–Carnap sort of conventionalism.
>
> In response, Barry Stroud (1965)[2] pointed out that the position Dummett calls "radical conventionalism" cannot possibly be Wittgenstein's. A convention, in the literal sense, is something we can legislate either way. Wittgenstein does not anywhere say or suggest that the mathematician proving a theorem is *legislating* that it shall be a theorem (and the mathematician would get into a lot of trouble, to put it mildly, if he tried to "legislate" it the opposite way).
>
> Basing himself on a good deal of textual evidence, Stroud suggested that Wittgenstein's position was that it is not *convention* or *legislation* but our *forms of life* (i.e. our human nature as determined by our biology-plus-cultural-history) that cause us to accept certain proofs *as* proofs. And Stroud's reply to Dummett's interpretation appears to have been generally accepted by Wittgenstein scholars.
>
> It appears to me that Stroud's reply, while correct as a response to Dummett's interpretation, does not speak to the real philosophical point Dummett was making. The real point is that if *either* Dummett *or* Stroud is right, then Wittgenstein is claiming that mathematical truth and necessity *arise in us*, that it is human nature and forms of life that *explain* mathematical truth and necessity. If this is right, then it is the greatest philosophical

discovery of all time. Even if it is wrong, it is an astounding philosophical claim. If Stroud does not dispute that Wittgenstein advanced this claim – and he does not seem to dispute it – then *his* interpretation of Wittgenstein is a revision of Dummett's rather than a total rejection of it.³

It is clear that Putnam is right to say that even Stroud's Wittgenstein is propounding a thesis that goes against the common opinion; but, at the risk of appearing obstinate, I do not think he is right to accept Stroud's emendation of my interpretation. For it is really a version of moderate conventionalism, in that it acknowledges something – namely, human nature or our form of life – that *determines* the consequences of the basic necessary truths, or of the conventions that directly confer necessity upon them. Admittedly, as Putnam remarks, it locates what determines that within us; it is not an external necessity. Nevertheless, if Stroud is really propounding an interpretation that conflicts with mine, it must involve that, given the basic necessary truths, or, equivalently, the basic linguistic conventions, human nature, or our form of life, determines what we shall take as their consequences: granted what we are like, we cannot but draw from our basic conventions the consequences we in fact draw.

It may be said that that is just as Stroud intended: he meant to present Wittgenstein's view as less radical than I had done. It seems to me, however, that such an interpretation misses Wittgenstein's primary contention. Certainly we do, by and large, agree on what the consequences are, what follows from what, what is a valid proof and what is not. This is a fact of our existence – of our form of life, if you wish to use that phrase – and, without it, mathematics, as we practice it, could not exist. But, on Wittgenstein's view, it is a *brute* fact: nothing explains it. It cannot be accounted for by appeal to any general feature of our nature; and so no general feature of our nature suffices to determine what, specifically, we take to be consequences of the truths whose necessity springs from our basic linguistic conventions – the "grammatical" remarks that register our conformity to those conventions. If our nature did determine what, for us, would constitute a consequence of them, then there would be necessary truths that were, by our lights, consequences of the fundamental conventions even though we had not yet recognized them as such; indeed, there might be such necessary truths that we should never recognize. A conventionalist of what Putnam calls the Ayer–Carnap type thinks that the conventions we have adopted for the use of the words "cylinder," "intersection," "plane," and "ellipse" of themselves determine the inescapable truth of the theorem connecting them, by an ineluctable meta-necessity. Wittgenstein, as interpreted by Stroud, thinks that they do so in virtue of our human nature, or our form of life. But Wittgenstein himself thought that *nothing* determines it in advance: only when we have accepted the proof and put the theorem in the archives does it *become* a consequence of the initial conventions.

The phenomenology of mathematical proof is, indeed, quite different from that of taking a decision or of making a stipulation. We do not, in the normal case, see ourselves as having any other option than to accept the proof; we cannot think of anything we can say to resist it. Wittgenstein is well aware of this obvious feature, and indeed emphasizes it. It is part of the brute fact: but, as I understand him, he thought that we should not be seduced by it into supposing there to have been anything which determined in advance that such a proof was waiting to be discovered, or that, once given, it would strike us as compelling.

The core of Wittgenstein's argument is the observation that the proof provides us with a new criterion. This observation is, however, susceptible of a wholly banal construction. When we know the theorem, our accepting that *this* is a cylinder and *that* a plane gives us a reason for saying that the figure determined by their intersection is an ellipse; and this is a reason that we did not have before. If this is all that is meant by saying that we have a new criterion, it is indisputable; but it tells us nothing about what a mathematical proof is, or about the status of the theorem that it proves.

Now Wittgenstein's official description of his method in philosophy is that it consists in assembling truths that no one could dispute; if we believe that this is a true description, we may be inclined to suppose that the banal interpretation of the observation about the new criterion is the intended one. But, if so, the observation tells us precisely nothing; if, so understood, it is an example of Wittgenstein's philosophy, then that philosophy is incapable of throwing any light on anything. It seems, therefore, that the official description of Wittgenstein's philosophical method cannot be the true one, and that, in particular, the observation about new criteria cannot be meant to be understood as a mere platitude.

If it is not a platitude, what is its content? It is a platitude if it is construed as compatible with assuming that the new criterion will always agree with the old criteria, when these are correctly applied in accordance with our original standards for applying them correctly; that is, with the assumption that, whenever we apply the new criterion correctly, we should have been justified by the original criteria in making the assertion that we do, even if we had failed to notice the fact. For instance, whenever we rightly judge, by the old criteria, that this is a cylinder and that a plane, and, applying the new criterion, judge their intersection to be an ellipse, we should have been justified by the old criteria in declaring it to be an ellipse, even though, had we not known the theorem, we might not have noticed that it was or even, as the result of some mistake, have judged it not to be one.

That, however, is precisely what we take the force of the proof to be. We normally take the proof to show that whatever is judged by the new criterion to be an ellipse *must* be an ellipse by the old criterion, rightly applied, provided that we have also rightly applied the terms "cylinder" and "plane." Seeking a more than banal interpretation of the central observation about new criteria therefore appears to be a hopeless task: to all appearance, it is not merely a delicate matter to state the Wittgensteinian alternative, but an impossibility. We might try the following: if the observation that the proof supplies a new criterion is not to be a platitude, then it must be possible for there to be an apparent counter-example to the theorem whose description as being a counter-example involves no specifiable mistake in the application of the original criteria for applying the terms "ellipse," "cylinder," and "plane." But to say that there cannot be a counter-example, and hence that any description of something as one must involve a mistake, is an expression of our acceptance of the theorem; and, since we do accept it, we do say that, and there is no questioning our correctness is saying it. It is useless to retort that it does not follow that there must be some *specifiable* mistake. There may obviously be a mistake that we are unable to specify, not having spotted it; but this is, once more, banal. It remains that every mistake must be intrinsically capable of being specified; there can be no such thing as a mistake that is in itself unspecifiable.

In order to arrive at a robust interpretation of the thesis about new criteria which will give some substance to Wittgenstein's view of mathematical necessity, we might try saying that we are not entitled to claim that, in arriving at a judgement in conflict with the theorem, any *particular* mistake will in all cases come to light. That, however, is again banal: what is needed is a claim that there need *be* no particular mistake to come to light. Such a claim would be incoherent: there cannot be a mistake that is not a particular mistake, any more than there can be a donkey that is not a particular donkey.

Must we conclude, therefore, that there is no admissible interpretation of the thesis that the proof supplies a new criterion other than the banal one? That appears to land us back in moderate conventionalism: the validity of the new criterion is a consequence of our adoption of the original criteria, a consequence that holds whether we recognize it or not. That certainly does not represent Wittgenstein's view, at least as I am interpreting him: according to him, its being a consequence depends wholly upon our recognizing it as a consequence. But it seems that can be maintained only if we put a more than banal construction upon the thesis about new criteria: and we have seen that it appears impossible to arrive at any coherent formulation of any such construction.

Where have we gone wrong? I believe that the fact is that Wittgenstein does not want us to attempt to imagine the circumstances as from a super-human viewpoint. We strive to differentiate the banal from the robust interpretation of the thesis about new criteria by talking about mistakes that we might in fact make, although we neither detect them nor currently possess any reason for supposing them to have occurred: in general, by talking about what would have been *true* even though we had not recognized it as true. But this is to adopt the externalist standpoint that it was the whole point of Wittgenstein's account to repudiate: to attempt to step outside the situation in which we are placed, and thus to pass beyond the limits of language and say what can only be shown. We possess certain criteria for the application of our words; we make, and detect, mistakes in applying those criteria; and, since our criteria overlap, we also declare that a mistake must have occurred in cases in which we have not detected any. And all that can be done, according to the view I am attributing to Wittgenstein, is to describe those criteria and their interaction.

We want to say that, if we have an apparent counter-example to the theorem, God must be able to see what mistake we have made in the application of our own criteria, even if we cannot. It seems that, if we say this, we shall have reduced the thesis about the new criterion to banality. In reaction, we may attempt to formulate our internalist thesis, defending the conception that our acceptance of the theorem constitutes the whole sub-stance of the proposition that we must have made a mistake by saying that, on the contrary, there need not have been any specific mistake for God to notice. But if we choose this option, we shall have been unfaithful to our acceptance of the theorem. This is, essentially, the core of Putnam's refu-tation of relativism and allied heresies: any attempt to state the general thesis must run foul of that actual practice which it claims to be the source of necessity and truth, and hence be self-refuting: it is an attempt to view our language and our thought from that external vantage-point which it declares to be inaccessible.

The resolution of the difficulty lies in our acquiescing in the impossibility of our so much as talking intelligibly about how things are in themselves – how they are as God apprehends them – independently of what we treat ourselves as having reason to say. If we acquiesce in this, then there are no two distinct interpretations of the thesis about new criteria to put in con-trast with one another. It can be admitted to be banal, thus vindicating Wittgenstein's description of his philosophical method; but, because it uses the only resources that we have, it also constitutes the account that has to be given of the character of mathematical proof and the source of mathe-matical necessity. It is vain and presumptuous to attempt to see reality through God's eyes: all we can do is to describe our own practices as we can view them through our own eyes. Considered as a constituent of those practices, what a mathematical proof does is to induce us to accept a new criterion as being justified by the criteria we already had. That, therefore, is the sole and sufficient account of mathematical proof and of the necessity of mathematical theorems. We are not to ask whether the new criterion is *really* so justified: justification is what we *count* as justification.

If I have interpreted Wittgenstein aright, his doctrine is internalism with a vengeance; it could hardly be called internal *realism*. To say that we cannot intelligibly talk about what is true independently of what we recognize as true is, in effect, to hold that there is no admissible notion of truth other than that of being accepted as true. The internalist thesis that necessity attaches to a statement only in virtue of its being treated as necessary proves to require holding also that truth can attach to a statement only in virtue of *its* being treated as true. The claim that there are true statements whose truth we do not at present recognize can be admitted only in so far as it relates to those we shall come to recognize as true. Truth *is* to be equated with being recognized, or, better, with being treated, as true.

On reflection, it is evident that the internalist thesis about necessity *must* imply the internalist thesis about truth. For we are not here concerned with the, to my mind misbegotten, concept of metaphysical necessity, and logically necessary statements interest us only in so far as they encapsulate principles of inference, fundamental or derived. The disagreement between defenders and opponents of the law of excluded middle, for example, is about the validity of certain forms of reasoning such as the dilemma. A defender of the law who had some ingenious means of recognizing every instance of it as a logical truth, while rejecting as invalid all those rules of inference ordinarily thought of as standing or falling with it, would be occupying a position indistinguishable in substance from that of an opponent of the law: it is deductive validity that concerns us for its own sake, and necessary truth only as an instrument in securing that. The whole point of establishing a logically necessary truth is to provide us with a more streamlined means of arriving at contingent truths; so, if the necessity of the necessary truth depends solely upon our according it that status, the truth of contingent truths arrived at by its means must also depend in part on that. It might be retorted that mathematicians value theorems for their own sake; but Wittgenstein, at least, appears to have held that they have no value save in so far as they can be applied.

The difficulty with externalism – with purporting to say how things are in themselves, independently of how they appear to us – is that it soon presents itself as an attempt to say the unsayable. It is of little use to console ourselves with the reflection that there nevertheless *is* the unsayable, and that its only disadvantage is that we cannot say it; to say that is to pretend that the unsayable is nevertheless thinkable, whereas, if it cannot be said, it cannot be thought either. It is at this point that realism and idealism seem to coincide: once you have recognized that what you were attempting to say was unsayable, and have abandoned the attempt to say it, then there is nothing that cannot be said. How do we know that things exist when we do not perceive them? We apply certain criteria for something's having existed during an interval within which we were not perceiving it; and so, if it satisfies those criteria, it *did* exist during that interval, which is to say that we are right to say that it did – according to *our* criteria. But, to the externalist, internalism appears to be one of those traps from which it is, unfairly but undeniably, impossible to escape. How do I know that I am not dreaming, or mad? It seems that I can, in principle, offer no reply: for anything I might adduce might merely be part of my dream or a product of my madness. So here: I cannot, by the nature of the case, cite an instance of a true statement that we have no ground to recognize as true. I can, of course, claim that the statement "There are true statements that we have no ground to recognize as true" would be generally recognized as true; but all this does is to display the internalist thesis, in the strong form in which I am discussing it, as itself unsayable. But that is not to refute it. It does not show that we can ever do more than describe what our practice is; and any consequence I draw from supposing some particular statement to be true although unackowledged will still be the apodosis of a conditional that I have shown that we have good reason, by our existing criteria, to accept.

Still, if realism and idealism, or, as I am here preferring to say, externalism and internalism, coincide, there can be no harm in being an externalist. The externalist has an advantage over the internalist, in that, of certain things that we say, it is our practice to claim that they represent how things are in themselves, independently of how we apprehend them. Granted, we can have no grounds for asserting anything that, according to our linguistic conventions, we do not have a ground for asserting; but, when we assert something as representing how things are in themselves, the internalist's objection is stifled, since he has no means of expressing his thought that it does not *really* so represent them, but merely accords with a linguistic convention allowing, or requiring, us to *say* that it does.

It seems that neither the externalist nor the internalist view can be established, since to establish either would require us to say the unsayable; both sides may comfort themselves that there still *is* the unsayable, but it will be a different unsayable that each is constrained to refrain from attempting to say. Putnam nevertheless argues that it is possible to demonstrate the externalist view to be incoherent. From the side of physics, quantum mechanics makes it impossible to maintain that we are able to say how things are quite independently of our observation of them, unless we are prepared to adopt the metaphysical extravagances of the many-worlds interpretation;

and, from the side of logic, the paradoxes block us from supposing that we can devise a language in which everything can be expressed.

The paradoxes – both the set-theoretic and the semantic – result from our possessing indefinitely extensible concepts: those of set, ordinal number, and cardinal number are all indefinitely extensible, as is that of a statement. An indefinitely extensible concept is one for which, together with some determinate range or ranges of objects falling under it, we are given an intuitive principle whereby, if we have a sufficiently definite grasp of any one such range of objects, we can form, in terms of it, a conception of a more inclusive such range. A sufficiently definite grasp of a language, for example, is for this purpose one yielding an intuitive conception of the notion of truth as applying to the assertoric statements of that language. Given this, we may always frame a richer language in which we can talk about the first language, in the sense of formulating semantic properties of it, and also say anything that we could say in that language. Hence there can be for us no all-inclusive language, any more than we can talk simultaneously about all ordinal numbers in the sense of all objects that we could ever recognize as falling under the intuitive concept *ordinal number*.

By the nature of the case, we can form no clear conception of the extension of an indefinitely extensible concept; any attempt to do so is liable to lead us into contradiction. Is it intelligible to suppose that a superhuman intelligence could form such a conception? The concept could not be given to that intelligence as indefinitely extensible; but might it not have a concept whose extension covered all and only those objects we are capable of coming to recognize as ordinal numbers? The question seems unanswerable; but we should be cautious in formulating the proposition that we cannot talk simultaneously about all objects falling under an intuitive concept given to us as indefinitely extensible. We can obviously frame some incontestably true statements about all such objects, for example, "Every ordinal number has a successor." What we cannot do is to suppose that a language admitting such statements obeys a two-valued semantics; but there is no difficulty in envisaging such a language as obeying intuitionistic logic. That will not, of course, satisfy the externalist, because the statements of such a language will not all be determinately true or false, and for the most elementary reason, namely that the quantification they involve is not over a determinate domain (or at least over one of which we can attain a definite conception). We here come upon a link between externalism, as I have been discussing it, and realism, in the sense in which I have frequently discussed it and in which it crucially involves the principle of bivalence, a link that justifies Hilary Putnam's use of the phrase "external realism." Since the focus is different, however, I shall continue to use the term "externalism."

We may thus accept that full-blown externalism is incoherent. That does not vindicate full-blown internalism, however, since it, too, is incoherent. Of the two, externalism is definitely the more congenial to common sense; but from where do we get so much as the idea of a distinction between how things are in themselves and how they appear to us? We get it from our own linguistic practices, that is, the practices in which we learn to engage in the course of becoming masters of our mother tongues. I am not meaning here to allude to the contrast between delusive and veridical appearances, or between carrying out a procedure incorrectly and carrying it out correctly, since those, in general, are just matters of rectifying one observation or procedure in the light of others; they are distinctions *within* the realm of the way things appear. What we need to fasten on are those practices which induce us, or compel us, to form a conception of how things are independently of any observations we make; and that on which I wish to concentrate is that of deductive inference. If we spoke a language devoid of all inferential practices whatever, then there would be nothing to debar us from equating the truth of a statement with its having been directly verified; more properly expressed, the speakers of such a language would have no need of, and would not in fact possess, any notion of truth for which they could conceive that it might apply to any statements they had not directly verified. There would be for them no distinction between the world as it is and the world as it impinged on them. The introduction of deductive inference into the practice of the speakers of such a language would immediately compel them to frame a broader conception of truth. Perhaps "truth" is too strong a term for the notion they would have to have, for they would not need, simply in view of their admission of inferential procedures, to differentiate between it and the notion of what may justifiably be asserted; but they would certainly need a conception of what can be *indirectly* established as assertible, even though it has not been *directly* so established, just because that is what, in any interesting case, inference does, namely to establish its conclusion indirectly.

I hope I may be forgiven for using an example I have used before, that of Euler's proof concerning the bridges at Königsberg. This proof certainly does not show that, whenever we have verified that someone followed a connected course involving his or her crossing every bridge, we shall thereby have verified that he or she crossed at least one bridge more than once, for this is by no means so. What it establishes, rather, is that any sufficiently detailed observations that serve to verify the former can be so arranged as simultaneously to verify the latter; more exactly, that, when we have so arranged our observations, we have an effective means whereby we can locate an error whenever our observations appear to verify the former and to falsify the latter. In any specific case, the opportunity to carry out such detailed observations may have irretrievably passed; we may have verified that the walker crossed every bridge, without having the detail to transform this into an observation that the walker crossed some bridge twice. In the light of Euler's proof, we nevertheless take the observations we have made as entitling us to assert that some bridge was (must have been) crossed twice.

In so doing – more exactly, in coming to engage in the practice of accepting and applying such proofs – we *extend* our notion of what justifies the assertion of such a statement; the proof really does induce us to adopt a new criterion. It may be said that internalism can take that in its stride. This just is one of our practices: we have the custom of taking such a thing as justifying the assertion; and the statement is true precisely inasmuch as we have that practice, and the circumstances which it requires us to take as justifying the assertion do in fact obtain. But that is too glib: the question is whether we should maintain the practice if we believed the claims of the internalist. It is like Cantor's paradise: Wittgenstein does not drive us out of it, but, if we believe him, it will cease to appear a paradise and we shall see no reason for remaining.

Our criterion for the validity of a proof of this kind is that it provides an effective method for transforming a sufficiently detailed current observation that verifies a statement of a certain form into a verification of a related statement of a different form. The practice of making inferences on the basis of proofs valid by this criterion involves our willingness, when we have verified a statement of the first form, to assert one of the second form, even though we have not verified it and can no longer do so; that is why we have in such a case an *indirect* justification. Our having learned to engage in this practice has induced in us a conception of how things are – must have been – even when we have not observed them to be so. Once we have this conception, it is integral to our perceiving the practice we learned as a sound one; we have a conception of the truth of a statement in terms of which an argument which invokes the theorem is to be seen as transmitting truth from premiss to conclusion. We are entitled to assert that the walker crossed at least one bridge twice because the proof shows that that is how it must have been; we did not, but we *could have*, observed it to be so at the time.

But full-blown internalism repudiates this conception of truth. According to it, it is our practice of applying proofs of this kind that *constitutes* the truth of the statement we infer. And, once we believe that, why should we continue to apply them? Doubtless, when we first adopted the practice of inferential reasoning, there was little choice in the matter; we were simply trained to do so. But we do not maintain it simply because it is what society expects us to do: we do so because it appears to us to have a rationale, that is, to be a method of ascertaining how things in fact are. The full-blown internalist would have us think that rationale an illusion; if we believe the internalist, only inertia can make us go on reasoning as before. Better to strive to eradicate within ourselves the delusive distinction between the world as it is and the world as it impinges on us.

Thus full-blown internalism can make our linguistic practices the whole source of necessity and of truth only by discrediting those practices, and, indeed, the concepts of necessity and truth themselves: that is *its* incoherence. Logic and physics bar us from being full-blown externalists; but full-blown internalism will lead us to dismiss as pointless the practices on which it so heavily insists. It thus appears that a reasonable position must lie between the two extremes; but where? Hilary Putnam has attacked externalism in its full-blown form, but opposes to it a rather moderate internalism; full-blown internalism he equally repudiates. One temperamentally disposed towards externalism might aim at being as much of an externalist as possible, while shunning the untenable full-blown version; but, conversely, one temperamentally disposed towards internalism might wish to remain as internalist as possible, without going to the extreme in *that* direction.

This presents us with three problems. Is there a coherent moderate externalism? Is there a coherent moderate internalism? And do they coincide?

Unquestionably there have been philosophers whose views have embodied both externalist and internalist doctrines, held in apparent harmony. Frege is a clear example. His celebrated principle that a term has meaning only in the context of a sentence is a strongly internalist one. It involves a rejection of the conception whereby to treat a term as referring to some particular object is to make a mental association between the term and the object, considered as directly apprehended by the mind from a standpoint outside our language and our thought. According to the context principle, nothing can be picked out as an object of thought save in some particular way, which will in principle be expressible in language. Hence the determination of the reference of a term must reduce to fixing the conditions for the truth or falsity of identity-statements connecting it with other terms: grasping which object the term refers to is nothing more than knowing the conditions under which statements purporting to identify it in other ways are true.

Equally internalist is the corollary derived by Frege from the context principle, that with any term there must be associated a criterion of identity. This says, essentially, that the world does not come to us already dissected into discrete objects; rather, it is we who, by adopting particular criteria for what is to count as being presented with the same object as before, slice it up into objects in one manner rather than another.

Despite his propounding these internalist theses, Frege was, notoriously, a staunch realist. The mathematician's task is to discover what is there; truth is to be utterly distinguished from what is taken to be true; the sun is what it is, regardless of what we think it to be. We express our thoughts in language, but, in grasping those thoughts, recognize them as being determined as true or as false in virtue of how things are and independently of whether we do or can judge of their truth or falsity. The conception that reconciles the internalist and externalist components of Frege's philosophy is expressed in the *Tractatus* in the metaphor of the grid. To describe the world at all, we need a grid, and might use one or another; but, given the grid, what constitutes a correct description is wholly independent of us.

Kant and Putnam are agreed that the grid does not resemble one of the projections by means of which we draw a flat map of part of the surface of the earth; for there, by representing it upon a sphere, we can get to the reality we project in different ways. Frege, for all his realism, was also in agreement with this; we cannot think about any object save in some particular way, and we cannot think about the world save within the framework of a system of senses expressed by a particular language. But that is only the first surrender externalism is called upon to make to internalism. Internalism contests Frege's unargued externalist assumption that the grasp we have of the thoughts we express entitles us to regard the world as determining each of them either as true or as false independently of our ability to decide its truth-value, as if we were able in thought to stand outside our means of arriving at judgements and envisage reality as rendering our thoughts true or false independently of those means. (I remain somewhat uncertain where Putnam stands on this question.) But, the internalist once having abandoned the firm ground of the realist conception of truth, is in some embarrassment over just what to replace it by. This is because, as argued earlier, the extreme internalist conception, which would simply identify the truth of a statement with our eventual sustained acceptance of it, while perhaps not actually incoherent, would render uninteresting and pointless a great deal that we regard as interesting and full of point. It would, in fact, ride roughshod over all that prompts us to strain after a full-fledged realist and externalist conception, whereas there is much in our "form of life" that does so prompt us and which it is nihilist to treat with scorn.

The internalist's problem is how to arrive at a conception of truth which does justice to these constituents of our form of life without allowing them to push us back into externalism. In particular, we need to acknowledge the degree to which the desire to attain a description of the physical world as it is in itself has motivated a good deal of science, even if it is in principle impossible to attain or even conceive of such a description and even if the aim has had to be forsworn at the most fundamental level. The completely objective may be unattainable, perhaps unimaginable, perhaps even nonsensical; but our drive to approximate to it is not to be dismissed as a mere product of a metaphysical error.

It is not merely that our means of determining truth are circumscribed; we also commit constant errors in applying them. To accommodate *this* feature of our form of life, Putnam's moderate internalist notion of truth invokes both the ideal and the subjunctive conditional; truth is what we should eventually arrive at were we to commit nothing that was a mistake by our own lights. This appeal is difficult to resist; yet it embodies a substantial externalist component. For it assumes that there is a fact of the matter concerning what we should do were we ideal human beings, rather than the imperfect ones that we are; what we should do were we to make no mistakes. By the nature of the matter, this is something that we cannot in all cases know: what justifies us in assuming that there is some specific thing that we should in those ideal circumstances do? Indeed, to put the question in this epistemological form is to make it too weak; it should be a metaphysical question, namely: if there *is* some specific thing that we should do, *what makes it the case that we should do that*, even though we cannot be sure what it is?

Wittgenstein was resolute in refusing to take an externalist view of subjunctive conditionals. A passage in the *Lectures on the Foundations of Mathematics* illustrates this vividly, and is the clearest evidence in favour of my interpretation of him. Wittgenstein says, of a calculation that we have not made and will never make, that it is wrong to say that God knows what its result would have been had we made it, for "there is nothing for God to know." What is the difference between a calculation and an experiment? According to Wittgenstein, it is simply that, having once made and checked the calculation, we treat its result as a criterion for our repeating the calculation correctly. It is only our doing the calculation and "putting it in the archives" that constitutes its result as being that obtained by doing it correctly; so, if we never do that calculation, there *is* no one correct result, and hence God cannot be said to know what that result is. There is, in other words, no determinate result which is that which we should get if we were to perform the calculation correctly according to our criteria for correctness.

This conclusion is the outcome of an unflinching application of Wittgenstein's ideas about rules; and it leads to a thoroughgoing internalism. He was certainly right to observe that, for the most fundamental of the rules that we follow, there is nothing *by which* we judge something to be a correct application of them. It certainly does not follow from this that, if we never do make such a judgement in some particular instance, there is no specific thing that would have been a correct application: to draw that inference, you need a general internalist premiss, that there is nothing to truth beyond our acknowledgement of truth. This premiss is totally implausible: and the conclusion induces a skepticism so profound that few can swallow it.

Suppose the calculation in question is an ordinary addition sum. One of the rules that make up the computation procedure is that, when one of the two final digits is 7 and the other 8, you write 5 in the units column of the sum of the two numbers and carry 1 to the tens column. To maintain that there is no determinately correct result of the calculation, you must say one of two incredible things. Either you must say that, until someone has done it, it is not determinate what would count as writing down 5 and carrying 1; or you must say that, although it is determinate what the outcome of each application of one of the constituent rules would be, it is not determinate what would be the outcome of a large but finite number of such applications. I do not know how many of the followers of Wittgenstein *really* believe either of these things; for myself, I cannot, and conclude that the celebrated "rule-following considerations" embody a huge mistake. If they do not, then, if no one judges the position of the door, there will be no fact of the matter concerning whether, if someone had judged it to be shut, that judgement would have been right; there will be no truth that we have not expressly acknowledged as such. But I have suggested that the argument begs the question: global internalism is required as a premiss to take us from the epistemology of rules to their metaphysical standing.

The moderate conventionalist view was never a solution to the problem of logical necessity at all, because, by invoking the notion of consequence, it appealed to what it ought to have been explaining; that is why it appears to call for a meta-necessity beyond the necessity it purported to account for. The conventionalists were led astray by the example of the founders of modern logic into concentrating on the notion of logical or analytic *truth*, whereas precisely what they needed to fasten on was that of deductive *consequence*, which it is helpful to think of in terms of the metaphor of patterns. Even the simplest judgement imposes a pattern upon reality, a pattern in common between the variegated circumstances which would verify it. To make the judgement requires us not merely to attend passively to the relevant circumstances, but, deploying the concepts involved in the judgement, to discern the appropriate pattern in them. A deductive step brings about a small shift in the pattern apprehended; a series of such steps brings us to discern a pattern previously quite unexpected. When the step requires two premisses, we first superimpose two patterns on one another, to extract a third. The discernment of a new pattern is not merely compatible with, but *requires*, a recognition that that in which it is discerned has not itself changed; it is this which renders the deductive argument valid, while the novelty of the pattern represents the epistemic advance. The rules of inference which govern the deductive transitions themselves consist in the recognition of a pattern; not of a pattern in reality, but of one in a set of judgements, which mediates the passage from the discernment of one simple or complex pattern in reality to the discernment of another. Certainly our ability to discern patterns depends upon the stock of concepts available to us, which we acquire with our language and to which to a very limited extent we ourselves add. We do not *impose* the patterns, however, but *discern* them, and the capacity of one pattern to be transformed into another is intrinsic, not created by our ability to perform the transformation.

This externalist account of deductive reasoning says nothing about the nature of the reality in which the patterns are discerned. I have argued that the admission of the practice of deductive inference requires a notion of truth not grossly internalist, but in some degree differentiated from the occurrence of a direct verification. On how great the distance is between the two will depend which rules of inference are to be recognized as valid, and how much compromise the internalist is compelled to make with externalism. But that is a further question, not to be enquired into here.

Notes

1   Michael Dummett (1959), "Wittgenstein's philosophy of mathematics," *Philosophical Review*, 68, 324–48.
2   Barry Stroud, "Wittgenstein and logical necessity," *Philosophical Review*, 74, 504–18.
3   Hilary Putnam, *Realism and Reason: Philosophical Papers*, vol. 3, pp. 115–38.

4 Putnam and the Skolem Paradox

Michael Hallett

One of the interesting things about Hilary Putnam's recent work, and just one of the many things that make him such a stimulating philosopher, is his attempt to use the framework of mathematical logic to support or undermine positions in general metaphysics. What is meant here, of course, is Putnam's various uses of results from that branch of logic known as model theory in defence of the position he calls "internal realism," or rather as part of a sustained attack on what he has called "metaphysical realism," to which internal realism is opposed. One key feature of Putnam's earlier deployment of model theory was his appeal to the so-called "Skolem paradox" and the famous "Downward Löwenheim–Skolem Theorem (DLST)," which lies behind this. A good deal of the concern here will be with this "paradox." But it is also worth devoting a little attention to the general structure of Putnam's use of model-theoretic arguments.[1]

1 The Model-theoretic Arguments

Let us start with some of Putnam's own statements of what metaphysical realism amounts to. In Putnam (1981), he says this:

> On this [metaphysical realist] perspective, the world consists of some fixed totality of mind-independent objects. There is exactly one true and complete description of "the way the world is." Truth involves some sort of correspondence relation between our words or thought-signs and external things and sets of things.[2]

And in a more recent characterization, Putnam says:

> The traditional metaphysical realist picture of language is the following: the metaphysical realist pictures the world as a totality of language-independent things, a totality which is fixed once and for all, and, at least in the case of an ideal language, one (and only one) reference relation connecting our words with that totality is supposed to be singled out by the very way we understand our language.[3]

From these statements it seems clear that there are two related doctrines central to Putnam's characterization of metaphysical realism. The first is that there is a fixed and unique language-independent world, which, following Putnam's preferred notation, we will call THE WORLD. The second involves a claim about our language, namely that there is a unique reference function, fixed and determined by THE WORLD, taking individual terms of our language, terms like "cherry," on to particular REAL-WORLD objects or kinds of object, like cherries. It is to attack both of these doctrines that Putnam employs model theory.[4]

To cast all this in terms which are amenable to model-theoretic treatment, we have to make the following assumptions. The first, a very strong assumption, has to be:

1 Our beliefs about the world, including our scientific theories, can be framed reasonably accurately as a theory Σ cast in a regimented language $\mathscr{L}(\Sigma)$ of the kind mathematical logic normally deals with.

Putnam tells us that as well as being an adequate representation of our theories, we can also assume that Σ contains statements of "operational constraints," in short (a) that the "observational" part of the vocabulary of $\mathscr{L}(\Sigma)$ is as referentially fixed as propositions can make it, and more generally (b) that all the important features of our linguistic practices are correctly formulable in the language $\mathscr{L}(\Sigma)$ and added to the theory Σ. We can even assume that Σ is as good as we can ever get it, and that $\mathscr{L}(\Sigma)$ has been adjusted accordingly – in other words that Σ is what Putnam calls "the ideal theory." $\mathscr{L}(\Sigma)$ will in general contain constant terms (which might be considered proper names), and function expressions which can then be applied to these. The set that results from closure under these functions we can call the set of closed terms (thus names and descriptions) of $\mathscr{L}(\Sigma)$; call it $C_{\mathscr{L}(\Sigma)}$, or simply C. We can also assume that the specified predicates and function symbols of $\mathscr{L}(\Sigma)$ are constant "names" for properties, relations, functions, and so on, in other words names for the appropriate kind of entity (thus n-place function names will name n-place functions of real world objects, etc.). Let these "names" be added to C to form a slightly more general set called *Names$_{\mathscr{L}(\Sigma)}$*, or N for short.

Given all these assumptions, the view of the fixity of reference can now be stated as the claim that there is a fixed function REF taking each name n of N on to an item in this language-independent totality, THE WORLD. Thus:

> 2   THE WORLD (which, of course, must contain all the things in REF[N]) is an interpretation of $\mathscr{L}(\Sigma)$ in the usual model-theoretic sense of interpretation; indeed we can call it the intended interpretation of the metaphysical realist speaker of $\mathscr{L}(\Sigma)$.[5]

In particular, this means that THE WORLD must be a complex thing in a rather special sense, a *relational structure* possessing a domain (or several domains) of objects, which contain(s) items correctly matching the names in N, thus co-operatively and rather miraculously matching the language $\mathscr{L}(\Sigma)$, matching it so well in fact that the question of truth or falsity can arise for any of the sentences σ of $\mathscr{L}(\Sigma)$.

The fixity and uniqueness of REFERENCE only imply that part of THE WORLD is fixed, that part made up of those pieces which our language $\mathscr{L}(\Sigma)$ can name, the pieces in REF[N]. But the doctrines of metaphysical realism demand more than this, namely that THE whole WORLD is fixed. If this is so, we can make this stronger notion of "fixed" quite precise, for we can say:

> 3   If f is any homorphism on THE WORLD to any other structure f [THE WORLD] (quite possibly with the same domain(s) as THE WORLD), and f is not the identity map, then f [THE WORLD] is an unintended interpretation.

This captures the view Putnam wishes to combat because it amounts to saying that THE WORLD, assumed to be fully independent of our language $\mathscr{L}(\Sigma)$, is *the* correct interpretation of this language: thus not only is the part of it REF[N] fixed, it is *all* fixed, and "fixed" here seems an appropriately language-independent notion. Note that this also gives us a very strong notion of "intended interpretation," i.e. much stronger than the usual "unique up to isomorphism."

By a convention, every so-called *valuation* or *satisfaction* function g from $\mathscr{L}(\Sigma)$ into THE WORLD will have the function REF as its fixed core, thus these valuations will vary only on the values that they give to the variables of $\mathscr{L}(\Sigma)$. Moreover, every such satisfaction function will make exactly the same sentences of $\mathscr{L}(\Sigma)$ true and false. Another way to put it is to say that these true sentences are determined by the function REF, and we can denote the true sentences so determined by REF(*True*) – the set of truths about THE WORLD which the fixed language $\mathscr{L}(\Sigma)$ is capable of formulating given REF.

With this arrangement, there is now a clear way of stating the purposes of the model-theoretic arguments. There are in effect three arguments here. It can be shown that: (i) even if it is *an* interpretation which satisfies REF(*True*), THE WORLD cannot be the *only* such interpretation, thus determining REF(*True*) will not in the least enable us to recapture REF, without an antecedent guarantee that we are dealing with the interpretation THE WORLD; (ii) moreover, even if we assume that we are dealing with REF, there will be no way of singling out THE WORLD from these other interpretations; and finally (iii) even if we know that we have THE WORLD and REF(*True*), we still cannot get REF. Consequently, the model-theoretic arguments aim to demonstrate something of an epistemological circle. There are in effect three unknowns here, THE WORLD, REF, and REF(*True*). REF(*True*) will not give us REF unless we already have THE WORLD, for we can only work backwards from the set of truths (if only somehow we could get our hands on this) to REF itself if we already know that we are dealing with THE WORLD (or a significant part of it), thus in particular if we already know that there is a unique WORLD which fits our language well enough to be an interpretation of $\mathscr{L}(\Sigma)$, which is close to saying that we have REF. (For note that it is not just the stuff of THE WORLD that is important, but the way it is arranged too.) Moreover, REF(*True*) even with REF will not give us THE WORLD. More precisely, there are unintended interpretations of $\mathscr{L}(\Sigma)$ in the sense of "intended" which we gave above, i.e. interpretations other than THE WORLD, which make exactly the same sentences of $\mathscr{L}(\Sigma)$ true as THE WORLD does and which will preserve REF if we so wish, at least in so far as this is propositionally possible.

Putnam has used essentially two different arguments, achieving the aims just stated by proving somewhat different things. The first type of argument uses some sophisticated model theory involving the *DLST*; this we will refer to as the *Löwenheim–Skolem argument*; the other is rather more straightforward, and we will call it the *permutation argument*.

The Löwenheim-Skolem argument, as its name suggests, is based on the Löwenheim-Skolem Theorem (*LST*). Let $\mathfrak{A}$ be any structure which has an infinite domain and is a model of any consistent set of first-order sentences Γ. The *LST* in general says that, given any infinite cardinality different from that of the domain of $\mathfrak{A}$, there is another structure $\mathfrak{B}$ of that cardinality which is essentially different from $\mathfrak{A}$ *only* in the matter of cardinality; in other words, whose distinguished objects are just the same as those of $\mathfrak{A}$, and whose properties and relations are essentially the same too (this is the first key point), and which *also* satisfies the sentences Γ (the second key point).[6]

We can even show that there is such a $\mathfrak{B}$ which must include any specified set X of elements of the domain of $\mathfrak{A}$, provided only that the cardinality of X does not exceed the desired cardinality for $\mathfrak{B}$.[7] What this shows, then, is that even if THE WORLD *is* a model of the sentences Σ (in other words, that Σ is a subset of REF(*True*)), then there are lots of other structures which also satisfy Σ (indeed, the whole of REF(*True*)) and which are not isomorphic to THE WORLD, hence certainly not "intended" in the strong sense, assuming of course that Σ demands that its interpretations be infinite. Thus, our theory Σ, which, recall, is supposed to be as good as we could possibly get it, cannot hope to pick out THE WORLD from among all other possible structures, even if it happens to be true of this WORLD. Hence, we have claim (i). This supposedly is meant to challenge the sense of claiming that THE WORLD is a unique interpretation, for we can never hope to know this, at least not in any ordinary, propositional way. As for claim (ii), the slightly more general result shows that we can demand that the "unintended" interpretations contain (apparently) all the things that REF can name, as far as Σ is concerned all the right things. Thus, if a and b are in THE real WORLD, and *a is to the right of b*, and if "a" and "b" and "is to the right of" correctly name a, b and *is to the right of* (as far as we can tell), then the theorem says that we can find a model of Σ which also contains THE real WORLD entities a, b and *is to the right of*, and where the sentence "*a* is to the right of *b*" is made true by these. Thus REF is apparently preserved, that is, as far as Σ can tell, for as examples like the Skolem construction show us, the reference of a term t might be radically different in cardinality in the new model. Even more extremely, if we so wish we could demand that $\mathscr{L}(\Sigma)$ has names for all the items in THE WORLD, and that these names must be attached to the right objects. There will still be unintended interpretations of Σ obtained by expanding the domain(s) of THE WORLD, i.e. adding inaccessible parts.

The *DLST* covers that part of the result which deals with infinite cardinalities *smaller* than that of $\mathfrak{A}$ (if there are any), and is what is essentially involved in the Skolem paradox. Both parts of the *LST* are highly nontrivial results, and by no means straightforward to prove. However, these results have the disadvantage of not being widely applicable outside the realm of first-order theories, whereas there seems no reason why what is here called the permutation argument should not work for any theory cast in an extensional logic.

The permutation argument itself involves no sophisticated logic. Nevertheless, it does rely on a fundamental theorem of basic model theory, namely:

Fundamental theorem. If two structures are *isomorphic*, then they are *elementarily equivalent*.

Two structures are said to be *elementarily equivalent* if they satisfy exactly the same sentences, and *isomorphic*, of course, if their forms are mirror images of each other, that is, if the cardinalities of their domains, their names, predicates, and functions, and the actions of these, all match in a sense which can be made quite precise. The theorem is the key to the permutation argument in the following sense.[8]

Suppose we are lucky enough in our choice of Σ for THE WORLD to be a model of it under the valuation sequence g, which must, of course, extend the reference relation REF, and which thus gives rise to the set of truths REF(*True*). (Thus, Σ is again a subset of REF(*True*).) Now proceed as follows. Take a one–one permutation π of the domain(s) of THE WORLD, in other words, a one–one function π such that when a belongs to the domain of THE WORLD $\pi(a)$ does too. Using π, we can generate a potentially new interpretation: suppose the n-place relation name r_j of the language $\mathscr{L}(\Sigma)$ denotes the elementary n-place relation R_j in THE WORLD; then define a new relation R_j^π on $\{\pi(a): a$ is in the domain(s) of THE WORLD$\}$ by

$$R_j^\pi (\pi(a_1), \ldots , \pi(a_n)) \text{ iff } R_j (a_1, \ldots , a_n)$$

We can guarantee that π is non-trivial in that at least one of the R_j^π will be different from its corresponding R_j. Take an R_j under which something but not everything falls in the k-th place, and let a be one of the things which does fall under R_j in the k-th place. Then as $\pi(a)$ put some object which does not fall under R_j in the k-th place. In this case, R_j^π will be different from R_j. The domain(s) of THE WORLD, only now with the new relations R^π, give us a new interpretation of the language $\mathscr{L}(\Sigma)$; call it THE permuted WORLD. Moreover, given the valuation sequence g, we can define a new sequence g^π for the new interpretation by putting $g^\pi(x) = \pi(g(x))$; this readily allows us to see that the new interpretation is isomorphic to the THE WORLD, but different from it in the sense that at least one term in the language is assigned a different object from that assigned to it by REF, for example our r_j. Nevertheless, the basic theorem assures us that the new interpretation is elementarily equivalent to THE WORLD, that is, to repeat, that it satisfies exactly the same sentences as this does, the sentences in REF(*True*). Thus, in short, we cannot work backwards from REF(*True*) alone to REF, and (i) is established.

Moreover, we can strengthen this argument a little in that we can in principle demand that the R^π are *also* elements of THE WORLD. For example, suppose under REF a denotes a and r_j denotes the one-place property R_j, and suppose further that $R_j(a)$. In THE permuted WORLD we can arrange it so that a denotes some $\pi(a)$ and r_j denotes the REAL

WORLD property R_k, with $j \neq k$, and $R_k(\pi(a))$. (Of course, the possibilites of doing this properly will depend on the richness of the language, though we will assume that this is not a problem here.) Thus we can stay completely within THE WORLD; even so REF(*True*) will not give us REF, thus establishing (ii).

This permutation argument seems to contain the bare, model-theoretic bones of the "cats/cherries" argument that Putnam (1981) puts forward, an argument based on an appropriate permutation of the words "cat" and "cherry." That argument is disarmingly, perhaps suspiciously, simple, though this rather formal presentation of it shows that, given the set-up, it is unimpeachable.

The fundamental theorem on which this argument rests, although straightforward to prove, is not at all trivial. The reason that it is a basic theorem of model theory is that it embodies an assurance about the way model theory approaches extensional mathematics. It is simply a fact that much of the time mathematics is interested in what might be called *isomorphism invariant* properties of structures, and when not interested in these is interested in structures from the point of view of their ability to preserve the truth of some specified sentences. In short, we might characterize a mathematician as someone (qua mathematician) who ought not to be disturbed by it being pointed out that it is not 4 which is the square of 2, but rather some other object of the same name and which happens to play the same role as the pretender, or perhaps as someone who would not be bothered by Benacerraf's argument in "What Numbers Could Not Be,"[9] or as someone not troubled by being told that it was not actually Homer who wrote the *Odyssey*, but rather someone else of the same name. The fundamental theorem provides an assurance that two isomorphic structures will in fact satisfy exactly the same sentences, thus that one kind of invariance, form invariance, entails the other, true sentence invariance. Hence, in so far as mathematics is interested in the latter, nothing will be lost when we switch from consideration of one model-theoretic structure to consideration of an isomorphic one, thus connecting one notion of invariance, which on the face of it has nothing to do with the language, to another, which does.

With this in mind, what Putnam relies on is the fact that, although REF(*True*) is, REF itself is not isomorphism invariant, something we knew from the moment we said that THE WORLD itself is not isomorphism invariant, in other words that the metaphysical realist, unlike the mathematician, *will* be worried by Benacerraf's arguments or by the claims about 4, and certainly by the claims about Homer. The permutation argument shows that we can deviate from REF, as we might also do in the case of the Skolem argument, but we do not thereby deviate from REF(*True*). What this means a fortiori is that REF cannot be pinned down by the attainment of true sentences, even by the pinning down of all of the intended truths, the set REF(*True*). It follows from this that any attempt to state, i.e. to formulate in sentences added to Σ, what it is that *does* pin down the reference relation will be just to add some more truths, or rather some more sentences which must be satisfied, and hence will be doomed to failure.

In summary, then, the Löwenheim–Skolem argument establishes (i) and (ii) above, and the permuation argument establishes (i) and (iii). The latter could also be used to establish (ii) if we assume that there are parts of THE WORLD not named by REF, for we could then (presumably) perform some permuation among these, thus leaving REF fixed, but abandoning THE WORLD. Although the arguments do not achieve quite the same results, on the whole the permutation argument is better because it is both simpler and more general. Even supposing our beliefs could be formalized in a regimented logical language, it seems unlikely that the *LST* would apply. On the other hand, the Skolem argument communicates a much stronger sense of the essential inaccessibility of the THE WORLD, which the permutation argument does not, a sense of the massive gap between our theories and the way THE WORLD might be. For this reason, if personal psychology is anything to go by, the latter is more disturbing.

In this connection, it is interesting to note that some versions of skepticism seem to derive their force from worries that true sentence invariance, or even isomorphism itself, is not enough. If we want to compare the two forms of argument to some traditional skeptical arrangements, then the first is perhaps analogous to the argument from the premise that the world only came into existence ten minutes ago, or that we are brains in vats (thus we are asked to contemplate a radically non-isomorphic but supposedly elementarily equivalent structure), and the second is analogous to the argument from the premise that the world doubled in size ten minutes ago (thus we are faced here with an isomorphic and thus also elementarily equivalent structure). Note also that in this case, too, the gap between our theories and the way the world might be, as presented by the skeptic, is much greater, and again more disturbing, in the non–isomorphism case than in the other. Be that as it may, however, in both cases the crux of the skeptic's point is that there can be structures elementarily equivalent to THE WORLD *but different from it*, and this difference in structure, moreover, is one which no knowledge (propositionally expressed) can hope to detect, no matter how perfect we make it. Note that Twin Earth thought experiments also trade on the fact that we are asked to suppose a structure which is isomorphic to our world, or at least isomorphic up to the crucial point, the composition of water, say, though the differences in structure cannot be confined to this. This is, perhaps, no accident, for intrinsic to the very idea of these thought experiments is that the same sentences will be made true by both the Earth world and the Twin Earth world while reference varies, thus again decoupling the reference of a term from the truth of a specified collection of sentences (perhaps those which are supposed to give the meaning of that term).

The message from all this seems to be that the original notion of REF-ERENCE from which we started cannot be a terribly useful one in any attempt to gain significant knowledge of the world, at least not without some account of how we might use REF to attach names to things. Presumably one of the ways in which science tries to work is by attempting to formulate true sentences or true theories about the world, and one of its tasks is surely to say what some of the pieces of the world are. The circle Putnam confronts us with then presents a dilemma. It might be thought that before we can say what the world is like, we have to get reference right as far as we can. But surely part of what is entailed in getting reference right is being able to make some true claims; but then the challenge to REFERENCE comes. Suppose we grant that there can be a first step of getting some of REFERENCE right, and suppose we subsequently succeed in stating some truths. What Putnam's arguments seem to show is that there can be no route back from these truths to more of REFERENCE, without already knowing a lot about what THE WORLD is like, and it is just for gathering this knowledge that we wanted REFERENCE in the first place. Putnam's conclusion is that we have to adopt a notion of reference which accepts the looseness involved here, a notion which is at least true sentence-invariant, when the theory is taken as a whole, where the notion of "true sentence" does not itself depend on any function like REFERENCE.

Given the framework, the arguments seem unimpeachable. But what of the model-theoretic set-up? First, there is the difficulty of assuming that all our knowledge is encapsulated by the regimented language $\mathcal{L}(\Sigma)$, a matter which will not be discussed here. Secondly, the use of model theory turns on attributing to metaphysical realism the belief that THE real WORLD is an appropriate model-theoretic structure. This is a little strange, in that, whatever basic material they might be taken to start from, model-theoretic structures are set theoretic entities, thus abstract, theoretical constructions that depend on a linguistic and theoretical framework. Surely sets are not built into the world and our interactions with it in anything like the same way that cats and cherries are. The problem of reference for the metaphysical realist is just that of how the terms of the language we use are to be linked up to stuff of THE WORLD, to thoroughly non-theoretical entities, entities which are not in the least dependent on our language. But the assumption (2) at the beginning is in effect that THE WORLD is indeed the right kind of theoretical entity, and thus must be a construction which is to a large extent a product of some of our language and some of our mathematical theory (or at least the claim must be that THE WORLD is perfectly mirrored by such a construction). This is most clearly shown in the very assumption that THE WORLD is an interpretation of our language at all, for, as remarked above, THE WORLD is miraculously co-operative in choosing to fit our language so well. The reason this parallelism between models and language works so well in model theory is that one starts from a structure for which all of the basic form is given from the beginning of the study (distinguished elements, number and type of basic relations, functions, etc.), and then a language is shaped to fit this; thus names are provided for the functions and so on. The language mimics the structure, and the fit, therefore, is not in the least a miracle. But this is patently not what goes on with our use of language with respect to the world. The structure of this is not given at the outset; indeed, the very problem of science is to discover it.[10]

The conclusion that the shape of the world is partly dependent on language is something Putnam wants to convince us of. This may indeed be right. But the key point here is whether Putnam's model-theoretic arguments are arguments for this conclusion. What Putnam attributes to the metaphysical realist is the combination of claims that THE WORLD is indeed language-independent, but that it does nevertheless fit the language, interpret it model-theoretically. It is this combination that is challenged by the model-theoretic results, this and the non-toleration of isomorphic copies.[11] But if metaphysical realism wants to insist on the full independence of THE WORLD, it seems highly counter-intuitive to adopt the further claim about the language fit. Indeed, Putnam's challenge might well be a challenge to *this* and not to independence.

Let us now turn to the Skolem paradox; as we will see, there is good deal of connection between the views that lie behind this paradox and some of those attributed by Putnam to the metaphysical realist.

2 The Skolem Paradox

As was mentioned above in the short account of the Löwenheim–Skolem Theorem, the procedure there is to produce a model which differs in cardinality from the the given one, and which thus cannot be isomorphic to this, let alone intended. The most striking example of this procedure yields the so-called *Skolem paradox*. Shortly stated in a way which stresses the paradox, it consists in this. Suppose $\mathfrak{A}$ is an intended model of first-order set theory *ZF*, thus a model in which the continuum is (surely) really uncountable. Then we can use the *DLST* to produce a transitive, *countable* model $\mathfrak{B}$, isomorphic to an elementary substructure of $\mathfrak{A}$, and hence elementarily equivalent to $\mathfrak{A}$, and in which, being transitive, the continuum must be "really" countable.[12] What makes this potentially paradoxical is that ZF is unable to tell the models $\mathfrak{A}$ and $\mathfrak{B}$ apart, for they satisfy exactly the same sentences. Moreover, since $\mathfrak{B}$ is isomorphic to an elementary substructure of $\mathfrak{A}$, it has the right structure – for example, it is not obviously weird in the way that non-standard models sometimes can be. One conclusion is then that set theory cannot pin down the notion of uncountability adequately (in one common formulation, it is "unavoidably relative" in this respect). So much the worse for set theory, it seems, uncountability being one of its fundamental notions. It is this conclusion from the Skolem argument that I want to question here.

In a sense, the remark above about the number 4 suggests why we should not be too worried about the existence of countable models of set theory. Surely being countable or uncountable is really nothing more than the satisfaction of certain sentences of set theory, just as being 4 amounts to nothing more than the satisfaction of certain sentences of arithmetic. Putnam remarks about set theory in "Models and Reality:" "But if *axioms* cannot capture the 'intuitive notion of a set', what possibly could?"[13] In a sense, this is precisely the right instinct, although spelling out its background and consequences in the case of set theory and the Skolem paradox is not simple.

One of the things that makes the situation complicated is the strong hold of the view that axiomatic set theory (ZF set theory, say) is responsible to its models together with the view (thus the similarity with the metaphysical realism Putnam describes) that there are theory-independent models to be responsible to. Of course, given this view, the Skolem paradox can easily be made to show that ZF does not live up to these responsibilities. One of the things that strengthens the impression of responsibility to models is the situation with arithmetic, not least the confrontation between arithmetic and the Gödel theorems. Suppose one takes the first-order axioms for number theory, say the usual PA axioms, and then the usual independent Gödel sentence G for PA. One of the standard reactions is to say that the sentence G, although false in some non-standard model, is nevertheless "a truth of arithmetic," and thus a truth which PA cannot deliver as a theorem. This view is instructive, for what this assertion really means is that "G is true in the standard model $\mathfrak{N}$ of arithmetic," thus again that there is such a thing as the standard model of arithmetic and that one can see on inspection that G is made true by it. But, as Dummett makes clear in his paper on the Gödel incompleteness theorem,[14] models of arithmetic are *not* theoretically independent things which we have access to in some mysterious way. In order for the claim that "G is true in the standard model $\mathfrak{N}$ of arithmetic" to carry any weight, there must be a precise theoretical account of the model

$\mathfrak{N}$, which is to say that we need a theory in which the description of $\mathfrak{N}$ can be given and which *shows* that G is true in it, and also a description of a model in which G fails; in short, a model theory of the right sort. Ordinary set theory is quite good enough for this, for it allows us to give a comprehensive description of the notion "model of PA," and then to characterize (up to isomorphism) the standard model $\mathfrak{N}$, perhaps as just the intersection of all the other models. The feeling that we do have access to something here other than the theory PA is, when worked out, correct. We *do* have access to $\mathfrak{N}$; but it is decidely not theory-independent, but stems rather from, say, a theory of sets, perhaps ZF, or even something weaker. It might even be correct to think of PA and ZF as stemming from quite different sources, different "intuitions" if you like, so the feeling that we can say what the standard model of PA is like independently of PA itself is partially justified. It is just not *theory*-independent, for the informal or "intuitive" ideas either about what the natural numbers are like or as to how set theory should be developed are embodied in precise theories. It is only this which allows us to make precise sense of a statement like "the Gödel sentence G is really *true* of the natural numbers," and thus to make use of it in a decision as to how to proceed when faced with the Gödel theorems.

Something like this must hold for set theory and the Skolem paradox too. Let us start by looking at the way in which it is usually explained that the Skolem paradox is in fact just a paradox, and does not amount to a contradiction.[15]

Let the intended ("correct") model be denoted by $\mathfrak{A}$, and its continuum by $\mathfrak{a}$; let the transitive, countable model constructed by means of the theorem be denoted by $\mathfrak{B}$, and its continuum by $\mathfrak{b}$. According to the usual explanation, the paradox would only give rise to a genuine antinomy if the object $\mathfrak{b}$ of $\mathfrak{B}$ were both countable and uncountable, and the standard argument points out that $\mathfrak{b}$ is not at the same time, and in the same sense, both. It is countable because we have employed the Downward Löwenheim–Skolem Theorem (along with the axiom of choice) to demand that it is so, and this means that there exists a function which takes the domain of the model (and hence the extension of $\mathfrak{b}$) one–one onto the "real" natural numbers considered as existing "outside" the model. At the same time, $\mathfrak{b}$ is "uncountable" for the model $\mathfrak{B}$ just because it satisfies σ, the sentence which says that the continuum is uncountable; but this just means that there is no function in the model $\mathfrak{B}$ which "counts" $\mathfrak{b}$, i.e. is one–one, and whose domain is $\mathfrak{b}$ and whose range is the set of natural numbers $\omega^{\mathfrak{B}}$ of $\mathfrak{B}$. These two assertions are not, apparently, in any sort of contradiction.

This talk of "inside" and "outside" is basically right, when looked at in the right way. But we have to be careful with it, for it can suggest the kind of pernicious relativity which the paradox is sometimes supposed to lead to.

This explanation might seem to encourage the impression that the theory *does* fail to pick out the "real" continuum a, for the *ZF* term for the continuum (call it τ) might equally well pick out b instead. And then we seem close to a position about the "relativity of meaning" of *ZF*. If it is assumed that, to acquire any meaning, the terms of *ZF* have to be interpreted by models – or, in other words, that without models the language of *ZF* is strictly meaningless – then from the fact that there can be various non-isomorphic models, the relativity of meaning follows immediately. To spell it out, according to this view the meaning of the $\mathscr{L}(ZF)$ term for the continuum is in fact something which depends on the pair of the linguistic item τ and the corresponding elements a, b, ... etc. of the various models. But since the pairs $\langle \tau, a \rangle$, $\langle \tau, b \rangle$ ... etc. are essentially different (because the second element of the pairs varies – these are not only non-identical but non-isomorphic), then the meaning of τ varies as the model does. Thus, according to this view, the term τ would only have a fixed meaning if the way it is interpreted by a model remains fixed, or more generally if the reference of the term remains fixed.[16] Thus, part of the problem seems to stem from thinking, on the one hand, of the *meaningless* theory *ZF* and of the models on the other, and then conceiving of the relationship between the two as one of interpretation in the model-theoretic sense, and indeed stems from assuming a fixed reference relation, just as the metaphysical realist does according to Putnam.

There is another difficulty, implicit in the description we have just given and which also seems be emphasized by this "inside"/"outside" explanation. The apparent relativity could, of course, be overcome if one of the models were to be picked out as the right one – and we do seem to be able to say immediately that $\mathfrak{A}$ is right and $\mathfrak{B}$ wrong. Thus it seems that we do know what the real model is like, with its real continuum and its real notion of uncountability. Hence, the impression can easily be given that we are relying on some mysterious extra-*ZF* knowledge of set theory, or, to put it another way, that set theory and *ZF* are two different things, and that the latter is simply an inadequate formalization of the former. Needless to say, belief in a mysterious extra-knowledge makes set theory an easy target to attack.

Let us respond to both difficulties. As was said, the "inside"/"outside" explanation is along the right lines, but, as laid out here, does not go quite far enough. Recall that in the case of arithmetic we demanded that the claim that G is true be spelt out theoretically, otherwise it has little explanatory force. Let us demand the same thing here, that is, that the Skolem paradox itself and the "inside"/"outside" explanation of it are spelt out theoretically.

The central technical result which produces the Skolem paradox is, of course, the *DLST*, and this is a standard result of first-order model theory. Here, theories are treated as uninterpreted calculi, certainly for some purposes, and the division between these calculi and the models they have is as sharp as it could be. Moreover, precisely what model theory does is to investigate the relationship between these uninterpreted calculi and their models, though we should stress that this should by no means be seen as a concession to the view that theories are in fact meaningless, or that "modelling" an uninterpreted calculus endows it with meaning. The investigation of the relationships between theories and their models must itself take place in some articulated theory *T*. And since models are (usually) taken to be sets of some kind, such a theory *T* must include principles governing the production of sets. Furthermore, to produce the paradox as we have given it, *T* must have available both the notions of countability and uncountability, and thus in effect the natural numbers $\mathfrak{N}$ and the real numbers $\mathfrak{R}$, some means of representing the formulae of *ZF* to itself, and hence some way of discussing the collection of axioms of *ZF*. In addition, it must be able to reproduce the standard Tarski satisfaction definition which yields the usual way of saying that a set of axioms is true in a model, and it must have the axiom of choice available. It should also have some means of comparing models, some way of saying that one model is isomorphic to another, or that the two are elementarily equivalent, or whatever, for, without any of these, we would not be able even to frame the *DLST*, certainly not in a form strong enough to produce the Skolem paradox. Lastly, to get the result which is at the bottom of this, *T* must have the axiom of foundation available, for this is crucial to the construction of the countable, transitive model $\mathfrak{B}$ from the model $\mathfrak{A}$.[17] Given this, it is obvious that our viewpoint is the theory *T*, and from this viewpoint it is quite clear which set is the continuum, namely *T*'s $\mathfrak{R}$, and it is perfectly clear which models of *ZF*'s continuum are intended (isomorphic to $\mathfrak{R}$, and thus to each other) and which ones are unintended.

Once we are clear that we are relying on a theory *T*, then we can give a perfectly clear and unmysterious sense to the notions of "inside" and "outside." After all, unlike THE WORLD in the view that Putnam attributes to the metaphysical realist, the models $\mathfrak{A}$ and $\mathfrak{B}$ are purely theoretical constructions, fully within our theoretical control. Thus, when we say that there is a mapping outside the model $\mathfrak{B}$ which goes from the natural numbers one–one on to $\mathfrak{b}$, then what we mean is that we can prove from *T* that there exists a mapping from $\mathfrak{N}$ one–one on to $\mathfrak{b}$; and when we say that there is no mapping inside $\mathfrak{B}$ from $\omega^{\mathfrak{B}}$ one–one on to $\mathfrak{b}$, what we mean is that we can prove in *T* (on pain of contradiction) that there is no object of $\mathfrak{B}$ which satisfies the *ZF* sentence "f is a 1–1 function from ω on to τ," and remember that *T* is supposed to be able to deal with notions like "*ZF* sentence" and "σ is satisfied by x," and so on. All this is quite consistent with knowing, from T's perspective, that $\mathfrak{b}$ and $\omega^{\mathfrak{B}}$ are both countable, i.e. that T can prove the existence of functions that take both of these sets one–one on to $\mathfrak{N}$.

Of course, T will recognize that ZF has non-isomorphic models, but the important point is that it itself has a perfectly good continuum available. Thus, T is only in a position to say that the ZF theory of the continuum is "inadequate" because it itself has an adequate one. This follows because part of what it means to point out the inadequacy of ZF with the Skolem paradox is to exhibit a model $\mathfrak{B}$ whose continuum $\mathfrak{b}$ is not isomorphic to the uncountable $\mathfrak{R}$ of T, which means accepting the $\mathfrak{R}$ of T as the standard, at least accepting the proof that it is uncountable, i.e. cardinally different from $\mathfrak{N}$. Thus, if there are lots of models available, and if for whatever reason we wish to hold on to the claim that the meaning of τ is determined by the reference it picks out, then T need not be bound by the assumption that the only criterion of the adequacy of models is their satisfying ZF theorems: T can appeal to another criterion, namely the ability to produce a continuum which is isomorphic to $\mathfrak{R}$. Here, it is not some inarticulable and mysterious "mathematical intuition" which picks out the right models of ZF, but rather the perfectly articulable theory T.

In short, either (for one theoretical reason or another) T will not be able to reproduce the reasoning behind the Skolem argument, or it will be able to, in which case it is not at all clear that the Skolem paradox raises any particular difficulty. The "inside"/"ouside" explanation is, indeed, the right one, but only if we are clear that it takes place within a theory T.

Comparing this now with the arithmetical situation, does it mean that there has to be a theory T given to us quite independently of ZF which enables us to sort all this out? And what about the point that T itself might be formulable as a first-order theory which is then itself vulnerable to the production of countable models and Skolem reasoning. What then of T's $\mathfrak{R}$?

We have to be a little careful here. In the case of number theory, we can make precise sense of the "intuition" that there is a "standard model" in which G is true because we can call on some set (or more general) theory to help, and the Gödel theorem can then be used (in the light of this, i.e. from the perspective of higher set theory) to show that the theory PA does not capture the standard model. (Note that this is only because there is a fuller account of arithmetic available.) The corresponding situation with the Skolem paradox seems to be that it can only be used to show that ZF is "inadequate" if there is a theory T which goes beyond ZF, which is acceptable, and which can produce the variety of models involved in the paradox. But is there a theory over and beyond ZF (or ZF-based) set theory which can be appealed to?

The short answer is that there is not. In saying this, the point is not that there is something supreme, sovereign, and untouchable about *ZF*. On the contrary, it really amounts to the rather mundane observation that *ZF* sums up the core of the set theory we have. On the one hand, there is nothing like a noumenal "model," some set theoretic reality over and above this which *ZF* is responsible to, in which *ZF* floats (to steal Putnam's picture of Quine's picture from both);[18] and on the other, there simply is not a generally accepted extension of *ZF*, despite all the effort that has gone into finding one. What this means is that *ZF* does not *formalize* set theory, in the sense that it presents a mathematical version of some independent set theoretic reality − it *is* set theory. From this point of view, Putnam's remark that it is the axioms that capture "the intuitive notion of set" is right, at least according to this way of looking at things. Once again, this is not to say that set theory has not been heavily influenced by intuitive ideas about what sets are like or what mathematical role they might have, and how set theory is to be incorporated into more traditional mathematical concerns. Indeed, this was the very stuff of the development of set theory. Rather, it is just to say that these ideas have been absorbed or overtaken, perhaps even supplanted, by *ZF*. Thus, we might say that *ZF* summarizes set theory. To put it yet another way: of course it is right to say that *ZF* is answerable to informal notions; but this answerability does not amount to "answerable to a model," and there is no grand "intended interpretation" in a theory-independent sense. And without assuming this, and without assuming further that models can themselves be treated set theoretically, we cannot get further "Skolemization" and neither paradox nor an infinite regress.[19] Something like these assumptions are attributed by Putnam to the metaphysical realist, and of course it is these from which the unpleasant consequences come.

But the Skolem paradox is not quite finished with. If there is no generally accepted extension of *ZF*, then what of the Skolem paradox? The question is surprisingly interesting, though the issues can be no more than touched upon here. The reason that the question is interesting is that *ZF* (not surprisingly, on reflection) can reproduce virtually all of the model theory we demanded above, although, of course, if it is consistent, then it cannot prove that it itself has a model. In particular, *ZF* can code formulas into sets in a fairly straightforward way, and it can produce just the right sort of definition of satisfaction and truth in a model (meaning that it clearly mimics Tarski's satisfaction definition). Given this, it is easy to prove the *DLST* in *ZF* in the strong form which is required for the Skolem paradox, for we can define the central notion of being an elementary substructure of a set *u* in terms of the satisfaction relation: an elementary substructure of *u* (as one might expect) is a subset of *u* which satisfies the same (Gödel

' numbers of) formulas as u.[20] As long as the axiom of foundation is taken to be present, so that the Mostowski Collapsing Lemma is a relatively straightforward consequence, then precisely the reasoning which is used in the derivation of the Skolem paradox can be deployed *within ZF itself*. When we do this, we get what amounts to an "internal" Skolem paradox. In fact, we get the following result concerning the predicate $C(x)$, the predicate which expresses the usual formulation of the countability of x:

(*) If the system ZF is consistent, then the predicate $C(x)$ is not absolute.[21]

By the same token, the predicate $\neg C(x)$ expressing the uncountability of x is not absolute either. (We will come back to absoluteness in a while.) If we want to, we can construct a sentence of $\mathscr{L}(ZF)$ which expresses the assertion "The system ZF is consistent (has a set model)," namely $\exists u \forall x [Ax(x) \rightarrow Val(x, u)]$, where $Ax(x)$ stands for "x is the Gödel 'number' of an axiom," and $Val(x, u)$ stands for "the ZF sentence with Gödel 'number' x is true in the set u." Needless to say, if ZF really is consistent, we cannot prove this sentence in ZF. However, with it (*) can be replaced by a single theorem schema of ZF.

The reason that this is highly interesting is that we can show fairly easily that ω is an absolute term (or set), and by the same techniques as are involved in the proof of (*) that $P(\omega)$ (or the continuum) is not. Thus, what the Skolem argument (and thus the *DLST*) in fact gives us is a precise way to contrast these two sets, the set of natural numbers and its power set or the continuum.

Again, this internal Skolem paradox is no antinomy. In fact, the situation here is precisely parallel to that which obtains in the case of the traditional and genuine antinomies. These antinomies were absorbed by the system ZF in the sense that this system makes use of the reasoning which led to the contradictions, yet it does not allow the derivation of the contradictions themselves. Thus, antinomies like Russell's are "internalized," or absorbed, and the contradictions they once carried are defused. For example, inside ZF the reasoning which leads to the Russell antinomy is employed in the proof of a theorem which says that there is no universal set, as Zermelo showed.[22] Similarly the reasoning of the Burali-Forti antinomy is used to establish just that there is no set of all ordinals.[23] In both cases the arguments are transformed from contradictions into *reductios* which refute the hypotheses from which they start, namely that there is a set of such-and-such a kind, or, more generally, that any arbitrary predicate defines a set. In the case of the Skolem argument, too, precisely the reasoning which led to the apparently paradoxical result leads here to the theorem cited above, or to the parallel result that $P(\omega)$ (or the continuum) is not absolute. This internalization is certainly not contradictory, certainly not paradoxical, and does not raise any special difficulties. In fact, it confirms the analysis we have given above.

It is important to see what has been gained from this. First, leaving aside any role the Russell antinomy may have had in the genesis of axiomatic set theory, one could say that in the context of *ZF*, what the (former) antinomy is about, as Zermelo saw, is just the fact that there is no universal set. Similarly, in the context of *ZF*, the Skolem paradox is really about the fact that we can specify a precise way of distinguishing the natural from the real numbers, in effect a way of saying something precise about the notion of (un)countability which we can then proceed to investigate. Looked at in this way, there is not even the suspicion of the view that the Skolem paradox is about set theoretic relativity or indirectly shows the incoherence of the set theoretic account of the continuum, and it shows in addition that the Skolem paradox is not at root about *ZF*'s possession of non-standard models, something which would follow from an application of the *Upward LST* as well. One can argue that this result reveals the real content of the Skolem paradox. For one thing, as was stated, the internalization of the paradox formalizes in *ZF* exactly the mathematical core of the reasoning that would be used by any model theory *T*, and makes precise the conclusions to which such reasoning can lead. For another, it also takes seriously the view that it is quite possible that we will not be able to go beyond the theory *ZF*. In a sense, then, this result minimizes the Skolem reasoning. As against this, all the implicit, *extra* assumptions which appear to lie behind the paradox as frequently presented, assumptions about the meaninglessness of *ZF* without models and so on, are left firmly out of the account.

We have to say something very briefly about absoluteness, Despite variations in the way it is presented technically, the principle behind the notion of absoluteness, as the name suggests, is one of invariance, in this case the singling out of those terms or formulas which keep the same value (in the latter case, truth-value) as the domain in which they are evaluated varies. As far as set terms are concerned, we can sum up the situation as follows. Suppose u is a set; then $u = \{x : \phi(x)\}$ for some appropriate property ϕ. Now suppose ψ is a property determining what we might then call a "domain," either a set or a class. (It does not for the moment matter whether this domain is "adequate" or not; we just assume it to be non-empty, and that the theory *ZF* can recognize whether or not whatever conditions we impose on ψ hold.) Now suppose we evaluate u in ψ, in other words form the set $\{x : \phi(x)\}^{\psi}$, which just means in effect that all the quantifiers in $\phi(x)$ are assumed to be restricted to ψ. (Informally, $\{x : \phi(x)\}^{\psi}$ is the set which ψ thinks is u.) Then $u = \{x : \phi(x)\}$ is absolute if for all ψ (satisfying certain minimal conditions, in particular that ψ obeys a specified finite fragment of the axioms) the set $\{x: \phi(x)\}^{\psi}$ is exactly the same as the original set $\{x: \phi(x)\}$, i.e. $\{x: \phi(x)\}^{\psi} = \{x: \phi(x)\}$. Correspondingly, then, u is not absolute if we can find a ψ satisfying the minimal conditions such that $\{x: \phi(x)^{\psi} \neq \{x: \phi(x)\}$. (It should be clear that invariance or absoluteness in this sense will not be a fixed notion; more and more things will be absolute as more and more conditions are put on the domains to be used for the evaluation.) We usually ask for the ψ to be transitive, and in this case we can state the outcome of non-absoluteness in an even simpler way. For instance, in the case that interests us here, the non-absoluteness of $P(\omega)$ amounts to saying something quite simple, namely that we can find a non-empty transitive ψ (satisfying whatever finite list of axioms we like, as well as the other minimal conditions, of course) such that $\psi \cap P(\omega)$ is not the same as $P(\omega)$. This in turn just means that whatever axioms we specify, then we can find a ψ "adequate" to these axioms but which fails to contain at least one subset of ω, i.e. one member of $P(\omega)$.

But if the result we have stated is the core of the paradox, and if the paradox as usually presented has been defused, does this mean that it is no longer very important for what it says about the set theoretical concept of the continuum? This is not at all the case.

In the first place, the fact that the set of natural numbers is absolute but that the continuum is not is of central importance in the various key proofs (due to Gödel and Cohen) that go to make up the overall result that the continuum hypothesis is independent of set theory, the result that shows, in short, that we do not know (on the basis of ZF) what the cardinal size of the continuum is. Thus, the difference between the natural numbers and the continuum shown by the Skolem paradox appears to be intimately linked to the most significant sequence of results in modern set theory. This independence in turn suggests that set theory's treatment of cardinality is incomplete, in that it, and the results that came after it, taken together show that there is a radical indeterminacy in the concept of cardinality. But we should be careful here. The considerations raised by independence results tell us neither that set theory gives us an inadequate account of the continuum, nor, more specifically, that the theory of cardinality is wholly inadequate. What they do tell us, rather more modestly, is that the application of this latter theory is subject to certain definite limitations. In so far as the independence of the continuum hypothesis points out a limitation, then the Skolem paradox (as presented in (*)) is indeed connected to this, as Skolem originally suggested that it might be.[24] This is significant and interesting; but it is hardly devastating in the way that the Skolem paradox is often seen to be.

But there is a way in which the result about the non-absoluteness of the continuum *might* be taken to indicate that there is something amiss with its set theoretic treatment. For if one could provide arguments against absolute sets, one would have arguments, now based on the core of the Skolem paradox, to show that the treatment of the classical continuum by *ZF* is unsatisfactory. And curiously, the original analyses given by Russell and Poincaré of the genuine antinomies did focus on the non-absoluteness of sets.

Perhaps the clearest short hint of the involvement of something like non-absoluteness in the antinomies is in the following passage from one of Russell's analyses of the paradoxes (1906), written before he had fixed on a solution, thus before he had stated the vicious circle principle (*VCP*). We find the following striking passage:

> [t]here are what we may call self-reproductive processes and classes. That is, there are some properties such that, given any class of terms all having such a property, we can always define a new term also having the property in question. Hence we can never collect all the terms having the said property into a whole; because when we hope we have them all, the collection we have immediately proceeds to generate a new term also having the said property.[25]

It might be instructive to try to see the kind of "self-reproduction" Russell is pointing to in the traditional antinomies.

Suppose, informally, we call ψ a temporary universe. Let ϕ be some property; then we seem to be able to define a set u as $\{x: x \in \psi \wedge \phi(x)\}$. Using the Law of Excluded Middle, it is immediate that either $u \in \psi$ or $u \notin \psi$. Now, let us suppose that ϕ is the property involved in the Russell contradiction, i.e. that $u = \{x: x \in \psi \wedge x \notin x\}$ and suppose further that $u \in \psi$. Then clearly we have straightaway that $u \in u \leftrightarrow u \notin u$, i.e. the Russell contradiction. Hence it must be the case that $u \notin \psi$. Suppose now that ϕ is the property $Ord(x)$. If ψ is transitive, we can easily show that $u = \{x: x \in \psi \wedge Ord(x)\}$ is a von Neumann ordinal, and thus cannot be a member of itself. But if $u \in \psi$, we would have, on the contrary, that u does belong to itself – again the well-known contradiction. Thus, again $u \notin \psi$. Consequently, if we accept the definition of u as a good one, the conclusion has to be that, at least with respect to these two properties, ψ is not the full universe – it is indeed only temporary, for there are perfectly good sets, like u it seems, which cannot possibly belong to it. Put in the terms appropriate to what has been set out in previous sections, we could say that what Russell shows is that there are ϕ such that for any ψ it must be the case that $\{x: \phi(x)\}^\psi \neq \{x: \phi(x)\}$. This is obviously close to the notion of non-absoluteness.[26] Put more in Russell's way, whenever we call a halt to the "process" of collecting together the ϕ, we find that there is at least one more ϕ that we have yet to account for, in this case u. In other words, as Russell puts it, ϕ is a "self-reproductive" property.

It is clear that the idea of the *VCP* itself owes much to this. Here, for example, is Russell's (1908) statement:

> Thus all our contradictions have in common the assumption of a totality such that, if it were legitimate, it would at once be enlarged by new members defined in terms of itself.
>
> This leads us to the rule: "Whatever involves all of a collection cannot be one of the collection;" or, conversely: "If, provided a certain collection had a total, it would have members only definable in terms of that total, then the said collection has no total."*

*When I say that a collection has no total, I mean that statements about *all* its members are nonsense.[27]

Putting this together with the comments on self-reproductive properties, the resulting view appears to be that collections should only be admitted as genuine sets when it can be shown that we reach some stopping point in the "gathering" of their members, that is to say, although we might go on adding to the universe of sets, we will not thereby go on adding members to the collection in question. What Russell is getting at here is that the "self-reproductive" antinomies exhibit something that might be described as "non-absoluteness from below" – the attempt to capture all of the ϕ in one breath (all sets that do not belong to themselves, all ordinals) does not work.

Now interestingly, although Russell's main focus in the 1906 analysis is the Burali-Forti antinomy, Poincaré's various analyses are concerned more with the Richard antinomy and with the similarity between this and the Cantor diagonal proof. Moreover, the analyses he gives demonstrate a clear connection between what Russell illustrates and the structure of the continuum. If we proceed as is normally done in *ZF*, then the continuum *is* introduced "in one breath" via the power set operation applied to ω. However, suppose instead we start from the natural numbers and allow ourselves only quantification over, or reference to, what has already been defined. The Cantor diagonal proof will then assure us that the set of all real numbers will never be reached, for it is always possible to define a new real number in the sense of one that cannot belong to what has already been defined. In short, the continuum seen in this way is also clearly "non-absolute from below."

Poincaré saw the Richard and Cantor arguments as representing two sides of the same phenomenon. Referring to "laws" which co-ordinate the natural numbers to the definable decimals, he writes:

Richard's proof teaches us that, wherever I break off the process, then there's a corresponding law, while Cantor proves that the process can always be continued arbitrarily far.[28]

He endorses what he says is Richard's own solution to his antinomy, namely:

> E is the aggregate of *all* the numbers that can be defined in a finite number of words, *without introducing the notion of the aggregate E itself*, otherwise the definition of E would contain a vicious circle; we cannot define E by the aggregate E itself.
>
> Now we have defined N [the new real number] by a finite number of words, it is true, but only with the help of the notion of the aggregate E, and that is the reason why N does not form a part of E.[29]

The point then seems to be this. When the specification of E is being given, there cannot be any reliance on the existence of E, for indirectly this (in Poincaré's view) is just what the specifications are trying to establish. However, once the existence of E has been accepted, then its existence can be relied upon in any attribution of meaning to the terms used in a further specification. Thus, what Poincaré points to is just the ability to use "old" sets of a certain kind, and available at a certain stage, to define "new" sets of an apparently similar kind, i.e. satisfying what looks to be the same property. The continual extension of lists of real numbers like E is quite acceptable from Poincaré's point of view. What is not acceptable, however, is the claim that there is a set $\Re$ of all real numbers (or all subsets of ω), and in particular the claim that this set is uncountable. For any claim to this effect will fall foul of the exhibition of a member of $\Re$ or $P(\omega)$ which is defined in terms of $\Re$ or $P(\omega)$ itself.

A direct connection to non-absolute sets in general is to be found in the following two remarks, the first from Poincaré's 1909 article:

> A "non-predicative class" [thus, one whose definition suffers from what Poincaré calls a vicious circle, and is consequently illegitimate] is not an empty class, but a class with uncertain [*indécise*] boundaries.[30]

The second comes in 1909:

> From this there emerges a distinction between two types of classification applicable to the elements of infinite collections, *predicative* classifications, which cannot be disrupted [*bouleversées*] by the introduction of new elements, and *non-predicative* classifications for which the introduction of new elements requires constant reshaping [*remanier*].[31]

Such potential "variation" in membership is just what Poincaré indicates in the case of the Richard paradox and the set of all reals. Thus he is pointing to something very similar to the phenomena exhibited by Russell's "self-reproductive" properties. With the extension of any of the collections given by these, the boundaries are indeed "uncertain," as Poincaré says, because later "creation" of sets will alter them. Again, as with Russell, the preference is for sets which reach "stability," thus reach a stage at which this boundary shifting will no longer take place.

It is somewhat doubtful whether Poincaré's views can be adequately crystalized in precise prescriptions. Nevertheless, it is possible to see two doctrines about sets at work in his description of, and opposition to, non-absoluteness of this kind, thus in particular to the full Cantorian continuum. First:

> A set (or any mathematical object) cannot be said to exist until there is a specification of it.

(Call this the *Linguistic Specification Thesis*, or *LST*.) The second is the further claim that:

> Before a set *u* can be said to exist, we must be in possession of specifications of all of its potential members; and to avoid "circularity" these specifications cannot make reference, either direct or indirect, to the set *u*.

(This we might call for convenience the *Individual Specification Thesis*, or *IST*.) It is immediately clear that these theses will automatically rule out acceptance of sets *u* which contain members *v* only specifiable by direct or indirect reference to *u*, thus sets like the classical $P(\omega)$. This also makes it completely clear that adoption of ordinary set theory, say *ZF*, must involve the rejection of *IST*. The interesting question is why.

One of Poincaré's reasons for adopting *IST*, and thus for rejecting collections which contain members only definable in terms of themselves, is denial of the thesis that objects exist independently of the means of selecting them and of the concomitant thesis that the basic task of mathematics is the singling out and describing of these pre-existent objects. It is clear that this latter position will involve rejection of the *LST*, and will also certainly clear the way for rejection of the full *IST*. For, as Gödel remarks (1944, pp. 127-8), if one believes that mathematical objects exist independently of any constructions we might make, then there is nothing wrong with the view that the function of definitions is not to create these objects but rather to single some of them out, and it is then quite justifiable to use unbounded quantifiers, or "circular definitions," in doing this.[32] But the central question in this context is whether set theory's rejection of *IST* commits us to this thesis of independent existence.

If it does, then it would seem that we are back to the "metaphysical realist" view of mathematics which was behind our original presentation of the Skolem problem, for recall that this seems to be based on a belief that there is a "universe of sets" (or a continuum) which exists independently of any attempt we might make to say what this is. If the purpose of the (first-order) axioms of set theory is to try to pin down this independent "universe," then it will surely have succeeded in doing so only if the "universe" (or the continuum) is a unique model of these axioms. But then the familiar difficulties arise, and the traditional lines of argument can consequently proceed, because the theory has lots of apparently equally good, and non-isomorphic, models. The conclusion is that we can never succeed in pinning down *the* "universe" or *the* continuum or whatever. It would seem that focus on the issues raised by non-absolute sets has not brought us much further.

But focus on the *IST does* bring us further. What it suggests is an extension or clarification of the view put forward in the original discussion of the Skolem paradox above. There it was stated that there is no universe which acts as *the* correct model to which set theory is responsible and which it might fail to capture. What further emerges from consideration of the *IST* is that set theory cannot really be concerned with individually specified objects at all, or rather, it is only derivatively so.

The basic point behind this was succinctly put by Russell in his *Introduction to Mathematical Philosophy*. He writes:

> This is only an illustration of the general principle that what matters in mathematics, and to a very great extent in physical science, is not the intrinsic nature of our terms, but the logical nature of their interrelations.[33]

This attitude is by no means new with Russell. In fact, it goes back to Hilbert's treatment of the foundations of mathematics propounded from the end of the nineteenth century on, an attitude that has largely shaped the modern meta-mathematical approaches to the foundations of mathematics of which model theory is now a key part. The core of this attitude consists precisely in a shift away from the view that mathematical theories are concerned essentially with the description of an independent reality, and towards the view that they are at root concerned, not with specifications in Poincaré's sense, but rather with tractable axiom systems.

The Hilbert view originates in his treatment of geometry, and with the attempt, in which he was completely successful, finally to divorce the study of mathematical geometry both from the study of physical space and the behavior of ideal bodies in it, and from the study of real number manifolds. This involved not just the provision of an axiomatization of geometry, but also that of an axiomatization of real number theory. And in giving this latter, Hilbert was quite explicit that the study of the arithmetical continuum can no longer be the study of a totality of Cauchy sequences or some other collection of individually specified objects, but rather must be about the precisely specified axiom system. Through this, one does give specifications of individual real numbers through Cauchy sequences or Dedekind cuts. But these are "constructions" within the axiomatic framework already laid down, and one is thus allowed to call on (but only on) this axiomatic framework and the theorems it can prove in carrying out these constructions. (Thus, one is circumscribed by the framework, yet free within it.) However, the axiom system one starts from is not "correct" or "justified" because it corresponds to some independent mathematical realm existing prior to it, and therefore defective if it fails to pin this realm down.[34] On the contrary, the very notion of an appropriate mathematical realm is something subordinate to, and dependent on, a full, mathematical investigation of the relevant axiom system, including its (possibly manifold) relations to other systems, the question of its categoricity, the examination of its consistency and the provision (if possible) of consistency proofs. The "correctness" or, better, adequacy of the axiom system lies in the results of this investigation, and the reference to individual objects (which will quite possibly be products of other *theories*, as is the case in model theory) will be part of this, but only part. In fact, Hilbert was clearly of the opinion that the more possible references the terms of a theory have (even a categorical theory), the better, for then more connections to other mathematical and physical theories are established, thus helping to establish the importance of the theory. In particular, according to this view, the appropriate notion of mathematical existence is not that of "pre-existence" in a theory-independent sense. Rather, mathematical existence is theory-dependent, tied to properties of or facts about the theory, thus about the axiom system, and above all tied to that of consistency.[35]

In the case of set theory, what we start from is a list of axioms with a rather simple, recursive structure. It is the "logical nature of the interrelations" that these give rise to which must be emphasized when we consider particular terms of axiomatic set theory, terms like that for the continuum. It will not be a simple matter to explain how we understand such a list and its consequences (or to explain what this understanding has to do with second-order formulations), and it may be a mistake (as Putnam has taught us in another context) to imagine that the understanding or meaning of the axioms can be specified in a simple recipe. To be sure, set theory *is* complex, difficult, and intriguing. But the complexity, difficulty, and intrigue lie in the "logical nature of the interrelations" between the statements expressible in its language, and about the terms that can be defined with the help of its theorems, and not in some baffling relation between the axioms and a set theoretic reality. (One of the lessons of Gödel's and Gentzen's work is that sets of axioms of apparently simple structure can give rise to immense complexity when we consider the "interrelations.") Understanding, then, will not be easy. But surely some of this understanding is manifest in what can very loosely be called usage, thus in the fact that set theory's continuum builds up, reproduces, and integrates the various standard ways in which the continuum of real numbers was and is employed in various other branches of mathematics.

It is sometimes said that the non-absoluteness of the set $P(\omega)$ shows that the extent of $P(\omega)$ is somehow tied to the extent or the "richness" of the universe.[36] If the position of the independent existence of mathematical objects is adopted, this might make the non-absoluteness of the continuum seem difficult to accept, and indeed throw doubt either on its coherence, or at least on the claim that it is adequately represented in a set theoretic framework. For this latter will suggest that understanding the "extent" of the continuum requires first understanding the "extent" of the "universe," and thus apparently some superhuman powers, the understanding of some vast, imprecise, and ultimately ineffable structure. But the kind of theory-dependent holism implied in Russell's remark, and embedded in Hilbert's approach, surely indicates a clear, and non-pejorative, sense in which the extent of the continuum "depends on that of the whole universe," in other words, one which does not at all suggest that we think of axiom systems as designed to capture some independently existing reality. We surely do not have to understand some vast infinity of "objects," some ungraspable collection, in order to understand the "universe of sets." Given the complexity of the "logical interrelations" exhibited by set theory in particular, it ought not to be too much of a surprise that we do come across notions which depend on a large fragment of a theory for their elucidation, and it has become clear in various ways, not least through the non-absoluteness result, that this is true of the set theoretic concept of the continuum. Indeed, this is further confirmed by the independence results and subsequent work on large cardinals, for this makes it clear that in some sense understanding the set theoretic concept of the continuum not only depends on a large fragment of the standard theory, but might also fluctuate with new principles.[37]

One of the apparent problems with this "theory-centred" point of view, certainly in the original form given to it by Hilbert, is that it seems to depend heavily on the notion of consistency, and, following Gödel's work, it will not be a simple matter to say why systems are consistent, if indeed they are. But surely this is a quite general problem, and has nothing specifically to do with the continuum or any problems the Skolem "paradox" might engender, or even with impredicative definitions or non-absolute formulae. Moreover, consistency was originally only one of the properties that the Hilbert programme was interested in, and the surprising complexity of the network of problems surrounding this by no means shows that the basic, theory-centred attitude is misguided.

3 Conclusion

In some ways, the analysis of the Skolem paradox offered above is close in spirit to that which Putnam offers in place of metaphysical realism. This, of course, ought to be no surprise. In both cases, the assumption on which the paradoxical conclusions are founded is that of the independent existence of an intended model of the language, a model which is then shown to have the unwelcome, if not unacceptable, property of being quite inaccessible. However, in spite of this similarity, there is not complete symmetry between the two cases. In the case of the Skolem paradox, it is the assumption of the theoretical independence of the realm of sets that it at fault. With metaphysical realism, on the other hand, although there might be other good reasons for abandoning the view of the complete theoretical independence of THE WORLD, it seems more plausible to question whether there could be the requisite fit between THE WORLD and our language that would allow THE WORLD to be a model of our theories.

Application of model theory certainly changes the terms of the debate, and this can only be beneficial, for philosophical questions cannot be properly addressed until one has succeeded in putting them in a clear and precise framework, something which, unfortunately, happens all too rarely. But this is just what Putnam has done in this instance, and we can only be deeply indebted to him for that.

Notes

I would like to acknowledge the generous and kind support of the Alexander von Humboldt Stiftung, the Akademie der Wissenschaften zu Göttingen, the Social Sciences and Humanities Research Council of Canada, as well as McGill University for the granting of a sabbatical year in 1990–1 during which this paper was prepared. I would also like to thank David Davies for his invaluable help in the writing of this, as well as Daniel Velleman for comments on related work. Whether he recognizes it or not, I have also been greatly helped by notes of, and conversations with, Mihaly Makkai.
  1   Putnam's uses of various forms of model-theoretic arguments for the purpose of challenging metaphysical realism are to be found in particular in Putnam (1978b, 1980, 1981, 1983, 1989).

2 Putnam (1981), p. 49.

3 Putnam (1989), p. 214. That Putnam sees the problem of reference as fundamentally involved seems clear from the introduction to Putnam (1983), and also (1978b).

4 It should be pointed out that these are not the only kinds of argument which Putnam deploys against metaphysical realism.

5 Suppose the function name "eldest daughter of" really applies to the function of being the eldest daughter, and that the name "Emmy Noether" really picks out Emmy Noether. We would not expect the term "eldest daughter of Emmy Noether" to pick out anything. However, for the sake of simplicity we can assume that in cases like this there is a conventional denotation which it picks out, say the number 0, while when the function has "Peter Clark" as argument, "the eldest daughter of Peter Clark" stands for the young woman we expect it to. Let us also assume that we have no names without denotation.

6 We are assuming, of course, that the underlying language is countable, i.e. of the smallest infinite cardinality.

7 See Bell and Machover (1977), pp. 169–70, Theorem 5.2.1, or Chang and Keisler (1973), pp. 67–8 and 109–10.

8 This was pointed out to me by Mihaly Makkai.

9 See Benacerraf (1965).

10 Perhaps this is part of Lewis's (1984) message. For example, he says: "Referring isn't just something we do. What we say and think not only doesn't settle what we refer to; it doesn't even settle the prior question of *how* it is to be settled what we refer to. Meanings – as the saying goes – just ain't in the head" (p. 226).

11 One instinct is that the correct "philosophical" response to skeptical paradoxes like that based on the doubling in size of the world is a shrug of the shoulders. This might indicate a tolerance for a certain amount of isomorphic copying.

12 Actually, the correct construction of $\mathfrak{B}$ is rather more complicated than this. See Hallett (forthcoming).

13 Putnam (1980), p. 3.

14 See Dummett (1963).

15 The standard resolution goes back to Skolem's (1923) original exhibition of the problem, pp. 143–4 (English translation, pp. 295–6).

16 This is close to the view in section (1) about the fixity of REFERENCE.

17 See Hallett (forthcoming).

18 See Putnam (1989), pp. 221–2.

19 The view suggested here that "models" just things we construct *in mathematics* is very well stressed by Tait (1986), e.g. p. 356. There is further discussion of this below, p. 90 and n. 34.

20 We can also, of course, prove a version of the completeness theorem in *ZF*, though we cannot prove in *ZF* that *ZF* has a model.

21 See Bell and Machover (1977), pp. 507–8.

22 See Zermelo (1908b), p. 265; p. 203 of the English translation.

23 This was originally shown by von Neumann (1928); see, for example, Kunen (1980), p. 17.

94   *Michael Hallett*

24 See Skolem (1923).
25 Russell (1906), p. 144. See also the various discussions in Poincaré (1906), pp. 304–10 (which corresponds to (1908), pp. 202–8; pp. 185–91 of the English translation) and (1909), p. 463 (which corresponds to (1913), p. 10; p. 47 of the English translation). Excellent general treatments of both the views of Russell and Poincaré can be found in Goldfarb (1988) and (1989).
26 Though Russell's condition is apparently stronger than absoluteness, for according to the explanation given above a property ϕ is absolute when it is possible to find at least one ψ such that $\{x: \phi(x)\}^{\psi} \neq \{x: \phi(x)\}$ not that this necessarily holds for *all* ψ.
27 Russell (1908), p. 63 and footnote.
28 Poincaré (1910b), pp. 46–7.
29 Poincaré (1906), p. 307 (which corresponds to (1908), pp. 206–7; pp. 189–90 of the English translation).
30 Poincaré (1906), p. 310 (which corresponds to (1908), p. 208; p. 191 of the English translation). See also Poincaré (1909), where he uses the terms "mutable" and "immutable" for similar phenomena.
31 Poincaré (1909), p. 463 (which corresponds to (1913), p. 10; p. 47 of the English translation).
32 This was also in effect pointed out by Zermelo and Ramsey. See Zermelo (1908a), p. 191 of the English translation) and Ramsey (1926), pp. 368–9 (which corresponds to (1931), pp. 41–2, or (1978), pp. 192–3).
33 Russell (1919), p. 59. I am assuming here that "term" means something like "theoretical construct."
34 Something like this view has been stressed recently by Tait (1986). He argues that there are not two separate streams in mathematics, the theory-independent and that stemming from the use of theories, the question then being how these streams match each other, but rather just one – the latter. Tait puts this in a somewhat different way, using the fact that there are *apparently* two separate criteria for mathematical correctness, that of truth and that of provability. He argues that in fact talk of two separate criteria is misleading, and that there is at root only one, that of provability.
35 For much fuller discussions of Hilbert's point of view, see Hallett (1990) and (1994).
36 See, e.g. Bell and Machover (1977), p. 509.
37 Although this cannot be discussed properly here, it must not be thought that the common use of the term "universe of sets" in treatments of set theory shows that there *is* some extra-theoretic realm of objects on which set theory relies and is responsible to.

References

Aspray, W. and Kitcher, P. (eds) (1988), *History and Philosophy* of Modern Mathematics. Minneapolis: University of Minnesota Press.

Bell, John and Machover, Moshe (1977), *A Course in Mathematical Logic.* Amsterdam: North-Holland Publishing Co.

Benacerraf, Paul (1965), "What Numbers Could Not Be," *Philosophical Review,* 74, 47–73. Reprinted in Paul Benacerraf and Hilary Putnam (eds) *(1983), Philosophy of Mathematics: Selected Readings,* 2nd edn, Cambridge: Cambridge University Press, pp. 272–94.

Chang, C.C. and Keisler, H.J. (1973), *Model Theory.* Amsterdam: North-Holland Publishing Co.

Dummett, Michael (1963), "The Significance of Gödel's Incompleteness Theorems," *Ratio,* 5, 140–55. Reprinted in Dummett (1978), pp. 186–201. Page numbers in the text refer to this reprinting.

Dummett, Michael (1978), *Truth and Other Enigmas.* London: Duckworth.

George, Alexander (ed.) (1989), *Reflections on Chomsky.* Oxford: Basil Blackwell.

Gödel, Kurt (1944), "Russell's Mathematical Logic," in Schillp (ed.) (1944), pp. 125–53. Reprinted in Paul Benacerraf and Hilary Putnam (eds) (1969, 1983), *Philosophy of Mathematics: Selected Readings,* 1st edn, Oxford: Basil Blackwell, pp. 211–32; 2nd edn, Cambridge: Cambridge University Press, pp. 447–69; and also in Gödel (1990), pp. 119–41. Page numbers in the text refer to the last mentioned reprinting.

Gödel, Kurt (1990), *Collected Works,* vol. 2. New York, Oxford: Oxford University Press.

Goldfarb, Warren (1988), "Poincaré Against the Logicists," in Aspray and Kitcher (eds) (1988), pp. 61–81.

Goldfarb, Warren (1989), "Russell's Reasons for Ramification," in C. Wade Savage and Anthony Anderson (eds), *Rereading Russell* (Minnesota Studies in the Philosophy of Science, Vol. 12), Minneapolis: University of Minnesota Press, pp. 24–40.

Hallett, Michael (1990), "Physicalism, Reductionism and Hilbert," in Andrew Irvine (ed.), *Physicalism in Mathematics,* Dordrecht, Holland: D. Reidel Publishing Co., pp. 183–257.

Hallett, Michael (1994), "Hilbert's Axiomatic Method and the Laws of Thought," in Alexander George (ed.), *Mathematics and Mind,* New York, Oxford: Oxford University Press.

Hallett, Michael (forthcoming), "Absoluteness and the Skolem Paradox" to appear in Peter Clark and Michael Hallett (eds), *The Skolem Paradox.*

Heijenoort, J. van (ed.) (1967), *From Frege to Gödel: A Source Book in Mathematical Logic.* Cambridge, MA: Harvard University Press.

Kunen Kenneth (1980), *Set Theory: An Introduction to Independence Proofs.* Amsterdam: North-Holland Publishing Co..

Lewis, David (1984), "Putnam's Paradox," *Australasian Journal of Philosophy,* 62, 221–36.

Neumann, John von (1928), "Die Axiomatisierung der Mengenlehre," *Mathematische Zeitchrift,* 27, 669–752. Reprinted in John von Neumann (1961), *Collected works. Vol. I: Logic, Theory of Sets and Quantum Mechanics,* Oxford: Pergamon Press, pp. 339–422.

Poincaré, Henri (1906), "Les Mathématiques at la Logique," *Revue de Métaphysique et de Morale*, 14, 294–317. Reprinted with some changes in Poincaré (1908), pp. 192–214.

Poincaré, Henri (1908), *Science et Méthode*. Paris: Ernest Flammarion. English translation as *Science and Method*, New York: Dover Publications.

Poincaré, Henri (1909), "La Logique de l'Infini," *Revue de Métaphysique et de Morale*, 17, 462–82. Reprinted in Poincaré (1913), pp. 7–31.

Poincaré, Henri (1910a), *Sechs Vorträge über ausgewählte Gegenstände aus der reinen Mathematik und mathematischen Physik*. Leipzig and Berlin: B.G. Teubner.

Poincaré, Henri (1910b), "Über transfinite Zahlen," in Poincaré (1910a), pp. 43–8.

Poincaré, Henri (1912), "La Logique de l'Infini", *Scientia*, 12, 1–11. Reprinted in Poincaré (1913), pp. 84–96.

Poincaré, Henri (1913), *Dernières Pensées*. Paris: Ernest Flammarion. English translation by John Bolduc as *Mathematics and Science: Last Essays*, New York: Dover Publications.

Putnam, Hilary (1978a), *Meaning and the Moral Sciences*. London: Routledge and Kegan Paul.

Putnam, Hilary (1978b), "Realism and Reason," in Putnam (1978a), pp. 123–38.

Putnam, Hilary (1980), "Models and Reality," *Journal of Symbolic Logic*, 45, 464–82. Reprinted in Putnam (1983), 1–25. Page numbers in the text refer to this reprinting.

Putnam, Hilary (1981), *Reason, Truth and History*. Cambridge: Cambridge University Press.

Putnam, Hilary (1983), *Realism and Reason: Philosophical Papers*, Vol. 3. Cambridge: Cambridge University Press.

Putnam, Hilary (1989), "Model Theory and the 'Factuality' of Semantics," in George (1989), pp. 213–32.

Ramsey, Frank Plumpton (1926), "The Foundations of Mathematics," *Proceedings of the London Mathematical Society*, 25 (second series), 338–84. Reprinted in Ramsey (1931), pp. 1–61, and also in Ramsey (1978), pp. 152–212.

Ramsey, Frank Plumpton (1931), *The Foundations of Mathematics and Other Logical Essays*. Ed. by R.B. Braithwaite. London: Routledge and Kegan Paul.

Ramsey, Frank Plumpton (1978), *Foundations: Essays in Philosophy, Logic, Mathematics and Economics*. Ed. D.H. Mellor. London: Routledge and Kegan Paul.

Russell, B.A.W. (1906), "On Some Difficulties in the Theory of Transfinite Numbers and Order Types," *Proceedings of the London Mathematical Society*, 4 (second series), 29–53. Reprinted in Russell (1973), pp. 135–64.

Russell, B.A.W. (1908), "Mathematical Logic as Based on the Theory of Types," *American Journal of Mathematics*, 30, 222–62. Reprinted in Russell (1956), pp. 59–102, and in van Heijenoort (1967), pp. 150–82. Page numbers in the text refer to the former reprinting.

Russell, B.A.W. (1919), *Introduction to Mathematical Philosophy*. London: George Allen and Unwin.

Russell, B.A.W. (1956), *Logic and Knowledge*. Ed. R.C. Marsh. London: George Allen and Unwin.

Russell, B.A.W. (1973), *Essays in Analysis*. London: George Allen and Unwin.

Schillp, P.A. (ed.)(1944), *The Philosophy of Bertrand Russell*. Evanston and Chicago: Northwestern University Press.

Skolem, Thoralf (1923), "Einige Bermerkungen zur axiomatischen Mengenlehre," reprinted in Thoralf Skolem (1970), *Selected Papers in Logic*, ed. Jens Erik Fenstad, Oslo: Universitetsforlaget, pp. 137–52. English translation in van Heijenoort (1967), pp. 290–301.

Tait, W.W. (1986), "Truth and Proof: The Platonism of Mathematics," *Synthese*, 69, 341–70.

Zermelo, Ernst (1908a), "Neuer Beweis für die Möglichkeit einer Wohlordnung," *Mathematische Annalen*, 65, 107–28. English translation in van Heijenoort (1967), pp. 183–98.

Zermelo, Ernst (1908b), "Untersuchungen über die Grundlagen der Mengenlehre, I," *Mathematische Annalen*, 65, 261–81. English translation in van Heijenoort (1967), pp. 199–215.

5 Reliability, Realism, and Relativism

Kevin Kelly, Cory Juhl, and Clark Glymour

1 Three Putnamian Theses

At one time or another, Hilary Putnam has promoted each of the following theses:

1 *Limiting reliabilism*: A scientific method is better in so far as it is guaranteed to arrive eventually at the truth in more possible circumstances.
2 *Truth as idealized justification*: Truth is idealized rational acceptability.
3 *Moderate relativism*: Truth is dependent, in part, upon the concepts, belief system, etc. of agent *x*.

Thesis (1) appears in two papers published in 1963.[1] Theses (2) and (3) appear in later works under the joint rubric of "internal realism."[2] Putnam has not explained how the semantic theses that constitute internal realism fit together with his earlier, reliabilist conception of scientific enquiry. Nor have his followers. Barrels of philosophical ink have been spilled on (3) in complete isolation from (1). Computer scientists, on the other hand, have furthered the study of (1) over the past three decades with no consideration of (2) or (3). So there remains an interesting and obvious question. Can the conception of method characteristic of Putnam's earlier work be squared in a precise and fruitful way with his later semantic views? In this chapter, we undertake to answer this question.

In section 2, we discuss Putnam's early methodological work in the context of thesis (1). In section 3, we adapt the techniques discussed in

Figure 5.1

section 2 to the analysis of the notion of idealized rational acceptability involved in thesis (2). Finally, we show in section 4 how to extend the limiting reliabilist standards discussed in section 2 to settings in which evidence and truth can both depend upon the scientist's conceptual scheme and beliefs.

2   Limiting Reliability

Putnam's concern with the limiting reliability of scientific method is evident in his critique of Carnap's inductive logic,[3] a critique informed by Kemeny's reflections on the role of simplicity in inductive inference.[4]

> I shall argue that one can show that no definition of degree of confirmation can be adequate or can attain what any reasonably good inductive judge might attain without using such a concept. To do this it will be necessary (a) to state precisely the condition of adequacy that will be in question; (b) to show that no inductive method based on a "measure function" can satisfy it; and (c) to show that some methods (which can be precisely stated) can satisfy it.[5]

We will fill in points (a), (b), and (c) in order to illustrate the role played by limiting reliability.

2.1   Reliable Extrapolation in the Limit

Consider the game of guessing the next item in a sequence of zeros and ones.[6] When shown the sequence (0, 0, 0) one might guess that the next entry will be 0. Of course, the data might continue (0, 0, 0, 1, 1, 1), suggesting 0 as the next entry. In general, a rule that outputs a guess about what will happen next from the finite data sequence observed so far will be referred to as an extrapolator or predictor (see figure 5.1).

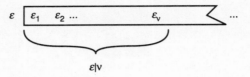

Figure 5.2

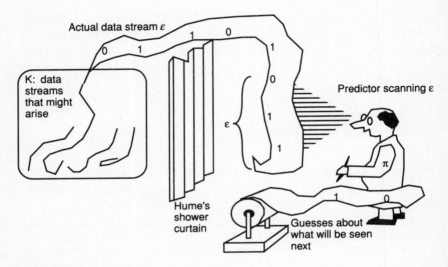

Figure 5.3

In this situation, the extrapolator gets to see more and more of the infinite data stream ε through time. At each stage n, ε_n is received, and by time n all of initial segment $\varepsilon|n$ is available for inspection (see figure 5.2).

We may know something in advance about what the data stream we are observing will be like. We might be told that all the sequences consist of a repeated pattern, or that they all converge to some value. Let K represent the space of all data streams that may arise for all we know or care.

The predictor and his or her situation can now be depicted as follows. Some $\varepsilon \in$ K is the actual data stream that π will face in the future. π reads larger and larger initial segments of ε and produces an increasing sequence of guesses about what will happen next. "Hume's shower curtain" prevents π from seeing the future, which would, of course, make prediction a bit too easy (see figure 5.3).

There are infinitely many possible methods for producing predictions. It remains to say what would count as a good method. It would be unreasonable to expect even the brightest extrapolator to be right *always*. It would also seem unreasonable to expect it to be right after some fixed time that can be specified a priori. Whatever that time is, there might be two possible extensions of the data that diverge only after that time. But we might hope at least that for each infinite data stream, there is some time (which may differ from one data stream to another) after which the extrapolator eventually "gets the gist" of the sequence and locks on to it, producing only correct predictions thereafter. We can think of this as a criterion of success for extrapolation methods in general. Let π be an extrapolator and let K be a specified set of data streams that we care about. Then

> π *reliably extrapolates* K in the limit $\Leftrightarrow$
> > *for each* possible data stream ε in K
> > > *there is* a time n such that
> > > > *for each* later time m,
> > > > > π's prediction is correct (i.e. $\pi(\varepsilon\,|\,m) = \varepsilon_{m+1}$).

This criterion of success reflects *limiting reliability*, since what is required of the extrapolator is convergence to the state of producing correct predictions, and this convergence is guaranteed over all of K, the space of data streams we care about. Whether or not reliable extrapolation is possible will depend heavily on the structure of K. If K contains only the everywhere-0 data stream, then we succeed over K by always guessing 0, without even looking at the data. If K includes all logically possible data streams, it is not hard to show that reliable extrapolation in the limit is impossible, no matter how clever our method might be. Then there are intermediate cases, as when K = *Rec*, the set of all data sequences that can be generated by a computer. That is just the example involved in Putnam's condition of adequacy for extrapolation methods:

(a) extrapolator π is *adequate* $\Leftrightarrow$ π reliably extrapolates Rec in the limit.

Putnam did not assume that this notion of adequacy would stand on its own. He was careful to explain that if no possible method is "adequate," then it is this condition of "adequacy" rather than Carnap's methods that must go. The condition is supposed to derive its force from the fact that it is both desirable and achievable.

2.2 Putnam's Diagonal Argument

Now we turn to the second step of Putnam's argument:

(b) no inductive method based on a "measure function" is adequate.

Before we can review Putnam's proof of (b), we must clarify what is meant by an inductive method *based on* a "measure function." Carnap's *c*-functions, or logical probability measures, are (in our set-up) conditional probability measures with special symmetry properties on the infinite product space E^ω, where E is an effectively enumerable set of atomic (mutually exclusive and exhaustive) possible observations. Such measures may be turned into extrapolation methods as follows. Let x be a particular observation and let $e*x$ be the result of concatenating x to finite sequence e. Let $c(e*x, e)$ be the probability that the next observation is x, given that e has been observed so far. Assume a fixed, effective enumeration $x_0, x_1, \ldots, x_n, \ldots$ of E. Then we can define predictor π_c so that π_c outputs the unique prediction assigned probability greater than 0.5 by c if there is one, and some "stall" character "#" otherwise.

$$\pi_c(e) = \begin{cases} \text{the first prediction } x \in E \text{ s.t. } c(e*x, e) > 0.5, \text{ if there is one} \\ \text{\# otherwise} \end{cases}$$

Observe that if $c(e*x, e)$ is recursive in e and in x (as Carnap's methods are), then π_c is also recursive.

It turns out that when c is one of Carnap's methods, the extrapolation method π_c has a special property, which is the only property of π_c that is relevant to Putnam's proof. Say that π is *gullible* just in case no matter what has been seen so far, if we feed observation x to π often enough, π will eventually start to predict that x will occur next. π is *recursively gullible* just in case there is some effective procedure that enables us to calculate in advance how many xs must be fed to π to get π to predict x next, for each finite evidence sequence e and for each x. To be precise, let x^n denote the sequence $(x, x, \ldots, x)$, in which x is repeated n times. Then we have:

π is *recursively gullible* $\Leftrightarrow$
  there exists a computable function f such that
    for each finite data segment e
      π predicts x after reading $f(e, x)$ successive xs added to e (i.e. $\pi(e*x^{f(e, x)}) = x$)

By an *inductive method based on a "measure function,"* we take Putnam to mean any extrapolation method π_c, where c is one of Carnap's *c*-functions. All such methods are recursively gullible. Thus (b) is implied by:

(b′)   If π is recursively gullible then π does not extrapolate Rec in the limit.

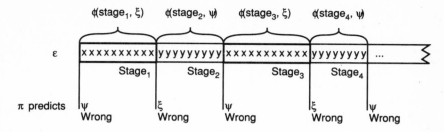

Figure 5.4

Putnam proves (b') by means of a diagonal argument. Since π is recursively gullible, we let $f(e, x)$ be a computable function that tells us how many xs we would have to add to e to get π to predict x as the next observation. At each stage, we check what π predicted at the end of the previous stage (say, x). Then we choose some datum $y \neq x$ and use f to calculate how many ys must be added to the data e presented so far to get π to predict y. We add this many ys to e, so that π makes a mistake after reading the last of the ys so added at this stage (see figure 5.4).

In the limit, π is wrong infinitely often. But ε is effective since it is defined recursively in terms of the recursive function f. Thus $\varepsilon \in$ Rec, so π does not extrapolate Rec.

Putnam mentions as a corollary that (b') remains true if recursive gullibility is replaced with the more perspicuous condition that π be recursive:

(b″)   If π is recursive then π does not extrapolate Rec in the limit.

This also implies (b) because $c(e^*x, e)$ is recursive in e and x, and hence when c is one of Carnap's methods, π_c is recursive.

(b″) follows from the fact that if π is recursive and is also able to extrapolate Rec, then π is recursively gullible.[7] For if we suppose that some recursive π extrapolates Rec, then if follows by (b') that π does not extrapolate Rec, which is a contradiction. To see that a recursive extrapolator of Rec is recursively gullible, suppose that recursive π extrapolates K. Define $f(e, x)$ to be the least number of consecutive xs that, when added to e, leads π to predict x. f is clearly computable if π is, so the only worry is whether π will eventually predict x at all. If π does not eventually predict x, then it is wrong all but finitely often on the data stream in which e is followed by all xs, which is also in Rec. But that contradicts the assumption that π extrapolates Rec.

2.3   *Hypothetico-deductivism*

Now we come to the last claim of Putnam's argument:

(c)   Some π extrapolates Rec in the limit.

The method that witnesses this fact is extremely simple. The idea is to enumerate predictive hypotheses, to find the first hypothesis in the enumeration consistent with the current data, and to predict whatever this hypothesis says will happen next. This basic architecture for choosing a hypothesis in light of data is known in the philosophy of science as the *hypothetico-deductive method* or the *method of conjectures and refutations*, in computational learning theory as *the enumeration technique*, in computer science as *generate-and-test search*, and in artificial intelligence as the *British Museum algorithm*. Putnam's interest in such proposals was inspired by an early article by Kemeny (1953) on methods that order hypotheses for test according to simplicity.

To adapt this venerable idea to the prediction of recursive sequences, we think of computer programs as hypotheses, so that the output of program p on input n is p's prediction about what will be observed at time n in the data stream. For concreteness, let computer programs be written in LISP. A LISP program (hypothesis) is correct for data stream ε just in case it makes a correct prediction for each position in the data stream.

Now we must confront an issue that looks like a mere detail, but that turns out to be the crux of Putnam's argument. Anybody who has written a program in LISP knows that LISP permits the programmer to write programs with "infinite loops." Such a program is incorrect for every data stream, since it fails to predict anything when it goes into an infinite loop. If such programs occur in an effective hypothetico-deductivist's hypothesis enumeration, one can never be sure whether the current attempt to derive a prediction is caught in a complex infinite loop or whether it will terminate at the next moment with a correct prediction. If he uses some criterion for cutting off lengthy tests and concluding that he has detected an infinite loop, he might throw out all the correct programs too early because their predictions take longer to derive than his criterion permits! If he insists on completing each derivation, he will freeze for eternity when testing a program with an infinite loop.

So the effective hypothetico-deductivist must eliminate all hypotheses with infinite loops from the hypothesis enumeration if he is to be a successful predictor. A program that never goes into an infinite loop is said to be *total*. An enumeration η of LISP programs is total if each program occurring in the enumeration is. On the other hand, the enumeration must be complete as well, in the sense that it includes a correct program for each recursive data stream. Otherwise, the hypothetico–deductivist will clearly fail if the un–represented data stream is in fact the one we receive. But it is perhaps the most basic fact of recursion theory that:

> *Fact 2.3.1*: An enumeration η of programs is either non–recursive or incomplete or non–total.[8]

In fact, this is not a special problem for the hypothetico–deductivist. It can be shown[9] that if $K \subseteq$ Rec is reliably extrapolable in the limit by some recursive π, then there is some recursive hypothesis enumeration that is total and complete for K. So in this sense every recursive extrapolator must somehow cope with fact 2.3.1.

Putnam's response to this inescapable limitation on computable extra–polation is to assume as "given" some non–comp table oracle producing a complete and total hypothesis enumeration η. When a computable process is provided with a non–computable oracle, it is said to be *recursive in* the oracle. Accordingly, let η be a hypothesis enumeration. Now we construct an extrapolation method π_η that uses the given enumeration η as follows:

$\pi_\eta(e)$:
find the first hypothesis p in η that eventually returns correct pre–dictions for all of e; predict whatever p says the next datum will be.

It is easy to see that:

> (c2)   If η is total then π_η is recursive in an oracle for η.

This is because the program for π can call for successive programs from the oracle η and then simulate each program received from the oracle for its agreement with e, the evidence received so far, producing its next pre–diction from the first such program found to agree with e. Since η is total, all consistency tests terminate. It is also easy to see that:

> (c3)   If η is total and complete then π_η extrapolates Rec in the limit.

Let ε be in Rec. Since η is complete and $\varepsilon \in$ Rec, some p occurring in η is correct for ε. Let p' be the first one (since there may be many correct programs). Then each preceding program p'' is incorrect in at least one of its predictions. Eventually, the data exposes each of these errors, and p' is the first program consistent with the data. It is never rejected, and its predictions are all correct. So once p' is at the head of the list, π_η never makes another mistaken prediction.

(c3) implies (c) and completes Putnam's argument. Putnam extends his arguments by announcing one more fact, namely:

(d)   Any recursive extrapolator that extrapolates $K \subset \text{Rec}$ can be improved to extrapolate one more data stream in Rec.

It is easy to see how. If π is recursive, then, as we saw in the proof of (b''), π is recursively gullible. By Putnam's diagonal argument we can use the gullibility function to produce a recursive data stream ε missed by π. Let p be correct for ε. Now we can "patch" π by having it predict according p until p is refuted, and thereafter switch to its own predictions. The resulting, recursive predictor π_p clearly succeeds wherever π does, but also succeeds on ε. Since π_p is recursive, we can diagonalize again, patch again, and so forth to form an infinite sequence π, π_{p_1}, π_{p_2}, . . . of ever better extrapolators of recursive data streams.

2.4   *Hypothetico-obscurantism*

Putnam concludes his argument as follows:

> This completes the case for the statement made at the beginning of the paper; namely, that a good inductive judge can do things, provided he does not use 'degree of confirmation' that he could not in principle accomplish if he did use 'degree of confirmation'.[10]

That is, if your extrapolator is π_c, where c is one of Carnap's c-functions, it will be recursively gullible, and no recursively gullible extrapolator extrapolates each data stream in Rec. But the hypothetico–deductive method π_η can extrapolate all of Rec, so presumably we should use π_η instead.

This sounds good – until we recall that the same objection applies to *all* computable predictors. By parity of reasoning, Putnam must also recommend that we use no computable methods because we could do more if we used the non-computable method π_η. The rub, of course, is that computability is the operative explication of what can be done using an explicit method. If Church's thesis is correct, then we cannot use π_η in the sense in which a method is ordinarily taken to be used or followed, so we cannot do more using π_η than we could using some computable method π. It would seem that Putnam agrees, since he asserts in the same article that an inductive method that is "never computable"[11] is "of no *use* to anybody."[12] So the apparent dominance argument against Carnap's methods fails. Carnap's methods are better in so far as they can be used. The uncomputable methods are better in so far as they would do more if they could be used.

So why should c-functions be branded as inadequate because, as computable methods, they cannot do as much as some useless, non-computable method? Putnam's answer is that π_η, though not recursive, is recursive in an oracle for η. And science should be viewed as having such an oracle "available" through some unanalyzed process of hypothesis proposal.

> I suggest that we should take the view that science is a method or possibly a collection of methods for *selecting a hypothesis*, assuming languages to be given *and hypotheses to be proposed*. Such a view seems better to accord with the importance of the hypothetico–deductive method in science, which all investigators come to stress more and more in recent years.[13]

But now a different difficulty arises. If Putnam's favourite method is provided access to a powerful oracle, then why are Carnap's methods denied the same privilege? The real question is whether there is a method π_c based on a conditional probability measure c that can effectively extrapolate all of Rec when provided with an oracle for η. But of course there is! Just define $c_\eta(x, e) = 1$ if $x = \pi_\eta(e)$ and $c_\eta(x, e) = 0$ otherwise. These constraints induce a joint measure on the infinite product space ω^ω by the usual measure extension lemmas, and $c_\eta(x, e)$ is clearly computable in η.

Putnam seems to have recognized this weakness in his original argument, for in his Radio Free Europe address he proposed the possibility of constructing a measure c for each hypothesis stream η so that $\pi_\eta(e) = \pi_c(e)$, for each finite data sequence e.[14] Then one may think of the c-function so constructed as implicitly "using" η. Now the objection to Carnap becomes more subtle. Carnap, together with contemporary Bayesians, insists that once a c-function is chosen, all changes in degrees of belief should be regulated by c as more data is read. But if c is a fixed, computable method then some hypotheses will be missing from its tacit η. Putnam's point is that it would be crazy, upon being shown that some total program p is missing from η, not to add p to η to form η' and to switch from c to $c_{\eta'}$. But a Carnapian committed to c from birth is not free to do so. In modern Bayesian jargon, such a move would be *diachronically incoherent*.

But again, the same argument applies to *all* computable predictors.[15] When it is pointed out that one's method π fails to "consider" total program p, one ought (by parity with Putnam's argument against Carnap's methods) to switch to some method π' that does everything π does, but that also "considers" program p.

This sounds good, but we must again be careful. We already know that for any fixed, effective method π we choose, we could have chosen a more reliable one, so every effective method is "inadequate" in the sense that using it prevents us from being as reliable as we might have been. But from this point of view, Putnam's objection against following a fixed, computable method is weak. It is like saying of a man who asks a genie for a huge amount of money that he was crazy not to ask for twice that amount. If every chosen amount could have been larger, then he cannot be crazy for choosing a particular amount. So by analogy, unless the process of modifying our current method to account for newly "suggested" hypotheses leads to limiting performance better than that of any *possible* recursive extrapolator, we should not conclude that using a fixed, recursive method π is crazy, even in the face of a second-guesser who points out how we could have chosen better as soon as we choose π.

But whether a methodological patcher relying on a hypothesis oracle η can do more than any fixed, recursive method will depend heavily on the nature of η. Where could η come from? Putnam's own examples arise from diagonalization. Consider some hypothetico–deductive method π_η, where η is effective. We can effectively recover some total p missing from η. Instead of adding p to the front of η, we insert p into η after the first program consistent with the data at the previous stage, to form η'. Now suppose we keep doing this over and over. The added programs will not interfere with convergence, since they are always inserted behind our current conjecture, so it is a lot better to proceed this way than to stick with η. But everything done here is effective, so all of this Camus-esque striving to escape the bourgeois rut of following a fixed extrapolation algorithm for life amounts to nothing more than following a fixed, recursive extrapolation algorithm for life, an algorithm whose own incompleteness can be effectively exposed by Putnam's diagonal argument!

Let us then turn to Putnam's suggestion that η be given, rather than formed effectively by diagonalization. This raises the possibility that π_η can do more than any effective method, as when η is complete and total for some $K \subseteq$ Rec for which no effective η is total and complete. Let us refer to such an η as *effectively transcendent*. But now a new problem arises: how are we to know that the enumeration η produced by a given source of hypotheses is, in fact, effectively transcendent? If we cast our lot with some π_η such that η is not effectively transcendent, then some fixed, recursive method π can do better than us!

It is hardly clear a priori that "creative intuition," "informal rationality," "common sense," or any other alleged source of hypotheses is effectively transcendent. Nor will it do for Putnam to appeal to scientific enquiry to determine the effective transcendence of a given hypothesis source, for it

Figure 5.5

can be shown that in a very weak sense of reliable success to be introduced shortly, no method, whether computable or not, can figure out whether a given hypothesis source (e.g. Uncle Fred) will in fact produce an effectively transcendent hypothesis stream η by studying its past performance.[16] Thus, the proposal to inductively investigate the status of a given hypothesis source is a cure far worse than the disease, because at least some non-computable method can extrapolate Rec. Moreover, it can be shown that no effective method can figure out whether the oracle is even total, let alone transcendent.[17]

We can add uncertainty about the hypothesis source to the definition of inductive success so that its significance for successful prediction is explicit. Our knowledge about the hypothesis source consists of some set S of infinite hypothesis streams, any one of which the source might generate, for all we know or care. Then reliable extrapolation using the source as an oracle can be defined as follows, where π now takes a finite, initial segment of η as well as a finite, initial segment of ε as input.

π reliably extrapolates K in the limit with a hypothesis oracle in S $\Leftrightarrow$
    for each possible data stream ε in K
        for each possible hypothesis stream η in S
            there is a time n such that
                for each later time m,
                    π's prediction is correct
                    (i.e. $\pi(\varepsilon|m, \eta|m) = \varepsilon_{m+1}$).

Without going into a detailed analysis of this intriguing success criterion, it suffices to observe that just as extrapolability *simpliciter* depends essentially upon the space of possible data streams K, extrapolability with a hypothesis oracle depends crucially on the space of possible hypothesis streams S. So we have the intuitive conclusion that we had better know a lot more than we do about our alleged oracles (e.g. "creative intuition," "informal rationality," "common sense") before we complain about how "inadequate" all the computable extrapolators are.[18]

There is yet another possible interpretation of Putnam's dissatisfaction with effective extrapolators. We have already seen that no recursive extrapolator succeeds over all of Rec, and that each such method can be improved, so there is no best. So no particular, recursive extrapolator is universal, in the sense that it succeeds over all of Rec. On the other hand, for each effective extrapolator π, there is some choice of an effective η so that the hypothetico–deductive extrapolator π_η succeeds on the same space $K \subset$ Rec of data streams that π succeeds over. We may think of hypothetico–deductivism as a recipe or architecture for building extrapolators in a particular way, using an effective hypothesis stream and a test procedure. Since for every effectively extrapolate K, some effective hypothetico–deductive method π_η extrapolates it, we may say that hypothetico–deductivism is a universal architecture for effective extrapolation. Universal architectures have the following desirable property: while no method built in the specified way is guaranteed to succeed over all data streams in Rec, at least the architecture does not stand in the way by preventing us from being as reliable as we could have been. In particular, a scientist wedded to a universal architecture is shielded from Putnam's charges of inadequacy, since completeness implies that there is nothing one could have done by violating the strictures of the architecture that one could not have done by honoring them. This is something of a let–down from Reichenbach's grand ambition of a universal method for science, but it provides the basis for a well-motivated "negative methodology" in which methodological principles ought at least not stand in the way of progress.[19]

Perhaps Putnam inherited from Reichenbach the notion that methodology proper should consist only of universal principles. From this it would follow that methodology should consist only of maxims or architectures, rather than of particular, concrete algorithms for extrapolation since the former can be universal and the latter cannot. On this reading, the "informal rationality" and "common sense" required to apply methodological maxims are a matter of making a maxim into a concrete plan for action, whether explicitly, or implicitly, in light of one's cognitive dispositions to produce conjectures on the basis of data in light of the maxim. This interpretation fits well with Putnam's hypothetico–deductivism, for as we have seen, hypothetico–deductivism is a universal architecture for extrapolation that yields a concrete method only when the hypothesis stream η is specified. But it still does not account entirely for Putnam's antagonism toward explicit, recursive methods. To say that a universal maxim is good when every explicit instance of it is "ridiculous"[20] makes about as much sense as the 1992 presidential polls, which placed a Democrat in the lead, but each particular Democrat behind.[21]

In short, Putnam's negative philosophical morals about "mindlessly" following computable extrapolation methods are not very persuasive. But ultimately, that is not so important. The lasting contribution of his argument was to illustrate how rich the study of effective discovery methods can be when approached from a logically sophisticated, recursion-theoretic perspective. Putnam exposed intrinsic, formal structure in the problem of effective extrapolation that his predecessors never dreamed of, and that most philosophers of science and statisticians still know nothing about. He set the stage for an approach to inductive methodology in which dogmas and preaching give way to formal facts about what is possible, regardless of what we insist we "must have." His analysis was tied squarely to the objective of getting correct answers eventually, a refreshingly straightforward alternative to evasive epistemologies based on coherence or some primitive notion of "theory justification," whatever that might be; epistemologies that make the *point* of following a reliable method obscure.

The special strength of Putnam's analysis, which is almost entirely missing from the methodological work of his contemporaries, is its exploitation of the strong analogy between the fundamental concepts of computation and induction. Our inductive abilities are fundamentally limited because the data stream can only be scanned locally. If it could be seen all at once, extrapolation would be trivial. But a computing machine's computational abilities are limited by its inability to write upon or scan an infinite memory store at once. This fact is manifested in our discussion of the hypothetico-deductivist's uncertainty regarding whether or not a given computation will halt. From a computer's point of view, the formal question of consistency becomes an internalized empirical question, and the machine's potentially infinite, ever-extendable memory can be viewed as a second, internalized data presentation, only some finite segment of which can be scanned at a given time. This strong analogy between the leading metaphors of induction and computation poses the prospect for a logical study of induction entirely parallel to modern mathematical logic, both in style and in content. As in mathematical logic, the fundamental objects of inductive logic become problems and relations of relative difficulty between them.

Finally, Putnam's recursion-theoretic methodological results make no recourse to measures and probability, the traditional mainstays of inductive logic. Putnam's attitude is that extrapolation over some range K of possible data streams is a fixed problem, and that methods like Carnap's, which update probability measures over possible observations, are just one proposed solution among many. Whether or not such methods are good solutions

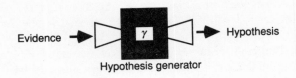

Evidence　Hypothesis

Hypothesis generator

Figure 5.6

to the prediction problem should drop out of a careful, comparative analysis. Nor does Putnam exempt probabilistic methods from failure over sets of data streams that the method is "almost sure" will not arise, as in Bayesian, "almost-sure" convergence theorems. Such theorems show only that each countably additive probability measure is willing to "bet its life" that it will get to the truth in the limit. In Putnam's analysis, the method is required to *really* succeed over all of K in virtue of its computational structure: he does not take the method's own word for its future success. Thirty years on, these proposals are still both radical and exciting.

2.5　Hypothesis Discovery and Hypothesis Assessment

The preceding discussion was about extrapolation methods, since Putnam's article puts matters this way, but his limiting reliabilist analysis applies just as well to other types of methodological problem. Sometimes a scientist desires to produce some correct hypothesis in light of the available data. Methods for doing this are called *logics of discovery* by philosophers, *estimators* by statisticians, and *learning machines* by cognitive and computer scientists. We will refer to methods that produce hypotheses on the basis of evidence as *hypothesis generators* (see figure 5.6).[22]

Hypothetico–deductive method is most simply conceived of as a hypothesis generator constructed out of a hypothesis enumeration η and a special criterion of hypothesis test, namely, consistency with the data:

$$\gamma_\eta^K(e) = \text{the first hypothesis in } \eta \text{ consistent with } e \text{ in K.}$$

Recall the criterion of reliable extrapolation in the limit. The idea was that the method should eventually "get it right" after some time, no matter which data stream in K is actual. We can also hope that our methods for discovery will eventually "get it right." In hypothesis generation, "getting it right" means producing a correct hypothesis. Recall, for example, that a LISP program is correct for infinite data stream ε just in case it correctly predicts each observation in ε. Generalizing that example, let *hypotheses* be objects in some countable set H, and let *correctness* be some relation

R between infinite data streams in K and hypotheses in H.[23] Now we can be precise about the notion of "consistency" assumed in our definition of hypothetico–deductive method: *e is consistent with h in K with respect to R* just in case there is some ε in K that extends e and that makes h correct with respect to R.

An *inductive setting* is a triple (K, R, H), where K is a set of infinite data streams over some recursive observation space E, H is a decidable set of objects called hypotheses, and R is an arbitrary relation between K and H. For example, Putnam's critique of Carnap's methodology essentially assumes that K = Rec, H = LISP, and R = Computes, where *Computes* $(\varepsilon, p) \Leftrightarrow$ for each n, p outputs ε_n on input n. Putnam's setting (Rec, LISP, Computes) will be referred to as the *computer modeling* setting.

Now we can define what it means for a hypothesis generator to "get it right eventually" in an arbitrary inductive setting (K, R, H):

γ *makes reliable discoveries in the limit given* K (with respect to R) $\Leftrightarrow$
    for each infinite data stream ε in K
        there is a time n such that
           for each later time m
           γ produces a hypothesis correct for ε
           (i.e. $R(\varepsilon, \gamma(\varepsilon|m))$)

This definition entitles γ to vacillate forever among correct hypotheses on some data stream in K. When γ does not so vacillate, we say that γ makes *stable* discoveries in the limit.[24] Plato, among others, took stability to be a key feature of knowledge, distinguishing it from mere true belief,[25] so stable discovery is an idea of some epistemological interest.

In the computer modeling setting (Rec, LISP, Computes), the extrapolability of K $\subseteq$ Rec in the limit implies reliable discovery in the limit is possible given K, and this claim holds both for effective and for ideal agents.[26] The converse is also true for uncomputable methods but is false for computable ones.[27] Both directions are false for effective and for ineffective methods when we move from computer modeling to arbitrary inductive settings.

The results for reliable discovery in the computer modeling setting mirror Putnam's results for extrapolation. No recursive γ makes reliable discoveries in the limit over all of Rec (this result, due to E.M. Gold,[28] strengthens Putnam's result), but the hypothetico–deductive method γ_η^K succeeds when provided with a total and complete enumeration η of LISP programs. There is no best, recursive, limiting discoverer of correct LISP programs. For each recursive generator, it is trivial to make an improved recursive generator that succeeds on one more data stream.[29] One difference between extrapolation

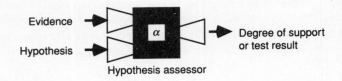

Hypothesis assessor

Figure 5.7

and discovery in the computer modeling setting is that there is no guarantee of a recursive, total and complete hypothesis enumeration for K when effective discovery is possible over K in the limit.[30]

A method that assigns degrees of warrant or support in light of the data is called a *confirmation theory* or *inductive logic*. A method that outputs 1 or 0, for "pass" or "fail," is called a *hypothesis test*. We shall refer to all these methods collectively as *hypothesis assessors* (see figure 5.7).

Some confirmation theorists view the assignment of a degree of warrant or inductive support to a hypothesis as an end in itself.[31] But assessment is more often viewed as a means for reliably determining whether or not a given hypothesis is correct. A natural analogue of the preceding success criteria suggests itself, where we view H as the set of hypotheses we might possibly be asked to assess:

α verifies H in the limit given K (with respect to R) $\Leftrightarrow$
    for each hypothesis h in H
        for each possible data stream ε in K
            $R(\varepsilon, h) \Leftrightarrow$
            there is a time n such that
                for each later time $m > n$, $\alpha(h, \varepsilon | m) > 0.5$.

Verification in the limit requires that α eventually place only values greater than 0.5 on h if and only if h is correct. When h is incorrect, α is free to vacillate forever between values above and below 0.5. When α eventually produces only values less than 0.5 if and only if h is incorrect, we say that α *refutes* H *in the limit given* K. When α both verifies and refutes H in the limit given K, we say that α *decides* H *in the limit given* K.

We have discussed hypothetico-deductivism as an architecture for building a prediction method π_η from a given hypothesis enumeration η. Hypothetico-deductivism can be viewed more directly as a proposal for building a hypothesis generation method γ_η from η as follows. Say that *h is consistent with e*, K $\Leftrightarrow$ for some $\varepsilon \in K$ $e \subseteq \varepsilon$. Now define the hypothetico-deductive method γ_η determined by η as follows:

$\gamma_\eta(e) =$ the first hypothesis h in η that is consistent[32] with e, K.

Consider the hypothesis h that at most finitely many 1s will occur in the data stream. This hypothesis is consistent with all finite data sequences, so hypothetico–deductivism is bound to fail. If, for example, h occurs prior to the first correct hypothesis h' in η, no evidence will refute h, and the hypothetico–deductive method will conjecture h forever, even if in fact the number of 1s in the resulting data stream is infinite. On the other hand, the trivial method that returns test result 1 if the last entry of e is 0 and 1 otherwise is an effective method that verifies h in the limit. So perhaps science would benefit by replacing the hypothetico–deductivist's narrow consistency test with a more reliable, limiting verification procedure α. Then, in our exemple, the hypothetico–deductivist would recommend producing the first hypothesis in η whose limiting verifier returns an assessment greater than 0.5. But this will not work if α vacillates between values above and below 0.5 forever on the first hypothesis, for then the hypothetico–deductivist will incorrectly conjecture the first hypothesis infinitely often.

A better proposal is this. Let η enumerate H, and let α be an assessment method. Let e be a finite data sequence of observations drawn from E. The *bumping pointer method*[33] $\gamma_\eta^\alpha(e)$ works as follows. First, construct an infinitely repetitive version η' of η as follows: $\eta' = \eta_0, \eta_0, \eta_1, \eta_0, \eta_1, \eta_2, \ldots, \eta_0, \ldots, \eta_n, \ldots$. This can be done recursively in η. Initialize a pointer to position 0 in η'. The pointer will move as initial segments of e are considered. If the pointer is at position i on initial segment $\varepsilon \mid n$ of ε, then on segment $\varepsilon \mid n + 1$, we leave the pointer where it is if $\alpha(\eta_i, \varepsilon \mid n + 1) = 1$, and move it to position $i + 1$ otherwise. $\gamma_\eta^\alpha(e)$ returns η_k, where k is last pointer position upon reading all of e (see figure 5.8).

Say that H *covers* K *according to* R just in case each data stream in K bears R to some hypothesis in H. Then we have:

> *Fact 2.5.1*:
> (a)   if rng(η) covers K according to R and α verifies rng(η) in the limit given K (w.r.t. R) then γ_η^α stably identifies R–correct hypotheses in the limit.[34]
> (b) γ_η^α is recursive in α, η.

(b) is immediate. To see (a), let $\varepsilon \in$ K. Since rng(η) covers K, we may choose $h \in$ rng(η) so that R(ε, h). Then for some n, we have that $\forall\ m \geq n$, $\alpha(h, \varepsilon \mid m)$ = 1. Moreover, h occurs in η' (the infinitely repetitive version of η constructed by γ_η^α) infinitely often, and hence at some position $m' \geq n$ in η'. Thus, the pointer cannot move beyond position m'. Now suppose h' occurs at some position m'' prior to m' in η' and $\neg$R(ε, h'). Then α returns 0 infinitely often for h' on ε. Thus, the pointer cannot remain at position m'' forever. So the pointer must remain forever at some correct hypothesis, and γ_η^α converges to this hypothesis.

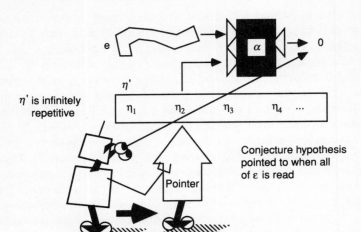

Figure 5.8

Recall Putnam's recommendation that we view science as a set of universally applicable maxims that require ingenuity to apply. We may think of the bumping pointer proposal γ_η^α and of hypothetico–deductive proposal γ_η as general maxims or architectures that yield different, concrete hypothesis generators for different specifications of η and of α. Recall that an architecture or maxim is universal or complete just in case it yields a successful method whenever there is one. What we have just seen is that the hypothetico-deductive architecture is not complete since some method can find the truth even when all hypotheses are all unfalsifiable, but no hypothetico–deductive method can succeed in such cases even in principle. This refutes Popper's bold conjecture[35] that the method of bold conjectures and refutations is our best and only means for finding the truth. But it remains to consider whether or not bumping pointer architecture is in fact universal. What is required is nothing less than a formal proof of completeness for a discovery architecture. In the next section we will see that in spite of the long-standing dogma that there is no logic of discovery, Putnam developed just such proof techniques to handle a purely logical problem posed by Mostowski.

2.6   *Transcendental Deductions of Convergent Reliabilism*

A *transcendental deduction* is a demonstration that some condition is necessary for knowledge of a certain kind. A transcendental deduction is *complete* if it yields both a necessary and a sufficient condition. If we think of stable, reliably inferred, correct hypotheses as knowledge (a view with a philosophical pedigree extending from Plato to the present day) then a complete transcendental deduction would be a necessary and sufficient condition for reliable inference in an arbitrary inductive setting (K, R, H). Among computational learning theorists, such results are known as *characterization theorems*. In 1965, Putnam and E. Mark Gold published in the same journal the same characterizations for reliable verification, refutation, and decision in the limit.[36] Complete architectures for assessment and discovery drop out as a by-product.

The Gold–Putnam result characterizes verifiability in the limit by computable methods in terms of the *computational complexity* of the correctness relation relative to background knowledge K. The relevant scale of computational complexity is known as the *Kleene* or *arithmetical hierarchy*. The basic idea is to define correctness in terms of quantifiers over a decidable relation, and to measure complexity in terms of the number of blocks of adjacent quantifiers of the same kind in the resulting expression. For example, suppose that some correctness relation R can be defined relative to K and H as follows:

$$\forall \varepsilon \in K, \, \forall h \in H, \, R(\varepsilon, h) \Leftrightarrow \exists w \exists x \forall y \forall z P(\varepsilon, h, x, y, w, z)$$

where $P(\varepsilon, h, x, y, w, z)$ is required to be recursive in the sense that it can be mechanically decided by a LISP program armed with an oracle for the data stream ε. Then we count the number of distinct blocks of quantifiers of the same type in the definition. Here we have the blocks $\exists \exists$, $\forall \forall$, so the count is two. Then we say that R is in the complexity class $\Sigma[H, K]_n^0$ just in case the first block of quantifiers in its definition consists of $\exists$s and there are n blocks in all. R is in the dual complexity class $\Pi[H, K]_n^0$ just in case there are n blocks of quantifiers in its definition starting with a block of $\forall$s, in which case $\overline{R} \in \Sigma[H, K]_n^0$. Finally, R is in complexity class $\Delta[H, K]_n^0$ just in case R is in both $\Sigma[H, K]_n^0$ and $\Pi[H, K]_n^0$. A standard fact of mathematical logic is that these classes form a hierarchy. Links in figure 5.9 indicate proper inclusion, with smaller classes to the left and larger ones to the right.

What Putnam and Gold showed was the following:

Theorem 2.6.1 (Gold, Putnam):
(a) H is *effectively verifiable in the limit given* K (w.r.t. R) $\Leftrightarrow$ R $\in$ $\Sigma[H, K]_2^0$.
(b) H is *effectively refutable in the limit given* K (w.r.t. R) $\Leftrightarrow$ R $\in$ $\Pi[H, K]_2^0$.
(c) H is *effectively decidable in the limit given* K (w.r.t. R) $\Leftrightarrow$ R $\in$ $\Delta[H, K]_2^0$.

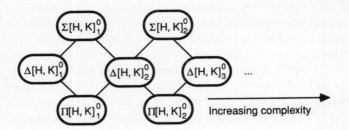

Figure 5.9

It suffices to consider only the first case, the other two following readily. ($\Rightarrow$) Suppose recursive α verifies H in the limit over K. Then by definition,

$$\forall \varepsilon \in K \forall h \in H, R(\varepsilon, h) \Leftrightarrow \exists n \ \forall m \geq n \ \alpha(h, \varepsilon|m) > 0.5.$$

where the relation "$\alpha(h, \varepsilon|m) > 0.5$" is recursive since α is. So $R \in \Sigma[H, K]_2^0$.

($\Leftarrow$) Let $R \in \Sigma[H, K]_2^0$. Then for some recursive relation S we have:

$$\forall \varepsilon \in K \forall h \in H, R(\varepsilon, h) \Leftrightarrow \exists x \ \forall y \ S(\varepsilon, h, x, y),$$

where x, y are vectors of variables. Assume some fixed, effective enumeration $x_1, x_2, \ldots, x_n, \ldots$ of the possible values for x and another effective enumeration $y_1, y_2, \ldots, y_n, \ldots$ of the possible values of y. We now define an effective mechanism for managing a pointer on the enumeration $x_1, x_2, \ldots, x_n, \ldots$ as follows: on data e of length n, the mechanism maintaining the pointer seeks the first position $k \leq n$ such that for each $j \leq n$, the decision procedure for $S(e, h, x_k, y_j)$ does not return 0. If there is no such k, then the pointer moves all the way to position n (see figure 5.10).

We define the method $\alpha(e)$ to say 0 whenever the pointer moves and to say 1 otherwise. Now we verify that α works. Let $h \in H$, $\varepsilon \in K$. Suppose $R(\varepsilon, h)$. Then $\exists k \ \forall j \ S(\varepsilon, h, x_k, y_j)$. Let k' be the least such k. Then the pointer can never be bumped past k', so α stabilizes correctly to 1. Suppose $\neg R(\varepsilon, h)$. Then $\forall k \ \exists j$ s.t. $\neg S(\varepsilon, h, x_k, y_j)$. Let x_k be arbitrary. Choose y_j so that $\neg S(\varepsilon, h, x_k, y_j)$. e is eventually long enough so that $S(\varepsilon, h, x_k, y_j)$ halts with output 0. So the pointer is eventually bumped past k. Since this is true for arbitrary k, and α produces a 0 whenever the pointer is bumped, α produces infinitely many 0s, as required.

The method constructed in the proof of this theorem can be thought of

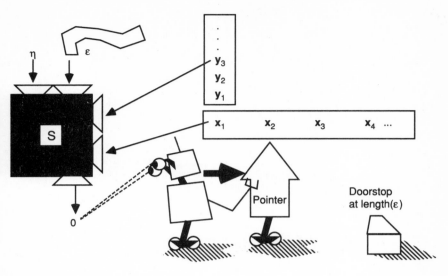

Figure 5.10

as an application of the bumping pointer architecture to hypothesis assessment. Thus, a corollary of the theorem is that bumping pointer assessment architecture is universal for verification in the limit.

The theorem can be extended to mechanical falsifiability and verifiability in the old, logical empiricist sense. Say that H is *effectively verifiable with certainty* given K (w.r.t. R) just in case there is an effective α such that for each hypothesis h in H and data stream ε in K, α eventually halts with 1 if and only if h is correct in ε. *Effective refutability* or *"falsifiability" with certainty* is defined similarly, except that α must halt with 0 just in case h is incorrect in ε. And *effective decidability with certainty* requires both verifiability and refutability with certainty. Then by the very definitions of the complexity classes, these cases are characterized, respectively, by $\Sigma[\mathrm{H}, \mathrm{K}]_1^0$, $\Pi[\mathrm{H}, \mathrm{K}]_1^0$, and $\Delta[\mathrm{H}, \mathrm{K}]_1^0$, yielding the correspondence between success criteria and complexity classes shown in figure 5.11.

We can also characterize stable discovery in a related fashion. The idea is that some effective discovery method works whenever any effective discovery method works, so the architecture for building discovery methods out of effective hypothesis enumerations and effective hypothesis assessors is complete in the sense of limiting reliability.

But there is an interesting twist. Contrary to the hypothetico–deductivists' intuitions, effective, reliable discovery of hypotheses in H is possible in the limit even when no ideal assessment method can even verify hypotheses in

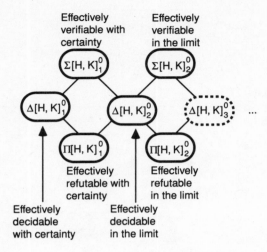

Figure 5.11

H in the limit. The following setting provides a simple illustration of this fact:[37]

$$\mathfrak{P}_0 = (K_0, R_0, H_0)$$
$$R_0(\varepsilon, i) \Leftrightarrow \varepsilon_0 = i \text{ or } i \text{ occurs infinitely often in } \varepsilon$$
$$K_0 = \omega^\omega$$
$$H_0 = \omega$$

Thus, the successful discovery method cannot succeed by using a reliable assessment procedure, since there may be no such procedure when some method can succeed! The trick is that the method is free to "pretend" that correctness is *more stringent* that it really is, where the more stringent correctness relation $R' \subseteq R$ is obtained from the original relation R by making some hypotheses incorrect where they were previously deemed by R to be correct. Then the discovery method can employ a reliable assessor α attuned to this "imaginary" notion of correctness, and whatever α judges correct will be correct, but not conversely.

This seems paradoxical. How could pretending that fewer hypotheses are correct for various data streams make it easier to find correct hypotheses? The answer is that making a correctness relation more stringent can also make it far less complex, just as planing wood from a rough surface can make it smooth. We can choose $R'_0 \subseteq R_0$ so that $R'_0(\varepsilon, i) \Leftrightarrow \varepsilon$ begins with i, for example, thereby reducing the complexity of R_0 from a hefty $\Pi[\omega, K_0]_2^0$ to a trivially manageable $\Delta[\omega, K_0]_1^0$. Thus, contrary to the usual hypothetico-

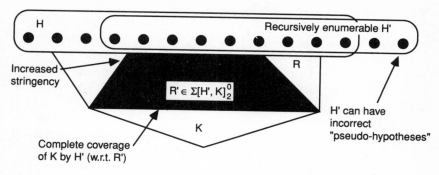

Figure 5.12

deductive view, reliable discovery in the limit can in be much easier in principle than reliable assessment in the limit.

It is possible to make R too stringent. The simplest and most stringent notion of correctness makes no hypotheses correct under any circumstances. But, of course, such a relation is also a useless guide for what to conjecture. Thus we must insist that in reducing complexity, we retain some correct hypothesis for each data stream in K. Moreover, we will need to enumerate the relevant hypotheses, so we insist that the remaining, correct hypotheses be in some recursively enumerable set.

Theorem 2.6.2:

Let (K, R, H) be an arbitrary inductive setting.

Correct hypotheses are effectively stably discoverable in the limit given K (w.r.t. R) $\Leftrightarrow$ there is some $R' \subseteq R$, H' s.t.

    (1) H' is recursively enumerable and

    (2) H' covers K according to R' and

    (3) $R' \in \Sigma[H', K]_2^0$

Corollary: The theorem still holds if we add the condition: (4) R' is single-valued (see figures 5.12).

($\Rightarrow$) Let recursive γ stably discover correct hypotheses in the limit given K according to R. Then we have:

$$\forall \varepsilon \in K\ \exists n\ \forall m \geq n\ \gamma(\varepsilon|m) = \gamma(\varepsilon|n)\ \&\ R\ (\varepsilon, \gamma(\varepsilon|m))$$

Choose H' as follows:

H' = the set of all hypotheses conjectured by γ.

Next, define R′ over H′ and K as follows:

$$\forall \varepsilon \in K, \forall h \in H', R'(\varepsilon, h) \Leftrightarrow \exists n \, \forall m \geq n \, \gamma(\varepsilon|m) = h$$

R′ is a subset of R by (5.1) and by (5.2). (1) follows from the definition of H′ and the fact that γ is recursive. (2) follows from (5.1) and (5.2). (3) follows from the form of (5.2).

($\Leftarrow$) Suppose conditions (1–3) are met for some R′ $\subseteq$ R, H′. Then let recursive α verify H′ in the limit given K with respect to the new relation R′, by theorem 2.6.1 and (3). Let η be an effective enumeration of H′ by (1). By (2) and by fact 2.5.1, the method γ_η^α is effective and stably discovers correct hypotheses in the limit given K w.r.t. R′. And if this hypothesis is correct according to R′ it is correct according to R since R′ $\subseteq$ R.

This is a proof that the bumping pointer architecture is a universal maxim for discovery, but *not* if we insist in addition that α be a reliable test, for when R is not $\Sigma[H', K]_2^0$, there can be no reliable test (in the sense of verifiability in the limit) even though the bumping pointer method for some less complex R′ $\subseteq$ R succeeds at discovery. It is remarkable that Putnam's purely logical work should have such powerful and immediate consequences for his philosophical thesis that scientific method should be viewed as a complete set of maxims.

The theorem also places Putnam's critique of Carnap's methodology in perspective, for the theorem shows that there is exactly *one* way in which effective discovery can be computationally harder than effective hypothesis assessment: it may be that no H′ satisfying (3) is recursively enumerable. The computer modeling setting has just this special feature, so that total programs are reliably discoverable but not assessable. In other settings, discovery can be much simpler than assessment, as in the case of the setting $\mathfrak{P}_0$ discussed earlier.

The general point, however, is that Putnam's style of analysis provides a framework in which completeness and other logical concerns arise for inductive methods in just the manner that they arise for proof systems and for algorithms for other tasks, irrespective of whether we consider discovery, assessment, or prediction. The results reviewed are only a small sample of what can be done. We can consider different notions of computability (e.g. finite-state automata rather than LISP programs), different notions of success (e.g. stabilizing to within a finite set of correct hypotheses), and different side constraints (e.g. Bayesian coherence). For each mixture of conditions, we can seek a complete architecture, as well as a classification of concrete inductive settings into intrinsically solvable and unsolvable cases.

Putnam's early work sketches a mathematical edifice for methodology, complete with rooms, unexplored halls, and a partially stocked tool chest.

Our question now is whether this edifice harmonizes or clashes with Putnam's more recent views about truth, when truth is viewed as an aim of reliable enquiry.

3   Convergent Reliabilism and Truth as Ideal Rational Acceptability

We now turn to the second of the theses introduced at the beginning of this chapter, which asserts that truth is a kind of idealized, epistemic justification. Putnam describes this conception of truth in his book, *Reason, Truth and History:*

> "Truth," in an internalist view, is some sort of (idealized) rational acceptability – some sort of ideal coherence of our beliefs with each other and with our experiences as those experiences are themselves represented in our belief system – and not correspondence with mind-independent or discourse-independent "states of affairs."[38]

The operative standards of coherence and rational acceptability are psychologically based:

> Our conceptions of coherence and acceptability are, on the view I shall develop, deeply interwoven with our psychology. They depend upon our biology and our culture; they are by no means "value free."[39]

But truth is not just coherence or rational acceptability, because truth is stable in time and not a matter of degree, whereas the rational acceptability of a statement changes as the evidence or circumstances change and is also widely regarded to be a matter of degree.[40] To account for stability, Putnam appeals to idealization:

> What this shows, in my opinion, is . . . that truth is an idealization of rational acceptability. We speak as if there were such things as epistemically ideal conditions, and we call a statement "true" if it would be justified under such conditions. "Epistemically ideal conditions," of course, are like "frictionless planes:" we cannot really attain epistemically ideal conditions, or even be absolutely certain that we have come sufficiently close to them. But frictionless planes cannot really be attained either, and yet talk of frictionless planes has "cash value" because we can approximate them to a very high degree of approximation.[41]

The frictionless plane metaphor is rather vague. Fortunately, we get a bit more:

> The simile of frictionless planes aside, the two key ideas of the idealization theory of truth are (1) that truth is independent of justification here and now, but not independent of all justification. To claim a statement is true is to claim it could be justified. (2) truth is expected to be stable or "convergent;" if both a statement and its negation could be "justified," even if conditions were as ideal as one could hope to make them, there is no sense to thinking of the statement as having a truth-value.[42]

Finally, Putnam provides us at the very end of his book with an explicit reference to truth as an ideal limit:

> The very fact that we speak of our different conceptions as different conceptions of *rationality* posits a *Grenzbegriff*, a limit-concept of the ideal truth.[43]

It is not hard to see how such views fit with Putnam's limiting reliabilist past. For we may conceive of *rational acceptability* as some hypothesis assessment function α, that somehow results from our cognitive wiring, our culture, and the accidents of our collective past together. Hypothesis h is then said to be true for a community whose standard of rational acceptability is α just in case α converges in some sense to a high assessment for h as evidence increases and "epistemic conditions" improve. We may think of ε as the data stream that arises for a community committed to an ideal regimen of ever-improving epistemic conditions concerning some hypothesis h.[44] Background knowledge K_{ideal} can be what the community knows ahead of time about how the data would come in if this regimen of improving epistemic conditions were to continue indefinitely.

Putnam claims to provide an "informal elucidation" rather than a formal theory of truth, but vague proposals license the reader to consider precise interpretations, and our discussion of Putnam's early work on induction suggests one. Let h be a hypothesis, and let ε be a data stream that might possibly arise under the assumption that we are committed to the continual improvement of our "epistemic conditions," so $\varepsilon \in K_{ideal}$. Then define:

$$\text{True1}_\alpha(\varepsilon, h) \Leftrightarrow \exists n\ \forall m \geq n\ \alpha(h, \varepsilon \mid m) > 0.5$$
$$\text{False1}_\alpha(\varepsilon, h) \Leftrightarrow \exists n\ \forall m \geq n\ \alpha(h, \varepsilon \mid m, h) \leq 0.5$$

This proposal defines truth in terms of what a hypothesis assessment method α does in the limit, a suggestion reminiscent of C.S. Peirce's definition of reality: "And what do we mean by the real? . . . The real, then, is that which, sooner or later, information and reasoning would finally result in, and which is therefore independent of the vagaries of me and you."[45] Peirce's motivation, like Putnam's, is to appeal to limits to wash out intuitive disanalogies between truth and rational acceptability. Therefore, we will refer to the general strategy of defining truth in terms of the limiting behavior of some methodological standard as the *Peirce reverse*. In particular, truth1_α is stable and independent of particular assessments by α, where α can be viewed as an arbitrary, socially or psychologically grounded standard of "rational acceptability," as Putnam intends.

Truth1_α is trivially verifiable in the limit by a community whose standard of rational acceptability is α because α is the community's standard of rational acceptability. The same triviality does not extend to discovery or to prediction, however. Recall that in theorem 2.6.2 a necessary condition for effective discovery is the existence of an effectively enumerable collection of hypotheses covering K w.r.t. R. This condition may fail even when each hypothesis is verifiable in the limit, as in the computer modelling setting. Moreover, since extrapolation does not depend upon the notion of hypothesis correctness, internal realism does not make extrapolation any easier. Thus, Putnam's analysis of extrapolation stands unaffected by the move to truth1. Finally, verifiability, refutability, and decidability with certainty are not trivialized by this proposal.

Putnam requires (in the above quotations) that a hypothesis and its negation cannot both be true. Clearly, truth1 does not satisfy this condition over arbitrary choices of α, for if α assigns 1 to both h and $\neg h$ no matter what the data says, both h and $\neg h$ will be true1. One solution would be to impose "rationality" restrictions on α that guarantee that the requirement in question will be satisfied. A natural such constraint would be that $\alpha(h, e)$ be a conditional probability. In that case, $\alpha(h, e) > 0.5$ implies $\alpha(\neg h, e) \leq 0.5$, so Putnam's requirement that h and $\neg h$ not both be true is satisfied by truth1_α.

There are other, equally intuitive conditions that Putnam could have imposed. For example, it would seem odd if both h and h' were true but h & h' were not true. But this is possible under the definition of truth1 even when α is a probability measure, since the probability of a conjunction can be much lower than the probabilities of the conjuncts, as in the familiar *lottery paradox*. In so far as Putnam's gambit is to wash out the standard, intuitive disanalogies between confirmation and truth by appeals to idealization and limits, he is unsuccessful.[46]

As we have already seen, Putnam has been critical of probabilistic methods anyway. Perhaps some different choice of rational acceptability standard α would guarantee that truth1_α is well behaved. But it turns out that no α satisfying a plausible constraint (being able to *count*) can provide such a guarantee. The argument for this fact is of special interest, since it adapts

126 *Kevin Kelly, Cory Juhl, and Clark Glymour*

Putnam's methodological diagonal argument to the investigation of internal realist semantics.

Let h_n be the sentence "as we progressively idealize our epistemic conditions in stages, observable outcome x occurs in at least n distinct stages of idealization." In our community, the sentence "there are at least n xs" is intimately connected with the practice of counting, in the sense that if we suppose the xs to be easily visible without a lot of effort, we can count and tally the number of xs seen up to the present, returning 0 until the tally reaches n, and returning 1 thereafter. That is what we do when we are asked if there are at least ten beans in a jar. We do not say "yes" until we pull out ten beans. Assume further than when considering $\neg h_n$, the method says 1 until n xs are counted and 0 thereafter. Any method that assesses hypotheses of form h_n, $\neg h_n$ by means of counting occurrences of x in this manner will be referred to as a *counting method*.

We need not say what counting is, since social practices are the primitive in the internal realist's elucidation of truth. It suffices that counting somehow returns a natural number n (the count of xs) for each finite data segment e presented to the counter. Indeed, we must be careful in our logical analysis of internal realism not to second-guess the practice of counting by asking whether its count of xs is correct relative to some independently specified number of xs in the data, since by the Peirce reverse, the truth about the number of xs in the data is fixed by the practice of counting and not the other way around. But our refusal to second-guess the accuracy of counting in this manner does not prevent us from listing some evident properties the practice of counting that make no reference whatsoever to what is "really" in the data:

(A) No matter what data e has been shown to the counter, we can feed a stream of data that keeps the count of xs fixed where it is forever.

(B) No matter what data e has been shown to the counter, we can feed a finite churk of data that makes the count of xs increases.

(C) The count of xs never goes down.

Not all obvious explications of our society's standards of rational acceptability are counting methods. For example, if the data stream is thought to be generated by independent tosses of a fair die, then $p(h_n) = 1$ for each n, and hence for each finite sequence e, $p(h_n, e) = 1$. Then $\alpha_0(h_n, e) = p(h_n, e)$ is not a counting method because a counting method cannot, by definition, output 1 for more than a finite number $h_1, \ldots h_n$ of hypotheses on finite evidence segment e. Now conditional probability measures are thought by many methodologists to provide a good approximation of our practices of rational acceptability, so it would be hard for us to make an absolute case here that our community's actual standard of rational acceptability is a counting method. But we can do something easier; we can make our case conditional on the charitable assumption that internal realism is more or less correct and that the English-speaking community is not radically confused about the meaning of "at least n xs will appear." To do so, we put the following question to the English speaking community:

(Q) Suppose that we never count more than two xs in the data for eternity. Is it true or false that at least a billion xs eventually appear in the data?

We suspect that almost everybody would say "false," and that most would agree that a method like α_0 that says 1 no matter what is observed *could* lead in the limit to a different truth1 assignment on hypotheses of form h_n than counting methods would lead to. In light of this and similar enquiries with similar results, we infer, roughly, that either (1) the community of English speakers does not understand the simple English statement "at least n xs will appear," or (2) it is internal realism rather than the community's understanding that is defective, or (3) internal realism is correct, the English-speaking community understands "at least n xs will appear," and the standard of rational acceptability that grounds usage for such hypotheses in our community is a counting method. Respect both for Putnam and for the English-speaking community dictates that we conclude:

(3) Our society's standard of rational acceptability is a counting method.

Let h_ω be the sentence "as we progressively idealize our epistemic conditions in stages, observable outcome x occurs in infinitely many distinct stages of idealization." Say that truth1$_\alpha$ can be *ω-incomplete* just in case for some data stream ε, each h_n is true1$_\alpha$, but h_ω is not true1$_\alpha$. And if there is some ε in which h_ω is true1$_\alpha$ and some $\neg h_n$ is true1$_\alpha$ then we say that truth1$_\alpha$ can be *inconsistent*. Now we may construct a Putnam-style diagonal agrument to show that:

Theorem 3.1:
If α is a counting method, then truth1$_\alpha$ can be either inconsistent or ω-incomplete.

Let α be a counting method. Suppose for *reductio* that truth1$_\alpha$ can be neither ω-incomplete nor ω-inconsistent. We present data as follows. By axiom (B), show α successive chunks of data that continue to make the count rise repeadedly, until α starts to return some value greater than 0.5 for h_ω. Such a time must come, else by axiom (C), we have that for all n, h_n is true1_α but h_ω is not, so Truth1_α can be ω-incomplete, contrary to assumption. As soon as α outputs a value greater than 0.5 for h_ω, we start presenting data in a way that will prevent the count from ever rising higher (by axiom (A)), until α's confidence in h_ω drops below 0.5. This must happen, else there is an n such that $\neg h_n$ is true1_α but h_ω is also true1_α, so truth$1a$ can be inconsistent, which is a contradiction. By repeating this procedure over and over (we do not have to count how many times we have done it) we end up (by axiom (C)) with a situation in which each h_n is true1_α but h_ω is not, so truth1_α can be ω-incomplete. Contradiction.

By analogy, Gödel's first incompleteness theorem shows that a system of arithmetic is either ω-inconsistent or incomplete. Although the "ω" has switched sides (curiously enough), the import is the same: a methodological substitute for truth (e.g. mechanical proof, limiting rational acceptability) does not measure up to our intuition that truth should be complete and consistent.

Putnam might very well embrace the result. He has expressed a guarded admiration for intuitionism, and intuitionistic truth can be gappy when no construction is available either for p or for $\neg p$. Nor has he claimed that internal realism's appeal to limits is supposed to "plug" these gaps. Thus, he may well have expected something much stronger than what we have shown, namely, that truth is actually incomplete. But whether or not the result was expected, it is interesting that it can be proved using the same sort of diagonal construction Putnam employed in his critique of Carnap's methodology. By interposing practice between the data stream and the method, Putnam's limiting reliabilist methodology is transformed into internal realist semantic theory. By playing the same game with different sets of sentences and output constraints on practices, one could no doubt prove more subtle and impressive things about internal realist truth.

Despite this potential for agreement, it is still worthwhile to consider some possible objections that an internal realist might raise, both to dispel them and to illustrate further how diagonal arguments bear on the internal realist's conception of truth. We have already addressed the objection that our argument assumes a "god's-eye view" of the data to second-guess α's performance. In our argument, truth is entirely fixed by the practice of counting, and the social practice of counting is a primitive characterized entirely by three axioms that make no reference to what "really" occurs in the data. No external "semantics" of any sort is imposed on the hypotheses in question aside from internal realist truth.

An internal realist might also object, in light of passages like the following, that our diagonal argument bases internal realist truth on a fixed method α:

I agree with Dummett in rejecting the correspondence theory of truth. But I do not agree with Dummett's view that the justification conditions for sentences are fixed once and for all by a recursive definition. . . . In my view, as in Quine's, the justification conditions for sentences change as our total body of knowledge changes, and cannot be taken as fixed once and for all. Not only may we find out that statements we now regard as justified are false, but we may even find out that procedures we now regard as justificatory are not, and that different justification procedures are better.[47]

But this is no objection to our argument, for if truth is defined as an ideal limit of rational acceptability, then truth is relative to the standard α of rational acceptability operative at the time, so truth changes as the standard α changes, but is fixed for eternity relative to a fixed standard, as Putnam requires. The diagonal argument shows that none of these successively adopted standards of rational acceptability grounds a notion of truth guaranteed to be both ω-complete and consistent, so long as it is a counting method. And we have already argued that our current α is a counting method.

Nor is it relevant to object that we assume α to be some recursive function of the data. We require only that α be a counting method satisfying the weak axioms (A), (B), and (C), which entails neither that α is recursive, nor even that α is definable.

A more promising response to our diagonal argument would be to adopt a less stringent convergence criterion for truth while retaining the basic spirit of the Peirce reverse, as follows:

$$\text{True2}_\alpha(\varepsilon, h) \Leftrightarrow \forall s > 0, \exists n \, \forall m \geq n \, 1 - \alpha(h, \varepsilon|m) < s$$
$$\text{False2}_\alpha(\varepsilon, h) \Leftrightarrow \forall s > 0, \exists n \, \forall m \geq n \, \alpha(h, \varepsilon|m) < s$$

A hypothesis is true2 if and only if the society's standard α of rational acceptability produces assessment values that move ever closer to 1, possibly not ever arriving there. Unlike truth1, truth2 does not require that the assessment value drop below some fixed threshold (0.5) infinitely often when h is not true. This laxity makes it possible to construct a community standard α of rational acceptability that guarantees that truth2$_\alpha$ is both ω-complete and consistent.[48] A method β that ensures falsity2$_\beta$ to be both ω-complete and consistent can also be constructed.[49]

But the internal realist is not home free, for he or she cannot find an adequate δ that jointly guarantees that truth2$_\delta$ and falsity 2_δ will be ω-complete and consistent.

Fact 3.2: If α is a counting method then
either truth2$_\alpha$ or falsity2$_\alpha$ can be either ω-incomplete or inconsistent.

To see why this should be so, we may extend our transcendental deductions to cover the notion of reliable success in the limit implicit in the definitions of truth2 and falsity2:

α *weakly verifies* H *in the limit given* K (with respect to R) $\Leftrightarrow$
    for each hypothesis *h* in H
        for each possible data stream ε in K
            R(ε, *h*) $\Leftrightarrow$
                for each real number $r > 0$
                    there is a time *n* such that
                        for each later time $m > n$,
                        $1 - \alpha(h, \varepsilon \mid m) < r$.

Of course, truth2 trivializes weak verifiability in the limit just the way truth1 trivializes verifiability in the limit. Weak refutation in the limit is defined dually, and weak decision in the limit requires that a single method both weakly verify and weakly refute H in the limit given K. Following the strategy of theorem 2.6.1 above, we arrive at a characterization of weak hypothesis assessment in terms of arithmetic complexity:

Theorem 3.3:
(a) H is effectively weakly verifiable in the limit given K (w.r.t. R)
    $\Leftrightarrow$ R $\in$ $\Pi[\text{H, K}]^0_3$.
(b) H is effectively weakly refutable in the limit given K (w.r.t. R)
    $\Leftrightarrow$ R $\in$ $\Sigma[\text{H, K}]^0_3$.
(c) H is effectively weakly decidable in the limit given K (w.r.t. R)
    $\Leftrightarrow$ R $\in$ $\Delta[\text{H, K}]^0_2$.

Combining this result with theorem 2.6.1, we have the complexity classification of our various notions of reliable hypothesis assessment shown in figure 5.13.

Consider clause (c) of theorem 3.3, which states that weak decidability in the limit is characterized by $\Delta[\text{H, K}]^0_2$ rather than by $\Delta[\text{H, K}]^0_3$, as might be expected by analogy with the other cases. (c) follows from the trivial fact that a weak, limiting decision procedure just *is* a limiting decision procedure, and decidability in the limit is characterized by $\Delta[\text{H, K}]^0_2$. This is what underlies fact 3.2. From a realist's point of view, the diagonal argument for fact 3.1 shows that h_ω (under the "obvious" realist interpretation) is decidable in the limit over arbitrary data streams in E^ω.[50] In light of (c), if both truth2$_\alpha$ and falsity2$_\alpha$ were guaranteed to be ω-complete and consistent, then α would weakly decide h_ω in the limit (according to the "obvious" realist interpretation of the hypotheses h_ω, h_n). But as we have just remarked, this

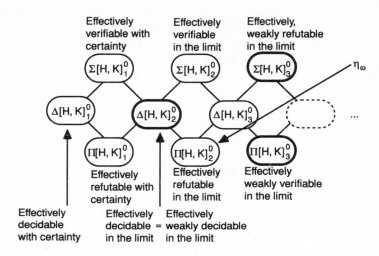

Figure 5.13

is equivalent to demanding that α decide h_ω in the limit, and this is impossible, since no method (effective or otherwise) can even verify h_ω in the limit (by the proof of theorem 3.1).

Parts (a) and (b) of theorem 3.3 explain, further, why truth2$_\alpha$ and falsity 2$_\beta$ can both be guaranteed separately to be ω-complete and consistent so long as they are based on distinct methods α and β. Correctness for h_ω, together with each h_n, $\neg h_n$, is a $\Pi[H, K]_2^0$ relation, and hence is both a $\Sigma[H, K]_3^0$ relation (so falsity2$_\beta$ works out) and a $\Pi[H, K]_3^0$ relation (so true2$_\alpha$ works out). But for both truth2$_\delta$ and falsity2$_\delta$ to work properly when based on a single method δ, correctness would have to be a $\Delta[H, K]_2^0$ relation, which it is not. Thus, someone possessed of both a weak, limiting verifier and a weak limiting refuter of h_ω is in a curious position. The first method will converge to 1 on h_ω if some x occurs infinitely often in ε and the second machine will converge to 0 on h_ω if no x occurs infinitely often in ε, but there is no way to assemble these two methods into a single method that has both properties.[51]

We finish this section with a proof of theorem 3.3. (a). (b) follows by duality. The proof is of independent interest, since it extends Putnam's program of transcendental deductions to a weaker criterion of success, and it also exhibits a universal architecture for this notion of success.

($\Rightarrow$) Suppose that α effectively, weakly verifies H in the limit given K (with respect to R). Then by definition

$$\forall \varepsilon \in K \; \forall h \in H, R(\varepsilon, h) \Leftrightarrow \forall \text{real } r > 0 \; \exists n \; \forall m \geq n \; 1 - \alpha(h, \varepsilon|m) < r$$

We can replace the quantifier over reals with a quantifier over rationals since for every real greater than 0 there is a smaller rational greater than 0. And we can effectively encode rationals with natural numbers, so that the quantifier over reals greater than 0 can be replaced with a quantifier over natural numbers. Since $1 - \alpha(h, \varepsilon \,|\, m) < r$ is recursive if α is recursive and r is a rational effectively encoded as a nautrsal number, we have that R $\in$ $\Pi[\text{H, K}]_3^0$.

($\Leftarrow$) Suppose that R $\in \Pi[\text{H, K}]_3^0$. Then for some recursive relation S we have

$$\forall \varepsilon \in \text{K } \forall h \in \text{H, } R(\varepsilon, h) \Leftrightarrow \forall \text{x } \exists \text{y } \forall \text{z } S(\varepsilon, h, \text{x, y, z}),$$

where x, y, z are vectors of variables. Let k be the length of x. Then for each $\mathbf{a} \in \omega^k$, $Q_\mathbf{a}(\varepsilon, h) \Leftrightarrow \exists \text{y } \forall \text{z } S(\varepsilon, h, \mathbf{a}, \text{y, z})$ is a $\Sigma[\text{H, K}]_2^0$ relation. An examination of the proof of theorem 2.6.1 reveals that we can construct a (rational valued) assessor $\alpha_\mathbf{a}(h, e)$ recursive in $\mathbf{a}$, h, and e so that for each $\mathbf{a} \in \omega^k$, $\alpha_\mathbf{a}$ verifies H in the limit given K w.r.t. $Q_\mathbf{a}$. Now we use $\alpha_\mathbf{a}$ to construct an effective, weak limiting verifier α of H given K (w.r.t. R) as follows. First, we effectively construct an infinite sequence θ of rationals that converges to unity (e.g. $1 - 1/2, 1 - 1/4, \ldots, 1 - 1/2^n, \ldots$) and we effectively enumerate ω^k as $(\mathbf{a}_1, \mathbf{a}_2, \ldots, \mathbf{a}_n, \ldots)$, so that each $\mathbf{a}_i$ is a k-vector of natural numbers. Now let $h \in \text{H}$ and finite data segment e of length j be given. We calculate $b = (\alpha_{\mathbf{a}_1}(h, e), \alpha_{\mathbf{a}_2}(h, e), \ldots, \alpha_{\mathbf{a}_j}(h, e))$, and set w = the greatest $x \leq j$ such that $b_1, b_2, \ldots, b_x$ are all greater than 0.5. Then output θ_w. Observe that each of these operations is effective (see figure 5.14).

Now we show that α works. Let $h \in \text{H}$, $\varepsilon \in \text{K}$. Suppose $R(\varepsilon, h)$. Then for each $\mathbf{a}_i$, $\exists \text{y } \forall \text{z } S(\varepsilon, h, \mathbf{a}_i, \text{y, z})$, so $Q_{\mathbf{a}_i}(\varepsilon, h)$. Then for each i, $\alpha_{\mathbf{a}_i}$ eventually produces only values strictly greater than 0.5. Let k be given. Then there is a time n such that for all $m \geq n$, $\alpha_{\mathbf{a}_1}(h, \varepsilon \,|\, m) > 0.5$, $\alpha_{\mathbf{a}_2}(h, \varepsilon \,|\, m) > 0.5$, $\ldots$, and $\alpha_{\mathbf{a}_k}(h, \varepsilon \,|\, m) > 0.5$. Thus, for all $m \geq n$, $\alpha(h, \varepsilon) > \theta_k$. Since k is arbitrary, we have that for all $r > 0 \; \exists n \; \forall m \geq n \; 1 - \alpha(h, \varepsilon \,|\, m) < r$, as required. Now suppose that $\neg R(\varepsilon, h)$. Then for some $\mathbf{a}_i$, we have that $\neg Q_{\mathbf{a}_i}(\varepsilon, h)$. Then for infinitely many m, $\alpha_{\mathbf{a}_i}(h, \varepsilon \,|\, m) \leq 0.5$. But for each such m, $\alpha(h, \varepsilon \,|\, m) \leq \theta_i$. Thus α weakly verifies H in the limit given K (w.r.t. R), as required.

4   Reliability and Relativism

We now turn to the third of Putnam's theses, moderate relativism. Putnam puts the matter in terms of reference:

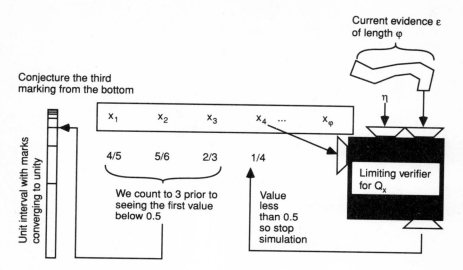

Figure 5.14

"What does the world consist of" is a question that it only makes sense to ask within a theory or description.[52]

a sign that is actually employed in a particular way by a particular community of users can correspond to particular objects *within the conceptual scheme of those users*. Objects do not exist independently of conceptual schemes.[53]

The passage reflects Kant's distinction between the world–in–itself and the world of experience. The world–in–itself does not come pre-partitioned into distinct individuals and relations so reference and truth make no sense in relation to it. But relative to the conceptual and perceptual apparatus of the perceiver, truth and reference are possible (see figure 5.15).

This sort of thing admits of degrees. *Coherentists* exclude the role of the world–in–itself altogether, insisting that any coherent set of beliefs is true because we believe it.[54] *Naive realists* insist that the conceptual scheme is irrelevant, so that experience is a direct apprehension of things in themselves. *Moderate relativism* covers the interesting ground between these extremal positions. Putnam pursues this moderate course, in which truth and evidence depend both upon the world–in–itself and upon our conceptual contribution: "Internalism does not deny that there are experiential inputs to knowledge; knowledge is not a story with no constraints except internal coherence; but it does deny that there are any inputs which are not themselves shaped by our concepts."[55] In traditional philosophy, the world-

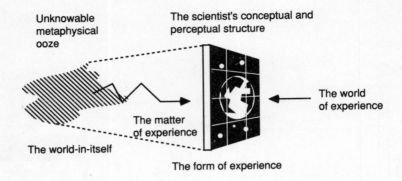

Figure 5.15

in-itself has been taken as the objective, external, or mind-independent component of truth, while conceptual scheme has been identified with the subjective, internal, or mental component of truth. In methodology, we do not care about the purely metaphysical distinction between objectivity and subjectivity. We care about methods and strategies, where the crucial issue is control. For our purposes, the world-in-itself is the component of truth that cannot be manipulated at will by us. The conceptual scheme is the component that can. In Putnam's terms, we adopt a *functionalist* perspective on the metaphysics of relativism, since that is all that matters for the purposes of reliabilist methodology. So, for example, Kant, who admitted a strong, subjective component in truth, was none the less a functional realist, since the took the conceptual scheme to be fixed for all humanity (though it might be different for other creatures).

4.1   Worlds-in-themselves

In general, a functionalist world-in-itself is some dependence of truth and evidence upon voluntary acts by the scientist. These acts may include belief change, conceptual change, experimental set-ups, changing what is meant by correctness, changing the color of your tie (in the case of social constructivist theories of truth), and finally, the act of making a particular conjecture. More precisely, let E once again be a set of possible observations. Let S be the set of finite strings over some suitably large alphabet. A *correctness assignment* for H will be some map $f: S \to \{1, 0, *\}$, where $*$ indicates "ill-formed", 1 indicates correctness, and 0 indicates incorrectness. Correctness might be truth, something stronger, or something weaker.[56] Let C be the space of all correctness assignments (see figure 5.16).

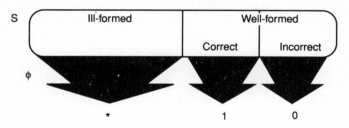

Figure 5.16

A hypothesis generator produces some hypothesis h and may perform some other semantically relevant acts summarized by $a \in A$. Thus the pair $\langle h, a \rangle$ $\in H \times A$ summarizes all of the scientist's semantically relevant acts at a given time. A world-in-itself is then a map that takes an infinite sequence of complete semantic acts $\langle h_1, a_1 \rangle, \langle h_2, a_2 \rangle, \ldots$ together with some specified moment n of enquiry, and returns to the scientist the datum x for stage n and the current truth assignment f for stage n. That is, a world-in-itself is most generally a map $\psi \colon ((H \times A)^{\omega} \times \omega) \to (E \times C)$ (see figure 5.17).

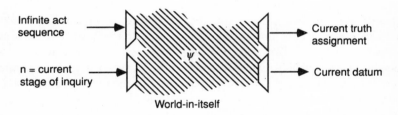

Figure 5.17

It is often assumed by relativist philosophers of science that only the scientist's current conceptual scheme (act) is relevant to the current truth assignment to hypotheses. Such worlds-in-themselves will be called *semantically immediate*. Some Marxists and feminists claim that one's entire ideological history is relevant to truth in the present. Worlds of this sort are *semantically local* but not immediate. The limiting conception of truth promoted by Peirce illustrates that the situation can be much more general, for in that case, the truth depends upon what is conjectured by the scientist forever. Such dependencies (reminiscent of the medieval problem of God's foreknowledge and future contingents) are *semantically global*. There are still other possibilities. Truth can depend only on the current time, quite independently of the acts of the scientist. Then we say that the world-in-itself is *semantically spontaneous*. This would be the case if the laws of nature slowly evolve through time independently of anything we do, as some cosmologists have entertained, or if hypotheses involve indexicals such as "now" or "this." If the truth assignment is constant, we say that the world-in-itself is *semantically fixed*. This is the position of an extremely naive realist.

All of these distinctions make sense for evidence as well, but we know of no published version of relativism that cannot be modeled with evidentially spontaneous or local worlds. For example, Kuhn's proposal is evidentially and semantically local. Quine's holism is semantically immediate (only the current "web" of belief matters) and evidentially spontaneous (if "evidence" is taken to be "surface irritation"). Naive convergent realism assumes that the world-in-itself is evidentially spontaneous and semantically fixed. This is the sort of setting assumed in Putnam's critique of Carnap, as reviewed in section 2 of this chapter. A wide range of philosophical positions can be parametrized in terms of various constraints on evidentially local worlds-in-themselves.

Finally, some worlds-in-themselves are functions whose values depend not upon what the scientist conjectures, but only upon acts independent of conjecturing. If we model a logical positivist setting by interpreting a to be a conventional choice of analytic truths or meaning postulates, then truth depends only on this choice, and the conjecture of an empirical (non-analytic) h would have no bearing on meaning or truth. Such worlds-in-themselves will be called *conjecture-independent*. By making truth depend upon all of one's beliefs, Quine insists that the world-in-itself is *conjecture-dependent*, if we take the conjecture to be added to the current set of beliefs. An economic prognosticator who brings down the market by predicting doom provides a more vivid example of conjecture-dependency.

4.2 Transcendental Background Knowledge

In relativistic settings, background knowledge is a set K of possible worlds-in-themselves. It may be objected that such transcendental knowledge is hopeless to obtain. But whatever our own views on the possibility of such knowledge may be, literary theorists, metaphysicians, and philosophers of language regularly propound transcendental theses as a matter of course. The naive realist considers only semantically fixed and evidentially spontaneous worlds-in-themselves, so that the world-in-itself collapses to a single data stream and a single notion of truth. Coherentists, at the other extreme, are sure that all that matters to truth or to data is which coherent set we decide to believe. The positivists knew that truth depends only upon the free act of adopting some special set of conventional, analytic truths. Quine knows the negation of this claim.[57] Kuhn knows that the scientist's training, colleagues, and stock of solved examples are what determine truth and evidence. He even speaks of scientists with different backgrounds as inhabiting different "worlds."[58] Hanson knew that evidence depends upon perceptual and conceptual "gestalts."[59] Social constructivists know that truth is a matter of community assent, so the world-in-itself is the causal disposition of the community to assent in response to how one interacts with the community. Many Marxists know that truth is a matter of one's political role.

We can also consider the transcendental knowledge implied by Putnam's internal realism. His moderate relativism is characterized by at least the following principles:

(P1) Reference depends upon the community's current conceptual scheme.[60]

(P2) Individuation depends upon the community's current theory.[61]

(P3) Experience depends upon the community's belief system.[62]

(P4) Truth is an ideal limit of rational acceptability under increasingly idealized epistemic conditions.[63]

(P5) Whether or not a given sequence of epistemic conditions is increasingly idealized depends on our knowledge.[64]

For simplicity, we will identify *conceptual schemes, knowledge,* and *theories* with *belief systems,* and we will also identify *experience* with *evidence.* We expect that *truth, individuation,* and *reference* are closely enough related to be assimilated to *truth* in our discussion. *Epistemic conditions* are something else again. We think of them as alterations to our local environment that affect our powers of observation (e.g. building larger and larger radio telescopes, peering more closely, etc.).[65]

Then Putnam's proposal seems to be this. Semantically relevant acts are triples $\langle B, \alpha, c \rangle$, where $B \subseteq H$ is the current belief system, α is the current standard of rational acceptability, and c is the current attempt to improve our epistemic conditions. The evidence at stage n depends immediately (as opposed to historically) upon the current belief system B and the current experimental set-up c, but is presumably not directly dependent upon the current α (though α may be a factor underlying *our* choice of B).[66] Accordingly, let $e_\psi(B, c)$ be the datum received from ψ in response to B and c.

Truth at stage n depends immediately upon α (as in our discussion of truth1_α and truth2_α) and immediately upon K (in so far as the data stream that would be produced under increasingly idealized choices of c will depend immediately upon K). Truth does not depend upon the actual c chosen by the scientist, however. It depends only on what the current α would do if c were, counter-factually, to be progressively idealized for eternity. Let P be the set of all programs or procedures for enumerating an infinite sequence χ of epistemic conditions, and let $p \in$ P. Let $p[n]$ be the epistemic condition output by p on input n. Let Improve(p) be the hypothesis "p enumerates an infinite sequence of improving epistemic conditions." Assume that Improve(p) $\in$ H. Let $f_{\psi(B,\alpha)}$ be the truth assignment for hypotheses in ψ relative to $\langle B, \alpha, c \rangle$ (recall that truth does not depend upon the actual choice of c). Then a rough reconstruction (along the lines of truth1)[67] of Putnam's transcendental knowledge is:

(a) $f_{\psi(B,\alpha)}(h) = 1 \Leftrightarrow$
$\forall p \in$ P, if $f_{\psi(B,\alpha)}(\text{Improve}(p)) = 1$,
then $\exists n \ \forall m \geq n$ such that $\alpha(h, \langle e_{\psi}(B, p[0]), \ldots, e_{\psi}(B, p[m]) \rangle) > 0.5$

(b) $f_{\psi(B,\alpha)}(h) = 0 \Leftrightarrow$
$\forall p \in$ P, if $f_{\psi(B,\alpha)}(\text{Improve}(p)) = 1$,
then $\exists n \ \forall m \geq n$ such that $\alpha(h, \langle e_{\psi}(B, p[0]), \ldots, e_{\psi}(B, p[m]) \rangle) \leq 0.5$

We take Putnam at his word that truth is stable, rational acceptability under increasingly idealized epistemic conditions, not stable rational acceptability under conditions we believe to be ideal or that we would be justified in asserting to be ideal. Putnam makes a great point of distinguishing internal realism from redundancy theories of truth and from Dummett's identification of truth with actual verification. But then, the truth about claims concerning epistemic conditions should also be internal realist truth, not actual warranted assertibility or willingness to believe.[68] Thus, we run the claim Improve(p) back through internal realist truth in the antecedents of (a) and (b). Since internal realist truth is relative to B, we still save (P5). But true to internal realism, idealization is more, on our account, than what we believe or are currently justified in believing about idealization.

Putnam insists that he does not intend internal realism to be a definition of truth. As a matter of fact, this reservation is warranted, since different truth assignments are consistent with (a) and (b) under a fixed choice of ψ, B, and α.[69] The problem is that the recursive call to $f_{\psi(B,\alpha)}$ in the antecedents of (a) and (b) may or may not "bottom out," depending on the structure of ψ and of α. Since examples can be found in which the alternative truth assignments are entirely symmetrical (up to permutation of 0s and 1s), it is hard to see what further restrictions of an internal realist sort could be added to (a) and (b) to pick out one of them in a non-arbitrary manner.

Relativistic dependencies can be much more mundane than in these

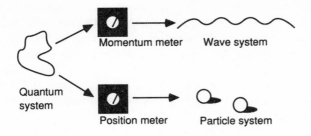

Figure 5.18

philosophical examples. In the case of the economic prognosticator who crashes the market, the truth-dependency is entirely causal, but the logic of the situation is the same: truth depends on what the prognosticator predicts. The power of suggestion of a psychoanalyst on the personality under study provides another such example. In a quantum system, the truth can depend essentially upon the scientist's free choice of an experimental act. Thus, believers in quantum mechanics think they know quite a bit about the structures of possible worlds-in-themselves (see figure 5.18). Indeed, it can be argued that Bohr conceived of quantum mechanics as a relativistic system in just this manner.[70] Relativity theory can be viewed as a relativistic system in which the free decision to ignite rocket fuel is the act relevant to the truth about simultaneity. And to make the matter as concrete as possible, whenever the hypothesis under investigation is contingent, the scientist's acts can help determine whether or not it is true (e.g. the scientist can murder the last non-black raven). So ordinary experimental investigation of contingent hypotheses can also pose a relativistic problem in the functional sense. In each of these cases, we take our "transcendental knowledge" K about functional worlds-in-themselves (truth dependencies) to be quite strong.

4.3   Convergent Relativism

The philosophy of science is still reeling from the relativistic and holistic blows leveled by Quine and by Kuhn. According to the usual story, scientific objectivity and hence scientific rationality have been undercut. Since the evidence depends upon the background and pet theories of the perceiver, different scientists following the same method can end up with different, justified conclusions.

Philosophy journals are stuffed with articles that accept the implication from non-trivial relativism to methodological nihilism, but which deny the antecedent. The story is that relativism happens to be benign in real historical cases, so rationality is saved by accident.[71] On the other side are the anarchists eager to exploit the barest hint of relativity to reject all prospects for general methodological norms and principles. But neither party challenges the inference from relativity to "anything goes."[72] Our strategy is just the opposite: to concede the possibility of strong versions of relativism and incommensurability while undermining the usual inference from relativity to methodological nihilism.

The first question is why the inference from relativism to "anything goes" is so popular. The logical positivists, like the phenomenalists and empiricists before them, started out as reliabilists. The point of formulating analytic reduction relations was to skirt the global underdetermination[73] of physical theory by data, for underdetermination precludes the reliability even of a god who can see all the data that will ever arrive in the future. But once the reductionist program was pursued in earnest, it became clear that the highly ambitious aim of "logically" reducing all knowledge to sense data was not going to pan out. The reductionist program had too much momentum to be halted by the mere rejection of its fundamental motivation, however. Instead, the language of sense data was exchanged for the fallible language of macroscopic physical objects in order to make reduction easier, and reliability was replaced with a new rationale for reductionism: *intersubjective agreement*.

> The condition thus imposed upon the observational vocabulary of science is of a pragmatic character; it demands that each term included in that vocabulary be of such a kind that under suitable conditions, different observers can, by means of direct observation, arrive at a high degree of certainty whether the term applies to a given situation. . . . That human beings are capable of developing observational vocabularies that satisfy the given requirement is a fortunate circumstance: without it, science as an *intersubjective enterprise* would be impossible.[74]

Notice the striking absence of concern that science be a *reliable* enterprise in the last sentence of this passage. Kuhn and Quine undercut this particular rationale for reductionism. The difficulty was not relativism per se. The positivists were relativists, but the relativism was contrived to be conjecture-independent since meaning was pinned to conventionally selected, analytic meaning postulates independent of the scientist's election to believe this or that contingent, empirical hypothesis. Analytic truths were taken to "frame" the language of science, and inductive methods were conceived as operating within this framework, leaving it undisturbed by their changing conjectures. Quine's holism made truth depend upon all beliefs, and Kuhn's evidential relativism made data depend upon paradigms partly constituted by shared beliefs and assumptions. Thus both proposals imply conjecture-dependency.[75]

In a conjecture-dependent world-in-itself, a shared method of hypothesis assessment and shared "conventions" do not guarantee shared conclusions, even in the long run. For suppose we were to follow something like the hypothetico-deductive method or its improvement, the bumping pointer method (introduced in section 2 above). If our hypothesis enumerations differ ever so slightly, or if our data streams differ in the slightest respect (e.g. from different optical perspectives on the same thing), we may end up with different conclusions in the short run. But in light of conjecture-dependent data, these slight differences of conjecture can lead to slight differences of data, which will lead to greater differences in conjecture, and so forth, until truth, evidence, and hence "justified conclusions" become very different for the two former colleagues. If precisely the same discovery methods were used, and precisely the same data were collected through time, even conjecture dependency would not undermine the late-positivistic aim of intersubjective science, but these exacting conditions are too fragile to carry much philosophical significance.

So relativism is a special problem for confirmation theorists who ground scientific rationality on intersubjective agreement. Is it a problem also for the limiting reliabilist? It may seem that the proposal to unite relativism and convergent reliabilism is a non-starter, for if truth changes through time, convergence to *the* truth makes no sense. But we can still attempt to isolate the circumstances under which a scientist can converge to his or her *own* truth, even though others may converge to their truths which differ from this. It cannot be objected that science is concerned with real truth rather than truth-for-me, since, under the hypothesis of relativism, there is no truth but truth-for-me. The real losers in relativistic science are not those who disagree with one another. The losers are those who are fooled for eternity according to their own, internal versions of falsehood. The proposal that scientific methods converge reliably to the relative truth when truth is not unique will be referred to as *convergent relativism*. Thus, we can unify Putnam's early, limiting reliabilism with his recent, moderate relativism.

There are perhaps two main reasons why convergent relativism has not captured the imagination of philosophers. First, the goal seems too difficult. It is one thing, so the story goes, to find the truth in a fixed, spoon-fed framework of concepts, but it is quite another to search among different conceptual frameworks to find one that is suitable. This observation is doubly flawed, however. It is by no means always trivial to find the truth in a fixed system, as the many negative results presented in the first section of this chapter attest. And finding the truth in the system of one's choice can make the problem of finding the truth *easier*, for the scientist may

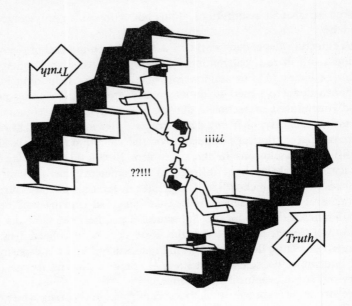

Figure 5.19

sidestep inductive difficulties by altering auxiliary assumptions, concepts, and so forth. This sort of stratagem is familiar from the old discussions of conventionalism.

In light of these comments, getting to the relative truth may now appear too easy. If truth depends upon you, then what is the point of enquiry? Just make your present beliefs true by an act of will, and be done with it! But this triviality holds only in the most extremal forms of coherentism, and does not follow for moderate relativism. If truth depends not only upon the investigator but also upon some independent reality over which the investigator has no control, then the scientist may not know just how truth actually depends upon what he or she does. This is the case in each of the intuitive examples of relativism discussed above. Under such circumstances, finding the truth about a given hypothesis may be difficult or even impossible.

4.4   Reliable Relativistic Discovery in the Limit

A relativistic hypothesis generator γ is just like its non-relativistic counterpart, except that it produces both a hypothesis h and some act $a \in A$ on the basis of the data provided, rather than just a hypothesis h.[76] Assuming that the world-in-itself ψ is evidentially local, the interaction between the world-in-itself ψ and method γ then determines an infinite play sequence *play* (γ, ψ), where γ produces its act and conjecture on the empty data sequence, ψ responds with a truth assignment and the next datum, and so forth, forever. For each position n, play (γ, ψ)$_n$ denotes some tuple $\langle a_n, h_n, x_n, f_n \rangle$ where $a_n \in A$ is the method γ's act, $h_n \in H$ is γs conjecture, $x_n \in E$ is the current datum returned by ψ, and f_n is the current truth assignment returned by ψ. Then we define sequences $A(\gamma, \psi)$, $H(\gamma, \psi)$, $E(\gamma, \psi)$, $C(\gamma, \psi)$ so that for each n, $A(\gamma, \psi)_n = a_n$, $H(\gamma, \psi)_n = h_n$, $E(\gamma, \psi)_n = x_n$, and $C(\gamma, \psi)_n = f_n$. So the model reflects the "hermeneutic circle" of relativism, in which the conceptual scheme depends upon the evidence and the evidence depends upon the conceptual scheme. But here the circle is bent into a spiral through time, so we have mutual dependency without circularity.[77]

Relativistic discovery admits of various different senses of success. Let γ be a relativistic hypothesis generator and let K be a set of evidentially local worlds-in-themselves. One sense of success requires only that after some time, the conjecture of γ is correct with respect to the acts of γ:

γ makes reliable discoveries in the limit given K $\Leftrightarrow$
> *for each* world-in-itself ψ in K
>> *there is* a time n such that
>>> *for each* later time m
>>>> the conjecture produced by γ in ψ at time m is correct at time m with respect to all the acts and conjectures ever performed or to be performed by γ in response to ψ.
>>>> (i.e. $C(\gamma, \psi)_m(H(\gamma, \psi)_m) = 1$).

This definition is general enough to apply at once to local and to global worlds-in-themselves. It is also quite liberal. Reliable relativistic discovery permits γ to vacillate forever both in its conjectured hypothesis and in its other semantically relevant acts. Thus it is permitted for γ to initiate "scientific revolutions" infinitely often, so long as after some time the hypothesis produced is correct relative to the conceptual scheme operative when the hypothesis is conjectured. Strange? Yes! But the possibility for such success is implicit in the standard relativistic philosophies, whether or not it is advertised. And when these relativisms are taken seriously (as we take them here), it is hard to say what would be wrong with this sort of success from a limiting reliabilist point of view.

Those who are subject to semantic vertigo at the prospect of an eternity of bounces between worlds or conjectures are free to impose extra, syntactic stability conditions on conjectures and on other semantically relevant acts in various combinations. Stable discovery requires that eventually both the acts and the conjectures stabilize to some specific choice of $\langle h, a \rangle$.

4.5   Anything Goes

P.K. Feyerabend's "anarchist" response to meaning variance and relativism in science has been summarized in the slogan "Anything goes." As we have seen, it is a limiting reliabilist commonplace that different methods are better in different inductive settings, so if "anything goes" means only that we should not force a fixed method on everybody, we do not need relativism to prove it. And if "anything goes" means that there is no universal architecture for relativistic discovery, it is mistaken both for relativistic and for naive realist science, as we shall see in the next section.

Perhaps "anything goes" means that it is wrong to force a particular conceptual scheme on the scientist, or to require him or her to stabilize to a particular such scheme. We may think of each shift in correctness and evidence due to the agency of the scientist as a *scientific* or *conceptual revolution*. Stable discovery fits with the intuition that each scientific revolution is a clean break with the past, so that convergent success can succeed only within a fixed conceptual scheme. Thus, after some time science should fix upon a particular scheme and diligently seek the truth within it. Unstable discovery embodies a more anarchistic attitude, in that it countenances an infinite number of conceptual revolutions. This kind of anarchism is in fact vindicated from the point of view of convergent relativism, because there are relativistic discovery problems that cannot be solved in the stable sense, but that can be solved in the unstable (anything goes) sense. For a trivial example, suppose that $K = \{\psi\}$ where ψ is semantically spontaneous so that at even stages of enquiry the only correct hypothesis is h and at odd stages of enquiry the only correct hypothesis is h', no matter what the scientist does. It is impossible to stabilize to a true hypothesis in ψ, even in the limit, but the trivial method that conjectures h', h, h', h, ... for eternity, irrespective of the evidence, succeeds in the unstable sense.

The preceding example made stabilization to a correct hypothesis impossible for purely semantic reasons. A more interesting example would be one in which stabilization is semantically possible, but reliable stabilization to a particular scheme–conjecture pair is not possible for properly epistemic reasons, because stabilization would prevent the scientist from seeing important data. To construct such a case, suppose the scientist's only semantically relevant act is to adopt one of two conceptual schemes, 1 or 0. Let ψ_1 be a world-in-itself in which h is true exactly when the current scheme is 1 and in which the current datum is 0 no matter what the scientist does. Let ε be a fixed data stream in which only 0s or 1s occur. In world ψ_2^ε, h is correct exactly when the current scheme is 1, and the data is produced as follows: a pointer is initialized to ε_0, and each time conceptual scheme 1 is visited,

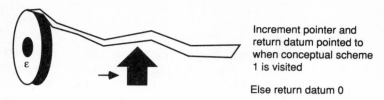

Increment pointer and
return datum pointed to
when conceptual scheme
1 is visited

Else return datum 0

Figure 5.20

the next entry in ε is presented as data. Whenever conceptual scheme 0 is visited, however, datum 0 is returned (see figure 5.20).

In world ψ_3^ε we have the same situation, but the role of schemes 1 and 0 is reversed. Thus, data are drawn by the same pointer mechanism from ε in scheme 0, datum 0 is always returned in scheme 1, and h is correct in scheme 0 but not in scheme 1. Finally, suppose that in each of the worlds under consideration, $\neg h$ is correct whenever h is not correct, and no other hypotheses are correct under any circumstances. Suppose we know in advance that the actual world-in-itself is either ψ_1, ψ_2^ε or ψ_3^ε, where it is certain that infinitely many 1s occur in ε. Thus, $K_0 = \{\psi_1\ \psi_2^\varepsilon,\ \psi_3^\varepsilon$: infinitely many 1s occur in ε).

Intuitively, the dilemma posed by the problem is that if the scientist is actually in ψ_1 and stabilizes the truth value of h after some time, say to 1, then he or she must eventually settle into performing act 1 forever. But then if the scientist had really been in ψ_3^f, he or she might never have seen a 1 in the data prior to deciding to settle down into act 1, so would never have discovered that in fact the truth value of h is 0 under act 1. This dilemma can be turned into a rigorous, relativistic version of Putnam's diagonal argument:

Fact 4.1: Effective, relativistic discovery is possible in the limit over K_0, but stable, relativistic discovery is not possible over K_0 even by an ideal method.

Proof: The effective scientist γ who succeeds in the unstable sense follows this strategy: he or she flip-flops between schemes 1 and 0 forever, producing hypothesis h in scheme 1 and hypothesis $\neg h$ in scheme 0 so long as only 0s are seen in the data. As soon as a 1 is seen, the scientist remarks which scheme a it occurred under and stabilizes to that scheme and the corresponding hypothesis (h if $a = 1$, and $\neg h$ if $a = 0$).

In ψ_1, γ alternates forever between schemes 0 and 1 and hypotheses h, $\neg h$, but γ's conjecture is always correct. In ψ_2^ε, eventually datum 1 appears under scheme 1 since γ visits scheme 1 at odd stages until a 1 is seen. Then

γ stabilizes correctly to $\langle 1, h \rangle$, which is correct for ψ_2^ε. By a similar argument, γ eventually sees a 1 under scheme 0 in ψ_3^ε, and thus stabilizes to act 1 and truth-value 0, which is correct for ψ_2^ε.

Now the diagonal argument. Suppose for *reductio* that γ stably succeeds over K_0. Then either (a) γ converges to $\langle 1, h \rangle$ in ψ_1 or (b) γ converges to $\langle 0, \neg h \rangle$ in ψ_1. Consider case (a). Let n be the time at which γ converges to $\langle 1, h \rangle$ in ψ_1. Let k be the number of times scheme 1 is visited by γ in ψ_1 up to stage n. Define ε so that ε has 0s up to k and 1 thereafter. Thus $\psi_3^\varepsilon \in K_0$. Moreover, the data seen by γ in ψ_3^ε are exactly the same up to stage n as the data seen in ψ_1 by γ. Since γ converges to scheme 1 at stage n, and since ψ_3^ε produces the same data under scheme 1 that ψ_1 does (namely, all 0s), γ converges to $\langle 1, h \rangle$ in ψ_3^ε which is incorrect. The cases for $\neg h$ are similar.

4.6   Relativistic Transcendental Deductions

Kant proposed both a moderate, metaphysical relativism and the notion of transcendental deductions. Since he thought that the human conceptual scheme is fixed, his transcendental deductions were not relativistic: they were directed at the character of this fixed scheme. But convergent relativism raises the prospect for rigorous, properly relativistic, transcendental deductions. And just as in the realist case, such results can be used to establish completeness for relativistic discovery architectures. The existence of such architectures for reliable, relativistic discovery overturns the quick inference from relativism to methodological nihilism.

For a simple example, when truth depends upon the current act of the scientist but evidence does not, we have an easy reduction to the situation in section 2. When evidence is spontaneous, each world-in-itself is characterized by a unique data stream ε_ψ (the one generated in successive times by ψ, regardless of what γ does). Since ψ is semantically immediate, we may let $f_{\psi(\langle h,a \rangle)}$ denote the correctness assignment produced by ψ at any time in light of semantic act $\langle h, a \rangle$. Now the characterization condition may be stated as:

Theorem 4.6.1:   Suppose the worlds-in-themselves in K are
    (a)   evidentially spontaneous and
    (b)   semantically immediate
Then correct hypotheses are effectively stably discoverable in the limit given K $\Leftrightarrow$
    there is some $R' \subseteq (E^\omega \times H)$, $S \subseteq (H \times A)$ s.t.
        (0) $\forall \psi \in K$, $\langle h, a \rangle \in H \times A$, $R'(\varepsilon_\psi, h) \Rightarrow f_{\psi(\langle h,a \rangle)}(h) = 1$ and
        (1)   S is recursively enumerable and
        (2)   S covers K according to R' and
        (3) $R' \in \Sigma[H', K]_2^0$

Condition (0) replaces the realist condition $R' \subseteq R$ in theorem 2.6.2. It is a relativistic way of saying that the act $\langle h, a \rangle$ is "correct" if R' says it is. Conditions (1), (2), and (3) mimic the conditions with the same numbers in theorem 2.6.2, where we take the pair $\langle h, a \rangle$ to be "correct" or "incorrect" for a world-in-itself ψ rather than for a particular data stream ε. The complete architecture for discovery will be a minor variant of the bumping pointer architecture that takes these minor alterations into account.

We have also characterized a special class of problems in which data also depend upon the current act of the scientist (Kelly and Glymour, 1992). When the scientist's history is relevant to the data presented (i.e. the world-in-itself can "remember"), the situation becomes more complex. Such historical dependencies can make success harder to achieve, because some desired datum may be forever unobservable for a scientist who has elected to perform some sequence σ of acts in his or her past.[78] These new difficulties are hardly unique to philosophical relativism, however, since they are familiar features of experimental science in general. In classical mechanics, it is usually assumed that we can perform essential experimental acts independently and get the same information, but in relativity theory[79] and in quantum mechanics,[80] this assumption is challenged. More concretely, experimental compatibility assumptions clearly fail in historical studies like archaeology, in which a pillaged or mismanaged site can shut the book on an ancient culture for eternity. Global relativism poses further technical challenges to the transcendental logician, issues we leave for future study.

4.7 Relativistic Theory-building

So far, we have viewed the scientist as producing a particular theory and other semantically relevant acts that may affect the correctness of this theory. Perhaps a more realistic situation portrays the scientist as building up a theory in response to data, sometimes removing hypotheses and sometimes adding them, with the intention of choosing new hypotheses so that the old ones remain true. In such a situation it is natural to suppose that a scientist is committed to the logical consequences of his or her conjectures, so we need to introduce a relativistic version of semantic entailment. Intuitively, h entails h' relative to method γ and time n just in case the correctness of h relative to γ at n implies the correctness of h' relative to γ at n.

$$K, h \models_{\gamma, n} h' \Leftrightarrow \forall \psi \in K, C(\gamma, \psi)_n(h) = 1 \Rightarrow C(\gamma, \psi)_n(h') = 1$$

The logical structure of relative entailment can vary radically from one time to the next. None the less, we might hope that for each h, there is a time after which h is entailed (with respect to the sense of entailment operative

Figure 5.21   Naive realist convergence

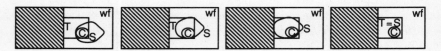

Figure 5.22   Positivistic convergence

at the time) if and only if *h* is correct (with respect to the sense of correctness operative at the time). Thus:

γ *non-uniformly discovers the complete truth given* K $\Leftrightarrow$

$\forall \psi \in$ K $\forall h \in$ H $\exists n \forall m \geq n$ C$(\gamma, \psi)_m(h) = 1 \Leftrightarrow$ K, H$(\gamma, \psi)_m \models_{\gamma,m} h$

Non-uniform theory construction is closer to the diachronic image of enquiry operative in many philosophy of science discussions.[81] In realist settings, truth and well-formedness are naively fixed, and truth stays put while science tries its best to home in on it in light of increasing data.[82] In figure 5.21, T is the set of all true hypotheses, wf is the set of all well-formed strings, and S is the set of hypotheses entailed by γ's current conjecture.

This picture is very little changed in the case of positivism. We must add to the picture the set C of all conventionally selected meaning postulates that tie down the language. Assuming with the positivists that enquiry is conjecture-independent (inductive methods do not fiddle with analytic truth) then the picture is the same, except that it is now guaranteed that the meaning postulates are well-formed and true (see figure 5.22).

If the meaning postulates C are changed, however, then there is a saltative break with the past. Positivists did not entertain the possibility of convergent success *through* changing conventions, and this is what left them vulnerable to the possibility of conjecture dependency raised by Kuhn and Quine, as we have seen.

Proponents of conjecture-dependency often assume that when truth depends on the scientist's conjectures, it meets them half-way to make science easier. Kuhn and Hanson speak of theory-ladenness, as though the theories we entertain color truth and the data so that truth and evidence always meet

Figure 5.23   Coherentism (positive conjecture dependency)

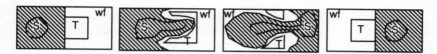

Figure 5.24   Sisyphusian relativism (negative conjecture dependency)

us half-way. Radical coherentists go further, and assume that truth unshakably chases us around, so long as certain unspecified standards of coherence are observed (see figure 5.23).

But once conjecture-dependency is out of the bag, we see that it is just as conceivable for truth to run away from us, in the sense that our conjectured theories are false because we conjecture them. Thus, a hypothesis could remain true as the scientist homes in on it, only to melt spitefully into falsehood (or even worse, into nonsense) the minute he or she comes to believe it, only to become true again after it is rejected. We refer such worlds-in-themselves as *Sisyphusian* (see figure 5.24).[83]

Sisyphusian relativism is not entirely a product of our malicious imaginations. If social constructivists are correct and truth is nothing more than the relevant community's assent to one's beliefs, then Sisyphusian relativism is a distinct possibility, for an offended community could out of spite reject, and therefore falsify, every one of the offender's announced beliefs.

Coherentism, the philosopher's ultimate refuge from skepticism, is not immune from these difficulties. Putnam has correctly remarked that coherentism is a dangerous position for a relativist, for it is vacuous if coherence is nothing at all, and if coherence is the same for everybody then it is naively objectivistic.[84] But if coherentism steers a moderate relativist course between these two extremes, so that coherence, itself, depends to some extent on the acts and history of the scientist, then Sisyphusian skepticism looms once again, for it may happen that what we believe is incoherent because we believe it.[85]

Sisyphusian relativism is much worse than the original, inductive skepticism that relativism (in its Kantian and positivistic incarnations) was summoned to defeat. Inductive skepticism tells us that belief might happen to be wrong for all we know. Relativistic skepticism tells us that belief might be self-defeating for all we know: a sorrier situation. All that stands in the way of such possibilities are the philosophers' claims to transcendental knowledge about how truth and evidence can possibly depend upon our acts. All that has happened is that ordinary scientific uncertainty has been replaced with a far more virulent transcendental uncertainty, and the material dogmas of science have been replaced with the metaphysical dogmas of the philosophers.

But Pandora's box is hard to shut once it has been opened. Perhaps it is vain to hope for a convincing, a priori argument against undesirable relativistic possibilities. But this does not leave us entirely helpless. At least we can reason backwards, by means of transcendental deductions, to determine what we would have to know about the world-in-itself for reliable, relativistic theory-building to be possible. If we are doomed to transcendental dogmatism, we can at least choose our dogmas to be as weak as they can be conditional on preserving some desired sense of reliability in scientific enquiry. In this manner, limiting reliabilist transcendental deductions can be used to constrain metaphysical theorizing. For example, since theorem 4.6.1 characterizes convergent success over conjecture-dependent worlds, it must exclude the possibility of Sisyphusian worlds. Inspection of the theorem will reveal that condition (0) is violated for every choice of R' when ψ is Sisyphusian.

4.8   Relativism, Logic, and Historicism

Our aim in this section of the chapter has been to extend Putnam's early, limiting reliabilism to settings in which theory-laden data and incommensurability run rampant. We have seen that there are transcendental deductions for convergent relativism that are quite parallel to those we obtained in the naive realist settings in the first section of the chapter. Despite this, it is interesting to observe that this basic strategy has already been anticipated – and *refuted* – some years ago by the cognoscenti of relativistic nihilism:

> The notion that it would be all right to relativize sameness of meaning, objectivity, and truth to a conceptual scheme, as long as there were some criteria for knowing when and why it was rational to adopt a new conceptual scheme, was briefly tempting. For now the philosopher, the guardian of rationality, became the man who told you when you could start meaning something different, rather than the man who told you what you meant.

Recall that a relativistic hypothesis generator is exactly a method that tells you what to conjecture and when to mean something different. Rorty claims that any such proposal must somehow presuppose meaning invariance:

But this attempt to retain the philosopher's traditional role was doomed. All the Quinean reasons why he could not do the one were also reasons why he could not do the other. . . . [As] soon as it was admitted that "empirical considerations" . . . incited but did not require "conceptual change" . . . the division of labor between the philosopher and the historian no longer made sense. Once one said that it was rational to abandon the Aristotelian conceptual scheme as a result of this or that discovery, then "change of meaning" or "shift in conceptual scheme" meant nothing more than "shift in especially central beliefs." The historian can make the shift from old scheme to the new intelligible. . . . There is nothing the philosopher can add to what the historian has already done to show that this intelligible and plausible course is a "rational" one. Without what Feyerabend called "meaning invariance," there is no special method (meaning-analysis) which the philosopher can apply.[86]

But as a matter of fact, nothing in our presentation presupposes invariance in meaning or truth of the scientist's conjectures; much less that such conjectures are translatable across conceptual revolutions. Stabilizing to one's own version of the truth does not require that past theories make sense or can be translated into one's current point of view. It does require knowledge of what past scientists accepted as evidence and what kinds of theory they conjectured when that evidence was accepted; but these are just the sorts of thing that Rorty claims the historian can teach us.

Rorty focuses on the question whether a particular shift in conceptual scheme is plausible or intelligible. But when we shift our attention to the reliability of general strategies for generating theories and changing meaning through time, the prospect arises for a genuinely logical analysis along the lines indicated above. Such analyses are something that a philosopher (or computer scientist, or historian, or anyone who pleases) can do and that amassing loads of historical case studies and explaining them informally would not do. We are not saying that one of these sources of insight into the workings of science is better than the other. Rorty is.

Perhaps the relativistic nihilist will respond with his or her ultimate weapon, namely, that even his or her relativism is relative. Since our logical investigation of relativistic induction assumes fixed, transcendental knowledge K, it assumes an Archimedean point which the nihilist is happy to pull out from under himself or herself. We have two responses.

First, this meta-relativism is a bold, transcendental thesis that is hardly entailed by the sorts of historical anecdote that historicists like Kuhn have proposed as evidence for their semantically and evidentially local versions of relativism. All that is indicated by such cases is (a) some dependence of truth and evidence upon one's history, and (b) a putative lack of translatability between paradigms. The scientific historian aspires, in fact, to tell us when revolutions occurred, which theories are incommensurable, and why certain shifts of meaning occurred. As long as the relativist can tell us about how the relativistic dependencies work, our apparatus for convergent relativism will apply.

Second, we may view the pulling out of the rug as the first step up a "hierarchy" of relativisms analogous to Tarski's hierarchy in the conventional theory of truth. As we move up this hierarchy, the world-in-itself may depend upon acts, that dependency may depend upon acts, etc., to any ordinal level. We expect that our convergent relativist gambit will apply, with a corresponding increase in subtlety and complexity, to fixed background knowledge concerning dependencies at any such level. If the nihilist insists that his or her ultimate relativism diagonalizes across each of these levels, then we no longer have a response, but neither do we know what is being asserted. Ultimate relativism, the relativism beyond all relativisms, belongs to the baffling realm of the greatest ordinal, the set of all sets, the liar paradox, and the neoplatonic One. If it takes this much to shut down Putnam's limiting reliabilist methodology, then it stands in excellent company.

Acknowledgments

We are grateful to Teddy Seidenfeld and to Wilfried Sieg for a useful discussion concerning issues in section 3. We are also indebted to Jeff Paris, at the University of Manchester, for some very useful suggestions concerning an earlier draft.

Notes

1 Putnam (1963a) and (1963b).
2 E.g. Putnam (1990).
3 Putnam (1963a).
4 Kemeny (1953).
5 Putnam (1963a), p. 270.
6 Instead of treating data as binary sequences, we could think of observations as being drawn from a recursively enumerable set E of mutually exclusive and exhaustive, possible observations. But binary data streams suffice for Putnam's argument, so we will assume that E is {0, 1}.
7 The following argument is from Gold (1965). A more recent version is given in Osherson et al. (1986).
8 Rogers (1987).

9   The idea is due to Barzdin and Freivalds (1972) and is applied in Blum and Blum (1975). Let π be a recursive prediction method. Define program p_e as follows: if $k <$ length(e), return e_k. Otherwise, feed e to π and thereafter feed the successive predictions of π back to π. Halt this process and output the kth prediction as soon as it is reached. If π extrapolates ε, then after some time n, π's predictions are all correct. Thus $p_{\varepsilon|n}$ computes ε. On the other hand, for each finite data sequence e, π extrapolates the sequence computed by p_e. Let e_0, $e_1, \ldots, e_n, \ldots$ be a computable enumeration of all possible finite data sequences. Then the enumeration of programs $p_{e_0}, p_{e_1}, \ldots, p_{e_n}, \ldots$ is computable, total, and complete over the set K of data streams extrapolated by π.

10   Putnam (1963a), p. 282.

11   No rational valued c-function is "nowhere computable" in the sense that no program can find any value of it, since for every particular pair $\langle\langle x, e\rangle, c(x, e)\rangle$, there is a program that waits for $\langle x, e\rangle$ and that produces $c(x, e)$ on this particular input. Indeed, this can be done for any finite number of inputs. The puzzling expression "never computable" must therefore mean "uncomputable" if Putnam's claim is not to be vacuously true.

12   Putnam (1963a), p. 276.

13   Ibid., p. 292, our emphasis.

14   Putnam (1963b), p. 302.

15   Cf. note 9 and (b″) above.

16   Effective transcendency is not *verifiable in the limit* over ω^ω, in the sense of section 2.5 below. Let α aspire to this task, with no preconceived ideas about what Uncle Fred will suggest (after all, we are *relying* on Uncle Fred for our new ideas). Then we may diagonalize as follows. Suppose α succeeds. Let η be a fixed, effectively transcendent hypothesis stream. We present η until α says 1, which must happen eventually, since α succeeds and η is effectively transcendent. Now we continue in an effective manner until α says 0, which must happen eventually, and so forth, for each finite sequence of total programs can be extended in an effectively transcendent way or in an effective way. Each time we switch back to η we make sure then next item in η is presented. In the limit, all of η is presented (perhaps with some more total programs) and hence the hypothesis stream presented is effectively transcendent, since η is. But α changes its mind infinitely often, and hence fails, contrary to assumption. Thus no α succeeds, whether computable or not. This is much worse than the original problem of extrapolating Rec, which is impossible only for *effective* methods.

17   Totality is not verifiable in the limit by an effective agent in the sense of section 2.5 below. Suppose recursive α succeeds. We fool α infinitely often by feeding it programs that simulate α and go into loops until α concludes that they will loop forever, at which point the loops all terminate. Specifically, suppose the finite sequence e of total programs has been presented to α so far. Let η be a fixed, effective, total hypothesis stream. We write a program that on input y simulates α on $e*X*\eta$ and that goes into a loop, waiting for α to conjecture some value ≤ 0.5 about the hypothesis of totality. As soon as such a value is produced by α, our program terminates the loop and outputs some

arbitrary value, say 0. Note that X is a free parameter. By the Kleene recursion theorem, X can be specified as the program p we have just defined, so it can feed itself to α in the simulation! Now if p stays in its loop forever, this is because α returns values greater than 0.5 forever, so α fails on $e^*p^*\eta$ which is not total, due to p, and we are done. If p exits its loop, this is because α's confidence in totality sagged at some point n in reading η during p's simulation. Then we really feed data $e^*p^*\eta$ to α until α really says 0, as p already determined in its simulation. Then we repeat the whole construction for a new internal simulation program p', and so forth, forever. Thus α's confidence in totality sags infinitely often on a total hypothesis stream, so α fails.

18 Similar considerations can be raised against the various arguments based on Gödel's theorem (e.g. Lucas (1961)) which are intended to show that minds are not computers. These arguments assume that the "genius" who (effectively) constructs the Gödel sentence and who "sees" (by following the proof) that the sentence constructed is true knows that the system for which he or she constructs the sentence is sound. But this presupposes a reliable soundness oracle for arithmetic systems, and we do not know that the geniuses in question are reliable oracles for soundness. Nor could we reliably find out by watching what these geniuses do whether they are reliable soundness oracles if in fact we are computable, by diagonal arguments similar to those rehearsed in the preceding footnotes.

19 Osherson et al. refer to maxims or architectures as strategies, and refer to cases in which maxims stand in the way of reliability as cases of restrictiveness. For a raft of restrictiveness results for recursive methods, cf. Osherson et al. (1986), ch. 4.

20 "There is no logic of discovery" – in that sense, there is no logic of testing, either; all the formal algorithms proposed for testing, by Carnap, by Popper, by Chomsky, etc., are, to speak impolitely, ridiculous: if you do not believe this, program a computer to employ one of these algorithms and see how well it does at testing theories! (Putnam, 1974, p. 268).

21 In section 3 we will see that Putnam's internal realist semantics provides a model for this absurdity, so perhaps he would endorse it.

22 The restriction to rational values eliminates problems about effectiveness later on.

23 Correctness is a very general notion. Correctness might be empirical adequacy (i.e. consistency with the total data to occur in ε) if hypotheses and observations are both drawn from some logical language. As in Putnam's discussion, we might also require that a correct hypothesis predict what will happen in ε. Or correctness might tolerate some number of mistaken predictions, or even an arbitrary, finite number. Simplicity and other properties of hypotheses may also be involved.

24 Add the condition that $\gamma(e \mid m) = \gamma(e \mid n)$ to the expression in parentheses.

25 Plato (1949).

26 Cf. Blum and Blum (1975).

27 Ibid.

28 Gold (1965).

29 Osherson et al. (1986).

30 This result was presented by Mark Fulk in a symposium at Carnegie Mellon University in 1989.

31 E.g. Horwich (1991) and Lycan (1988).

32 In our setting, say that *h is consistent with e*, K $\Leftrightarrow$ for some $\varepsilon \in$ K $e \subseteq \varepsilon$.

33 This method and the following argument were introduced in Osherson and Weinstein (1991) in the first-order hypothesis setting.

34 rng(ε) denotes the range of ε, or the set of all items that occur in ε.

35 Popper (1968).

36 Putnam (1965), Gold (1965). In personal correspondence, Putnam insists that his paper on Mostowski's problem was conceived quite separately from the paper on Carnap's methods. He does use inductive enquiry as a metaphor to motivate his construction, however. Gold clearly took the characterization result to have methodological significance, as did Putnam's student Peter Kugel (1977).

37 The trivially effective discovery procedure "$\gamma(e) =$ the last entry in *e*" makes reliable discoveries in the limit in this setting. On the other hand, let α be an arbitrary assessor, assumed for *reductio* to succeed in the limit in $\mathfrak{P}_0$. To show that α does not verify ω in the limit, assign α hypothesis 0 to investigate. Feed 111 . . . until α reports some value ≤ 0.5. Then fill in with 0s until α reports a value > 0.5, and so forth. Each such time must arise else α fails on the data we continue to feed, waiting for α to change its mind. If we make sure that a 0 is added each time α changes its mind, the result is a data stream for which 0 is correct, but α's confidence drops below 0.5 infinitely often.

   Let $\gamma(e) = e_1$. γ is trivially effective, and makes reliable discoveries in the limit. We show that ω is not verifiable in the limit given ω^ω (w.r.t. R_0) – even by an effective agent – by means of a simple Gold–Putnam diagonal argument, let α be an arbitrary assessor, assumed for *reductio* to verify ω in the limit given ω^ω (w.r.t. R_0). Pick hypothesis 2. Start out with 0, so that if 2 ends up being correct (according to R_0), it is not for the trivial reason that the data stream we feed has 0 in position 0. Now feed 2 until α's confidence rises above 0.5. This must eventually happen, else α's confidence always remains below 0.5 on a data stream with infinitely many 2s. When it happens, feed all 0s until α's confidence falls to or below 0.5, which again must happen, else α is eventually always more than 50 percent sure of 2 on a data stream that has only finitely many 2s and that does not have 2 in position 0. Continuing in the fashion, we produce a data stream with infinitely many 2s on which α's confidence vacillates above and below 0.5 infinitely often, so α does not verify 2 in the limit given ω^ω (w.r.t. R_0). Contradiction.

38 Putnam (1990), p. 50.

39 Ibid., p. 55.

40 Ibid.

41 Ibid.

42 Ibid., p. 56.

43 Ibid., p. 216.

44 This commitment to a *fixed* regimen of improving epistemic conditions will be relaxed considerably in section 4 below.

45 Peirce (1958), p. 69.
46 Teddy Seidenfeld and Wilfried Sieg provided helpful comments concerning these issues.
47 Putnam (1989), p. 85. The context of this passage is an attack on Dummett's proposal that rational acceptability be defined in terms of a simple, Tarski-style recursion on formula complexity, according to intuitionist semantics. We treat the passage, out of context, merely as a potential source of objections among those familiar with Putnam's expressed views.
48 We are indebted to Jeff Paris for suggesting the following construction: define $\alpha(h_\omega, e) = 1 - (1/\#_x(e))$, where $\#_x(e)$ is the current count of xs in e, and for each n, let $\alpha(h_n, e) = 1$ if $\#x(e) \geq n$ and $= 0$ otherwise. Now if the count goes up forever in ε, then h_ω is true2_α and each h_n is true2_α; and if exactly n xs are counted in ε, then for each $k > n$, h_k is false2_α and for each $k' \leq n$, k' is true2_α.
49 Define $\alpha(h_\omega, e) = 1/\#_x(e)$. If the count of xs goes up forever in ε, α goes to 0 and if only finitely many xs are ever counted, α stops short of 0 forever.
50 For brevity and mathematical clarity, we revert to the realist mode of expression, but the discussion can be reworked into a more "internally realistic" version parallel to the proof of theorem 3.1.
51 By similar reasoning, it can be seen that weak, limiting verification does not guarantee the existence of a reliable discovery procedure, either. This is why Reichenbach's straight rule estimates only rational-bounded intervals around limiting relative frequencies, rather than limiting relative frequencies themselves. The exact value of a limiting relative frequency hypothesis is weakly verifiable in the limit, but that fact does not help one to discover them.
52 Putnam (1990), p. 49.
53 Ibid., p. 50.
54 Isaac Levi's (1983) position is exactly this.
55 Putnam (1990), p. 54.
56 We might have added other kinds of semantic status, including well-formed but no truth-value, and so forth. Nothing of interest depends on these choices in what follows.
57 Quine (1951).
58 Kuhn (1970), pp. 111–12.
59 Hanson (1958), ch. i.
60 Putnam (1990), p. 50.
61 Ibid., p. 49.
62 Ibid., p. 50.
63 Ibid., pp. 55–6.
64 Putnam (1989), p. xvii.
65 "Consider the sentence 'There is a chair in my office right now.' Under sufficiently good epistemic conditions any normal person could verify this, where sufficiently good epistemic conditions might, for example, consist in one's having good vision, being in my office now with the light on, not having taken a hallucinogenic agent, etc." (Putnam, 1989, p. xvii).
66 Notice that the statement "evidence depends upon α" is metaphysically ambiguous. On the one hand, it could mean that we have no control over how our

choice of α affects the evidence, in which case the dependency would belong to the world–in–itself. On the other hand, it could mean that we happen to use α in our process for generating B, and that it is the dependency between B and the current evidence that is out of our control. Then the dependency in question results from our own choices (i.e. we could choose B without using α), and is not properly considered to reflect the structure of the world–in–itself. The matter can be subtle. Have we *chosen* α if it has no rote in shaping B? Is B really our belief system if α had no role in shaping it? Answers to such questions can incline us to cast dependencies either to the side of the world or to the side of the scientist.

67   It is a simple matter to rework the account along the lines of truth2.

68   Putnam seems to fudge this point in (1989), p. xvii. Picking up from the quote in note 65, we have: "How do I know these are better conditions for this sort of judgment than conditions under which one does not have very good vision, or in which one is looking into the room through a telescope from a great distance, or conditions in which one has taken LSD? Partly by knowing how talk of this sort operates (what the 'language game' is, in Wittensteing's sense), and partly by having a lot of empirical information. There is no single general rule or universal method for knowing what conditions are better or worse for justifying an arbitrary empirical judgment." Here, Putnam shifts from the internal realist truth about increasing idealization to what we know about increasing idealization. Those are two very different things.

69   To see that multiple truth assignments are consistent with (a) and (b) for a fixed choice of ψ, α, and B, suppose that $P = \{p_0, p_1\}$, where $p_0[n] = 2n$ and $p_1[n] = 2n + 1$. Let B be a fixed belief system. Let $e_\psi(B, x) = 1$ if x is odd, and 0 otherwise. Thus $\langle e_\psi(B, p_0[0]), \ldots, e_\psi(B, p_0[m]), \ldots \rangle$ is a sequence of 0s and $\langle e_\psi(B, p_1[0]), \ldots, e_\psi(B, p_1[m]), \ldots \rangle$ is a sequence of 1s. Let $\alpha(\text{Improve}(p_1), e) = 1$ if e contains only 1s, and let $\alpha(\text{Improve}(p_1), e) = 0$ otherwise. Dually, let $\alpha(\text{Improve}(p_0), e) = 1$ if e contains only 0s and let $\alpha(\text{Improve}(p_0), e) = 0$ otherwise. Define $S(p', p) \Leftrightarrow \exists n \, \forall m \geq n$ such that $\alpha(\text{Improve}(p'), \langle e_\psi(B, p[0]), \ldots, e_\psi(B, p[m]) \rangle) > 0.5$. Then we have $S(p_1, p_1)$, $S(p_2, p_2)$, $\neg S(p_1, p_2)$, and $\neg S(p_2, p_1)$. Thus, (a) is satisfied when Improve(p_0) is true (relative to B, α) and Improve(p_1) is not, and when Improve(p_1) is true (relative to B, α) and Improve(p_0) is not.

70   Faye (1991), p. 194.

71   E.g. Toretti (1990), p. 81.

72   Isaac Levi is a notable exception to this rule. His views are quite different from ours, however.

73   A hypothesis is *globally underdetermined* just in case the infinite data stream ε can be the same whether or not the hypothesis is true.

74   Hempel (1965), p. 127, n. 10, our emphasis.

75   Rorty seems to agree with this interpretation: "To say that we have to assign referents to terms and truth–values to sentences in the light of our best notions of what there is in the world is a platitude. To say that truth and reference are 'relative to a conceptual scheme' sounds as if it were saying something more than this, but it is not, as long as 'our conceptual scheme' is taken as simply a

reference to what we believe now – the collection of views which make up our present-day culture. This is all that any argument offered by Quine, Sellars, Kuhn, or Feyerabend would license one to mean by 'conceptual scheme'" (Rorty, 1980, p. 276).

76   i.e. $\gamma: E^* \to (A \times H)$.

77   If the world-in-itself is not evidentially local, then the circle is of a more interesting sort that must be handled with more powerful machinery than we will develop here.

78   Kelly (forthcoming), ch. 11.

79   The idea is that irregular features of the global topology of space-time can become forever causally disconnected from observers on some world lines (Malament, 1977).

80   In some developments of quantum logic, experimental compatibility is a central concept (Cohen, 1989, p. 25).

81   For example, consider the diachronic model in Lakatos (1970).

82   For a non-relativistic development of the logic of non-uniform or "incremental" theory construction, cf. Kelly and Glymour (1989).

83   Sisyphusian relativism is covered by Proposition III.D.1 in the case of semantic immediacy, for in that case it will be impossible to satisfy condition (2).

84   Putnam (1990), p. 123.

85   This may be seen in a precise way if we define relative satisfiability along the lines of our definition of relativistic entailment. E.g. say that h is satisfiable relative to γ at time n just in case h is correct relative to γ at n in some possible world-in-itself.

86   Rorty (1980), pp. 272–3.

References

Barzdin, J.M. and Freivalds, R.V. (1972), "On the Prediction of General Recursive Functions," *Soviet Mathematics Doklady*, 12, 1224–8.

Blum, M. and Blum, L. (1975), "Toward a Mathematical Theory of Inductive Inference," *Information and Control*, 28, 125–55.

Cohen, D.W. (1989), *An Introduction to Hilbert Space and Quantum Logic*. New York: Springer.

Faye, J. (1991), *Niels Bohr: His Heritage and Legacy*. Dordrecht: Kluwer.

Gold, E.M. (1965), "Limiting Recursion," *Journal of Symbolic Logic*, 30, 1, 27–48.

Hanson, N.R. (1958), *Patterns of Discovery*. Cambridge: Cambridge University Press.

Hempel, C.G. (1965), *Aspects of Scientific Explanation*. New York: Macmillan.

Horwich, P. (1991), "On the Nature and Norms of Theoretical Commitment," *Philosophy of Science*, 58, 1.

Kant, I. (1950), *Prolegomena to any Future Metaphysics*, trans. L. Beck. Indianapolis: Bobbs-Merrill.

Kelly, K. (1992), "Learning Theory and Descriptive Set Theory," *Journal of Logic and Computation*, 3, 1, 27–45.

Kelly, K. (forthcoming), *The Logic of Reliable Inquiry*. Cambridge, MA: MIT Press.

Kelly, K. and Glymour, C. (1989), "Convergence to the Truth and Nothing but the Truth," *Philosophy of Science*, 56, 2, 186–220.

Kelly, K. and Glymour, C. (1992), "Inductive Inference from Theory-Laden Data," *Journal of Philosophical Logic*, 21, 391–444.

Kemeny, J. (1953), "The Use of Simplicity in Induction," *Philosophical Review*, LXII, 391–408.

Kugel, P. (1977), "Induction, Pure and Simple," *Information and Control*, 33, 276–336.

Kuhn, T.S. (1970), *The Structure of Scientific Revolutions*. Chicago: University of Chicago Press.

Lakatos, I. (1970), "Falsification and the Methodology of Scientific Research Programmes," in I. Lakatos and A. Musgrave (eds), *Criticism and the Growth of Knowledge*, Cambridge: Cambridge University Press.

Laudan, L. (1980), "Why Was the Logic of Discovery Abandoned?," in T. Nickles (ed.), *Scientific Discovery, Logic, and Rationality*, Boston: D. Reidel.

Levi, I. (1983), *The Enterprise of Knowledge*. Cambridge, MA: MIT Press.

Lucas, J.R. (1961), "Minds, Machines, and Goedel," *Philosophy*, 36, 120–4.

Lycan, W. (1988), *Judgement and Justification*. New York: Cambridge University Press.

Malament, D. (1977), "Observationally Indistinguishable Spacetimes," in J. Earman, C. Glymour, and J. Stachel (eds), *Foundations of Space–Time Theories*, vol. VIII, Minnesota Studies in the Philosophy of Science. Minneapolis: University of Minnesota Press.

Osherson, D. and Weinstein, S. (1991), "A Universal Inductive Inference Machine," *Journal of Symbolic Logic*, 56, 2.

Osherson, D., Stob, M., and Weinstein, S. (1986), *Systems that Learn*. Cambridge, MA: MIT Press.

Peirce, C.S. (1958), "Some Consequences of Four Incapacities," in Philip P. Wiener (ed.), *Charles S. Peirce: Selected Writings*. New York: Dover.

Plato (1949), *Meno*, trans. B. Jowett. Indianapolis: Bobbs-Merrill.

Popper, K. (1968), *The Logic of Scientific Discovery*. New York: Harper.

Putnam, H. (1963a), " 'Degree of Confirmation' and Inductive Logic," in A. Schilpp (ed.), *The Philosophy of Rudolph Carnap*. Lasalle, IL: Open Court. Reprinted in *Mathematics, Matter, and Method, Philosophical Papers*, vol. I., Cambridge: Cambridge University Press (1979). All page citations refer to the more recent source.

Putnam, H. (1963b), "Probability and Confirmation," *The Voice of America, Forum Philosophy of Science*, 10, US Information agency. Reprinted in *Mathematics, Matter, and Method, Philosophical Papers*, vol. I., Cambridge: Cambridge University Press (1979), 293–304.

Putnam, H. (1965), "Trial and Error Predicates and a Solution to a Problem of Mostowski," *Journal of Symbolic Logic*, 30, 1, 49–57.

Putnam, H. (1974), "The Corroboration of Theories," in *The Philosophy of Karl Popper*, vol II. La Salle: Open Court.

Putnam, H. (1989), *Realism and Reason: Philosophical Papers*, vol. III. Cambridge: Cambridge University Press.

Putnam, H. (1990), *Reason, Truth and History*. Cambridge: Cambridge University Press.

Quine, W.V.O. (1951), "Two Dogmas of Empiricism," *Philosophical Review*, 60, 20–43.

Reichenbach, H. (1938), *Experience and Prediction*. Chicago: University of Chicago Press.

Reichenbach, H. (1949), *The Theory of Probability*. London: Cambridge University Press.

Rogers, H. (1987), *The Theory of Recursive Functions and Effective Computability*. Cambridge, MA: MIT Press.

Rorty, R. (1980), *Philosophy and the Mirror of Nature*. Princeton, NJ: Princeton University Press, and Oxford: Blackwell.

Savage, L.J. (1972), *The Foundations of Statistics*. New York: Dover.

Toretti, R. (1990), *Creative Understanding: Philosophical Reflections on Physics*. Chicago: University of Chicago Press.

6 Logic, Quanta, and the Two–slit Experiment

Michael Redhead

The two–slit experiment has always provided a major focus for debates on the interpretation of quantum mechanics (QM). In brief the experiment consists in allowing a beam of electrons of well–defined momentum to impinge on a screen which incorporates two parallel slits, and detecting the electrons emerging from the slits on a second screen, equipped for example with a photographic emulsion which will respond to the impact of an electron. The intensity of the beam can be reduced so that on average at a given time only one electron is passing through the device comprising the two screens, the one with the two slits and the detector screen. But nevertheless, QM predicts that an "interference" pattern will build up on the detector screen, quite unlike the mere summation of the patterns one would obtain if one or other of the slits were open but not both together. The electrons behave like localized corpuscles in respect of their detection at the second screen, but in respect of the interference pattern the behavior is characteristic of classical wave behavior, so in this experiment it appears that the electrons are displaying wave–like behavior in their passage through the slits in the first screen, but particle–like behavior in respect of their detection at the second screen. But how can an electron behave both like a wave *and* like a particle? That is the essence of the paradox posed by the two–slit experiment.

Referring to Figure 6.1, S_1 and S_2 are the two slits in the first screen, and Δ_j is a small-volume element enclosing a piece of emulsion that can record whether the electron hits the detector screen at a point located in Δ_j.

Denote by A_1 the proposition asserted at the time t that the electron is detected that the electron *had* passed through the slit A_1 at the earlier time t' at which the beam impinges on the first screen, and by A_2 the proposition at t, that the electron *had* passed through A_2 at t'. Furthermore denote by

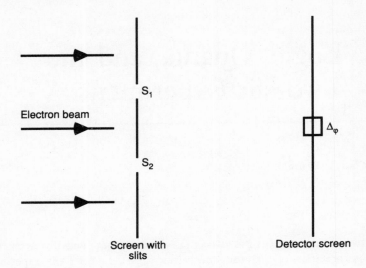

Electron beam

S_1

S_2

Δ_φ

Screen with
slits

Detector screen

Figure 6.1

R_j the proposition that the electron triggers the detector at time t in cell Δ_j, then we are concerned in explaining the two–slit experiment with evaluating the conditional probability Prob $(R_j \mid A_1 \vee A_2)$.

Let us first see how, treating the electron as a particle, which has passed through one or other slit, leads to the wrong sort of pattern on the detector screen. Let me evaluate Prob $(R_j \mid A_1 \vee A_2)$ according to classical ideas on the meaning of conditional probability.

$$\text{Prob } (R_j \mid A_1 \vee A_2) = \frac{\text{Prob } (R_j \wedge (A_1 \vee A_2))}{\text{Prob } (A_1 \vee A_2)} \tag{6.1}$$

$$= \frac{\text{Prob } ((R_j \wedge A_1) \vee (R_j \wedge A_2))}{\text{Prob } (A_1 \vee A_2)}$$

where I have used the distributive law of classical logic to write

$$R_j \wedge (A_1 \vee A_2) = (R_j \wedge A_1) \vee (R_j \wedge A_2) \tag{6.2}$$

now

$$\text{Prob } ((R_j \wedge A_1) \vee (R_j \wedge A_2))$$
$$= \text{Prob } (R_j \wedge A_1) + \text{Prob } (R_j \wedge A_2) - \text{Prob } (R_j \wedge A_1 \wedge A_2)$$
$$= \text{Prob } (R_j \wedge A_1) + \text{Prob } (R_j \wedge A_2)$$

since $A_1 \wedge A_2$ is a logical contradiction

$$= \text{Prob } (R_j \mid A_1) \times \text{Prob } (A_1) + \text{Prob } (R_j \mid A_2) \times \text{Prob } (A_2)$$

So, finally

$$\text{Prob } (R_j \mid A_1 \vee A_2) \tag{6.3}$$

$$= \text{Prob } (R_j \mid A_1) \times \frac{\text{Prob } (A_1)}{\text{Prob } (A_1) + \text{Prob } (A_2)}$$

$$+ \text{Prob } (R_j \mid A_2) \times \frac{\text{Prob } (A_2)}{\text{Prob } (A_1) + \text{Prob } (A_2)}$$

$$= \tfrac{1}{2} \text{Prob } (R_j \mid A_1) + \tfrac{1}{2} \text{Prob } (R_j \mid A_2)$$

if I assume a uniform incident beam, so $\text{Prob } (A_1) = \text{Prob } (A_2)$.

Now (6.3) is just the equally weighted summation of the patterns I would get if S_1 or S_2 were alone opened, and exhibits none of the features of QM interference. In order to reproduce such interference it would be necessary to assume that $\text{Prob } (R_j \mid A_1)$, for example, depended on whether S_2 was opened or closed, but this would admit a mysterious non-local action between opening and closing S_2 and what the electron was doing as it went through S_1. It is the hope of avoiding what Reichenbach (1944) refers to as "causal anomalies" that has inspired much of the discussion of the interpretation of the two-slit experiment.

The approach of the orthodox Copenhagen interpretation to this problem is simply to claim that when the electron is passing through the slits in the first screen, and displaying wave-behavior, it is meaningless to introduce propositions like $A_1 \vee A_2$ which express a typical particle notion, that the electron goes through one or other slit. So the whole of the above discussion is quite illegitimate according to the Copenhagenists because it involves conditioning on a meaningless proposition. The main argument in Reichenbach (1944) is to suggest that one can regard $A_1 \vee A_2$ as meaningful in the context of the two-slit experiment, but in order to avoid causal anomalies we must regard $A_1 \vee A_2$ as neither true nor false, but accorded a third truth-value, viz. indeterminate. This approach of employing a three-valued logic to interpret the two-slit experiment was taken up enthusiastically by Putnam (1957). But in Putnam (1965a, pp. 30–1) he was quite dismissive: "In Reichenbach's approach . . . it is simply assumed that statements about macro-observables have the conventional two truth values while statements about micro-observables may have a third truth value;

but this radical dichotomy between macro- and micro-observables is not derived from anything but simply built into the theory ad hoc." In brief the three-valued logic approach formalizes but does not explain the phenomenon of interference. In "A Philosopher Looks at Quantum Mechanics" (1965b, p. 100), Putnam makes no reference to quantum logic and concludes "*no* satisfactory interpretation of quantum mechanics exists today."

But then Putnam (1969) took up the idea of a bivalent but non-distributive logic as a resource for removing the paradoxes associated with the interpretation of QM. Technically the idea goes back to Birkhoff and von Neumann, who showed in 1936 that in a certain sense a non-distributive logic could be "read off" the mathematics of the Hilbert space formulation of quantum mechanics. To see what is going on I present a brief resumé of the non-distributive logic approach concentrating on those features emphasized by Putnam (1969, 1974). In classical physics the state of a system is identified with a location in phase-space and we can introduce elementary propositions p of the form $e(P)$ specifying that the state of the system lies in the subset P of the phase-space Ω. The logical connectives, conjunction, disjunction, and negation acting on the elementary propositions now translate into the familiar Boolean operations of intersection, union, and set-theoretic complement under the correspondence associating propositions p with subsets P. In QM the maximally specific state of a system is identified with a ray or one-dimensional subspace of a Hilbert space H. We can now introduce elementary propositions u of the form $e(U)$ specifying that the state of the system lies somewhere in the subspace U of H and the logical connectives "$\wedge$," "$\vee$," and "$\sim$" are now defined by their translation into the lattice operations of meet, join, and orthocomplement in the lattice of subspaces of H. The resulting "logic" is easily seen to be non-distributive.

Now, however, comes the decisive step. We introduce *new* elementary propositions of the form $(\Delta)_Q$ which assert that the observable Q possesses a value which lies in the Borel subset Δ of possible values for Q. We now introduce the idea of a "real" state or Putnam state as it is described in Redhead (1987), which is to be sharply distinguished from the QM state. The proposition $(\Delta)_Q$ is identified with the proposition $e'(U)$, specifying that the Putnam state lies in the subspace U of H which is now defined by the statement that, *if the QM state* were confined to U, then with probability one the result of measuring Q would lie in Δ. It is easily checked that U = ran $(P_Q(\Delta))$ where $P_Q(\Delta)$ is the projection operator associated with the Borel set Δ via the projection-valued measure associated with the hypermaximal operator that represents Q in the Hilbert space formulation of QM. The logical connectives acting on the $(\Delta)_Q$ propositions are now to be understood as translating into the lattice operations on the subspaces U via the correspondence $(\Delta)_Q \mapsto e'(U)$. The whole scheme is really quite complicated

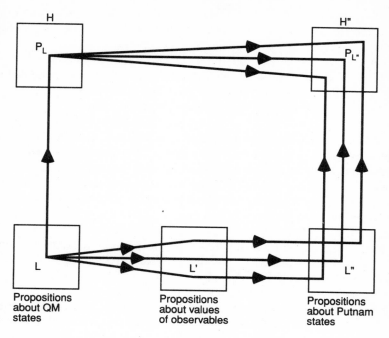

H   H"

P_L $P_{L''}$

L   L'   L"

Propositions   Propositions   Propositions
about QM   about values   about Putnam
states   of observables   states

Figure 6.2

and I have tried to summarize the situation in a schematic form in Figure 6.2.

L denotes a proposition about the specification of the QM state of the form $e(U)$ as described above. L' is a proposition of the form $(\Delta)_Q$ telling us about the values of observables. On a realist construal of QM each L-proposition is associated with a non-denumerable infinity of L'-propositions. Each L'-proposition is now associated via the correspondence $(\Delta)_Q \mapsto e'(U)$ with an L"-proposition specifying the location of what we have called the Putnam state. Each L-proposition is associated with a subspace of the Hilbert space H, and may be identified via its range with a unique projection operator P_L acting on H. Similarly each L"-proposition is associated with a unique projection operator $P_{L''}$ acting on a Hilbert space H", the space of Putnam states, which is formally identical with H. But conceptually H" and H must be sharply distinguished, a one–many map existing between the P_L and the $P_{L''}$ as illustrated in Figure 6.2.

In order to complete the logical scheme we require the specification of a truth valuation mapping propositions such as L or L" on to the two-element Boolean algebra of truth values, 0 and 1. For L-propositions, denoting $e(U)$ by u, it appears that we require the following admissibility criterion:

> A_1: Val: $\{u\} \to B_2$ is an admissible valuation iff there is a one-dimensional subspace N such that for every subspace M, Val $(m) = 1$ iff $N \le M$; where $\le$ denotes the subspace relation.

A_1 ensures that the quantum mechanical state is associated with the ray N, whose existence is asserted in A_1. For the L″-propositions the situation is more subtle. Let us restrict discussion for the moment to a finite-dimensional Hilbert space, so avoiding problems of observables with a continuous spectrum. Then for a proper realist semantics we would like to impose the admissibility criterion:

> A_2: Val: $\{u\} \to B_2$ is an admissible valuation iff the following conditions are satisfied:
> (1) Val $(u) = 1$ iff Val $(\sim u) = 0$.
> (2) If Val $(n) = 1$, and $N \le M$, then Val $(m) = 1$.
> (3) In any orthonormal basis $\{|\,q_i\rangle\}$ of H″, where $\{q_i\}$ are the eigenvalues of some maximal observable Q, Val $(q_j) = 1$ for some j and hence from (1) and (2) Val $(q_i) = 0$, $\forall i \ne j$.

Here q_j is a convenient shorthand for the proposition $e'(Q_j)$, where Q_j is the one-dimensional subspace generated by the eigenvector $|\,q_j\rangle$.

The third condition is the crucial one ensuring that every maximal observable has a unique definite value, thus implementing our realist intentions. It will also follow that non-maximal observables are assigned unique definite values as a result of A_2 (see Redhead, 1987, p. 165). The trouble is that there simply are no A_2-admissible valuations for Hilbert spaces of dimension ≥ 3.

Faced with this situation Putnam proceeds as follows. Consider a maximal observable Q in a Hilbert space of dimension $N \ge 3$. Then Putnam identifies the statement "Q has a value" with the disjunction $q_1 \vee q_2 \vee \ldots \vee q_N$. This is not only true but tautologically so. However, says Putnam, this does not mean that there is some specifiable j for which q_j is true. Now in classical logic the disjunction carries an existential commitment. We can write $(\exists i)\, q_i \equiv q_1 \vee q_2 \ldots \vee q_N$. Putnam is effectively retaining this classical result but using it to *define* what he means by $(\exists i) q_i$. Effectively Putnam is claiming that Q has a value but there is no value which it has! Consider now some other maximal observable R with eigenvectols $\{|\,r_i\rangle\}$ distinct from $\{|\,q_i\rangle\}$. So the associated operators $\hat{Q}$ and $\hat{R}$ do not commute (Q and R are so-called incompatible observables). Then

$$(\exists j)r_j \underset{\text{df}}{=} r_1 \vee r_2 \ldots \vee r_N$$

is also tautologically true. Indeed, consider the two statements:

S_1: $(\exists i)q_j \wedge (\exists j)r_j$
S_2: $(\exists i)\,(\exists j)\,(q_i \wedge r_j)$

S_1, according to Putnam, expresses realism and is tautologically true. In classical logic S_1 and S_2 are logically equivalent, but not so in quantum logic. S_2, indeed, is a logical contradiction, and this is regarded by Putnam as expressing complementarity, that although Q and R individually have values, it is contradictory to assert that they possess simultaneous values. It is of course, the failure of the distributive law that allows us to deny that S_1 and S_2 are equivalent propositions and hence to "reconcile" realism and complementarity.

Putnam (1969) tried to apply these ideas to elucidating the two-slit experiment. He pointed out that the derivation of the empirically incorrect summation result (3) depended on employing the distributive law (2). If (2) was disallowed we would be prevented from getting the wrong result – of course, that is a rather limited objective, quite insufficient for showing how to get the right result! But it was pointed out almost immediately by Gardner (1971) that in the particular case in question the distributive law is, in a certain trivial sense, actually true. To see what is going on let us identify the propositions A_1, A_2, and R_j with the relevant projection operators. For A_1 this is $P_{|\psi_1\rangle}$ the projector onto the state $|\psi_1\rangle$ which is the time-evolution at time t of the state which would arise at time t' if the slit S_1 alone were open. Similarly A_2 is associated with the projector $P_{|\psi_2\rangle}$ where $|\psi_2\rangle$ is the time-evolution at time t of the state which would arise at time t' if the slit S_2 alone were open. Finally R_j is associated with:

$$P_j = \int\limits_{x\varepsilon\Delta} dP(x);$$

where $P(x)$ generates the projection-valued measure associated with the position operator X.

Gardner then pointed out that:

$$\left.\begin{array}{l} P_j \wedge P_{|\psi_1\rangle} = 0 \\ P_j \wedge P_{|\psi_2\rangle} = 0 \\ P_j \wedge (P_{|\psi_1\rangle} \vee P_{|\psi_2\rangle}) = 0 \end{array}\right\} \tag{6.4}$$

where 0 denotes the null-projector. So the right-hand side and the left-hand side of equation (6.2) come out to be trivially equal, each side being the null-projector, so each side of the equation represents a logical contradiction.

Essentially what Gardner was pointing out was that states picked out by P_j are never in the linear span of $|\psi_1\rangle$ and $|\psi_2\rangle$. (A mathematically rigorous proof of this result for the two–slit experiment was provided by Gibbins and Pearson, 1981.)

Faced with this situation, Friedman and Putnam (1978) gave a quite different analysis of the two–slit experiment and its connection with quantum logic. But that paper cannot really be understood without taking account of the general way in which Putnam's views on quantum mechanics changed during the 1970s, in particular his rejection of the idea that knowing simultaneous values for incompatible observables would be impossible since it would correspond to knowing a logical contradiction. Indeed, in 1981 Putnam published a crucial paper entitled "Quantum Mechanics and the Observer," in which he expounded his argument for believing that it was not contradictory to know such simultaneous values. I shall analyze the content of this paper shortly, but for the moment let us see how this conclusion appears to motivate the 1978 approach.

The fact that incompatible propositions are logically contradictory corresponds, as we have seen, to the fact that the meet of the projectors corresponding to the associated Putnam states is the null-projector. This arises because we are using a lattice-theoretic (LT) version of quantum logic in which the binary logical connectives are interpreted in terms of the lattice operations, which are defined for all pairs of elements in the (projection) lattice. But already Kochen and Specker (1967) had employed a partial-Boolean-algebra (PBA) version of quantum logic in which the binary connectives are restricted to compatible pairs of projectors, lying, that is, in a common Boolean sub-algebra of the full non-Boolean projection lattice of the Hilbert space. This PBA version of quantum logic is exactly suited to what Putnam has in mind; the quantum-logical contradictions which he had previously identified with the impossibility of simultaneously knowing the values of incompatible observables could no longer be formulated in the PBA version of the logic. But there now arises a problem in formulating a conditional probability in terms of a joint probability as in (6.1) since the conjunction of the incompatible propositions R_j and $A_1 \vee A_2$ is no longer allowed. So a new formulation of conditional probability has to be invoked in terms of a "transition probability."[1]

I begin with some terminological conventions. I shall use the symbol P for a projector to denote ambiguously (1) the *projection operator* $\hat{P}$, (2) the *observable* P associated with the projection operator $\hat{P}$, (3) the *subspace* of Hilbert space which is the range of $\hat{P}$, (4) the *proposition*: [P] = 1, where [P] denotes the value of P, (5) the *proposition*: the state vector lies in the range of $\hat{P}$. Moreover, if P is associated with the Borel set Δ via the projection-valued measure associated with an observable Q, then (6) the *proposition*:

[Q] ε Δ. Note that senses (4) and (6) are equivalent under the assumption of FUNC, viz.:

FUNC: $[f(Q)] = f([Q])$

for any Borel function f of the observable Q. The senses (1) through (6) of the symbol P should always be clear from the context. Finally I use the convention that $P|\phi\rangle$, for an arbitrary QM state $|\phi\rangle$, shall always mean the normalized state:

$$\frac{P|\phi\rangle}{||P|\phi\rangle||}$$

With these conventions in mind I shall now explain how to understand the conditional probability $\text{Prob}_{|\phi\rangle}(F|P)$ as a transition probability. I understand this quantity as the probability that the proposition F is true given that the initial QM state is $|\phi\rangle$, and that a *maximal* measurement has established the value one for a *one-dimensional* projector P. According to standard ideas in the theory of measurement (the projection postulate), the QM state after the measurement has made a transition to $P|\phi\rangle$ and hence:

$$\text{Prob}_{|\phi\rangle}(F|P) = \text{Prob}_{|\phi\rangle}(F|P_{P|\phi\rangle}) \tag{6.5}$$
$$= \text{Prob}_{P|\phi\rangle}(F)$$

But this analysis for maximal measurements cannot be applied as it stands to the two-split experiment, where I have to evaluate $\text{Prob}_{|\phi\rangle}(R_j \mid P_1 + P_2)$, where I have replaced $P_{|\psi_1\rangle}$ by P_1 and $P_{|\psi_2\rangle}$ by P_2 in my former notation. The important point to note here is that $P_1 + P_2$ is a two-dimensional projector (i.e. its range is two-dimensional). So (6.5) cannot be applied directly.

Friedman and Putnam now note, however, that in quantum logic:

$$P_{|\phi\rangle} \Rightarrow P_{(P_1+P_2)|\phi\rangle} \leftrightarrow (P_1 + P_2) \tag{6.6}$$

where $\leftrightarrow$ denotes material equivalence and $\Rightarrow$ denotes logical entailment in the quantum logic. Since

$$P_{(P_1+P_2)|\phi\rangle}$$

and $P_1 + P_2$ are *compatible* propositions, the definition of material equivalence is just the classical one

$$A \leftrightarrow B \underset{\text{Df}}{=} (A \supset B) \wedge (B \supset A)$$

where $\supset$ is the usual material implication of classical logic.

In virtue of (6.6) Friedman and Putnam claim that we can substitute the one-dimensional projector

$$P_{(P_1+P_2)|\phi\rangle}$$

for the two-dimensional projector $P_1 + P_2$ and hence, applying (6.5), obtain

$$\begin{aligned}
\text{Prob}_{|\phi\rangle} \, (R_j \mid P_1 + P_2) \\
= \text{Prob}_{|\phi\rangle} \, (R_j \mid P_{(P_1+P_2)|\phi\rangle}) \\
= \text{Prob}_{(P_1+P_2)|\phi\rangle}(R_j)
\end{aligned} \qquad (6.7)$$

which yields, of course, the correct empirical interference pattern.[2] Substitutivity of materially equivalent propositions in conditionalization is, of course, not generally a truth-preserving move. This is particularly obvious if we understand conditional probabilities as conditionals with a probabilistic consequent, so Prob $(A \mid B) = p$ is analyzed as B $\square\!\!\rightarrow$ (Prob (A) $= p$). Since any two false propositions are materially equivalent we cannot expect substitution to preserve the truth-value of the counter-factual conditional. But if the material equivalence is provable from some background proposition then, on the Lewis analysis of counter-factuals, for example, substitution *is* permissible. The question of whether substitution is also allowed when the material equivalence of the antecedents in the counter-factual is only provable *quantum-logically* from a background proposition which cannot be *conjoined* with either of the antecedents may, however, be regarded as problematic.

Be that as it may, this solution of the two-slit problem is certainly ingenious, and I turn now to consider how the argument connects with Putnam (1981). In fact I shall show that knowing simultaneous values for incompatible observables cannot be independently established as Putnam seems to think, but can only be established on the basis of a quantum-logical argument based on (6.6).

Putnam's argument that one can simultaneously know the values of incompatible observables is based on his analysis of a thought experiment which I shall now explain. The exact details have been somewhat simplified so as to bring out the point at issue in the clearest possible way.

Consider a particle which can escape through a shutter briefly opened in the wall of a small confining box, and which, if it does so escape, is detected by a spherical photographic emulsion with its centre located at the shutter. (Putnam himself treats of a photon escaping from a box with absorbing walls, so the photon either escapes and is detected or does not escape and is presumably absorbed, but this just makes the physics more complicated to represent accurately.) The set-up is illustrated in Figure 6.3.

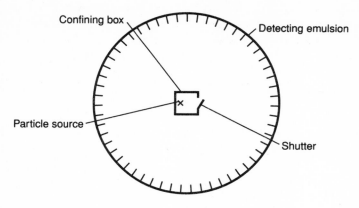

Figure 6.3

After the shutter has been opened and closed the QM state for the particle can be expressed as:

$$|\psi\rangle = \frac{1}{\sqrt{2}} (|\psi_{in}\rangle + |\psi_{out}\rangle) \tag{6.8}$$

where $|\psi_{in}\rangle$ is a state confined to the interior of the box and $|\psi_{out}\rangle$ is a state confined to the exterior or the box, and I assume for the sake of simplicity that the shutter is kept open for just such a length of time that the probability of the particle escaping from the box is a half. Putnam himself insists that $|\psi\rangle$ in (6.8) is represented in the Hilbert space appropriate to the particle *and* the photographic emulsion. For the moment I prefer to keep things simple and let $|\psi\rangle$ describe just the particle as stated. Later I shall indicate what happens when I describe both the state of the particle and the photographic emulsion, as Putnam requires.

Suppose I divide the whole of space into discrete cells Δ_i and define projection operators associated with these cells as before, P_i^{in} if Δ_i lies inside the box and P_i^{out} if Δ_i lies outside the box. Then clearly

$$|\psi_{out}\rangle = (\sum_i P_i^{out})|\psi\rangle \tag{6.9}$$

and

$$|\psi_{in}\rangle = (\sum_i P_i^{in})|\psi\rangle \tag{6.10}$$

172   *Michael Redhead*

where the summation in (6.9) is over the cells outside the box, and the summation in (6.10) is over the cells inside the box, and I again use my convenient convention that states are only specified modulo normalization.

I also note that

$$\sum_i P_i^{in} + \sum_i P_i^{out} = 1 \qquad (6.11)$$

and

$$P_j^{out} \Rightarrow \sum_i P_i^{out} \qquad (6.12)$$

$$\Rightarrow \sum_i P_i^{in} + \sum_i P_i^{out} \qquad (6.13)$$

Since all the P_i^{in} and P_i^{out} are compatible, (6.12) is just the classical result that if the particle is in the jth cell outside the box then it is *somewhere* outside the box, while (6.13) is the classical result that if the particle is in the jth cell outside the box, then it is *somewhere* (i.e. either inside or outside the box).

Now suppose at some appropriate time t I measure P_k^{out}, where Δ_k encloses a small piece of the emulsion, and find the value 1 (i.e. a mark on the emulsion appears in Δ_k at time t), then we know the proposition P_k^{out} (i.e. at time t the particle was located in Δ_k). But Putnam now claims that *in virtue* of knowing P_k^{out} we also know that the particle is outside the box and this (says Putnam) means knowing the value of

$$P_{|\psi_{out}\rangle}$$

which of course does not commute with P_k^{out}. At this point it is important to notice that $|\psi_{out}\rangle$ should be understood as referring to a superposition of coupled states of the particle and the emulsion, and P_k projects on to one component in this entangled superposition in which the mark has appeared in Δ_k. The above analysis can easily be adapted to this situation, which is the one actually envisaged by Putnam, by considering appropriate projections in the tensor product space of the particle and all the atoms in the emulsion. I leave it as an exercise to the interested reader to check that everything goes through in this more complicated setting in exact parallel with the simple mathematics I have described.

So the conclusion of the argument is that observing the mark on the emulsion in Δ_k, I thereby know the values of two incompatible observables. But this just seems confused. From (6.12), identifying j with k I have:

$$P_k^{out} \Rightarrow \sum_i P_i^{out}$$

so in words, if the particle is somewhere *specifically* outside the box, then it is somewhere outside the box! But P_k^{out} commutes with

$$\sum_i P_i^{out}$$

so there is no question of knowing incompatible propositions in virtue of knowing that the particle is in Δ_k *and* it is somewhere outside the box. Notice also that:

$$P_{|\psi_{out}\rangle} \Rightarrow \sum_i P_i^{out}$$

so if we knew that the state of the particle was $|\psi_{out}\rangle$ then we would know that it was outside the box. But the implication does not go the other way. Essentially Putnam's mistake boils down to claiming:

$$P_k^{out} \Rightarrow P_{|\psi_{out}\rangle}$$

apparently on the mistaken assumption that one can equate

$$P_{|\psi_{out}\rangle} = P_{(\sum_i P_i^{out})|\psi\rangle}$$

with

$$\sum_i P_i^{out}$$

But at this point we can rescue Putnam's argument provided we employ the quantum-logical entailment:

$$P_{|\psi_{out}\rangle} \Rightarrow P_{(\sum_i P_i^{out})|\psi\rangle} \leftrightarrow \sum_i P_i^{out} \qquad (6.14)$$

which is a simple generalization of the entailment (6.6) employed in the Friedman–Putnam paper. In fact, (6.14) says, given that we know the QM state is $|\psi\rangle$, then we can infer the material equivalence of the two compatible propositions associated with

$$P_{(\sum_i P_i^{out})|\psi\rangle}$$

and

$$\sum_i P_i^{out}$$

Since the propositions are compatible, material equivalence is just the familiar classical Boolean notion, but the entailment is of course only valid quantum-logically (remember that $P_{|\psi\rangle}$ does *not* lie in the same maximal Boolean subalgebra as

$$P_{(\sum_i P_i^{out})|\psi\rangle}$$

and

$$\sum_i P_i^{out})$$

Thus knowing P_k does allow us to know

$$P_{(\sum_i P_i^{out})|\psi\rangle}$$

as Putnam claims.

There is certainly no hint in Putnam (1981) that he sees the need for employing quantum logic in arriving at his conclusion about knowing simultaneous values for incompatible observables. I submit that without this move the argument of the 1981 paper cannot be sustained.

So, to conclude, the motivation for the move to a PBA version of quantum logic in the Friedman–Putnam paper cannot be established independently, as Putnam seems to believe, but only on the basis of presupposing such a quantum logic. But there is nothing viciously circular here; indeed, a pleasing consistency in the whole treatment of the two-slit problem is manifested by our discussion.[3]

Notes

1   By "transition probability" I mean here not the probability of a transition from one quantum state to another, but the change or revision in a probability assignment to a proposition occasioned by a transition from one quantum state to another.

2   In fact what has been *derived* here is just the so-called Lüders rule for extending the projection postulate to non-maximal measurements. For detailed reaction to the Friedman–Putnam proposal and its merits vis-à-vis the Copenhagenist treatment of the two-slit experiment see Hellman (1981), Bub (1982), and Stairs (1981). In this chapter I concentrate on a different aspect of the problem, viz. the relation with the argument in Putnam (1981).

3   In his reply Putnam stresses that in his 1981 paper he was using a strong ontological reading of von Neumann's "Moving Cut" interpretation of the measurement problem in quantum mechanics. Since this strong reading overlooks the fact that suitable correlation experiments will give different statistical predictions according to the location of the cut, I tried to interpret Putnam's argument in terms of the more standard weak reading, i.e. that the location of

the cut is irrelevant so far as measurements of observables associated with the original object system on its own is concerned.

Putnam now concedes that the strong reading is inconsistent essentially for the reason I have just given, and moreover we are now in agreement that on the weak reading Putnam's 1981 argument can still be rescued formally by utilizing the quantum logic employed in his 1978 paper with Michael Friedman.

In discussion with Hilary Putnam I have been helped to see the issues more clearly and am very grateful for his reciprocal acknowledgment in the introduction to his reply.

References

Birkhoff, G. and von Neumann, J. (1936), "The Logic of Quantum Mechanics," *Annals of Mathematics*, 37, 823–43.

Bub, J. (1982), "Quantum Logic, Conditional Probability, and Interference," *Philosophy of Science*, 49, 402–21.

Friedman, M. and Putnam, H. (1978), "Quantum Logic, Conditional Probability, and Interference," *Dialectica*, 32, 305–15.

Gardner, M. (1971), "Is Quantum Logic Really Logic?," *Philosophy of Science*, 38, 508–29.

Gibbins, P. and Pearson, D. (1981), "The Distributive Law in the Two–Slit Experiment," *Foundations of Physics*, 11, 797–803.

Hellman, G. (1981), "Quantum Logic and the Projection Postulate," *Philosophy of Science*, 48, 469–86.

Kochen, S. and Specker, E. (1967), "The Problem of Hidden Variables in Quantum Mechanics," *Journal of Mathematics and Mechanics*, 17, 59–87.

Putnam, H. (1957), "Three-Valued Logic," *Philosophical Studies*, 8, 73–80.

Putnam, H. (1965a), "Philosophy of Physics," in F.H. Donnell, Jr. (ed.), *Aspects of Contemporary American Philosophy*, Wurzburg: Physica-Verlag, Rudolf Liebing K.G., pp. 27–40.

Putnam, H. (1965b), "A Philosopher Looks at Quantum Mechanics," in R.G. Colodny (ed.), *Beyond the Edge of Certainty: Essays in Contemporary Science and Philosophy*, Englewood Cliffs, NJ: Prentice-Hall, pp. 75–101.

Putnam, H. (1969), 'Is Logic Empirical?," *Boston Studies in the Philosophy of Science*, 5, 216–41.

Putnam, H. (1974), "How to Think Quantum-Logically," *Synthese*, 29, 55–61.

Putnam, H. (1981), "Quantum Mechanics and the Observer," *Erkenntnis*, 16, 193–219.

Redhead, M.L.G. (1987), *Incompleteness, Nonlocality, and Realism: A Prolegomenon to the Philosophy of Quantum Mechanics*. Oxford: Clarendon Press.

Reichenbach, H. (1944): *Philosophic Foundations of Quantum Mechanics*. Berkeley, CA: University of California Press.

Stairs, A. (1981), "Quantum Logic and the Lüders Rule," *Philosophy of Science*, 49, 422–36.

7 Carnap's Principle of Tolerance, Empiricism, and Conventionalism

Thomas Ricketts

After more than half a century, logical positivism still exercises a powerful influence on the philosophical imaginations of those who have imbibed the analytic tradition. Logical positivism's suspicion of any first philosophy higher or deeper than natural science and its ideal of clarity, together with the use of logical techniques to achieve that clarity, still inform much philosophizing. Moreover, contemporary philosophical programs continue to be motivated in significant measure by the perceived failings of logical positivism. Nowhere are both sides of the logical positivist legacy more evident than in Hilary Putnam's writings in philosophy of science, philosophy of mathematics, and philosophy of language. Repeatedly, Putnam, sharing positivist standards of clarity, develops trenchant criticisms of positivist positions. These criticisms then serve to motivate the alternative views that Putnam has over the last thirty years presented for our consideration.

Two central facets of positivism have especially attracted Putnam's fire: its commitment first to empiricism in the guise of the so-called verificationist theory of meaning, and second to conventionalism in the philosophy of mathematics. The leading positivist idea here is that any genuinely factual statement is associated with verification conditions – observationally ascertainable possibilities the obtaining of which would confirm the statement. With an important exception, grammatical sentences that are not associated with verification conditions are cognitively meaningless pseudo-statements. The exceptions are the statements of logic and mathematics. Observation is irrelevant to assessing the truth and falsity of these statements so that they are not factual statements. Instead, their truth or falsity is secured linguistically, by the rules of language.

This general view receives its most detailed development in Rudolf Carnap's book *The Logical Syntax of Language* (1937a) and closely allied papers, most notably "Testability and Meaning (1936)." Here, it might be urged, the clarity Carnap achieves both in setting forth linguistic rules and in describing formally what verification conditions are makes patent the untenability of the positivist combination of empiricism and conventionalism. This is not, in my opinion, the primary lesson to be extracted from *Logical Syntax*. Rather, from the specification of the positivist picture there, we learn that positivism is not essentially a combination of empiricism and conventionalism.

Throughout his career, Carnap is concerned to distinguish pseudo-problems from substantive questions. He reports in his intellectual auto-biography in the Carnap Schilpp volume: "I was depressed by disputations in which opponents talked at cross purposes; there seemed hardly any chance of mutual understanding, let alone of agreement, because there was not even a common criterion for deciding the controversy."[1] Early on, Carnap became convinced that much of traditional philosophy involves just such fruitless wrangling; and throughout his career he returns to the debate between realists and idealists as an example. Carnap's concern with pseudo-problems leads him to an extraordinarily deflationary position in *Logical Syntax*. Here, I will argue, Carnap rejects any notion of truth-in-virtue-of. Although Carnap aims to clarify the distinction between factual truths and formal or linguistic truths, his explication does not draw on any notion of truth, on a notion of something's making a statement true. As a result, many familiar objections to positivism are not applicable to *Logical Syntax*. In particular, objections to verificationism commonly misevaluate the status of Carnap's empiricism and so fail to recognize that his rejection of traditional philosophy is, in the end, an ad hominem criticism, albeit a deep one. Furthermore, it is not apt to attribute to Carnap a conventionalist philosophy of mathematics. Such an account addresses the question "What is the nature of pure mathematics and its applications in science?" that Kant, Frege, Russell, and Schlick all variously address. A rejection of this question is implicit in *Logical Syntax*.

My goal in this chapter is to present the core of an interpretation of Carnap's program in *Logical Syntax* that will support these claims. I am more interested in figuring out what Carnap was trying to do there, how he intended various ideas to fit together, than in evaluating the extent of his success. I will not be talking about Carnap's post-1936 work in semantics. In *Logical Syntax*, he presents the principle of tolerance as his guiding maxim and indicates that it is the key to avoiding pseudo-problems: *"In logic, there are no morals.* Everyone is at liberty to build up his own logic, i.e. his own form of language, as he wishes. All that is required of him is that, if he wishes to discuss it, he must state his methods clearly, and give syntactical rules instead of philosophical arguments."[2] My interpretation will be, in effect, an extended gloss on this principle.

Although critics of positivism have tended to ignore the principle of toler-ance, Putnam insightfully discusses it in his Herbert Spencer lecture, "Phi-losophers and Human Understanding (1983)." He rehearses the familiar objection that the verification principle is self-refuting for being neither empirically verifiable nor analytically true. Later Putnam observes that Carnap might respond to this objection by invoking the principle of tolerance and claiming that the verification principle is not a statement but a proposal. (We will see that this is exactly the status that empiricism has for Carnap.) Putnam continues:

> However, this principle of tolerance, as Carnap called it, *presupposes the verification principle*. For the doctrine that no rational reconstruction is uniquely *correct* or corresponds to the way things "really are," the doctrine that all "external questions" are without cognitive sense, *is* just the verifica-tion principle. To apply the principle of tolerance to the verification principle itself would be circular.[3]

Here is one natural way to unpack this terse argument. According to the principle of tolerance, there is no right or wrong in the choice of a logic, of a language. So, if the principle is to be maintained, it cannot be legitimate to enquire whether a given language has the resources to represent fully the way things really are. Carnap can exclude this question only by appealing to the verification principle: he must argue that because there are no observa-tional grounds for judging whether a language has the resources necessary to represent the way things really are, there is no genuine question here. Since the principle of tolerance thus depends on an appeal to the verifica-tion principle, he cannot, without circularity, appeal to the principle of tolerance to maintain that the verification principle is, properly speaking, a proposal, not a principle.

This objection supposes that Carnap, in adopting the principle of toler-ance, assumes an explanatory burden of excluding the general question of the representational adequacy of a language, and of discrediting the general notion of fact, of the way the world is, that ineliminably figures in the formulation of the question. It is the explanatory or justificatory character of the burden that makes appeal to the principle of tolerance in defense of empiricism viciously circular. So construed, Putnam's objection trenchantly encapsulates an interpretation that makes Carnap into an empiricist epistem-ologist. I believe that the empiricist theory of knowledge Putnam credits to

Carnap is an example of the sort of *philosophical* position – in Carnap's pejorative sense of "philosophical" – that Carnap disparages in *Logical Syntax*. I hope to show that his recommendation of empiricism does not involve any vicious circularity.

A parallel point arises in connection with a very different-looking objection to Carnap. We find in *Logical Syntax* remarks like:

> the investigation will not be limited to the mathematico-logical part of the language . . . but will be essentially concerned also with synthetic, empirical sentences. The latter, the so-called "real" sentences, constitute the core of science; the mathematico-logical sentences are analytic, with no real content, and are merely formal auxiliaries.[4]

and

> In material interpretation, an analytic sentence is absolutely true whatever the empirical facts may be. Hence, it does not state anything about facts . . . A synthetic sentence is sometimes true – namely, when certain facts exist – and sometimes false; hence it says something as to what facts exist. *Synthetic sentences* are the *genuine statements about reality*.[5]

In the context of *Logical Syntax*, these two remarks can suggest that the truth of analytic sentences is fixed by syntactic stipulation, while the truth-values of synthetic sentences are determined by reality. We have then the following picture. By the stipulation of a language, a logical structure is imposed on descriptions of empirical reality. This structure enables users of the language soundly to infer empirical truths from empirical truths. The analytic sentences, those whose truth is fixed by the stipulation of a language, are contentless auxiliaries for such inferences. Kurt Gödel understands Carnap's philosophy of mathematics along these lines; and he advances a very general and persuasive objection to this viewpoint in an unpublished paper, "Is Mathematics Syntax of Language?" The application of arbitrarily stipulated syntactic rules will not generally take us from empirical truths to empirical truths. We will not accordingly be justified in using a Carnapian language to reason about empirical matters, unless we have some reason to believe that the syntactic rules specifying the consequence relation "do not themselves imply the truth or falsehood of any proposition expressing an empirical fact."[6] Gödel calls syntactic rules satisfying this condition *admissible*. Moreover, he thinks that if a set of syntactic rules is not admissible, then it is incorrect to call the sentences whose truth follows from the rules "contentless" and to contrast them, in this respect, with real, empirical sentences. A proof of admissibility is then required to underwrite the foregoing contrast of analytic and synthetic sentences. The admissibility of a set of syntactic rules implies the consistency of the language specified by those rules. In particular, a proof of admissibility for the syntactic rules for one of Carnap's languages would also be a proof of the consistency of the mathematics formalized in the language. On the basis of the second incompleteness theorem, Gödel notes that the proof of the consistency of the languages that interest Carnap requires the use of mathematics at least as powerful as that expressed inside the language. The justification, then, of a set of syntactic conventions requires the use of mathematics comparable to the mathematics that the conventions are supposed to stipulate. Thus, the mathematics required for the proof of admissibility cannot itself be taken to be true by syntactic convention without vicious circularity.

Carnap's writings do not unambiguously support attribution to him of the conventionalism that Gödel criticizes. In particular, this conventionalism is incompatible with the principle of tolerance, in the unqualified form in which Carnap states it. Gödel observes that the conventionalist will not be justified in taking the mathematics formalizable in some language to be a contentless auxiliary for science, unless the rules of the language can be shown to be admissible. Gödel's definition of admissibility employs a language-transcendent notion of empirical fact or empirical truth. Here it is important to note the role that this notion of empirical fact plays in his argument. He urges that we are justified in taking the analytic sentences of a Carnapian language to be conventionally stipulated truths only if the premises needed to establish admissibility are available in advance of the stipulation. This explanatory task arises only in the context of a language-transcendent notion of empirical fact. The requirement of a non-circular proof of admissibility cannot be supported without use of this notion. This notion of empirical fact imposes morals in logic on the conventionalist. Carnap, in adopting the principle of tolerance, rejects any such language-transcendent notions. Gödel's objection illuminates the difficulty in embedding a conventionalist account of mathematics inside a realist metaphysics; but the conventionalism that Gödel thinks gives *Logical Syntax* its philosophical point is on all fours with the philosophical positions that Carnap disparages.[7]

If, though, Carnap is not a conventionalist, how are we to understand his informal characterization of analytic and synthetic sentences just cited? Later in *Logical Syntax*, he in effect warns us to be very careful how we take such remarks; for these characterizations of the analytic–synthetic distinction are paradigms of what Carnap in (1937a) part V calls pseudo–object sentences. These, he tells us, are those which are "formulated as though they refer (either partially or exclusively) to objects, while in reality they refer to syntactic forms, and specifically to forms of the designations of those objects with which they appear to deal."[8] Carnap's examples of pseudo–object sentences together with their syntactic rephrasings are more informative than this characterization, which Carnap concedes is "informal and incorrect."[9] For instance, the material mode pseudo–object sentence

Five is not a thing, but a number,

should be rephrased

"Five" is not a thing-word, but a number-word.[10]

And

The word "luna" in the Latin language designates the moon,

should be replaced by

There is an equipollent expressional translation of the Latin into the English language in which the word "moon" is the correlate of the word "luna."[11]

Pseudo–object sentences then include those that putatively speak of such semantical relations as designation or description between words and things as well as generalizations about things, properties, and facts.[12] Carnap believes that pseudo–object sentences are, at best, highly misleading. They suggest the availability of language-transcendent notions of reference, ontology, and facts, and so the availability of a perspective from which to enquire after the correctness of various logics. The use of these sentences then tempts us to raise pseudo–questions in the absence of any context that defines the considerations relevant to the questions, a context that gives content to the questions. Carnap advocates that pseudo–object statements be replaced by syntactic claims restricted to a single language or well-defined class of languages.[13] These syntactic statements should not be viewed as strictly synonymous with the associated pseudo–object statements. Carnap's point is rather that syntactic statements can serve any clearly conceived purposes in logical investigations that pseudo–object statements serve.

The earlier quoted characterization of the analytic–synthetic distinction does not, then, invoke language-transcendent notions in order to set forth the distinction that Carnap is trying to capture in syntactic terms. Rather, Carnap here provides an example of a vague classification of sentences that can be replaced by a precise syntactic classification. In the syntactic recasting of the analytic–synthetic distinction any notion of truth-in-virtue-of goes by the board. This is the beginning of an interpretation of Carnap's remarks, but only a beginning. We still need to enquire after the ends in pursuit of which a syntactic definition of analyticity can without loss replace the philosophical characterization.

It is instructive to approach Carnap's (1937a) project by considering the continuities and discontinuities between his view of logic there on the one hand and Frege's and the young Wittgenstein's views on the other. My brief survey will highlight a number of motivations and guiding assumptions that frame Carnap's project.

In the Schilpp volume autobiography, Carnap credits Frege with a decisive influence on his own philosophical development.[14] There are four interconnected assumptions that underlie Carnap's work that it is plausible to think that he absorbs from Frege. First, Carnap adheres to Frege's antipsychologism. Carnap throughout his career sharply distinguishes the psychologist's empirical investigation of cognition from logic. He holds that, in traditional theory of knowledge, psychological and logical enquiries have been entangled. He believes that, in so far as questions concerning knowledge and evidence are not psychological questions, they concern logical relations among statements.[15] Second, Carnap follows Frege in his antiempiricism towards mathematics. Carnap takes it as evident that there is a principled difference between mathematics and natural science. A mark of this difference is the irrelevance of observation to the evaluation of mathematical statements. Third, Carnap is attentive to Frege's criticisms of crudely formalist accounts of pure mathematics as a sort of notational game. Frege formulates logic by exhibiting a formal system, his *begriffsschrift*. The syntactic identification of axioms and inference rules does not signify that the *begriffsschrift* is merely a notational game and not also a full-fledged language for the communication of judgements. We will see that Carnap's distinction between pure and descriptive syntax, after a fashion, recasts this Fregean point.

The fourth point is the most important and the most elusive: Carnap inherits logocentrism from Frege. Frege elaborates no philosophical foundations for logic, no theory of the subject matter or the epistemology of logic. Frege's attitude is that any enquiry must draw on, and so presuppose, logic. There is then no perspective from which to theorize *about* logic. The fundamental principles of logic can only be displayed: they admit no extralogical justification.[16] Carnap also assigns to logic a fundamental regulative role in enquiry. We observed that Carnap complains of "disputations in which opponents talked at cross purposes" because there was no basis for "mutual understanding," no "common criterion for deciding the controversy." Carnap believes that many such wrangles can be avoided, if investigators formulate hypotheses in a syntactically described language. This description fixes a consequence relation for the language; and only in the context of such a relation can one statement be said to support, oppose, or be irrelevant to another. A consequence relation is thus a basic and indispensable part of a common criterion for adjudicating disputes: it grounds agreement on the relevance of further statements to the hypothesis under consideration. There is, of course, an important difference between Frege's and Carnap's conception of the regulative role of logic. Frege holds to a universalist conception: there is a single set of logical principles implicit in rational thought and discourse. In *Logical Syntax*, Carnap embraces a pluralism: the framework that Frege believes logic provides for all thought and enquiry is, for Carnap, language-specific. Something important of Frege's logocentrism survives this transition. Carnap believes that there is no appeal to anything outside of a language that makes that language with its consequence relation correct. There is no question of justification that arises as regards the choice of a language, for any question of justification presupposes that a consequence relation is in place. In logic, there are no morals.

In sketching the development of his views on mathematics, Carnap says:

> I had learned from Frege that all mathematical concepts can be defined on the basis of the concepts of logic and that the theories of mathematics can be deduced from the principles of logic. Thus the truths of mathematics are analytic in the general sense of truth based on logic alone.[17]

This remark is puzzling. First, Carnap is well aware of the inconsistency in Frege's formulation of logic. Second, Frege seeks to establish analyticity of arithmetic by deducing arithmetic truths from logical laws and explicit logical definitions of the arithmetical vocabulary. In *Logical Syntax*, Carnap treats it as a matter of technical expedience whether mathematical symbols are introduced by definitions or whether they are taken as primitive.[18] Furthermore, he does not identify analyticity with derivability in any language. How then did Frege teach Carnap that mathematics is analytic?

Frege presents logic by setting forth a formal language with syntactically described axioms and inference rules that formulate logical principles. In *The Foundations of Arithmetic* (1978), he characterizes the analytic–synthetic distinction as follows: a true statement is analytic, if it is provable from logical laws plus explicit definitions; it is synthetic otherwise. He says almost nothing there by way of describing what logical laws or provability amount to: his previous and subsequent technical writings address these questions. Frege casually remarks that he does not intend to redefine "analytic" but only to capture "what earlier writers, in particular Kant, meant."[19] Significantly, despite this aim, Frege offers no defense of his definition. Like a working mathematician, Frege does not in practice sharply distinguish between clarification by analysis and clarification by replacement.[20]

Frege's attitude here is that he has clarified the philosophers' vague notion of analyticity by offering a precise demarcation of analytic truth in formal terms. Frege thus converts the distinction between analytic and synthetic into a precise formal one. The question of the analyticity of arithmetic is thereby removed from the sphere of philosophical debate and becomes a matter that can be settled by deriving the laws of arithmetic in the *begriffsschrift*.

Frege thus offers an example of the unified formal treatment of both logic and mathematics. With this, he provides Carnap with, first, a strategy for replacing vague philosophical characterizations of the difference between mathematical statements and scientific statements with a precise, principled formal characterization. It is Frege's attempted execution of this strategy that teaches Carnap that mathematics is analytic. Of course, Carnap's rejection of Frege's universalist view of logic gives the label "analytic" a different significance in his mouth than it has in Frege's. Furthermore, Carnap (1937a) attempts to implement Frege's strategy at the meta-level by developing a general characterization of analytic-in-L. However, alluding to this attempt, Carnap, in a popular exposition of his ideas, echoes Frege's (1978) remarks, saying, "The terms 'analytic' and 'synthetic' have already been used in traditional philosophy; they are especially important in the philosophy of Kant; but up till now they have not been exactly defined."[21]

Carnap's understanding of the significance of Frege's work as well as his rejection of Frege's universalist view of logic is importantly shaped by Carnap's study of Wittgenstein's *Tractatus*. In the Schilpp autobiography, Carnap cites Wittgenstein as the philosopher who, after Frege and Russell, most influenced his thought.[22] However, in *Logical Syntax* and associated writings, Carnap criticizes many features of Wittgenstein's views, and does so in terms that are, for him, harsh.[23] Let us then consider briefly what Carnap in *Logical Syntax* appropriates from the *Tractatus* and what he rejects.

Most importantly, Carnap gets from Wittgenstein a view of logical truth that denies that logical truths are a species of truth. For Frege, logical truths are what are deducible from fundamental logical laws; these logical laws are themselves evident, maximally general truths. Frege believes that logical laws and non-logical laws alike univocally have content, express a sense, are true. Logic is thus a science in the same sense in which physics or geometry are sciences, only a more general science than these. Wittgenstein explicitly rejects this view of logic in the *Tractatus* (6.123 ff). Logic measures the content of statements so that "If p follows from q, then the sense of 'p' is contained in the sense of 'q'" (5.123); and statements that mutually imply each other say the same (5.141). The presence in language of statements with sense, the statements of natural science, guarantees the presence of statement-like formations that appear to be true independently of the truth or falsity of other statements, formations that follow from every statement. Thus lacking truth-conditions, Wittgenstein says that these statement-like formations are tautologies that say nothing. (4.461; 4.4611; 5.142). This feature is palpable in the expression these tautologies receive in Wittgenstein's truth-table notation for the expression of compound statements. (See 4.42–4.46.) Wittgenstein then maintains that tautologies, in contrast with the statements of science, lack sense (*sinnlos*). Their truth – in so far as senseless formations of signs may be called "true" at all – is linguistically secured. Here Carnap takes Wittgenstein to have achieved a deep insight into the nature of logic. I will consider in the next section how Carnap (1937a) understands this status.[24]

Wittgenstein is also a principal source for Carnap's identification of logic with logical syntax. Wittgenstein, reacting against the ontological foundations Russell offers for logic, insists that for the establishment of a perspicuous notation it is unnecessary to talk about what signs mean; rather one should speak only about the signs themselves. (See especially the 3.33s.) Carnap shares Wittgenstein's hostility to giving ontological foundations for logic, as evidenced in his treatment of *designation* as a pseudo-object notion. Carnap also embraces the suggestion that the logician should restrict herself to talk of signs, but his appropriation of this idea is accompanied by the rejection of two central features of Wittgenstein's view. Wittgenstein, while rejecting Frege's and Russell's view of logic as the maximally general science, follows them in believing that there is just one logic – that any adequate logical notation is fully equivalent to any other. With the principle of tolerance, Carnap rejects this logical monotheism. Indeed, Wittgenstein's rejection of the Frege–Russell view in favor of a view of tautologies as notationally secured, contentless sentences facilitates Carnap's adoption of a pluralism in logic. Second, Wittgenstein tells us that logical form is what statements and reality have in common that enables the first to describe the second. This common form, though, is not itself describable. There are then no sentences that set forth the logical syntax of language. Carnap believes that the work of the Hilbert school and Gödel refutes this view. There is no inconsistency or intrinsic unclarity in these treatments of metamathematical questions; for their sentences about proofs are simply sentences that are concerned with "the *structures of possible serial orders* (of a definite kind) *of any elements whatsoever.*"[25] Lingering doubts about the legitimacy and status of logical syntax should be removed when we, via Gödelization, realize, "All the statements of pure syntax follow from these arithmetical definitions and are thus analytic sentences of elementary arithmetic."[26] Logical syntax is analytic, not nonsensical.

Finally, in the *Tractatus* Wittgenstein tells us that philosophy is not itself a science, that there are no philosophical propositions. Rather, philosophy is the activity of clarifying the (non-philosophical) statements of natural science (4.111–4.112). This clarification is presumably provided by analyses of these statements, by rewriting these statements in a logically perspicuous language, a language that obeys logical syntax (3.325). Carnap credits Wittgenstein with first exhibiting "the close connection between the logic of science . . . and syntax."[27] He, however, believes that Wittgenstein's views on the ineffability of logical syntax lead him astray. 4.112 states, "Philosophy aims at the logical clarification of thoughts . . . A philosophical work consists essentially of elucidations." Carnap takes the *Tractatus* itself to be such a philosophical work so that its remarks are examples of elucidations. He concludes that on Wittgenstein's view, "the investigations of the logic of science contain no sentences, but merely more or less vague explanations which the reader must subsequently recognize as pseudo-sentences."[28] Carnap thinks that there are questions that are not addressed by the statements of natural science, the statements that are formalized by what he calls material mode sentences – questions that do not disappear once the clarity that comes with formalization is achieved. These are logical questions about languages for science. Carnap believes that a number of questions that have exercised philosophers can be reformulated as, or replaced by, questions concerning the syntax of formalized theories.[29] These questions are addressed by applying the analytic theory of logical syntax to the languages under consideration.

Carnap's principle of tolerance is coeval with his embrace of logical syntax. In the late twenties Carnap became actively interested in disputes in the foundations of mathematics. He observes in the foreword to *Logical Syntax* that a universalist conception of logic requires that proposals in logic "must be proved to be 'correct' and to constitute a faithful rendering of 'the true logic'."[30] This attitude in turn fuels debates concerning the status and legitimacy of principles that figured in various formalizations of parts of mathematics, principles like the axioms of reducibility, infinity, and choice as well as the law of excluded middle. These controversies appeared to exhibit the same ill-defined, sterile wrangling that Carnap saw in traditional philosophy. In 1931 he had the liberating vision of applying the sort of meta-mathematical ideas that figured in the work of Hilbert and Gödel to the construction of "a general theory of linguistic forms."[31] Logical syntax, Carnap believes, enables him to make sense of their being alternative languages, alternative logics, alternative frameworks for enquiry. Fruitless controversy in the foundations of mathematics can now be replaced by the development and meta-mathematical investigation of languages that formalize the methods of proof advocated by the various foundationalist schools. In order to gain a fuller appreciation of Carnap's aims in *Logical Syntax*, we need to consider a basic question, one that will bring us back to Gödel's and Putnam's criticisms of Carnap.

What do sheer syntactic descriptions of languages have to do with logic? How do these syntactic descriptions set forth standards that regulate enquiry? Such questions do not arise for Frege, who sets forth his logic in the *Grundgesetze* in syntactic terms: he displays the formulas that are logical axioms; and he states his inference rules syntactically. Frege believes that humankind has a common store of thoughts, and that his logical notation, when extended by the addition of non-logical vocabulary, is adequate for the expression of those thoughts that figure in scientific enquiry. Before presenting the axioms and inference rules of his logical system, Frege has endeavored to impart to his readers an understanding of his notation. Relying on this instruction, Frege anticipates that his readers will recognize the axioms to be true and the inference rules to be sound. Something of the same view is present in the *Tractatus* as well. There Wittgenstein maintains that differences among languages are in the end notational: "Definitions are rules for translating from one language into another. Any correct sign-language must be translatable into any other in accordance with such rules: it is *this* that they all have in common" (3.343). Carnap, in adopting the principle of tolerance, and with it a logical pluralism, gives up any overarching notion of content, like those present in Frege or the *Tractatus*. Some differences among languages are not just differences in formulation. There is, then, no notion of content or sense to which Carnap can appeal in order to explain what is captured by a particular syntactically framed rule.

Section 2 of *Logical Syntax* is entitled "Languages as Calculi." Carnap informally characterizes a calculus as a system of formal rules that "determines in the first place the conditions under which an expression can be said to belong to a certain category of expressions [formation rules]; and in the second place, under what conditions the transformation of one or more expressions into another or others may be allowed [transformation rules]."[32] Carnap maintains that natural languages as well as the more regimented notations of mathematics can be described as calculi. The rules of chess are also a calculus. Carnap tells us, "In the widest sense, logical syntax is the same thing as the construction and manipulation of a calculus, and it is only because languages are the most important example of calculi that, as a rule, only languages are syntactically investigated."[33] What, though, is the relation between languages that scientists use or might use and abstract calculi? An answer to this question is, I believe, crucial for appreciating the point of Carnap's syntactic constructions.

The relation between calculi and languages is treated in Carnap's distinction between pure and descriptive syntax. Pure syntax investigates the formal properties of calculi by developing the consequences of the syntactic rules that define the calculi. Descriptive syntax is concerned "with the syntactical properties and relations of empirically given expressions."[34] Descriptive syntax thus might set forth the syntactic properties of German sentences, although Carnap believes that the formation and transformation rules for natural languages are so complicated as to render their statement unfeasible.[35] What is significant is an underlying assumption that formation and transformation rules are somehow implicit in the use speakers make of a language. Carnap voices this assumption when, much later in (1937a), he casually remarks:

> We have already seen that, in the case of an individual language like German, the construction of the syntax of that language means the construction of a calculus which fulfils the condition of being in agreement with the actual historical habits of speech of German-speaking people.[36]

I believe that Carnap's underlying assumption goes in the other direction as well. Not only can the syntax of the language in principle be read off from "speech habits;" via coordinating definitions analogous to those that Carnap believes link mathematical geometry to physical geometry, the syntax of a calculus determines habits that would make one a speaker of a language with that syntax.[37] Neither in *Logical Syntax* nor, to my knowledge, in surrounding writings does Carnap specify the speech habits that would make a group into speakers of a language with such-and-such transformation rules. I think that he believes that descriptions of the habits or usage relevant here can be given in logically non-tendentious terms, without invoking notions of meaning or reference. From Carnap's broadly behaviorist orientation as regards psychology, I take it that speakers' dispositions to affirm or deny some sentences on the basis of others are the sort of speech habit he has in mind.[38]

We now have the makings of an answer to our question concerning the point of Carnap's syntactic constructions. Carnap (1937a) describes two calculi, Language I and Language II. He puts forward Language I, primitive recursive arithmetic, as a language that captures the restrictions on proof procedures advocated by more constructive mathematicians; Language II, a version of the simple theory of types, is a language suitable for classical mathematics and for the expression of the natural sciences that employ classical mathematics. These claims about these two calculi presuppose that we envision the exacting use of them by rational investigators. Only when we think of these calculi as languages in use do they have the interest Carnap assigns to them.

There is, Carnap thinks, more to a language than syntax, more to the use of language than the usage that makes an individual a speaker of a language with a certain syntax.[39] Syntax says nothing about the use of protocol sentences "by means of which the results of observations are expressed."[40] Under the prodding of Neurath, Carnap identifies protocol sentences with sentences that apply an observation predicate to a spatio-temporal region. The notion of an observation predicate belongs, he tells us, "to a biological or psychological theory of language as a kind of human behavior, and especially as a kind of reaction to observations."[41] Carnap contents himself with a rough-and-ready characterization of observation predicates, one that he expects behaviorist psychologists to refine. Basically, a predicate in a group's language is an observation predicate, if the speakers largely agree in their dispositions to apply or withhold the predicate, under suitable conditions, to demonstrated regions on the basis of current observations.[42] Carnap believes that this conception of observation predicates captures the intersubjective dimension to the use of protocol reports by investigators to confirm or disconfirm empirical hypotheses.

We are now in a position to understand the informal characterizations of the analytic–synthetic distinction that, on their face, support Gödel's conventionalist reading. I have mentioned how in *Logical Syntax* Carnap develops sample syntactic descriptions of two languages. In these and in informal discussions, he divides transformation rules into L-rules (logical rules) and P-rules (physical rules). Intuitively, the L-rules fix the logic of the language and the P-rules axiomatize some body of theory in the language. We must not, however, read this distinction between L-rules and P-rules through the lens of the later controversy about analyticity. In that debate, some defenders of analyticity seek to clarify the analytic–synthetic distinction by sharply distinguishing change of language (identified with change of L-rules) from change of theory within a language (change of P-rules). However, Carnap (1937a) views P-rules as much as L-rules as being definitive of a language. From the syntactic viewpoint, a change in P-rules is as much a change of language as a change in L-rules.[43]

The first three parts of *Logical Syntax* are devoted to syntactic descriptions of Languages I and II. In Part IV, "General Syntax," Carnap presents the tentative beginnings of the dreamt-of general theory of linguistic forms. Here he advances a general definition, applicable across languages, of the analytic or L-valid sentences of a language. The general definition is stated in syntactic terms, and does not rely on the informal distinction between L-rules and P-rules. This distinction is, in effect, the one that Carnap aims to clarify in formal terms. He supposes that we are given the formation and transformation rules of a language, with no separation of transformation rules into L-rules and P-rules. The transformation rules are assumed to determine a consequence relation over the language. The valid sentences are those that are consequences of the null class of sentences; the contra-valid sentences are those that have every sentence as a consequence. The determinate sentences comprise the valid sentences together with the contra-valid ones. Carnap now defines the primitive logical vocabulary of the language along the following lines: the logical vocabulary is the largest vocabulary such that every sentence in the language constructed solely from that vocabulary is determinate. A valid sentence is analytic just in case either it is a valid logical sentence (i.e. a sentence that contains only logical vocabulary) or every sentence obtainable from it by substitution of non-logical vocabulary for primitive non-logical vocabulary is valid.[44]

Carnap does not require that consequence relations be recursively enumerable. In Languages I and II, he defines consequence relations that make every purely mathematical sentence determinate. Every mathematical sentence is thus either analytic or contradictory. He anticipates that the addition of further rules, P-rules, to these languages will not greatly swell the logical vocabulary, and so the class of analytic truths. The general definition "analytic" will then yield the desired results, when applied to languages that might be proposed for the formalization of science.[45] When Carnap embraces Tarski's work on truth, *truth* replaces the syntactic notion of *validity*. As a result, this approach to characterizing analyticity via a language-general distinction between logical and descriptive signs is no longer available to him.[46]

Carnap motivates his general syntactic characterization of logical versus descriptive vocabulary with the following remark:

> If a material interpretation is given for a language S, then the symbols, expressions, and sentences of S may divided into logical and descriptive, i.e. those which have a purely logical, or mathematical, meaning and those which designate something extra-logical – such as empirical objects, properties, and so forth. This classification is not only inexact but also non-formal, and thus is not applicable in syntax. But if we reflect that all the connections between logico-mathematical terms are independent of extra-linguistic factors, such as, for instance, empirical observations, and that they must be solely and completely determined by the transformation rules of the language, we find the formally expressible distinguishing peculiarity of logical symbols and expressions to consist in the fact that each sentence constructed solely from them is determinate.[47]

When Carnap speaks of a material interpretation for a language, he is conceiving of the language not just as a calculus, but as used by a community of investigators to formulate claims. In the quoted passage he describes the features of used languages that correspond to the syntactic classification of expressions into the groups labeled "logical" and "descriptive." Carnap says that descriptive expressions, in contrast to the logical ones, designate extra-logical items. At the outset of *Logical Syntax*, he has told us that notions of meaning and designation play no role in logical syntax.[48] His characterization here of the logical–descriptive distinction is another example of his use of a suspect pseudo–object statement. Not surprisingly, he quickly puts it aside as "inexact" and "non-formal." He then bids us reflect that "the connection between logico-mathematical terms are independent of extra-linguistic factors" like empirical observations and urges that this independence is what the general syntactic classification captures. Here he replaces the pseudo–object characterization with one that is still informal and inexact but that is couched in psychological terms, in terms of the use of language. His idea here is that the transformation rules for a calculus entirely fix the use of the logical vocabulary, though not the descriptive vocabulary. When we conceive of the calculus as a language in use by speakers whose "speech habits" fully conform with the rules, then we are conceiving of speakers who, qua speakers of a language that instantiates that calculus, are disposed or committed to accept the valid sentences and reject the contravalid ones. The use of the logical vocabulary is fixed in that the speakers are thereby already committed as regards the sentences that contain essentially only logical vocabulary, including all sentences constructed solely from logical vocabulary. There are, however, sentences containing descriptive vocabulary that are indeterminate. The use of this vocabulary is not, then, fixed completely by the transformation rules. Carnap's initial pseudo–object characterization of the difference between logical and descriptive vocabulary points toward this differentiating feature of their use. He replaces the pseudo–object characterization with a still vague characterization in terms of linguistic and extra-linguistic factors influencing the use of sentences of the language. When we think of a calculus as a language in use, Carnap's general syntactic definition of logical and descriptive vocabulary provides a precise way of capturing this idea.

Carnap's understanding of the analytic–synthetic distinction thus displaces, more than analyzes, the notion of truth-in-virtue-of. For the general syntactic definition of "analytic" gets applied to materially interpreted languages – used or potentially used languages – via coordinating definitions that specify the linguistic behavior that would make individuals the speakers of a language with a given syntax. Any notion of something's making the sentence true, of anything's justifying the speaker's dispositions or commitments to affirm the sentence, drops out. I believe that this attitude is reflected in Carnap's offhand remarks about truth. For example, in lecture II of (1935), in introducing the notion of a determinate sentence, he remarks, "Thus the determinate sentences are those whose truth-value is determined by the rules of the language."[49] In the next section of the lecture, Carnap mentions the distinction between L-rules and P-rules, alluding to the formal definition of this distinction in (1937a). He goes on to define the analytic–synthetic distinction and to gloss it, saying, "The synthetic sentences are those which assert states of affairs."[50] Carnap sees no contradiction in a sentence which "asserts a state affairs," having its truth or falsity "determined by the rules of the language." Here it is palpable how emptied these philosophical notions become in Carnap's hands.[51]

Carnap's more careful discussion of the notion of truth in §60b of *Logical Syntax* reinforces this conclusion. He believes that the distinction between truths and falsehoods is not syntactically reproducible for languages incorporating a descriptive vocabulary;[52] but here he does not regret the absence of a truth-predicate. First, he notes that the Liar paradox shows that "customary usage of the terms 'true' and 'false' leads . . . to contradiction."[53] More importantly, Carnap maintains that the truth-predicate is dispensable in science. Carnap believes that singular predications of "true" are disquotationally eliminable in favor of the use of the sentence that is the subject of the predication.[54] Uses of the word "true" in logic to generalize into sentential positions to express generalizations like

If a conjunction is true, then so is each of its conjuncts,

may be replaced by logical syntactic terms:

A conjunction has as L-consequences each of its conjuncts.[55]

Carnap does not go so far as to call truth a pseudo-concept. After all, "truth" compares favorably with "entelechy," since the clearest and most frequent uses of the former can be straightforwardly paraphrased.[56] Still, Carnap's remarks in §60b indicate that he believes that the truth-predicate has no clear use except in so far as it is disquotationally eliminable or replaceable in logical generalizations by syntactic terms.

Let us re-examine Gödel's objection to Carnap from this interpretive perspective. Gödel argued that the conventionalist is justified in taking mathematical truths to be conventionally stipulated truths only if it has been proved that the syntactic stipulations do not imply the truth or falsehood of any empirical statement. Because any such proof requires the use of mathematics comparable to that formalized in the language, he concludes that the justification for the conventionalist position is flawed by a vicious circularity. In contrast with Gödel's conventionalist view, Carnap's places no justificatory weight on consistency proofs. Of course, a language which is known to be inconsistent is unsuitable for the formalization of either mathematics or empirical science. A Carnapian may then adduce a consistency proof for a language that formalizes classical mathematics, perhaps in order to establish the admissibility of the L-rules vis-à-vis the observational sublanguage, i.e. to show that the language may be used to observationally test hypotheses.[57] The consistency proof is not intended to establish that the mathematics formalizable in the language is true in virtue of syntactic convention. Rather, the proof establishes a formal fact about the language that may be cited in advocating its use to formalize some theory. There is no vicious circularity in the use to this end of whatever mathematical resources are required. Carnap himself does discuss the consistency of his Language II. He is well aware of the consequences of Gödel's second incompleteness theorem for consistency proofs and observes that, since his consistency proof outstrips even the resources of Language II, it has limited interest when measured against the ambitions of Hilbert's program.[58]

At the outset I noted the centrality of Carnap's interest in distinguishing genuine issues from pseudo-problems. The logical syntactic description of various languages is a tool to this end. Faced with seeming disagreement between investigators, the Carnapian logician can set forth a language that formalizes the common ground that both parties bring to their disagreement – the logic they both accept (L-rules) and a shared background of empirical assumptions (P-rules). In favorable cases, this logical work will exhibit that the disputants have advanced incompatible hypotheses; moreover, hypotheses that in the shared language imply contradictory observation sentences. The disputed issue can then be addressed, if the investigators are able to position themselves to make observations that will prompt affirmation or denial of these observation sentences. Carnap does not believe that, in this circumstance, observation simply settles matters. Citing Poincaré and Duhem, Carnap takes a holistic view of theory testing and goes on, in a Quinean vein, to remark:

> No rule of the physical language is definitive; all rules are laid down with the reservation that they may be altered as soon as it seems expedient to do so. This applies not only to the P-rules but also to the L-rules, including those of mathematics. In this respect, there are only differences in degree; certain rules are more difficult to renounce than others.[59]

Formalization, or rational reconstruction, of the debate is to enable us to understand exactly what sort of difference exists between investigators as well as the role that linguistic factors – the linguistic usage that makes the investigators speakers of a given language – and non-linguistic factors, especially observation, play in the resolution of the dispute. So, in the envisaged case, rational reconstruction represents the difference between investigators to be a disagreement over an indeterminate sentence in a shared language. Suppose the investigators are able to make the observations relevant to their disagreement and that one of the theories is observationally disconfirmed. The formalization enables us to track the response an investigator makes in response to the observations. She may add to the P-rules of the shared language, advancing a new theory that conforms to the expanded set of observation reports. In addition to advancing a new theory, she may modify the P-rules of the language. Finally, the speech dispositions of an investigator may change to the point where a sentence that was previously L-valid for her ceases to be so. Of course, formalization may reveal that there is no common ground between the disputants. They may not share a common language, a common logic. In this case, their dispute is just verbal.

Carnap dismisses traditional philosophical questions as pseudo-questions because he does not "know how such questions could be translated into the formal mode or into any other unambiguous clear mode."[60] He believes that philosophers will not countenance the construal of their questions as syntactic claims about languages coupled perhaps with the expression of a preference for the use of some languages rather than others. I think that he anticipates that the reaction of the logicians whom he also took to be involved in pseudo-debates will be different: they should be happy to see their claims construed as syntactic claims about languages and welcome the disappearance of pseudo-debates over "correctness" in logic. Without discussion Carnap assumes that philosophers will not acknowledge the propriety of expressing their theses in a particular language where their views are simply P-valid sentences without observational consequences. He accordingly recommends:

> If one partner in a philosophical discussion cannot or will not give a translation of his thesis into the formal mode, or if he will not state to which language-system his thesis refers, then the other will be well-advised to refuse the debate, because the thesis of his opponent is incomplete, and discussion would lead to nothing but empty wrangling.[61]

Just here we encounter Carnap's empiricism. Throughout his career, when he disparages philosophy as entangled in pseudo-problems, he is contrasting philosophy with science. After the adoption of the principle of tolerance and the shift to logical pluralism, he tries to clarify this, to him, intuitive difference as a difference in language. Scientific theorizing is formalizable in languages in which investigated hypotheses are observationally confirmable. The exacting use of a language whose indeterminate sentences have this feature, is, Carnap suggests, what distinguishes science from traditional philosophy: it is through the employment of these empiricist languages that scientists avoid the fruitless squabbles evident among traditional philosophers. Carnap endorses the evidential standards captured by these empiricist languages and advocates that in so far as we enquire after sentences that are not L-determinate, we should restrict our enquiries to claims formulated in empiricist languages. This advocacy of empiricism is advocacy of the use of a range of languages, not the affirmation of a sentence within a particular language. Empiricism is not a theoretical matter; there is no right or wrong to it, for in logic there are no morals. Carnap's advocacy is backed up only by his endorsement of the evidential standards, the language use, that he believes typify science. It is in this sense, then, that Carnap's application of the criticisms "pseudo-problems" and "nonsense" is ultimately ad hominem.

Carnap (1936) is explicit on the status of his empiricism:

> It seems to me that it is preferable to formulate the principle of empiricism not in the form of an assertion – "all knowledge is empirical" or "all synthetic sentences that we can know are based on (or connected with) experiences" or the like – but rather in the form of a proposal or requirement. As empiricists, we require the language of science to be restricted in a certain way; we require that descriptive predicates and hence synthetic sentences are not to be admitted unless they have some connection with possible observations, a connection which has to be characterized in a suitable way.[62]

The conclusion of this remarks alludes to Carnap's search after a criterion for empirical meaningfulness. Following him, I have spoken of empiricist languages. He wants to clarify empiricism by characterizing empiricist languages generally using syntactic terms and the psychological term "observation predicate." Carnap (1936) characterizes empiricist languages by stipulating syntactic conditions for the introduction of non-observational descriptive predicates into a language. Today it is generally conceded that this strategy was unsuccessful in capturing the distinctive feature of scientific enquiry. Carnap's disparagement of philosophy thus retains a measure of the obscurity he condemns in philosophy. Had he been successful here, the term "empiricist" would have been transformed into a descriptive syntactic predicate of languages that could be used to commend use of a class of languages. This commendation would, however, still be simply advocacy of some languages over other. Success or failure here does not affect the sort of criticism Carnap is making.

We are now in a position to consider Putnam's objection from Carnap's vantage point. Putnam urges that the principle of tolerance depends on empiricism, for only by invoking empiricism can Carnap dismiss the question of the correctness, the descriptive adequacy, of a language as a pseudo-question. Putnam's challenge, however, assumes that the notion of fact, of the way things really are, is sufficiently clear that Carnap owes us an argument for rejecting it. Carnap would view matters differently. He would ask for a clarification of this notion. It is, I believe, difficult to envisage a clarification that would both satisfy him and bear the weight of Putnam's challenge. For example, from a Carnapian perspective, my conception of "the way things really are" is represented by the language that formalizes my total theory. I might then stipulate that a language is correct just in case it includes a sublanguage that translates my language. This notion of correctness does not supply a reason for rejecting the principle of tolerance; rather it reflects a refusal on my part to countenance any language that is not a notional variant on my own, and so an outright rejection of Carnap's logical pluralism.

Like the principle of empiricism, the principle of tolerance itself is not a thesis, but a proposal, the expression of an attitude or standpoint. The principle of tolerance is not formulatable as a statement in a Carnapian language. There is no question of "correctness" that is applicable to it. By giving it this non-statemental status, Carnap seeks to avoid the "mysticism," the resort to self-stultifying elucidations, that he criticizes in the *Tractatus*.

We would, however, miss the point of Putnam's objection were we to dismiss it on account of the obscurity of the notion of *fact* that figures in it. Putnam is objecting to Carnap's conception of clarification, to the position that the clarification of a thesis requires the statement of the thesis in an empiricist language. Putnam (1983) calls "any conception according to which there are institutionalized norms which define what is and is not rationally acceptable a *criterial* conception of rationality."[63] He reads Carnap as setting up the exacting use empiricist languages (including logical languages, like syntax languages, that lack descriptive vocabulary) as criterial for clarity and rationality. The target of his criticism is not so much just Carnap's empiricism, as my initial presentation of it suggested; Putnam rather objects to the position that rationality is constituted by the use of an empiricist *language*. It is this entire conception, not just the selection of empiricist languages, that Putnam argues admits of no non-circular justification.[64]

This criticism again, I believe, overestimates Carnap's philosophical ambitions. When the *Tractatus* asserts, "What can be said at all can be said clearly" (Preface; see 4.116), Wittgenstein invokes a notion of clarity that is constituted by the logic to which language, thought, and reality all conform. In contrast, Carnap's requests for clarification do not draw on some theory, some constrictive view, of what clarification must amount to. He is open to considering whatever is offered by way of clarification. He, however, advocates that when we find ourselves puzzled by some claim, we should formalize the claim in a syntactically described language. It is not a part of his view that clarification is *constituted* by formalization. It is precisely this sort of philosophical overlay that he eschews in *Logical Syntax*.

Notes

I have learned much from conversations with John Carriero, Burton Dreben, Gary Ebbs, Michael Friedman, Steven Gross, Edward Minar, and especially Warren Goldfarb on the ideas in this chapter.

1 Rudolf Carnap (1963), "Intellectual Autobiography," in Paul Arthur Schilpp (ed.), *The Philosophy of Rudolf Carnap*, LaSalle: Open Court, p. 45.

2 Rudolf Carnap (1937a), *The Logical Syntax of Language*, trans. A. Smeaton. London: Routledge and Kegan Paul, §17, p. 52. See also p. xv, and Carnap (1963), p. 44.

3 Hilary Putnam (1983), "Philosophers and Human Understanding," in *Realism and Reason: Philosophical Papers*, vol. 3. Cambridge: Cambridge University Press, p. 191.

4 Carnap (1937a), p. xiv.

5 Ibid., §14, p. 41.

6 Kurt Gödel (forthcoming), "Is Mathematics Syntax of Language?," Fassung V (Gödel Archives item 04046), p. 2, in Kurt Gödel, *Collected Works*, vol. 3, ed. S. Feferman et al., Oxford: Oxford University Press.

7 This is not to say that Gödel's incompleteness theorems do not pose problems for Carnap's project in *Logical Syntax*. My disagreement lies with Gödel's particular identification of those problems.

8 Carnap (1937a), §74, p. 285.

9 Ibid. Indeed, this characterization of pseudo–object sentences is itself a pseudo-object sentence. Compare Carnap's qualification of his remark in §2, p. 7, that the sentences of syntax are concerned with the forms of sentences.

10 Ibid., §74, p. 286.

11 Ibid., §75, p. 289. Carnap had previously offered a syntactical characterization of translation in §§61–62.

12 See especially ibid., §§75, 76, and 79.

13 See ibid., §78. See also Rudolf Carnap (1935), *Philosophy and Logical Syntax*. London: Kegan Paul, Trench, Trubner and Co., lecture II, sec. 5, pp. 75–8.

14 See Carnap (1963), pp. 5–6, 12, and 25.

15 See Carnap (1937a), §§72 and 86.

16 This attitude is evident in the introduction to Gottlob Frege (1893), *Die Grundgesetze der Arithmetik*, vol. 1. Jena: H. Pohle. See especially p. xix. I discuss Frege's logocentrism in more detail in (1986a), "Objectivity and Objecthood: Frege's Metaphysics of Judgment," in L. Haaparanta and J. Hintikka (eds), *Frege Synthesized*, Dordrecht: D. Reidel Publishing, pp. 65–95, and in (1986b) "Generality, Meaning, and Sense in Frege," *Pacific Philosophical Quarterly*, 67, pp. 172–95.

17   Carnap (1963), p. 46.

18   See Carnap (1937a), §84. In Carnap's Languages I and II, mathematical vocabulary is primitive.

19   Gottlob Frege (1978), *The Foundations of Arithmetic*, trans. J.L. Austin. Evanston: Northwestern University Press, §3, fn. 1, p. 3. See also §89, pp. 101f.

20   See Frege's striking discussion of this topic in (1983), "Logik in der Mathematik," in Hans Hermes, Friedrich Kambartel and Friedrich Kaulbach (eds), *Nachgelassene Schriften*, second edn, Hamburg: Felix Meiner, pp. 227–9.

21   Carnap (1935), lecture II, pp. 53f.

22   Carnap (1963), p. 25.

23   See Carnap's criticism of Wittgenstein's "mysticism" in (1935), lecture I, pp. 37–8.

24   Here I am indebted to Burton Dreben (1990), "Quine," in R. Barrett and R. Gibson (eds), *Perspectives on Quine*, Oxford: Basil Blackwell, p. 86.

25   Carnap (1937a), §2, p. 6.

26   Ibid., §19, p. 57. This remark is problematic, given the mathematical strength of the notions Carnap allows as syntactic.

27   Ibid., §73, p. 282.

28   Ibid., §73, p. 283.

29   See ibid., §83. For example, Carnap believes that the question of the relation of biology to physics should be replaced by, as we would put it, the question of the interpretability of a given biological theory in a given physical theory.

30   Ibid., p. xiv.

31   Carnap (1963), p. 54. See also Carnap (1937a), p. xv, the final paragraph, for an expression of this sense of liberation.

32   Carnap (1937a), §2, p. 4. Transformation rules are Carnap's inference rules.

33   Ibid., §2, p. 5.

34   Ibid., §2, p. 7.

35   We find here the antecedent of Carnap's later distinction between semantics and syntax on the one hand and pragmatics on other.

36   Carnap (1937a), §62, p. 228.

37   See ibid., §25.

38   For an expression of Carnap's behaviorism from this period see, for example, (1959), "Psychology in Physical Language," in A.J. Ayer (ed.), *Logical Positivism*, New York: Free Press. Original publication in (1932), *Erkenntnis*, 3. Carnap does not think that notions of meaning and reference will enter into descriptions of language use in descriptive syntax. In (1937), he treats these notions as allegedly logical notions that should be replaced by syntactic surrogates. Nor does Carnap think that the speech habits that make one a user of a calculus are to be described by reference to speaker's beliefs and intentions. In (1937a) he already attempts to analyze psychological attitudes as sentential attitudes. The notion of a language is thus presupposed in the notions of belief and intention.

39   See Carnap (1937a), §2, p. 5.

40   Ibid., §82, p. 317.

41 Rudolf Carnap (1936), "Testability and Meaning," *Philosophy of Science*, 3, p. 454. Although "Testability and Meaning" is published after Carnap's acceptance of Tarski's truth definitions, in the paper Carnap draws only on logical syntactic notions. I take it then to belong with Carnap's pre-semantic logical syntax writings.

42 For Carnap's own characterization, see (1936), pp. 454f. Carnap's observation predicates are then close kin to Quine's observation sentences, as Quine notes. See Quine (1969), "Epistemology Naturalized," in W.V. Quine, *Ontological Relativity and Other Essays*, New York: Columbia University Press, especially pp. 87–8.

43 See Carnap (1937a), §51, p. 180.

44 Carnap develops his general syntactic definition of the analytic–synthetic distinction in §§50–2 of (1937). He modifies the definition of "analytic" in ways that do not affect my discussion in (1936), pp. 451–3.

45 See Carnap (1937a), §50, pp. 178f, and §52, pp. 185–6, the part entitled "Examples."

46 See Rudolf Carnap (1942), *Introduction to Semantics*. Cambridge, MA: Harvard University Press, §13, pp. 58–9.

47 Carnap (1937a) §50, p. 177.

48 Ibid., §2, p. 5.

49 Carnap (1935), lecture II, p. 49.

50 Ibid., lecture II, p. 53.

51 See Carnap (1937a), §52, p. 186, the end of the "Examples" section.

52 Ibid., §60b, p. 216. See also ibid., §63, pp. 236f, and (1935), lecture II, pp. 47ff. In making such claims, Carnap has in mind languages with an extensive descriptive vocabulary of observational and non-observational predicates suitable for the formalization of a branch of science. Also it should be noted that by the standards of (1937), Tarski's truth definitions do not legitimate true-in-L as a logical syntactic notion. The stumbling block here lies not in the set theory needed in the metalanguage; Carnap is well aware that his "higher syntactic" definitions of L-validity have this feature too. It is rather the use within a Tarski truth definition of descriptive predicates to state satisfaction conditions for descriptive predicates that disqualifies truth from being a syntactic notion.

53 Carnap (1937a), §60b, p. 215. Carnap does go on to note that by eliminating impredicative uses of "true" via the distinction between object-language and metalanguage the paradox can be avoided.

54 Ibid., §60b, p. 216.

55 Ibid., §60b, pp. 216–17. The use of "true" in logic to generalize into sentential positions has, from Carnap's viewpoint, the drawback of not making explicit the relativization of logical claims like these to a single language or group of languages. Carnap is committed to taking the first statement of the logical law to be a pseudo-object statement.

56 See Carnap's discussion of the the concept of entelechy in (1937a), §82, p. 319.

57 In ibid., §82, pp. 318f, Carnap alludes in passing to the issue of admissibility as regards the protocol sublanguage of a language for science.

58 See ibid., §34i, p. 129.

59   Ibid., §82, p. 318.
60   Carnap (1935), lecture III, p. 79.
61   Ibid., lecture III, pp. 80f.
62   Rudolf Carnap (1937b), "Testability and Meaning (Continuation)," *Philosophy of Science*, 4, p. 33.
63   Putnam (1983), p. 188.
64   I am especially indebted to Gary Ebbs in this paragraph.

8 Putnam's Doctrine of Natural Kind Words and Frege's Doctrines of Sense, Reference, and Extension: Can They Cohere?

David Wiggins

Hilary Putnam has been apt to emphasize all the differences between the deictic doctrine that he advocates for the understanding of our understanding of natural kind substantives and the accounts of the meanings of these expressions that would have had to be offered by his predecessors in the philosophy of meaning. Delighting in iconoclasm, he has sought at various times to include within the ambit of his entertaining criticisms of his predecessors such figures as Aristotle, the Scholastics, Locke, Mill, Frege, linguistic philosophers, analytical philosophers, philosophers of linguistics, indeed practically everyone.[1]

In this chapter, I set out Putnam's proposal and show how it broke the mold for one kind of philosophical analysis. But then I try to show that we may deploy Putnam's proposal most convincingly if, first, flying in the face of Putnam's wish, we try to place it within the framework of Fregean sense and reference; but that, having done that, we can do even better if we seek to integrate the deictic proposal, significantly but desirably adjusted at one key point, with an extant, neglected but even more time-honored tradition of semantic speculation, a tradition, not empiricist, in which there is already a clear place for Putnam's insight into the functioning of natural kind words.

I begin by reminding you of the contents of the paper "Is Semantics Possible?" This is a paper that Putnam read to a conference in Brockport, Long Island, in 1967 (one that I myself knew for a long time only from the notes taken at the conference by my former student, Ronald de Sousa, to whom I must owe my first appreciation of its significance).[2] It was in this paper that Putnam first introduced the idea that to impart the meaning of a natural kind term is to impart certain core facts, (1) the *stereotype* – the facts an ordinary speaker needs to know in order to use a natural kind term – and (2) the *extension*, the identification of the latter being the province of experts. Or, as I would say (see below), it was in this paper that Putnam introduced the idea that the sense of thing-kind words standing for natural kinds is reality-invoking or extension-involving.

Putnam led up to his conclusion by criticizing incisively and amusingly the easy (or fall-back) supposition that the right way to give the meaning of "lemon," "tiger," "water," or whatever/would have to be by an analysis into simpler terms or by giving necessary and sufficient conditions. I worried, when I read de Sousa's notes, that Putnam filed no report of an analytical philosopher (contrast one philosopher of linguistics) with his trousers down actually attempting such a thing. But, then, by 1967, linguistic philosophers were a canny bunch; and, it quickly appeared to me that Putnam's failure to identify such an attempt was not a cause for criticism. The thing that mattered was that the problem of natural kind words was not to be solved by tact or good taste or by the refusal to recognize that these expressions constituted a special question for the philosophy of meaning.

On this matter, as on others, ideas were in short supply. But it must be recorded that, for the slightly similar case of proper names, there did exist from well before 1960 an important minority opinion, which (perhaps under the influence of Geach and Anscombe) Michael Dummett took very seriously and which (under Dummett's influence) I myself took maximally seriously (indeed believed and preached to my students from 1959 onwards). This was that a proper name has its meaning, affects the truth-conditions of the sentences in which it occurs, by standing for its bearer: and that there is no other way to give the sense of a proper name than to say which object it is the name stands for.[3] It was not then out of the question, even in that distant epoch, to say that the senses of proper names were reality-invoking or object-involving. Nor, among those who held the minority opinion, was it an unfamiliar question what it would involve to make room for this in Fregean semantics. (The notion of *Art des Gegebenseins* seemed to be ready-made for such an attempt. See below.) What was still missing in linguistic philosophy and (stranger still) in the philosophy of science was any perception of the need to say something similar for potentially predicative expressions like "lemon," "tiger," "water."[4]

Back now to "Is Semantics Possible?" Not only, Putnam insisted, were philosophical analyses of "lemon," "tiger," "water," laughably inadequate. The only explanation of anyone's supposing that there could be such an analysis was sheer negligence of the whole mise-en-scène, the whole social-cum-technological context on which we all depend in order to come to understand one another. (This context is what we depend upon even to understand what we find in a dictionary.) Philosophers who were ready to suppose that there could be an analysis of the meaning of "lemon" or "tiger" were ignoring both the division of mental labor and the role of the authorities or experts who sustain our shared understanding of natural kind words. Philosophers should cease to complain about the fact the dictionaries are "cluttered up with colour samples and with stray pieces of empirical information (e.g. the weight of aluminium) not sharply distinguished from purely linguistic information," Putnam said. They should take that fact seriously as a clue to the real situation, the situation he himself wanted (however schematically) to describe.

Confining oneself to the ideas of "Is Semantics Possible?," but departing a little from his mode of exposition there, one can put the positive proposal Putnam wanted to advance as follows: where the instructor's grasp of extension is authoritative (or is downstream from an authoritative identification of that extension), an instructor could initiate a learner into the meaning of the word "lemon" as follows:

> This is a lemon. (Here the instructor displays a specimen.) A thing is a lemon if it resembles this (the specimen) or this (another displayed specimen) or this (a third specimen) in the relevant way. I say *the relevant way*. But to understand better what that way is you must enquire, just to the extent necessary for your purposes, into the nature of these three things that I am showing you.

The philosophical claim is that (however artificially) such a demonstration or ostension reconstructs the ordinary teaching and learning of thing-kind words. It reconstructs the transactions that take place between those who know and those who do not know what a given substantive means.

I suspect that it is hard for those who have been introduced to philosophy by those who have understood the point of such a proposal to appreciate the novelty it enjoyed when Putnam introduced it. But, before I say any more of this novelty or touch upon the tractability of the doctrine to the theory of sense and reference or its affinity to certain rationalist ideas, three points need to be registered.

First, the doctrine, which is sometimes loosely called "the indexical theory", does not, on a true understanding, imply any close similarity between natural-kind substantives and indexicals or demonstratives. If "lemon" or "tiger" or "water" had any real resemblance to "this" or "that" or "now" or "today," these substantives might in other contexts, and without change of lexical meaning, pick out other kinds of thing than the kinds that we denominate lemons, tigers, or water. But the point of the theory is to attach the meaning of these words to the real natures, more or less well known, of the actual lemons, tigers, and water that we have encountered. Therefore we must not compare "water" to a demonstrative. The theory is a deictic theory in just one sense: it is the theory of the *deixis* by which we can, under special and favorable conditions, attach a word to a kind of thing.

Secondly, the doctrine does not extend to all thing-kind words. Occasionally, in later papers, Putnam was tempted to apply it to substantives like "pencil." But that was a pity, indeed threatened the shipwreck of a good idea. "Pencil" denominates a functional or instrumental kind.[5] Such a kind might well be defined (even in the strict, old-fashioned acceptation of "define"); and this is just as well, because almost the only nomological generalization one will discover by investigation of the class of pencils is the undependable generalization that one can write or draw with a pencil. There is little or no resemblance here to the case where the ostension of a natural kind invites us to extrapolate freely across the observed properties of its exemplars in the search for interesting generalizations about its nature.

This point leads to a third, which might itself have been the occasion for a whole paper, but is not the occasion for the whole of this chapter. In this area there are problems of the underdetermination of meaning by *deixis* and problems of the proper repesentativeness of specimens (problems analogous to those that Goodman in *The Structure of Appearance* called "constant companionship" and "imperfect community"). Room must be made within the theory of this demonstrative practice for an instructor to make his or her pupil (1) understand whether it is a species that is being indicated or a subspecies/variety – is it rose or *Rosa rugosa?* – or (2) understand that something specific, not something generic is to be identified – tiger (say) not *Felis.*[6] Ostension had better not be the magical solution to the problem of natural kind predicates. (I shall return to this point below.)

So much in outline for the new theory of natural kind words. Now one might ask why it was so difficult for our sort of philosophy to arrive at this deictic or extension-involving conception of their meaning? And how indeed was the barrier (whatever it was) ever surmounted?

I shall leave it to Hilary Putnam to answer the second question – unless modesty forbids. But about the first, there is at least one thing that cries out to be said. This thing is very obvious, but, since it occurred to me altogether afresh when I was reading a review in *Mind and Language* (1990, 5, 3) of the book *Representations and Reality* – which is Putnam's recent critique of many philosophical positions, not least of functionalism – I shall yield to the temptation to begin there.

After expanding Putnam's deictic theory in his own way, the reviewer writes:

> But why should water beliefs, so understood, pose a problem for the functionalist? He will not be able to capture the content of such beliefs by alluding to their characteristic causal connections with experience alone. Rather, the important connections will be those between the current water thought, a past demonstrative thought about certain samples then in front of the subject, and the theoretical belief that such substances fall under some fundamental classification which may be revealed by investigating the causal properties of those substances. It is these connections which will ensure that the thought is indeed about water and they are part of that thought's causal role.

I read that once and, with "water beliefs" and "current water thoughts" and the ambiguity of the latter, something stirred in memory. I read the passage again and I got the thing I was searching for. It was J.L. Austin's memorable footnote, "There will not be books in the running brooks until the dawn of hydrosemantics."[7] I am sure I am too easily amused. But now that (for "water" at least) we have got ourselves a hydrosemantics – now that the running brooks are in the books[8] (even if not yet vice versa) – it is time to consider the question why in the 1950s and well into the 1960s it seemed so irresistibly comical to contemplate the very idea of hydrosemantics. What was so unthinkable in the idea of a hydrosemantics even for "hydor" ("water")? Answer: this was unthinkable because, even though everyone knew that Quine had exposed a grave circularity in all extant attempts to explain from a standing start the analytic – synthetic distinction, that did not seem to matter very much. It did not matter because analytic philosophers thought they could still reach principled consensus on what was analytic. So what real reason was there to question the separation of language from the world, to let the brooks into books, or even to let water itself into the semantics of "water"? What reason was there to modify the idea that philosophy consisted in analysis? Analysis and the search for non-circular necessary and sufficient conditions could continue.[9]

By attacking the very idea of analyticity (a supposedly salutary exaggeration), the Quinean onslaught had overextended itself and miscarried. The point about Putnam's "Is Semantics Possible?" is that it was part of the more modest, and far more effective, second onslaught on the idea of analyticity. This second attack is not targeted on the existence of definable single criterion concepts, *vixen* (=*female fox*), *oculist* (=*eye-doctor*). Nor is it an attack on the analyticity of "a vixen is a female fox," "an oculist is an eye-doctor." What it is targeted upon is the attempt to *generalize* from those (however undeniable) small successes. "A theory which correctly describes the behaviour of perhaps three hundred words has been asserted to correctly describe the behaviour of tens of thousands of general names" (Putnam, "Is Semantics Possible?," *Philosophical Papers*, vol. 2, p.141) In other words, what obstructed the discovery (or rediscovery, as I claim) of the necessity for a deictic view of natural kind names was the failure of our philosophical community at large to think right through to the end all the problems and limitations of the analytic–synthetic distinction. It is no accident that Putnam, who had spent as long as anyone in re-examining the distinction, should have been the rediscoverer (or co-rediscoverer with Kripke) of the deictic view of natural kind words. What is astonishing, if anything is, is that these things have still not been thought through,[10] have still not impinged as they should on the practice of philosophy, and that philosophers of science (either of Carnap's and Reichenbach's generations or even of later generations) have not been at the forefront of this enterprise.

I believe that the explanation of all this has something to do with the self-declared nature of empiricism. But I find the point hard to pin down, and it is now time for me to go on to redeem my promise to show how the extension-involvingness of natural kind words will cohere with the theory of sense and reference.

On 24 May 1891, Frege wrote Husserl a letter about the sense and reference of predicates, and he included in it an instructive and remarkable diagram (see figure 8.1). Let me first gloss this diagram in familiar ways. Then, after proposing a small repair to Fregean doctrine under the third column, let me try to show how neatly the deictic proposal can be assimilated within the scheme.

About column 1, let us simply remark that grasping the sense of a sentence is a matter of grasping under what conditions it attains to the true. In preference to saying that, in the strict sense of "designate" or "refer," the true is the reference or designation of a sentence, let us say that the true is the semantic value – Dummett's term – of the sentence. (Let us think of reference itself as a special case of semantic value.)

Now column 2. Here let us bear in mind that, strictly and literally interpreted, the claim that "sense determines reference" is compatible with the denial of the *priority* of either.

Because it is rarely quoted, let me start by recalling to you Frege's remark, in *Ausführungen uber Sinn und Bedeutung*, about the fictional names

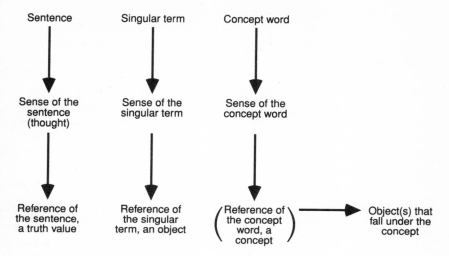

Figure 8.1

"Nausicaa" and "moly." In so far as "Nausicaa" is allowed any sense, Frege says its literary signification depends upon its behaving *as if* (*als ob*) it designated some girl. (Similarly, the kind name "moly" gets what sense it has by behaving as if it designated a particular herb, namely the herb that in *Odyssey*, Book X, Hermes gives to Odysseus in preparation for his encounter with Circe. The name is still there, ready and waiting for any pharmaceutical product with similar or comparable apotropaic powers.) Now this is the case of fiction. But implicit in the claim about about fiction is a simpler claim about the case of fact. The simpler claim is that in the non-fictional case a name has a sense by behaving as if it has – or simply by having – a reference. A name has its sense, then, by somehow presenting its object. To grasp the sense of a name is to know (in the manner correlative with the mode of presentation that corresponds to this somehow) which object the name is assigned to.

To speak as Frege does of sense as "mode of presentation" suggests then nothing less than this: there is an object that the name presents and there is a way in which the name presents it, or a conception, as I shall say, of that object. A conception of an object is an account of how things are, a body of information (not necessarily correct in every particular), in which the object itself plays some distinct role.[11] Note, however, that such a conception or body of information will normally be open-ended, imperfect and corrigible. Only rarely (if ever) could it be condensed into a completed description of the object. But why should one ever have expected that there would be any description of x that is synonymous with a given name of x? What it is reasonable to expect is only this: that the particular body of information about x to which the sense of some particular name of x is keyed will generate various different descriptions of x that might serve in a suitable context to identify x.

Properly possessed then, the conception of an object x that sustains the sense of a name that is keyed to that conception is a way of thinking about x that fixes (with the help of the world, the world being what helps create the conception) which object the object in question is. Which object the object is is precisely what is mastered by him or her who comes to understand the name with the sense corresponding to that conception.

Now perhaps we can effect the transition to Frege's third column. Just as grasping the sense of a name or singular term and its contribution to truth-conditions is grasping the particular conception of that object corresponding to the name's mode of presentation of what it stands for, and just as we give the term's sense by saying in a manner congruent with that conception what the term stands for, so grasping the sense of the predicate and its contribution to truth-conditions consists in grasping the predicate's mode of presentation of the concept it stands for, and we give the predicate's sense by saying what concept it stands for. And just as in the case of a singular term we show this sense in preference to that sense by exploiting one mode of presentation rather than another to say which object this is – drawing upon one body of information in preference to another in filling out our identification of the object – so similarly, in the case of a predicate, we show this sense in preference to that, e.g. the sense of "horse" rather than the sense of (say) "*Equus caballus*," by exploiting one mode of presentation rather than another to say which concept this is. We prefer (say) the body of information one might expound by saying "A horse is a certain animal with a flowing mane and tail; its voice is a neigh; and in the domestic state it is used as a beast of burden and draught, and for riding upon" over the body of information that identifies such creatures by classifying them as perissodactyl quadrupeds, locates their species among the genus *Equus* and the family *Equidae*, and then dwells on other zoological features.

With this suggestion – entailing that there can be different accounts of one and the same thing, the Fregean concept *horse* or *Equus Caballus* – I can look forward to a possible conclusion about stereotypes, namely this: that Putnam's stereotypes approximate to those special conceptions that correspond to the various senses of the various expressions that stand for natural kinds; that stereotypes are particular special ways of thinking in identificatory fashion about such kinds and their specimens. That will indeed be my proposal, but there are confusions to be avoided here, and there is a departure from Putnam. We must hasten more slowly.

To avoid confusion, we must take care to present Frege's theory in column 3 as perfectly general with respect to all predicates and *then* say what is so special about natural kind words among predicates. It will also be necessary to indicate at some point what sort of thing Fregean concepts are. Thirdly, conceptions of a horse being in this picture conceptions *of* the concept horse (i.e. conceptions of what it is for something to be a horse), we must be as clear as possible about the difference between a conception, something that goes with sense, and a concept, which is something on the level of reference – lest we fall into the old error of confusing sense and reference.

So let us return to the analogy between names in general and predicates in general, that is between columns two and three. If we take the analogy in the manner proposed, then it makes good sense of Frege's insistence, in the letter to Husserl and elsewhere, that the reference of a predicate cannot be any object or objects that it is true of. Just as singular terms without reference are unfitted to figure in the expression of a judgement possessed of a significance that enables us to move forward, as we must, to a truth-value, and just as a name capable of figuring in the expression of a judgement that can constitute knowledge must have reference, so must any predicate that aspires to this status. But many predicates essential to the expression of good information do not have anything they are true of. Therefore their Fregean reference is not any object they are true of. Thus, as Frege says in the letter cited,

> With a concept word, it takes one more step to reach the object than it does with a proper name, and this last step may be missing – i.e. the concept may be empty – without the concept words ceasing to be scientifically useful. I have drawn the last step, from concept to object, horizontally in order to indicate that it takes place on the same level, that objects and concepts have the same objectivity. In literary use it is sufficient if everything has sense; in scientific use there must also be *Bedeutungen*.

So on this account of things, the claim that a predicate has a concept as its reference does not bring out what is distinctive of natural kind terms or of Putnam's proposal concerning them. "Round square" has a reference, "blue" has a reference, "pencil" has a reference. You come to know this reference, which is nothing other than the concept, by coming to know what it would take (whether that be possible or impossible) for a thing to be a round square, blue, or pencil. And now, as one special case of this, there are terms, such as "lemon" or "tiger," where to grasp what it would take for something to be a lemon or a tiger or whatever it is, you need exposure to the extension of the term. In this case – if the argument of "Is Semantics Possible?" were correct – there is no grasping the reference or concept otherwise than through the extension. Here (at least) we cannot have reached the understanding that we do have by coming to grasp a strict lexical definition. For there is no strict lexical definition. So whereas the reality-involvingness of proper names amounts to their being reference-involving, the reality-involvingness of natural kind terms amounts to their being *extension*-involving. The schema itself of sense and reference neither demands that idea about extension nor excludes it, but it accommodates it.

On this account, we could say that he or she who understands "horse" and knows what Victor and Arkle both are, viz. horses, grasps a general rule for accepting or rejecting the sentence "*x* is a horse" according as it collects or fails to collect for arbitrary item *x* the verdict true. And, equally we could say that he or she who knows what Victor or Arkle are has got a grasp of the concept *horse*. These two accounts of the concept come to the same thing.[12]

At this point I suppose I must digress for a moment to say one word about one well-known and entirely general difficulty in Frege's scheme, a difficulty which has nothing to do with extension-involvingness, namely Frege's supposed need to deny that concept horse is a concept. If the view I take of these things is right, then the reference of horse is indeed something predicative but only in the following restricted sense. The term "horse" can be combined with the copula and article to give the predicative phrase "is a horse." The phrase "is a horse" is, in Frege's terminology, an unsaturated expression. If you wish, you can assign the phrase a semantic value. But to say that is not to say that that phrase has a reference. The predicative phrase is not what has the reference: "horse" is what has the reference. In other words, the way back to the truth that the concept horse is a concept is to take the copula seriously and distinguish "horse" from "is a horse." If I say that there is something that Victor and Arkle both are, then the thing they both are is *horse*, not *is-a-horse*. What we quantify over is concepts. But a concept is the sort of thing which we can connect to a subject of discourse by the copula. The concept has a predicative role, i.e. a role in predication, but it is complete in itself, not unsaturated.[13]

There is more to say on this subject, as there is on the analogy that Frege wanted to see between predicates and functions, but the time has come to sum up and move on to the next stage, which is to show how easily the deictic theory can be placed at column 3 within the framework of Fregean semantics.

In the case where we can only explain what is the reference of a predicate by something like the method that Putnam describes, because no strict analytical definition exists or could exist, what we who know the sense have to recapitulate for someone else who does not know the sense of a given substantive is that which we have ourselves learned by commerce in the world at large with the objects that satisfy, fall under or exemplify the concept. In practice, and so in the theory of this practice, any specification of such a concept will have to depend directly or indirectly on exemplars. That is Putnam's point. But surely the exemplars themselves cannot be given by bare unfocused presentation, unsupported by collateral explanation (cf. above). No presentation, one might say, without focus, and no focus without elucidation. When we fix the sense of an expression with a predicative role by giving its reference and give its reference by showing to or alluding to exemplars, what we need to impart to one who would learn the sense is both factual information *and* a practical capacity to recognize things of a certain kind, the information sustaining and regulating the recognition and the recognition making possible the correction and amplification of the information that first sustained the recognition. What we need to impart, we might say, is an identificatory or recognitional conception. It is this that corresponds to the sense of a natural kind term. The sense of such a term must correspond, then, to a recognitional conception that is unspecifiable except as the conception of things like this, that, and the other specimens exemplifying the concept that this conception is a conception of.

At this point it may be said that what I have just claimed is not the same as what Putnam claimed. I shall attend to that in a moment. But there will be a more basic disquiet, at the fact that, if you follow my suggestion about accommodating the doctrine of extension-involvingness, then you will find yourself saying: "That which supports the sense of the substantive 'horse' is a certain identificatory conception of the concept '*horse.*' Is this not an intolerable convergence in terminology?" I shall attend to the first of these worries in the course of allaying the second.

The convergence of "conception" and "concept" is ugly perhaps, but it does not signify any confusion. It is clear what the terms "conception" and "concept" mean here and clear what they have to do, namely quite different work. Not only that: it is perfectly possible to replace the term "conception." There are at least three ways of doing this, each of them illuminating in its own way.

In the first place we can replace the term "conception" by an expression of Evans's and we can say instead that there are two ways of thinking about the concept horse or about horses. Either one can think about what Victor is as a familiar domestic animal (as a beast of burden or mount) or one can think of what Victor is as a perissodactyl quadruped belonging to the genus *Equus* and the family Equidae. These are two different ways of thinking of one and the same concept.[14]

The second possibility is surely – is it not? – to replace the word "conception" by Putnam's word "stereotype". Or should this be doubted?

At the beginning of his article "Is Semantics Possible?," Putnam introduced the deictic theory by saying that in order to impart the meaning of a
thing-kind word one has to impart certain central facts, the stereotype, and
the extension. But what did Putnam mean by stereotypes? And what did
he think was the relation of stereotypes and extension? When Putnam spoke
of the stereotypes that support our normal understanding of the meaning
of thing-kind words, he may sometimes have been thinking of the little
engravings one sometimes finds in dictionaries like Larousse. (Indeed such
engravings are full of theoretical interest in these connections. They are
deictic reminders.) Normally, however, what Putnam means by a stereotype is a fund of ordinary information or a collection of idealized beliefs that
one needs to grasp in order to get hold of the meaning of a thing-kind word.
So a stereotype is rather like what you find – or one proper part of what
you find – in the text of a good dictionary or encyclopedia (which is not, of
course, to say that it resembles an analytical definition).

What, then, must the relation be between the stereotype and the extension? Putnam himself was insistent that the core facts that determine the
meaning of thing-kind word were two perfectly separate kinds of fact, as if
the stereotype could be explained or specified in a manner entirely independent of the question of its extension. The extension was the special
province of experts and could be quite dark to possessors of the stereotype.
But I find something strange in this separation. Of course the stereotype
is different from the extension, but this is not to say that the first can be
explained without allusion to the second. To defend his own way of separ-
ating stereotype and extension Putnam himself claimed that he possessed
the stereotype of elm and the stereotype of beech but did not know the
difference between an elm and a beech.[15] Reports have it that he has studi-
ously defended this ignorance over twenty years in order to defend his
opinion that one can understand a word by grasping the stereotype without
having a grasp of the extension. Nevertheless, if Putnam is as vague as he
says he is about the difference between an elm and beech, then I think one
has a good right to doubt the degree of his comprehension of these words.
If he entirely lacks the capacity to tell elms and beeches and to distinguish
them, then there is something that he is missing. To insist that this thing he
is missing is nothing *semantic* would become an upholder of the separation
of language from the world or of the full analytic–synthetic distinction. But
these are the distinctions Putnam's own work has done so much to dis-
credit. Would it not be better to say that the stereotype is the stereotype of
this or that concept and that grasping the stereotype represents the beginning of an identificatory capacity, a capacity that the expert manifests more
completely than the non-expert? In the case of the non-expert the capacity
can be rudimentary, but surely it is identificatory. It is a capacity which
could *advance* to the point where it became the capacity of an expert.

There is a third way to avoid saying that the conception which supports the sense of the word "horse" is a conception of the concept horse. This is to redraft one's description of the whole situation in terms inspired by Leibniz's theory of clear and distinct ideas. The thing we most badly need here is what Leibniz called a clear but confused (i.e. non-distinct) idea.

In Leibniz's account of ordinary human knowledge, a clear idea of horse is not an image or a likeness of horse. It is that by the possession of which I recognize a horse when I encounter one. (What clarity in an idea contrasts with is not confusedness or non-distinctness, but obscurity.) A clear idea of horse is confused or non-distinct if, even though I can recognize a horse when I encounter one, I cannot enumerate one by one the marks which are sufficient to distinguish that kind of thing from another kind of thing. My understanding is simply practical and deictic. What I possess here I possess simply by having been brought into the presence of the thing. ("Being brought into the presence of a thing" translates Leibniz's own words.)[16] Our idea of horse will begin to become *distinct* as we learn to enumerate the marks that flow from the nature of a horse and that distinguish a horse from other creatures.

What Leibniz shows us how to describe here is nothing less than the process by which clear but indistinct knowledge of one and the same concept begins life anchored by a stereotype to examples that are grouped together by virtue of resemblances that are nomologically grounded. But then this knowledge gradually unfolds the concept in a succession of different and improving ideas (or conceptions – as we might have said). Rather than tell again the old Lockean story of nominal and real essence and face again the question what makes them essences of the same thing, we can now describe the process by which a clear indistinct idea becomes a clear distinct idea, then a clear adequate idea.[17]

Which brings me to my last remark. When we reconstruct the first stages of the process, from the moment where there is ground to credit language-users with possession of a stereotype for horse, to credit them with possession of a stereotype of the very same thing as we have a better and more informative stereotype for, and when we reflect that at that stage there could scarcely have *been* any experts, we may think that, strictly speaking, what Putnam should have stressed was not the necessity of experts but the necessity of the possibility of experts.

Notes

1   See for instance the recent exposition that he gives in *Representation and Reality*. Cambridge, MA: MIT Press.

2 Eventually this paper was published in M. Munitz and H. Kiefer (eds) (1970), *Language, Belief and Metaphysics*. Albany: SUNY Press, and in (1970), *Metaphilosophy*, 3.

3 See G.E.M. Anscombe (1959), *Introduction to Wittgenstein's Tractatus*. London: Hutchinson, pp. 41, 42, 44, Michael Dummett (1958–9), "Truth," *Proceedings of the Aristotelian Society*, XXIV, 141–62.

4 If you doubt that, well read the reply to Putnam in the Brockport volume (or ask me for my recollections of the strange experience of trying to expound Putnam's theory to an incredulous audience at a meeting of the British Association for the Philosophy of Science in the early seventies).

5 In discussion, Hilary Putnam reminded me that at this point he had been reporting a discussion with Rogers Albritton, in which they had been envisaging circumstances under which it was found that all extant pencils had a certain microstructure. But *all* pencils, however manufactured and for whatever specialized purpose? This would be magic. Or (more likely) there would have to have been a practical joker somewhere in this story.

6 These problems are more tractable than the problems they superficially resemble and that were thrown up by the resemblance (or no-universals) theory of universals defended by Russell and H.H. Price. They are more tractable because here *deixis* can be supported by context and by verbal explanations that are unconstrained by special requirements of ontological parsimony. See the explanations envisaged below.

7 Dummett (1958–9), p. 21.

8 For a closer approximation to the (natural meaning) hydrosemantics the exiled Duke must really have had in mind at *As You Like It* II.i 12, cf. Paul Valéry's celebration of the Source Perrier.

9 Indeed it still continues, to judge by the aims and ambitions that are prescribed by most of the participants in the group effort to solve fox x – if necessary by brute force – in the equation: (knowledge) = (belief + x).

10 Not anticipating that Kripke would be charged with violating some supposed distinction between metaphysics and the philosophy of language, and falsely supposing that, after Kripke's excellent observations on the differences between the statuses of necessity, analyticity and *a priori*, all these things would inevitably be thought through to the end, I rashly elected in (1980), *Sameness and Substance*, Oxford: Basil Blackwell, to call certain truths, truths that rest on what things (objects or kinds) both individuatively are and cannot help but be, conceptual truths. I little thought that my "conceptual" would be read as an evasive synonym of "analytic," or that I would be seen as seeking to save some of the most implausible theses of linguistic philosophy. Why *should* a concept, why should what a thing or kind essentially is, be something that arises on the language side of a barrier that keeps the world from flowing into the word? I had expressly denied in the same book that language was protected by such an exclusion zone.

11 See John McDowell (1977), "On the Sense and Reference of a Proper Name," *Kind*, 86, 59–85; David Wiggins (1976), "Frege's Problem of the Morning Star and the Evening Star," in M. Schirn (ed.), *Studies on Frege*, II, *Logic and Philosophy of Language*. Bad Canstatt: Friedrich Frommann Verlag.

12 What then does it turn on whether concept C_1 is or is not the same as concept C_2 The question is difficult, but it does not represent a difficulty one brings on to oneself by talking of concepts. Concepts are not philosophical artifacts. They are general things we are committed to thinking about when we quantify over what predicates stand for. Once we see this, we shall not rush to offer any perfectly general answer, along the lines of Axiom V of Frege's *Grundgesetze*, or some modalization of this. For some important contributions to a piecemeal treatment of the problem, see Hilary Putnam (1975), "On Properties," *Philosophical Papers*, Cambidge: Cambridge University Press, vol. 1.

13 For the semantics of the copula and other aspects of the difficulties that Frege encountered with the concept *horse*, see David Wiggins (1984), "The Sense and Reference of Predicates: A Plea for the Copula," *Philosophical Quarterly*, 34, 311–28.

14 See Gareth Evans (1982), *The Varieties of Reference*, ed. J. McDowell, Oxford: Clarendon Press, ch. 1 .

15 See "The Meaning of 'Meaning' " in Putnam (1975), vol. 2.

16 See "Meditationes de Cognitione, Veritate et Deis" (Gerhardt IV), p. 422; *Discourse on Metaphysics* (ibid. §24–5); *New Essays*, pp. 254–6.

17 But only in a sense of "adequate" that must (I hold) be purged of certain other Leibnizian preoccupations, e.g. the idea that, at the limit, as human knowledge approximates to God's knowledge, a posteriori knowledge will be able to be replaced by a priori demonstrations.

   More generally, and against the idea that extension-involvingness itself only reflects a stage in the development of scientific understanding, see *Sameness and Substance* pp. 210–13.

9 On Putnam's Proof that We Are Not Brains in a Vat

Crispin Wright

In the *Meditations* Descartes made skeptical play first with dreaming and then, more radically, with the idea that all conscious mental activity might be the creature of the notorious Demon. It is usually supposed that philosophy in this century has merely changed the example when its discussions proceed in terms of the nightmare of brain-in-a-vathood. Here is how Hilary Putnam describes the nightmare in *Reason, Truth and History*:

> Imagine that [you] have been subjected to an operation by an evil scientist. Your brain has been removed from your body and placed in a vat of nutrients which keep [it] alive. The nerve-endings have been connected to a super-scientific computer which causes [you] to have the illusion that everything is perfectly normal. There seem to be people, objects, the sky, etc.; but really all [you] are experiencing is the result of electronic impulses travelling from the computer to the nerve-endings. The computer is so clever that if [you] try to raise your hand, the feedback from the computer will cause [you] to "see" and "feel" the hand being raised. Moreover, by varying the program, the evil scientist can cause [you] to "experience" (or hallucinate) any situation or environment the evil scientist wishes. He can also obliterate the memory of the brain operation, so that [you] will seem to yourself to always have been in this environment. It can even seem to [you] that you are sitting and [hearing] these very words about the amusing but quite absurd supposition that there is an evil scientist who removes people's brains from their bodies and places them in a vat of nutrients.

However, Putnam goes on to modify and embellish the story in a couple of respects. The predicament is generalized, and the Evil Scientist drops out. He writes:

Instead of having just one brain-in-a-vat, we can imagine that all human beings (perhaps all sentient beings) are brains-in-a-vat . . . Of course, the evil scientist would have to be outside – or would he? Perhaps there is no evil scientist, perhaps (though this is absurd) the universe just happens to consist of automatic machinery tending a vat full of brains and nervous systems . . . Let us suppose that the automatic machinery is programmed to give us all a *collective* hallucination, rather than a number of separate unrelated hallucinations. Thus, when I seem to myself to be talking to you, you seem to yourself to be hearing my words. Of course it is not the case that my words actually reach your ears – so you don't have (real) ears, nor do I have a real mouth and tongue. Rather, when I produce my words, what happens is that the efferent impulses travel from my brain to the computer, which both causes me to "hear" my own voice uttering those words and "feel" my tongue moving, etc., and causes you to "hear" my words, "see" me speaking, etc. In this case we are, in a sense, actually in communication. I am not mistaken about your real existence (only about the existence of your body and the "external world," apart from brains). From a certain point of view, it doesn't even matter that the "whole world" is collective hallucination; for you do, after all, really hear my words when I speak to you, even if the mechanism isn't what we suppose it to be.[1]

Why the changes? There is a superficial advantage. The standard version of the story, which features the Evil Scientist and the brain operation, has the victim effectively incommunicado. In Putnam's version, by contrast, the existence of a *plurality of* communicative minds is not, at least prima facie, called into question. So we are free to discuss the issues arising without any existential absurdity, or so it seems. But of course the real significance of Putnam's modifications goes deeper – in fact, there are a number of ways in which they matter, which will emerge in due course.

The usual philosophical purpose of such a fantasy is to raise philosophical questions concerning the status of our beliefs about the material world. We strongly believe that we are in no such predicament as vathood. But how, unless we can back that belief up with hard evidence, is it anything more than a prejudice? And how, in that case, is any more flattering a verdict to be delivered on the ramified system of specific beliefs about the material world which we actually hold?

For much of what follows, I shall proceed as if the discussion in *Reason, Truth and History* is best received as addressed to the skeptical problem which such fantasies raise. However, I think that that is, ultimately, a mistaken interpretation. Putnam's real project is, as so often, to embarrass the metaphysical realist. But the achievement of his discussion in that direction will be easier to appraise after we have reviewed it in the context of epistemological skepticism.

How exactly do such fantasies wreak *general* skeptical damage? The answer might seem obvious. In intention at least, the fantasy will be so constructed as to be beyond defeat by any possible evidence. If it follows from its indefeasibility that I cannot reasonably be assured that the fantasy is false, then neither can I reasonably be assured that my relationship to the external world is not, in the way depicted, radically otherwise than I normally take it to be. And that, presumably, undercuts my right to assurance in all the great multiplicity of propositions which belong with the more congenial picture of the world, and of my interaction with it, which I actually hold.

But this rather loose train of thought misses an important distinction. The standard brain-in-a-vat fantasy is, whereas Putnam's is not, consistent with the *truth* of most of my beliefs about the material world. It may be that the purposes of the Evil Scientist do not require him to be a deceiver, and that most of the information I am fed is genuine. By contrast, Putnam's version of a world wholly constituted by a group of brains in a vat and the attendant automatic machinery is already inconsistent with almost everything I actually believe about the physical universe. This discloses a more substantial consequence of Putnam's modifications to the standard story: an explicit skeptical argument built upon Putnam's version can be significantly simpler. Let R express the epistemic notion – knowledge, warranted belief, or whatever – which the skeptical argument challenges. Then its first claim will be to the effect that

   Not R not [BIV],

i.e. that there is no knowing, or warrantedly believing, etc. that one is not a brain in a vat. But reflect that if R is transmissible across entailment, so will "not R not" be. So given transmissibility, it follows that if the above claim is true, so is

   not R not [P],

for any proposition, P, entailed by – so whose negation is inconsistent with – the original fantasy. If the fantasy is Putnam's, the negations of almost all my beliefs about the external world will thus be appropriate substituends for P, and it will follow directly that I cannot know, have warrant for, etc., any of those beliefs. If, on the other hand, the fantasy is the standard version, it is at least not possible so directly to conclude

   not R not [P]

for most substitutions for P of that kind. (Exceptions, of course, will be propositions concerning the physical condition and spatial deployment of my body.)

The difference, in other words, is this: a skeptical argument which works with Putnam's fantasy can directly transmit our (putative) lack of warranted assurance that the fantasy is false into a lack of warranted assurance that most of our ordinary beliefs about the material world are true. But no such direct transmission is possible if the argument works with the standard fantasy. Rather it will need to be argued in addition first that, even though their truth would be strictly consistent with the fantasy, my warrant for almost all my beliefs about the material world would still somehow be undermined by the truth of the fantasy; and, second, that, in order to be warranted in holding those beliefs, I require not merely that the fantasy be as a matter of fact false but some *assurance* that it is so. Argument for both points can be provided. But additional presuppositions have to be made. Putnam's version importantly simplifies the implicit presuppositions of the attendant skeptical paradox.[2]

As is familiar, Putnam argues that his version,

> although it violates no physical law, and is perfectly consistent with everything we have experienced, cannot possibly be true. *It cannot possibly be true*, because it is, in a certain way, self-defeating.[3]

The key to his argument is a simple comparison between the thought that I am a brain in a vat and the thought that I do not exist: viz. that a necessary condition of my ability to think either thought is that it be false. At times Putnam writes as though the comparison is driven by a causal *theory* of reference – a theory according to which the reference of an expression would actually be determined by the obtaining of a favored kind of causal relation between tokenings of it and the entity or kind of entity for which it stood. It is therefore important to realize, for anyone skeptical whether such a theory of reference could be correct, that none is strictly needed for Putnam's purpose. It will suffice if reference is merely, in appropriate cases, a *causally constrained* relation – that elephants, for instance, would not be the reference of "elephant," as standardly used in English, if there were not appropriate causal relations between real elephants and tokenings of the term. Allowing that this much causality is necessary for reference in relevant cases is quite consistent with repudiating any suggestion that references generally can be identified by their satisfaction of certain causal conditions (let alone that the concept of reference can be given a causal analysis).

The relatively conservative character of Putnam's appeal to causation is, of course, a strength of his discussion. The heart of his argument is summarized in the following passage:

> when the brain-in-a-vat (in the world where every sentient being is and always was a brain-in-a-vat) thinks "there is a tree in front of me" his thought

does not refer to actual trees. On some theories . . . it might refer to trees in the image, or to the electronic impulses that cause tree experiences, or to the features of the program that are responsible for those electronic impulses. These theories are not ruled out . . . [by the causal constraint] for there is a close causal connection between the use of the word "tree" in vat English and the presence of trees in the image, the presence of electronic impulses of a certain kind, and the presence of certain features of the machine's program . . .

By the same argument, "vat" refers to vats in the image in vat English or something related (electronic impulses or program features), but *certainly not to real vats* [my emphasis], since the use of "vat" in vat English has no [relevant] causal connection to real vats . . . Similarly, "nutrient fluid" refers to a liquid in the image in vat English, or something related (electronic impulses or program features). It follows that if [the brains'] "possible world" is really the actual one, and we are really the brains-in-a-vat, then what we now mean by "we are brains-in-a-vat" is that *we are brains-in-a-vat in the image* or something of that kind (if we mean anything at all). But part of the hypothesis that we are brains-in-a-vat is that we aren't brains-in-a-vat in the image (i.e. what we are "hallucinating" isn't that we are brains-in-a-vat). So, if we are brains-in-a-vat, then the sentence "we are brains-in-a-vat" says something false (if it says anything). In short if we are brains-in-a-vat then "we are brains-in-a-vat" is false. So it is (necessarily) false.[4]

The essential claim here is that tokenings of the expression "brain-in-a-vat" in the thought of an envatted thinker, working in a language – let us say: BIVese – lexically indistinguishable from English, would not sustain the right kind of relations to actual brains and vats to qualify as referring to brains in vats. Whatever, if anything, such tokenings did succeed in referring to, it would not be to brains in vats. But then, were we brains in vats, so Putnam's thought seems to be, the attempt to configure our true situation in thought would necessarily miss its mark – our thoughts would have as their truth-conditions, if they had any, some type of situation distinct from and incompatible with the real situation: our being brains in vats. So, Putnam concludes, the hypothesis is self-refuting, and necessarily false in consequence.

Putnam remarks that it took him a long time to convince himself that this exceedingly slippery train of thought is right. I have, myself, thought very different things about it at different times. It is only too easy, when one tries to make it fully explicit, to hit on formulations which invite good but inessential objections – objections to dispensable features imported by the particular formulation. I shall spend some time on one illustration of that. Eventually, I shall agree with Putnam that there is a sound argument in the vicinity, which, moreover, supports the advertised conclusion. But I do not think it is one which fits all of his advertisement for it. In particular, I do not think that there is any sound route to the conclusion that, in the way we would like, the nightmare is refuted.

I will begin with a formulation – due to Allan Gibbard[5] – which arises quite naturally out of the passage last quoted. Let us agree that the etiology of tokenings of "brain in a vat," as they might feature in the thought of an envatted thinker, would not involve brains and vats in such a way as to allow those tokenings to denote brains in vats. Suppose that they would denote instead — let us say – brains in vats*. Then it seems we may assert:

> (i)   If I were a BIV, then the sentence "I am a BIV," as thought by me, would be true iff I were a BIV*.

We do not know much about BIVs*, but we do at least know that they are not BIVs – since denoting a BIV* involves not denoting a BIV. It presumably follows that

> (ii) If I were a BIV, I would not be a BIV*.

Whence, pooling the consequents of (i) and (ii), we have that

> (iii) If I were a BIV, then the sentence "I am a BIV," as thought by me, would be false.

And now it appears to follow that I am not a BIV. For suppose I am. Then "I am a BIV," as thought by me, is false. (Presumably modus ponens is unexceptionable with subjunctive conditionals.) Whence, disquoting, I am not a BIV, contradicting the supposition.

There, then, is one way of portraying the advertised *reductio*. But is it cogent? There are three immediate doubts about its premises. The first concerns premise (ii). It does not follow from the fact that "brain in a vat" as used by a long-term envatted thinker would not denote brains in a vat that the reference which it would have – if any – would be to some kind of thing *exclusive* of brains in a vat. What obstacle is there to the idea that "brain in a vat" in BIVese would denote some more general determinable kind, of which brains in a vat would be a determinate instance? Specific causal theories of reference might, in tandem with the detail of Putnam's story, generate such an obstacle. But then the theoretical commitments of the argument are going to be that much greater – we lose the advantage of the very light play with causality I dwelt on above.

The second and third doubts both relate to premise (i). First, what sort of conditional is it? Subjunctive, of course. But not all subjunctive conditionals are counter-factuals. Imagine you and I are lost in the mist on Crinkle Crags. I peer at the map and say, "If we were here, then we would have passed the point where we should have turned to the east to remain on the main ridge." So far from intending a counter-factual, I say this precisely to float a disturbing possibility which we are unfortunately in no position to exclude. Call such a conditional an *open* subjunctive. Then it is likely to seem that, if the Gibbard version is not merely to beg the question, its premises should be open rather than counter-factual. After all, the argument, if sound, should have the power to move an agnostic to the conclusion that he or she is not a brain in a vat. It can hardly do that if premise (i) is presupposed to be a counter-factual from the outset and only supported as such. But what is the train of thought which supports it if not something like the following?

> If I were a BIV, the dominant causal sources of my uses of "brain," "vat," etc., would be different, and the term would consequently come to denote something – call it a BIV* – quite other than the denotation it actually has.

And in this the presumed counter-factual character of the thought is quite explicit.

The third doubt is that the premise as formulated assigns a reference to "BIV" as used by a brain in a vat. So it simply bypasses the possibility, which Putnam's own text was careful to register, that isomorphs of English words tokened in the psychological activity of an envatted consciousness might have no reference at all – that envatted "thought" would to some substantial extent – perhaps altogether – lack content.

It might be thought straightforward to remedy this. Rewrite premise (i) as

> (i)   *If I were a BIV, then the sentence "I am a BIV," as thought by me, would not be true,

and drop premise (ii). Then assume that I am a BIV and proceed via modus ponens and disquotation as before. But this, of course, would be subject to the first concern above, if BIVese were assumed contentful – BIVese "I am a BIV" would not say that I am a BIV, but a positive causal theory of reference would appear necessary to license the conclusion that it would say something untrue. If, on the other hand, it is taken that long-term envatted thought is not a possibility, then the disquotation at the end of the argument would be invalid. For then the case would be that being a BIV would divest one's uses of "I am a BIV" of content; and contentless expressions do not disquote.

The fourth concern about the Gibbard version corresponds to a basic and very commonly felt kind of difficulty with Putnam's argument, whatever the detail of one's preferred formulation. The worry is, roughly, that the argument shoots at an unstable target. Consider an analog. Let E express the supposition that the color predicates of English come to denote the diametrical opposites of their actual denotations in the circular color spectrum. Then we have

(i)   If it were the case that E, then the sentence "Grass is green" would be true iff grass was red.

But presumably merely changing the language would not change the color of grass; so

(ii)   If it were the case that E, grass would not be red.

It follows that

(iii)   If it were the case that E, then the sentence "Grass is green" would not be true.

Suppose you now learn that – perhaps by recent edict of government – E *is* actually the case. Then, by a parallel modus ponens step, "Grass is green" is not true; whence, disquoting, grass is not green – and changing the language *has* changed the color of grass!

The intuitive reservation runs something like this. Premise (i) enjoins that, were it the case that E, then the sentence "Grass is green" would have a different content. So the falsehood of that sentence, when we envisage learning that E is actually the case, cannot be taken to imply the falsehood of the proposition – viz. that grass is green – which it *actually* expresses. And so too with the Gibbard argument. When I suppose that I actually am a brain in a vat, the thought goes, I in effect hypothesize a change in the language in which the argument is expressed; and whatever the argument then succeeds in showing, it cannot be assumed to correspond to the originally intended conclusion.

As I say, an objection of this general kind is very common, though the details of its expression vary. Eventually, I shall sustain what is, I suppose, a descendant of it. For now, though, assuming that the Gibbard version is shown not to be persuasive by the foregoing, I wish merely to note a pair of emergent constraints on a better construal. We must avoid making any assumption that brains in a vat would have a language, or about its semantics; and we must avoid any play with subjunctive conditionals, especially all whose antecedents hypothesize, whether implicitly or explicitly, a state of affairs whose obtaining would contribute towards determining the semantics of the language in which the argument is being run.

What are the suppositions which really drive Putnam's train of thought? There seem to be essentially two. One is the thought that *this* language – the one which we are using to reflect on these matters – permits correct, homophonic characterization of the references, satisfaction-conditions, and truth-conditions of meaningful expressions within it; in short, that this language *disquotes*. The second is that the language, or simulacrum of a language, which would be operated by a brain in a vat could not contain any expression referring to brains in a vat. That suggests the following basic premises:

(i)   My language disquotes.
(ii) In BIVese, "brain in a vat" does not refer to brains in a vat.

And now we may apparently proceed very directly. Thus:

(iii) In my language, "brain in a vat" is a meaningful expression.
(iv)   In my language, "brain in a vat" refers to brains in a vat – from (i) and (iii).

Hence

(v)   My language is not BIVese – from (ii) and (iv).

But

(vi) If I am a brain in a vat, my language, if any, is BIVese – definition of BIVese.

So

(vii) I am not a brain in a vat. QED.

This looks solid. But but we need to negotiate two objections. The first concerns disquotation. Anthony Brueckner[6] canvasses a worry which, applied to the above formulation, would come to the thought that even the very modest degree of semantic externalism involved in supporting premise (ii) will cancel the authority of the subject with respect to the content of expressions in his or her language. If I do not, at least before the argument is completed, know whether I am a brain in a vat or not, then I do not know what if any kind of thing is so related to my tokenings of "brain in a vat" to qualify as its reference. So I do not know what "brain in a vat" refers to, and am in no position, as at line (iv), to identify it by disquotation.

The proper reply to this, it seems to me, is to allow that there may well be a kind of identifying knowledge of content which, if semantic externalism is true, we do not possess. But if so, such identification is not a precondition of intelligent disquotation. Suppose the envatted brains do think determinate thoughts – that the components in their thought-symbolism are so related to real items that they constitute BIVese as a genuine language, apt for the expression of truths and falsehoods. Then whatever that language is, it may presumably be correctly used in homophonic characterizations of reference and truth-conditions. Let it be that I do not know whether I am speaking English or BIVese; still I do know that, whatever "snow" refers to in my language, I may identify its reference by *using* that very word. Is that not enough to justify the disquotation?

I envisage the reply that, if that is as far as my knowledge goes, I am justified no further than in affirming merely that the instance of the disquotational scheme,

"Snow" refers to snow,

is a true *sentence* – that

" 'Snow' refers to snow" is true –

and that I am in no position to affirm *its* disquotation. But that is mere legislation. Consider a parallel with proper names. A subject's possession of identifying knowledge of the bearer of a name is no necessary condition for his or her legitimately using the name, or for others' ascribing to him or her thought-contents in whose specification they use the name. It is no solecism to say that a thinker knows that "the Scarlet Pimpernel" denotes the Scarlet Pimpernel, but has no identifying knowledge of the Scarlet Pimpernel – does not know who the Scarlet Pimpernel is. It ought, in parallel, to be no solecism to allow that I know that "Snow" refers to snow, even if, to whatever extent is enjoined by semantic externalism, I may not know *which* kind of stuff is snow or which thought the thought that "Snow" refers to snow is. In order comprehendingly to disquote the sentence, " 'Snow' refers to snow," I do not need, in any sense jeopardized by semantic externalism, to *identify* the thought that "Snow" refers to snow. It is enough if, courtesy of the appropriate external circumstances, I *have* that thought, on the appropriate cue.

A related point may be made concerning subjects' authority for their own thought-contents and the threat to it which semantic externalism has often, in recent literature, been thought to carry. Such authority does not depend on identification of the contents of one's attitudes, in whatever is the jeopardized sense. It is enough that my second-order beliefs – beliefs that I believe, or desire, or hope, etc., that P – be reliable: that it tends to be true that I believe, or desire, or hope, etc., that P just when I think that I do. And if that would be so but for semantic externalism, then it is quite unclear what difference semantic externalism could make. Unreliability would be a matter of *not* being disposed to believe that I believe, etc., that P just when in fact I do. But why should the consideration that the content of the belief that P is in part determined externally, by real-world relations which I may have no knowledge of, provide a reason for thinking that such a situation is more likely than it would be otherwise? Does the opposing thought not merely trade on overlooking that the content of my second-order beliefs will *likewise* be externally determined – that it will, as it were, covary with externally determined variation in the content of my first-order attitudes?

I suggest that there is no sound concern about the use made of disquotation in the argument, though there is much more to say about how externalism does impinge on self-knowledge. I will come back to the matter.

The second objection worries about the role of the first person in the argument. The thought seems compelling that, if the argument is valid, it ought to make no difference if its tokens of the first-personal pronoun and possessive are uniformly replaced by tokens of something which is for you, the assessor, a coreferring expression – say, "CW." But it does make a difference. Suppose you are given

(i)   CW's language disquotes.
(ii)   In BIVese, "brain in a vat" does not refer to brains in a vat.
(iii) In CW's language, "brain in a vat" is a meaningful expression.

The argument then proceeds:

(iv)   In CW's language, "brain in a vat" refers to brains in a vat – from (i) and (iii).

Hence

(v)   CW's language is not BIVese – from (ii) and (iv).

But

(vi)   If CW is a brain in a vat, CW's language, if any, is BIVese.

So

(vii)   CW is not a brain in a vat.

The glaring problem is line (iv). Without supplementary information, you cannot validly infer anything from (i) and (iii) about how to *specify* what is the reference of "brain in a vat," as used in CW's language. All you can infer is that a specification in CW's language would be homophonic. That is the same thing as (iv) only if it is presupposed that your language – the language in which the argument is presented – is CW's.

Suppose your language is not CW's – suppose in fact that CW is a brain in a vat, the scenario differing from Putnam's only in that the vat, the contained brains, and the attendant automatic machinery are situated in a vault in the British Museum. Then the falsity of the conclusion of the argument need pose no threat to the truth of its premises. Let it be that CW's language – BIVese, on the present supposition – does indeed disquote and contain "brain in a vat" as a meaningful phrase. You may then infer that some disquotational sentence in BIVese which mentions and uses "brain in a vat" is true. But, without further information, that is all you may infer. There is nothing to contradict premise (ii), that in BIVese, "brain in a vat" does not refer to brains in a vat. So the argument, when formulated non-first-personally, is invalid.

But we should reply that if *all* that faults it is its suppression of the premise that the language of its hero is the language in which it is formulated, then we ought to sustain the first-personal formulation. For is not one effect of running the argument in the first person just to ensure that this premise is true?

And that, it seems to me, is right. The first-personal formulation *is* valid. Moreover, there seems no good objection to its premises. Surely this language in which I am working does disquote; surely "brain in a vat" is one of its meaningful expressions; surely brains in a vat could not refer to brains in a vat, whether BIVese is a language or not. So does that not do it? What objection can there be to a valid argument whose premises are recognized as true?

Consider the third-personal version which adds the following additional initial premise:

(o)   The following argument is formulated in CW's language, which coincides with that of you, the assessor, in the meaning assigned to all the expressions involved save possibly that assigned to "brain in a vat" and "BIVese."

Armed with this information you are now in a position – assuming all expressions in the argument are used univocally – both to recognize that line (iv) is validly inferred from lines (i) and (iii), and that it is inconsistent with line (ii). Consequently you can recognize the argument as valid. What you are not able to do, if this is the limit of your information, is to ratify the argument as a valid derivation of the proposition that CW is not a brain in a vat, since nothing in the stated premises entitles you to a view about what the conclusion of the argument at line (vii) amounts to – it is, e.g. consistent with everything you know that "brain in a vat" in CW's language means: Frenchman, and "BIVese": French.

What the first-personal version adds to the third-personal version augmented by (o) is, of course, exactly a putative closure of this gap: it is as if the words "save possibly that assigned to 'brain in a vat' and 'BIVese'" had been deleted from (o). But now, even this strengthened premise would not significantly change matters if it so happened that "brain in a vat" was an expression of my language which I did not understand, or only imperfectly understood, or if there was some indeterminacy about its content. And this is the crux. Earlier I argued that semantic externalism should not be viewed as generating any difficulty for disquotation or for knowledge of the contents of one's own attitudes. But I left it open that there might be a *kind* of identifying knowledge of one's own thought-contents which, if semantic externalism is true, we do not after all possess. What, it seems to me, has driven those who have expended significant effort looking for invalid moves in the argument is a worry which is actually consistent with acknowledging both that the argument is valid and that its premises are, plausibly, correct. The worry is whether fully exorcizing the skeptical doubt which brain in a vat examples and other similar stories raise would not require precisely the kind of identifying knowledge of content which semantic externalism itself proscribes. If that is right, then no argument which, like Putnam's, presupposes that content is a function, at least in part, of external factors – of the real relations holding between elements in our thought and the external world – can ever succeed in dispelling the basic intuitive concern.

We need, then, to address two questions. Is there a kind of identifying knowledge of content which we might have wanted to claim but which is called in question even by the very modest degree of semantic externalism involved in Putnam's argument? And is it the case that finally putting the specter of brain-in-a-vathood to rest would demand this kind of knowledge? I think the answer to the first question is "yes"; the second matter is less straightforward, but eventually I shall suggest that, in a way, the specter survives to haunt us still.

It is part of the way we ordinarily think about self-consciousness that we regard the contents of a subject's contemporary propositional attitudes as something which, to use the standard term of art, he or she can *avow* –

something about which his or her judgements are credited with a strong, though defeasible, authority which does not rest on reasons or evidence. No doubt it would be disturbing if plausible forms of semantic externalism called this conception into question. But, so far as I can see, there is, for the reason alluded to earlier, no threat. The perceived threat derives from the consideration that a subject has no such special, non-inferential authority in relation to external affairs; nor therefore, in particular, in relation to external affairs that enter into the determination of the content of his or her attitudes. The response was that since the contents of his or her second-order attitudes are determined in tandem with those of his or her first-order attitudes, externalism opens up no new way in which his or her actual psychology might diverge from his or her self-conception; whatever determines the content of the belief that P will eo ipso determine what belief it is that a subject who credits himself or herself with the belief that P believes himself or herself to possess.

Granting this is consistent, however, with recognizing that a certain transparency of content *is* surrendered by externalism. And what this comes to is actually something perfectly definite. Externalism poses no threat to the *synchronic* identification of the contents of one's attitudes. But it does raise an issue about *diachronic* identification: specifically, about the identification of the contents of attitudes held in the past. For obviously, if what thought I express by tokening a sentence is in part determined by external factors of which I may be unaware, then I may also be unaware of sufficient of a change in those factors materially to affect what belief I express by a token of the same sentence on a subsequent occasion. So avowals of the form, "I used to believe that P," or "When I was a boy of six, I already believed that P," are opened by externalism to a new kind of defeasibility; sufficient external change of the right kind may defeat such a claim even when it is perfectly sincere and there is no question of a failing of memory.

Even so, it does not seem that much of shake-up is engendered in our ordinary idea of the non-inferential authority of a subject's self-conception.[7] The practice of granting authority to what a subject has to say about his or her former beliefs and desires can perfectly well rest on deep general contingencies – as so many of our practices do. Most people are good at recognizing faces; and such recognition typically takes place spontaneously, without conscious inference. Clearly it is only against a background in which the world is not replete with look-alikes that we can possess such a skill. But our ordinary practice takes that fact for granted. So too, our ordinary practice may be viewed as taking it for granted that in the ordinary run of things semantically relevant external factors are not prone to change in reference-altering ways, still less to unmonitored such change. A picture associated with the practice of treating subjects as authoritative about former thoughts – the picture, roughly, of the contents of the mind as a kind of object, penetrated to the essence in ordinary self-knowledge – this picture *is* a casualty of semantic externalism. But the reasonableness of the practice need not be impugned by the demise of the picture.

The answer to our first question, then, is that semantic externalism has no evident bearing on the authority with which we identify our thoughts; but that it has a conceivable – though in practice negligible – bearing on the authority with which we *re*identify them. The second question is accordingly: would a finally satisfactory exorcism of the specter of brain-in-a-vathood demand such reidentification of thoughts in a context in which its possibility is jeopardized?

It will help here to construct an example where a skeptical suggestion does resist exorcism by a Putnam-style argument for just this reason. Recall twin earth where all water-like stuff is XYZ but which otherwise resembles the earth as an identical twin. But change the example to ensure that any instantiation of a natural kind found on earth is matched by one of the same natural kind on twin earth, and conversely. What remains, then, is the duplication of objects and events. Suppose moreover that twin earth is not a counter-factual state of the earth but an actual planet somewhere, and that earth and twin earth are quite unique in the similarity they bear to each other. And now let me be smitten with the paranoid fantasy that, at some point in my life, I will be – from my point of view – undetectably transferred there, never again to see family and friends, etc. (it is a nice question why I should *mind*), and never to learn what has happened.

Perhaps I can reassure myself by a judicious appeal to semantic externalism. The fantasy involves that once on twin earth, I will remain long enough – say ten years – for the changed causation of my uses of the word "Edinburgh," e.g., to effect a shift in its reference. If my fears materialize, then at some point by "Edinburgh" I will no longer mean: Edinburgh. That suggests an argument of now familiar structure:

(i)   My language disquotes.
(ii) In the language – Twenglish – of those who have been sufficiently long on twin earth, "Edinburgh" does not refer to Edinburgh.
(iii) In my language, "Edinburgh" is a meaningful expression.
(iv) In my language, "Edinburgh" refers to Edinburgh – from (i) and (iii).

Hence

(v)   My language is not Twenglish – from (ii) and (iv).

But

(vi)   If I have spent the last ten years on twin earth, my language is Twenglish.

So

(vii)   I have not spent the last ten years on twin earth. QED.

The reasoning is valid, and its premises are true. And the putatively comforting reflection is not merely that I can run this argument now, to prove that so far all is well; but also that I will be able to dust the argument off and use it at any *future* time – so I know now that my fears will never be realized. My future on earth is seemingly assured on purely semantic grounds!

Obviously, this is ineffectual. It is ineffectual because an argument of just this form can be sound in the mouth of a Twenglish speaker. Reflect that, according to the modified twin-earth story above, the semantics of English and Twenglish do not diverge except in the references assigned to proper names and other singular terms. So the only words in premise (ii) whose meanings are liable to vary between English and Twenglish are "Twenglish" itself, "twin earth" and "Edinburgh." Now since the twin-earth story does not just concern objects but involves that all earthly events, including sociolinguistic events, have twin-earthly counterparts, it follows that whatever occurred on earth to confer reference on earthly uses of "twin earth" will have been matched by counterpart occurrences on twin earth conferring reference on twin-earthly uses of "twin earth." It is not perhaps absolutely forced that the latter will consequently refer to earth, but let us suppose that reference-fixing descriptions like "the only planet in the universe which is a perfect twin of the earth" have featured prominently in the sociology of the term on earth. In that case, premise (ii) will be true in the mouth of a Twenglish speaker, and uses of "Twenglish," "twin earth," and "Edinburgh" in Twenglish will refer to English, earth and twin-Edinburgh respectively. Plainly, in this case, I *will* indeed be able to run the argument from true premises at any future time; but this has no bearing whatever on the realizability of my fear.

We need not trouble over the exact formulation of the modest semantic externalism which drives the thought that the reference of my uses of "Edinburgh" would change in due course, were a transfer to twin earth to take place. It is enough that replacing an object which plays a certain kind of role in the causation of one's use of a name by another which proceeds to play the same kind of role is taken to suffice, under the right circumstances and in due course, for the latter to supplant the former as the referent. *Without* this externalism, the argument could not get off the ground, for there would be no case for premise (ii); it would be open to an objector to say, for instance, that, no matter how long I were to stay on twin earth after transfer, the reference of my uses of "the earth" would always remain to the earth. But *with* the externalism in place, and under the circumstances envisaged, I will be in no position to detect the changes in reference which occur as a result of transfer; so in no position to know whether, for instance, the satisfaction-conditions of "the only planet in the universe which is a perfect twin of the earth" have changed in tandem with the reference of "the earth." Using the argument against the paranoid fantasy requires that I be able to affirm that what I can now express by, e.g., "In fifteen years' time, I will not have spent the preceding ten years on twin earth" will share its truth-conditions with what I can affirm in fifteen years' time by "I have not spent the last ten years on twin earth." The argument entails that the latter will then be true. But, once I take the fear seriously, I must recognize that I will be in no position in fifteen years to reidentify the thought then expressed as essentially that expressed now by "In fifteen years' time, I will not have spent the preceding ten years on twin earth;" and indeed, that if my fear has been realized, the truth of the future thought will be no fulfillment of the present thought. In short: the externalism which drives premise (ii) also, in the circumstances of the example, hinders my identification now of the content of crucial claims made at future times; and the proof that those claims will be correct when made consequently gives me nothing I can use to allay my fears.

The question now is: does the proof that I am not a brain in a vat lose its significance in the light of this reflection? Clearly it *would* do so if used to assail the standard version of the fantasy, featuring the Evil Scientist and envatting surgery carried out when I am already linguistically mature. For in that case there is a *type* of thought – that which I express by the words, "I am not a brain in a vat," at points in my life at which I have not yet been envatted – on which I can target my attention and desire afterwards, even though I cannot then express thoughts of that type by the same form of words. I can target it, for instance, as: the type of thought I would have expressed by the words, "I am not a brain in a vat," when I was first old enough to understand them. *That* is the type of thought which I wish to be assured has no true instance; and it is, especially, the instance of that type apt to be rendered true or false by my present situation which I very much want to be true. But I cannot assure myself that it is so by running the proof that I am not a brain in a vat, since the externalism needed to sustain an analog of premise (ii) – without which the argument cannot proceed – will also compromise my ability, as soon as I take the nightmare seriously, to identify the thought which I want to be true as the conclusion of the argument: the thought that I am not a brain in a vat.

But of course it is different if we are concerned with Putnam's fantasy – another respect in which his changes matter. According to Putnam's version, we have *always* been envatted brains, tended by automatic machinery, in a universe where that is all there is. In order for the proof that I am not a brain in a vat to miss its intended mark in the fashion indicated, we have to be able somehow to fix our thought on the intended mark – the proposition which we want the proof to disprove but which, in consequence of the operative externalism, we cannot certify whenever we want that it does disprove. But how is this to be done? There is no change in my status in Putnam's scenario, so no relevant semantic change: reference to the type of thought I would have expressed by the words "I am not a brain in a vat" when I was first old enough to understand them will fix on nothing other than the type of proposition expressed by uses of "I am not a brain in a vat" at all times in my life.

The temptation may be to respond that there plainly are two possible types of thought to be considered: that which a normal human subject can establish by Putnam's proof and that which he or she could establish – prescinding from any worry about the possibility of envatted thought – were he a brain in a vat. And what we need is an assurance that it is a thought of the former type which we establish when we run the proof. But the temptation, though understandable, is confused. In order for the proof really to concern a thought of the latter, unwanted type, I have to suppose that I am really a brain in a vat as I run it. And that is a supposition which, according to the externalism governing the argument, I can make only if it is false. So there is all the assurance we could need!

"But surely a community of brains in a vat could work through just these thoughts, and so convince themselves quite spuriously that they were not brains in a vat?" No, they could not. Maybe they might work through these *words*, and soundly convince themselves of something. But only creatures which are not brains in a vat can have these *thoughts*.

Putnam's argument, I suggest, is thus a transcendental argument which works. The question is, how much does it prove, and about what?

First, on skepticism: say that a hypothesis H is *semantically auto–disruptive with respect to a language L* if and only if, were H true, some elements in the L-expression, S, of H would differ in meaning in such a way that S would no longer express H. " 'Green' means: red," for instance, is semantically auto–disruptive with respect to English. And now define H as *absolutely* semantically auto-disruptive – *absaud* – if and only if for *any* expression, S, of H, in whatever language, if H were true some elements in S would so differ in meaning that S would no longer express H.

Granted that, in order to entertain any particular hypothesis, some kind of recourse is necessary to a symbolic expression of it, it follows from the above characterization that the thinkability of any absaud hypothesis requires its falsehood – for if the hypothesis were true, no symbolism would express it. There are two corollaries: first, that any reason to suppose that such a hypothesis is understood is reason to suppose it false; second, in consequence, that no skeptical argument can reasonably be supposed cogent which satisfies both the following conditions:

(i)   What is in fact an absaud hypothesis is claimed by one of its premises to be beyond evidence for or against, and so beyond justified disbelief; but

(ii) Following the argument requires understanding that hypothesis.

For (ii), and the absaudity of the hypothesis, require that the argument can be followed only if the hypothesis is false; and reason to think the argument cogent obviously requires reason to think it can be followed. So reason to think the argument cogent requires reason to think the hypothesis false; that is, by (i), reason to think one of its premises is untrue; that is, reason to think it is not cogent.

In these terms, Putnam's essential point is very simple: it is that the hypothesis that I am a brain in a vat, in the context of the relevant type of externalism and the further detail which he supplies, is an absaudity. For thinking it requires the use of symbols tokenings of which are causally linked to actual items in ways in which no tokenings by the brains in a vat in his scenario can be. The thinkability of the hypothesis implies its falsehood, and it therefore poses no skeptical threat.

What apparently limits the epistemological significance of this result is that, as in effect already remarked, good skeptical arguments seem to have no need to make play with absaud hypotheses. Interestingly, the Cartesian Demon is presumably an absaudity. But the supposition that I am now dreaming, for instance, or the supposition that I was envatted yesterday, are not. The class of skeptical arguments in which we are interested all seek to exploit the putative first-person undetectability of some cognitively disabling state. What interest can it have if some examples of such states on which discussion has traditionally focused turn out to involve absaudity unless they *all* do? Otherwise, the conclusion should be merely that some traditional skeptical arguments employ inept examples. If our concern is with the general bearing of undetectable cognitive impairment on our scheme of putative knowledge and justified belief, then the failure of certain rather lurid (putative) illustrations of such impairment is of no consequence unless there is reason to think that such failure necessarily afflicts any illustration.

That is too fast. Earlier we remarked on a distinction between direct and indirect strategies of skeptical argument. The direct strategy, recall, trades on the evidence-transcendence of a hypothesis which, if true, would be immediately inconsistent with most of what we ordinarily believe about the relevant subject matter – in the present context, the material world. Its key thoughts are that if warranted belief is transmissible across entailment, then lack of warrant to disbelieve will be likewise; that evidence-transcendence enjoins lack of warrant to disbelieve; and, hence, that we lack warrant to disbelieve the negations of, i.e. to hold, most of our beliefs about the material world. The indirect strategy, by contrast, works with a hypothesis which is again presumed evidence-transcendent, at least for its subject, but whose truth is not actually inconsistent with the class of beliefs that the skeptical argument is concerned with. The strategy is to argue, rather, that those beliefs, even if their truth does not require the falsity of the hypothesis, are not appropriately *warranted* unless the hypothesis is false – that their being warranted requires that they have a pedigree which is inconsistent with the truth of the hypothesis; that warrants have to be recognizable; and hence that warrant for such beliefs requires justification – allegedly impossible – for our taking the hypothesis to be false. This is the way it goes, for instance, with the dreaming hypothesis. The skeptic charges that no subject at any time has warrant for the belief that he or she is not then dreaming. To be sure, one can dream what is actually taking place. But beliefs formed on the basis of the apparent perceptual experience that features within a dream do not have the pedigree of actual perceptual warrant. Justification of those of my beliefs which I take to be perceptually warranted by my current experience would thus depend on justification for the belief that I am not now dreaming which, according to the skeptical contention, is impossible.

There is no space now to review the detail of the indirect strategy in any depth. Suffice it to say that it has, as it were, significantly many more moving parts than the direct strategy and is to that extent more likely to break down.[8] The striking point is therefore that, at least as far as the hypotheses so far mentioned are concerned, the division between the absaud and the non-absaud corresponds exactly to that between those of them which are apt to subserve the direct strategy of skeptical argument and those which are available only for the purposes of the indirect strategy. If I have always been a brain in a vat, with the background detail as in Putnam's scenario, it follows directly that almost all my beliefs about the material world are false. If Descartes' Demon has practiced massive deception on me as far as the material world is concerned, then again, it follows directly that almost all my beliefs about the material world are false. But if the thought is merely that, for all I can show to the contrary, I might now be dreaming, then it is at least consistent to suppose that what I am now dreaming is actually true, even if, qua dreamer, I am thereby deprived of any good grounds for believing it. Likewise, if the story is that I was envatted last night in such a way as to give rise to no gross discontinuity in my experience, then it is again quite consistent to suppose that beliefs which I have formed since envatment should be true.

The following thought accordingly occurs: has Putnam perhaps at least shown that the *direct* strategy of skeptical argument necessarily aborts? That is, is it the case that any hypothesis at the service of the direct strategy – a hypothesis of sufficient logical strength to be directly inconsistent with most of what we believe about e.g. the material world – has to be an absaudity? It would certainly constitute significant epistemological progress if this were so.

Obviously there are, from the skeptical point of view, risks in making play with hypotheses of such strength. If, for instance, the hypothesis works like Putnam's version of the brain-in-a-vat hypothesis, by canceling the very existence of most of the material world we believe in, then it will be committed to some deviant story about the etiology of the uses of material-world vocabulary that feature in our thought, and may very well clumsily impinge, in consequence, on the semantics of symbols that feature in its own expression. But while – at least in the presence of the kind of semantic externalism which has informed our whole discussion – it is difficult to see how such a hypothesis could fail to be semantically disruptive, it is hard to be clear a priori that it would have to be semantically *auto-disruptive*.

On reflection, though, this does not matter; mere semantic disruption is enough. Avoiding absaudity is in any case no guarantee, if you want to be a skeptic, of avoiding the trouble given by Putnam's argument. For the argument can easily be adapted to the refutation of *any* semantically disruptive hypotheses, whether or not the disruption extends to its own expression. Consider a skeptical hypothesis whose semantic disruption is confined just to a single predicate. Then:

(i)   My language disquotes.
(ii) In a language, L, differing from mine, if at all, only in respects dictated by the truth of H, "F" does not refer to F's.
(iii) In my language, "F" is a meaningful expression.
(iv) In my language, "F" refers to F's – from (i) and (iii).

Hence

(v)   My language is not L – from (ii) and (iv).

But

    (vi)   If H is true, my language is L – from (ii).

So

    (vii)   H is not true. QED.

So now it would seem that the direct strategy of skeptical argument against our material-world beliefs has a *very* tall order to fill: somehow or other, it must devise a hypothesis which is both directly inconsistent with most of our material-world beliefs and *wholly semantically conservative* – wholly consistent with the satisfaction of whatever causal conditions are involved in determining that all our material-world expressions have the references which they actually have. One might well scent the possibility of an a priori demonstration that those are incompatible requirements.

But the skeptical imagination is nothing if not resourceful. Reflect that one sure-fire way to avoid semantical disruption is to leave the past alone, so that whatever causal constraints have been observed in the socio-linguistic history which has determined the actual references of our expressions continue to be observed in the story. Reflect too that one way of ensuring that most of our beliefs about the material world are false is to have most of what we take to be the material universe not exist. Then the obvious way for the direct-strategy, material-world skeptic to have at least some of his or her cake while eating the rest is, accordingly, to propose a hypothesis whereby the material world was, until recently, much as we had always taken it to be, but has recently largely ceased to be. Such a story might be, for instance, one in which the Evil Scientist envats a large number of us, sets up the attendant automatic machinery, and then, by a fitting nemesis, accidentally destroys himself up along with the rest of the material universe. Or let the Evil Demon have lain doggo up until yesterday, when he destroyed the material world in which I believe and first assumed his classic Cartesian role. Such a hypothesis will subserve the direct strategy when targeted against our beliefs concerning the present and future states of the material world, but – provided the cataclysm is supposed to have been of some recency – should not be semantically disruptive at all. It remains to be settled whether Putnam's argument can indeed subvert all direct-strategy forms of material-world skepticism which aspire to a certain generality; but it is clear that the generality involved must at least embrace our beliefs about the past.[9]

I conclude that the epistemological significance of Putnam's proof is limited at best. But earlier I conjectured that, by its author's intention at least, the real bearing of the proof might be less epistemological than metaphysical. I shall finish by pursuing this a little.

The view of the world which Putnam calls metaphysical realism is certainly nothing very precise. It involves thinking of the world as set over against thought in such a way that it is only by courtesy of a deeply contingent harmony, or felicity, that we succeed, if we do, in forming an overall picture of the world which, at least in its basics, is correct. This is what commits the metaphysical realist to the possibility that even an ideal theory might be false or seriously incomplete. And the same kind of thinking surfaces in the idea that the world comes prejointed, as it were, into real kinds, quite independently of any classificatory activity of ours. Once one thinks of the world in that way, one is presumably committed to the bare possibility of conceptual creatures naturally so constituted as *not* to be prone to form concepts which reflect the real kinds that there are. The real character of the world and its constituents would thus elude both the cognition and the comprehension of such creatures.

Putnam's brains in a vat are exactly such creatures: minds doomed by the character of their interaction with the world they inhabit, and by the nature of that world, not to have the concepts they need in order to be able to capture in thought that world's most fundamental features and the nature of their relationship with it. The modifications which Putnam effected in the standard version of the brain-in-a-vat story thus enable it to serve as a kind of parable for a kind of cognitive predicament which metaphysical realism is committed to regarding as a real possibility in any case. And the following argumentative strategy is thereby opened up: show that the brain-in-a-vat fantasy is false in a way which depends only on features essential to its being the right kind of parable and you have provided an argument which will show that *any* such parable is false. But possibilities are things that might be realized, and when they are, there has to be some *specific* way in which they are realized – some specific description of the state of affairs which realizes them. Metaphysical realism is committed to the possibility of a certain kind of dislocation, or uncrossable divide between reality and our cognitive activity. If that possibility were realized, there would, accordingly, have to be some correct, specific account of the way in which it was realized. And that is just to say that something like the brain-in-a-vat story would have to be true. The details might naturally be very different; but the essential overall structure would be the same. It would be an account whereby, despite the apparent cognitive richness of our lives, we were somehow so situated as not to be enabled to arrive at the concepts which fundamentally depicted the character of the real world and the nature of our interaction with it.

Possession of a general method for refuting any such account would thus apparently put us in a position to convict metaphysical realism of something akin to Ω-inconsistency. An Ω-inconsistent system of arithmetic, recall, is one which, for some arithmetic predicate, F, both contains a proof that there is an x such that not Fx and proofs of each statement of the form, Fn, "n" being a numeral. Simple inconsistency is avoided only because the recognition that each Fn is provable cannot be accomplished via means formalizable within the system. The metaphysical realist would be committed to claiming, correspondingly, the irrefutability of the hypothesis that we are in a cognitive predicament of a certain very general sort, even though for each *specific* description of such a situation, the claim that we are in *that* situation would be open to definite refutation.

The unclarities about what is essential to metaphysical realism may seem to make it hard, at first blush, to assess the dialectical promise of this line of criticism. But in fact I think it is quite clear that it will fail. The difficulty is that Putnam's proof does not represent a general method for disproving *any* specific version of the relevant kind of possibility; at best, it represents a general method for disproving any specific version *which we can under-stand*. Any impression to the contrary involves temporarily forgetting that the falsity of the brain-in-a-vat hypothesis is established conditionally on its thinkability. But the sort of dislocation whose possibility is arguably implicit in metaphysical realism does not involve that its victims can conceptualize their predicament; quite to the contrary – their predicament consists in part precisely in the fact that they are debarred from arriving at the concepts necessary to capture the most fundamental features of their world and their place in it. There is nothing akin to Ω-inconsistency in the thought that a certain type of situation is possible – that we ourselves may be in such a situation – although any instance of the type whose specific characteristics we can conceptualize can be demonstrated not to obtain. The only conclusion licenced is merely that if the type is realized, we will not be able to understand the specific form in which it is so.

And this I think is the real basis of the dissatisfaction that so many have felt with Putnam's proof. The trouble is that we easily slip into inept formulations of it. The dissatisfaction is ineptly formulated, for instance, when presented as the idea that there are two relevant types of thought which the sentence "We are not brains in a vat" might express, depending whether we are brains in a vat or not, and that we need an assurance, which Putnam's proof cannot give us, that the one we succeed in refuting is the right one. When the doubt is expressed like that, we have all the assurance we need just in the proof that we are not brains in vats. But the real specter to be exorcized concerns the idea of a thought *standing behind* our thought that we are not brains in a vat, in just the way that our thought that they *are* mere brains in a vat would stand behind the thought – could they indeed think anything – of actual brains in a vat that "We are not brains in a vat." The specter is that of a thought whose truth would make a mockery of humankind and its place in nature, just as our true thought that they are merely brains in a vat makes a mockery of the "cognitive" activity of the envatted brains. What we should really like would be an assurance that there is no such true thought: an assurance not just that most of what we think is actually true – for semantic externalism might well deliver that result for the brains in a vat – but that we are on to the right categories in terms of which to depict the most general features of the world and our place in it; and can be reasonably assured that we are thinking about such matters in the right general kind of way.

But of course, if there were such a true thought, standing behind us as it were, it would no more be available to us than the thought that they are merely brains in a vat would be available to the envatted brains. And none of the concepts required to entertain the non-specific doubt, that there might be such a true thought, seems such that our very possession of it suffices, in the presence of a plausible semantic externalism, to ensure that the doubt is false. That is the assurance we would like to have, and it is unclear whether reflective philosophy can deliver it. But if it can, it will not be by argumentative manipulation of intelligible, specific descriptions of the kind of predicament, epitomized by the brains in a vat, to whose possibility metaphysical realism is committed. By the same token, a proper disenchantment with the metaphysical realist outlook must be motivated in a different way.[10]

Notes

This version of the paper is that originally read at the Gifford Conference. A shortened version of it has appeared in (1991), *Proceedings of the Aristotelian Society*, XCII, 67–94.

1   Hilary Putnam (1981), *Reason, Truth and History*. Cambridge: Cambridge University Press, pp. 5–7.
2   The indirect strategy is the focus of attention in my (1991), "Scepticism and Dreaming: Imploding the Demon," *Mind*, C, 87–116.
3   Putnam (1981), p. 7.
4   Ibid., pp. 14–15.
5   Offered in discussion of an unpublished paper of Anthony Brueckner's, "Semantic Answers to Skepticism," read at the University of Michigan in Fall 1989.
6   In (1986), "Brains in a Vat," *Journal of Philosophy*, LXXXIII, 148–67.

7 I here diverge from the response to the situation of Paul Boghossian in his (1989) "Content and Self-Knowledge," *Philosophical Topics*, XVII, 1, 5–26. See especially his §11.

8 And does indeed do so – see my (1991).

9 Does this point to a loophole for the skeptic to exploit? Do these limited direct-strategy (LDS) arguments slip between both Putnam's argument and the "implosive" counter-argument developed against the indirect strategy in my (1991)? Reflect that there is nothing to stop our exporting into the indirect setting the sort of skeptical hypotheses which LDS arguments will feature; hence, if the counter-argument of "imploding the Demon" is sound, an issue will be raised in any case about the inference from the (putative) impossibility of accumulating evidence against such hypotheses to the claim that there is no warrant for their denial. But once that inference is placed sub judice, then LDS skepticism is going to have trouble making a case for its premises unless it can independently find fault either with elements in the apparatus deployed in the indirect strategy of which the direct strategy has no need but which the implosion exploits, or with the implosion itself. So at worst there is no *extant* LDS skeptical paradox – the skeptical work, if it can indeed be done, is still to do. I hope to discuss the matter more fully on another occasion.

10 Though no one who has heard or read this chapter has yet suggested so, it is quite possible that others have published convergent thoughts on the subject, and I owe an apology to anyone who has. There is now, of course, a very large body of published discussion of Putnam's proof and the limited time I had in which to compose a paper for the Gifford Conference meant I had no opportunity for a properly scholarly survey and indeed had little option but to ignore the secondary literature altogether. An exception was Anthony Brueckner's paper referred to in n. 6 above. The immediate stimulus to think again about the topic was provided by the Brueckner colloquium referred to in n. 5; and by the intervention of Allan Gibbard in that discussion. I have been much helped by discussions with Allan Gibbard, Bob Hale, Stephen Yablo, and Hilary Putnam, and by colloquia at Edinburgh, the Oxford Ockham Society, Kings College London, CUNY Graduate Center, Michigan, and Nottingham at which I have read versions of this chapter.

10   Comments and Replies

Hilary Putnam

1   Simon Blackburn on Internal Realism

Precisely because our outlooks differ totally, I was delighted by Simon Blackburn's chapter, which presents our differences (as they appear from his point of view) with admirable sharpness and clarity. But because Blackburn does not distinguish between what I actually say and consequences which he claims to derive from my views, I am concerned that a reader who tries to deduce my views from Blackburn's criticisms of them will get the wrong idea. It is, therefore, necessary to begin by saying a word or two in explanation of the term "internal realism," as I use it. What follows is just an attempt to stress key points (points that tend to be misunderstood), however, and not a substitute for the more detailed statements that I have published elsewhere.[1]

"Internal realism"[2] is the name that I once gave to a picture of what truth comes to, rather than what most philosophers would call a "theory of the nature of truth" (by which philosophers today understand a reduction of the notion of truth to concepts which do not presuppose it or such related concepts as "reference"). On that picture, a statement is true just in case a competent speaker fully acquainted with the use of the words would be fully rationally warranted in using those words to make the assertion in question, provided she or he were in a sufficiently good epistemic position. Although I no longer accept that picture,[3] I emphasize that this formula was meant to connect the notion of truth to the way in which words are *used* (including the speech act of assertion) and to the notions of rational acceptability and of sufficiently good[4] epistemic conditions, and I still believe that our understanding of the notion of truth is intricately interwoven with our understanding of those notions.

But what are "sufficiently good" epistemic conditions? They are conditions under which one can tell if the assertion in question is true or false! Obviously, if the formula "an empirical statement is true just in case, etc." in the preceding paragraph had been intended as a reduction, it would be flagrantly circular. But, as I have already said, it was not so intended. The point of the picture was to combine realism with a concession to moderate verificationism (a concession I would no longer make, by the way): the concession was the idea that truth could never be totally recognition-transcendent.[5]

At the same time, I rejected – and I continue to reject – the idea that the use of words is fixed once and for all by something like a set of algorithms.[6] Learning to use words is more like learning to play a musical instrument than like learning to extract square roots. Sensitivity is involved, and so is informal rationality, and there is room for individual creativity. Yet there are reasonable and unreasonable, warranted and unwarranted, ways of using words. I continue to think of truth, like warrant, as fundamentally a normative notion.

A second claim[7] of "internal realism" – one I have not at all given up; the one I have increasingly emphasized in my writings, and the one at which most of Blackburn's fire is directed – concerns notions like "object," "entity," "property," and "existence." I have argued that it makes no sense to think of the world as dividing itself up into "objects" (or "entities") independently of our use of language. It is *we* who divide up "the world" – that is, the events, states of affairs, and physical, social, etc., systems that we talk about – into "objects," "properties," and "relations," and we do this in a variety of ways. "Object," "entity," "property," (and "relation") have not one fixed use but an ever-expanding open family of uses. Because "exist" and "entity" are conceptually linked, the same is true of "exist."

One example is so familiar as to run the danger of seeming trivial; we may partly describe the contents of a room by saying that there is a chair in front of a desk, and partly describe the contents of the same room by saying that there are particles and fields of certain kinds present. But to ask which of these descriptions describes the room as it is "independent of perspective," or "in itself," is senseless. *Both* descriptions are descriptions of the room as it really is. In saying this, I am, of course, contesting a metaphysical claim which many philosophers – including, I suspect, Simon Blackburn – wish to make about modern science, namely that science, and science alone, describes the world "as it is independent of language." I suspect that it is because I contest this thesis (contest its very intelligibility) that I provoke attacks like Blackburn's.

A controversial corollary of this claim – one Blackburn discusses – is that, given the variety of different ontologies that can legitimately be adopted to describe one and the same state of affairs, statements which are inconsistent if taken at face value (e.g. "there are mereological sums," "mereological sums do not exist") can both be true (that is, each can be true in the way of speaking – in the case of mereology, the formalized language – to which it belongs). I refer to this phenomenon as "conceptual relativity," and it is on my doctrine of conceptual relativity that Blackburn focuses his fire.

Blackburn's Charges

Blackburn brings two main charges against the position I have just described:

1   That I am committed to holding that "genuinely inconsistent descriptions of things" can be true.
2   That I reject the regulative ideal of unifying our knowledge.

In addition:

3   Blackburn tries to show that the sorts of ontological issues to which the doctrine of conceptual relativity is addressed pose no real problem for metaphysical realism. I shall address the two charges in the present section, and claim (3) in the next.

Re charge (1)

Blackburn writes as if I *hold* that "genuinely inconsistent propositions" can be true. Of course, I do not hold this. When I said that propositions which are inconsistent from the point of view of classical semantics can be true, I was criticizing "classical semantics," not endorsing the conclusion Blackburn ascribes to me.

As Blackburn mentions, one of my examples[8] is the dispute over the existence of mereological sums. I imagined a mini-world in which there are just three individuals, and at least one of them is wholly black and at least one is wholly red. If our ontology includes individuals but not mereological sums, then the sentence:

(A)   There is an object which is partly red and partly black.

is false. (I call a particular first-order language with this ontology "Carnap's language.") However, if we adopt an ontology which includes mereological sums, then the sentence (A) becomes true. (I call a particular first-order language with this second ontology "the Polish logician's language.") My claim was that the question

"Do mereological sums *really* exist?"

is a senseless one. We can use the words "object" and "exist" so that such "objects" as mereological sums "exist" (by adopting the Polish logician's language) or we can use the same words so that it will be true to say that "there are no such objects" (by adopting Carnap's language). If we make this latter choice, we shall have to say that there is no object in the mini-world which is partly red and partly black. But the mini-world itself does not *force* us to talk one way or to talk the other way.

Now, two remarks, one on the content of this view and one on its tenability.

On the content: in one of the works Blackburn cited, I pointed out that the Polish logician's language can be "translated" into Carnap's language by various logical tricks. Under one such interpretation, (A) above receives the translation:

(B) There is an object which is red and an object which is black.

Notice that if we adopt this interpretation of (A), the sentence (A) of the Polish logician's language becomes consistent with the following sentence (C) of Carnap's language (which, taken at face value, is identical with the negation of (A) in the Polish logician's language):

(C) There is no object which is partly red and partly black.

Since the status of the apparent "inconsistency" between (A) and (C) (when these sentences are in two different languages, as described) depends on which way we choose to interpret the Polish logician's language in Carnap's language, one cannot simply argue that:

(A) is true in the Polish logician's language. But (C) is true in Carnap's language. Therefore, if internal realism realism is right, genuinely inconsistent propositions can be true.

For, if I am right, (A) and (C) need not be (and, I would argue, should not be) regarded as "genuinely inconsistent." The fact that the words "object" and "exist" are used differently in the two languages is what blocks Blackburn's conclusion.

On its tenability: Blackburn seems to anticipate this answer, and replies, in effect, "Well then, you are just saying that 'object' and 'exist' have different meanings. We just have to distinguish between 'uninterpreted and interpreted sentences' and classical semantics takes care of the problem for us." What is wrong with this line is that the difference between the two uses of "object" and "exist" I have described is a very different phenomenon from the one we normally refer to as a "difference in meaning." To point out that one possible relative interpretation of the Polish logician's language in Carnap's language maps (A) on to (B) is not to make a remark about the "meaning" of the words in (A) in any sense of the word "meaning" that an ordinary speaker (or a linguist) would recognize.

Suppose that instead of considering individuals in a mini-world, we consider objects on a table. If the sentence "There are three objects on the table" were genuinely inconsistent with the sentence "There are seven objects on the table," even when the first sentence occurs in a vernacular description and the second occurs in a version which employs the notion of a mereological sum, then I would face the charge Blackburn makes. But it makes no difference to our predictions or actions which of these schemes we use. Nor are these schemes equivalent only in the weak sense of what is sometimes called "empirical equivalence," but, as I pointed out in the works Blackburn cites, each sentence in one of them can be correlated in an effective way with a "translation" in the other scheme, and the sentence and its translation will have the same truth-value and the same explanatory power.[9]

However, as I just remarked, the kind of "translation" just referred to does not provide what we would ordinarily regard as a linguistically synonymous expression. Moreover, these "translations" (the technical name for them is "relative interpretations") are not unique; the mereological sum version can be interpreted in the version without mereological sums in more than one way. But the question "Which translation scheme, if any, preserves the *meanings* of the sentences being translated?" is a bad question. The ordinary notion of "meaning" was simply not invented for this kind of case.

In contrast, a metaphysical realist would say "Well, all that is involved *is* a difference in meaning of a perfectly ordinary kind. The fact is just that 'object' sometimes includes mereological sums and sometimes excludes them" (in fact, Blackburn does say something very much like this); but this reply assumes that of course mereological sums are objects (otherwise one could not include them in one's ontology), and the choice of different "meanings" of the word "object" is just a choice of a subclass from a universe, or fixed totality, of all objects. Here I part company with Blackburn. I believe there are different uses of "object" and no metaphysically privileged use (and thus no sense to the notion of a totality of all objects fixed once and for all). In particular, the idea that there is a fixed, clear, notion of "object" (or "exist") in which it makes sense to ask "Are mereological sums objects?" (or "Do they really exist?") is one I reject. But I do not reject the idea that in an ordinary sense of the phrase "state of affairs" the "same state of affairs" can be described either by saying that "There are three objects on the table" or "There are seven objects (counting mereological sums) on the table."

Incidentally, saying that two different versions are about "the same state of affairs" or describe "the same physical system" or " the same event" is itself sometimes a part of a commonsense version of what we are doing; accepting such a version does not require us to elevate "states of affairs," etc., to the the status of a universal ontology.[10]

Re charge (2)

Blackburn's basis for the second charge is the following argument: internal realism holds that genuinely inconsistent propositions can be true. But genuinely inconsistent propositions cannot be conjoined in any one language. Thus, if internal realism is right, there are truths (pairs of sentences, each true in its own language) which cannot be conjoined. So we must give up the idea that all truths can be conjoined if we accept internal realism, and this would be to give up the regulative ideal of the unity of knowledge.

Since I have rejected the first premise, this argument has already been answered. Indeed, an example Blackburn himself uses seems to me to show the implausibility of his claim that any acknowledgment of conceptual relativity is a rejection of the unity of knowledge. Suppose scientific knowledge, or total knowledge (science, history, philosophy, etc.), or ideal versions of these, were formalized. Imagine two different formalizations (I would say, trivially different formalizations), which are alike except that in the first formalization numbers are identified with sets (as in von Neumann set theory) and in the second formalization numbers are assumed as abstract entities over and above the sets. It is easy to see that any factual statement that can be expressed in one of the resulting formalized languages has a reasonable "translation" into the other, in the sense of "translation" just discussed. Of course the sentence "Numbers are identical with sets" in the first language would not normally be translated into the second, nor would the sentence "Numbers are distinct from sets" in the second language normally be translated into the first; but these sentences are surely not statements of fact, but expressions of the conventions that structure these two languages.[11] The fact that I cannot conjoin a convention which underlies one way of speaking and a convention which underlies a different way of speaking is surely no real limitation on the unity of knowledge.

It may help the reader if I compare my position to the positions of Carnap and Quine. My position resembles Carnap's (in "Empiricism, Semantics, Ontology") inasmuch as I hold that differences in ontology *sometimes* amount to no more than differences in how we use words. But unlike Carnap, I do not rest the distinction between questions which have to do with the choice of a linguistic framework and empirical questions on an absolute analytic–synthetic distinction. Whether something is or is not "conventional," i.e. whether what is at stake is no more than a question of how to talk, is itself something to which empirical facts are relevant. There is continuum stretching from choices which, by our present lights, are just choices of a way of talking to questions of what are plainly empirical fact, but there is nothing here which is *guaranteed* to be true no matter what the facts may turn out to be.[12] What I would criticize Quine for is the suggestion that a distinction between fact and language-choice which is not absolute, not drawn once and for all unrevisably, is of no use.

The Price of Metaphysical Realism

Blackburn addresses this issue very clearly at one point in his chapter. I have in mind the following passage:

> One way of attacking metaphysical realism would be to find an internal inconsistency in it. A combination giving rise to such an inconsistency might be that of a determinate ontology, and an indeterminate or conventional identity relation. Thus we cannot both believe in a determinate, unique, mathematical ontology, containing numbers and sets, and also hold that whether we identify numbers and sets is a matter of convention. For either the ontology, which is not "up to us," has numbers as well as sets, in which case it would be a mistake to identify them, or it has only sets, in which case it would be a mistake to separate them. A determinate ontology takes away our freedom with identity; conversely, freedom with identity undermines the view that there is a determinate ontology. . . The point is undeniable, but it is not clear why a realist of any kind should be troubled by it. . . . the means of avoidance are to hand: one draws the ontology so that nothing genuinely "up to us" is determined by it (for example, in the numerical case, by sticking with sets and construing arithmetic as not concerned with objects at all).

So the means of avoidance "in the numerical case" – the means of avoiding an admission that the decision to identify/not to identify numbers with sets is a matter of convention – is to "draw the ontology" so that numbers do not exist (i.e. so that all statements about numbers are reconstructed as universal quantifications over infinite sequences).[13] What is amusing about this suggestion is that the metaphor of *drawing the ontology* suggests precisely the view Blackburn wishes to deny – the view that the ontology is something we can "draw," i.e. that it is "up to us." I take it that this is not what Blackburn wanted to say (although it is a point at which his text deconstructs itself in the fashion literary theorists discuss so much nowadays); I take it that what Blackburn means is that we should believe – because it is true – the view that there really are sets and there really do not exist any such things as numbers. If I thought I understood what such an assertion might mean, I would ask Blackburn how the devil he knows! But the fact is that never in my life, even when I counted myself as a metaphysical realist, did I think that kind of talk had any meaning at all. A sensible realist had better be able to allow that some ways of "drawing the ontology" (an expression I like, by the way) are equally right.

A curious feature of Blackburn's resolution of the ontological issue with respect to mathematical objects is that it contradicts Blackburn's own previous position. In *Spreading the Word*,[14] Blackburn's view is that we should assume that nothing exists (in the supposed strong metaphysical realist sense of "exist" that Blackburn believes in) except "the natural world" (including our reactions to it). Nevertheless, according to Blackburn, we are justified in speaking *as if* various other things existed (in several places Blackburn lists moral, mental, and mathematical facts, along with counterfactuals), and, as Blackburn also says in the present chapter, in using the word "true" in these domains, even though they do not belong to the natural world: this is called taking a "projectivist" attitude towards the discourses in question. Mathematical statements, in particular, are not "true" (on this earlier position) in the sense of being true of mathematical objects, for there are no such non-natural objects, but are true (when they are) in the sense that some of them are "grounded in practice." Blackburn's insistence on bivalence as a property of truth does not extend to areas about which he is a projectionist: thus, about mathematics he wrote:[15]

> Arithmetical truths gain their status as something more than mere formalisms because numbers matter; they are what we count and measure with, and because of this we are not free to invent propositions about them as we wish. But it is quite unclear how far this constraint goes. It seems to compel just one ordinary arithmetic. But mathematicians can devise systems which contain conflicting accounts of how many infinite numbers there are, and how they are packed. [Here Blackburn is referring to the existence of large cardinals, and certain other questions in set theory. Is one of these true, and the other not? Perhaps the correct account of how mathematical truth is grounded in practice shows that the grounding does not extend so far, and that we have here a *matter for choice* [emphasis added].

So in *Spreading the Word*, the properties of sets were allowed to be, in certain respects, possibly a "matter of choice"! (Of course, Blackburn would point out that when he took the earlier position, he was "drawing the ontology" so that sets were not really included at all.) Yet in the present chapter, denying precisely the position Blackburn put forward earlier is the means we are said to have "to hand" to avoid internal realism!

I presume that Blackburn has given up the doctrine of *Spreading the Word*, perhaps because he has come to see that mathematics is so interwoven with empirical science that to be a projectionist about sets and functions and a realist about electrons makes no sense, as Quine has long argued. But Blackburn need not fear that recognizing that there is an element of choice in mathematics means saying that everything is a matter of choice. Blackburn worries that "Putnam can try insisting that *all* questions of identity are up to us." But Putnam would not be caught dead "insisting" on that. It is not up to us whether Blackburn and Dummett are identical, or whether 2 + 2 and 17 are identical, or whether the null set and the unit set of the null set are identical. Yet it *is* up to us whether the number 2 is identical with a set, and if so, which set it is identical with. Saying that a few – but by no means most – identity questions call for a convention seems to Blackburn to be giving up the very notion of existence; to me, it seems to be giving up only a metaphysical fantasy, a fantasy that is, perhaps, built into the grandiose word "ontology."

But if Blackburn will not allow us to regard any identity question, even the question as to whether we should identify numbers with sets, as a question calling for a convention, what price shall we have to pay? Philosophers disagree, and have disagreed since Kant, over the question of whether points are/are not identical with limits (of convergent sequences of regions). Since Whitehead, we have known how to formalize Kant's claim that points in space are "mere limits" (by identifying points with, say, equivalence classes of convergent sequences – of course, identifying sequences with sets is something that itself can be done in more than one way). Do we have to "draw our ontology" so that points exist over and above regions and sequences of regions? Or do we have to "draw our ontology" so that there are only regions ("Space consists only of regions," Kant wrote), and construe geometry as not concerned with points at all? And how are we to know which of these ways of "drawing our ontology" is metaphysically correct?

Philosophers have long disagreed, and disagree today, over the relation of commonsense objects – tables and chairs – to their matter. Quine believes that a table is identical with its matter, that its matter is the electromagnetic, gravitational, etc., fields that occupy the volume in question, that fields are simply collections of space–time points with certain properties, and that, in consequence, tables and other physical objects are, in the last analysis, identical with space–time regions. David Lewis believes that they are identical with mereological sums of time-slices of molecules. Saul Kripke believes that they are distinct from their matter, on the grounds that they have different modal properties from their matter (the table could have consisted of different molecules; it could have occupied a different place). Our ordinary language can be rationally reconstructed (i.e. formalized) in accordance with any one of these doctrines, and our description of such states of affairs as there being three glasses on the table will not be affected. Indeed – and this is what Blackburn objects to – I would say that these different formalizations just provide us with different ways of describing what is, by commonsense standards, the same state of affairs. Blackburn complains that "we are not given . . . any help [by Putnam] in understand how much of the commonsense standard we are being asked to abandon, or why we should do so," but of course I am not asking us to abandon *any* part of the commonsense standard, of the commonsense practice (for such I take it to be) of regarding it as no real question at all whether a table is "identical with the region it occupies in space–time or with the mereological sum of time-slices of molecules that it contains." What I am asking us to "abandon" is the idea that such a question must have a non–conventional answer.

The price to be paid for taking the "way" that Blackburn finds so inviting (and so "to hand"), then, is refusing to admit that any of these ontological questions is a pseudo–question. But, as my quotation from *Spreading the Word* indicates, not even Blackburn is really willing to pay that price – or at least, he is not consistently willing to pay that price.

My Attitude to Ontological Relativity

Blackburn devotes more than a third of his chapter to an attempt to saddle me with Quine's notorious doctrine of ontological relativity.[16] Briefly, my view is that the model-theoretic argument is not a proof of ontological relativity but rather a *reductio ad absurdum* of ontological relativity and of the "naturalism" that underlies Quine's arguments for ontological relativity. (I put the word "naturalism" in shudder quotes here, because, whatever one's attitude towards naturalism may be – I suppose that, as a theist and a practicing Jew, I cannot call myself a "naturalist" in the sense in which John Dewey, who introduced it, used that term – the Quinian usage is *weird*. In Quine's sense, to be a "naturalist" is to believe that there is nothing to be said about science except what science itself can discover about science, i.e. there is no distinctive activity of philosophy apart from science. I would like to note that Dewey himself was not a "naturalist" in *this* sense.)

Blackburn worries about whether non-intentional facts (his "base totality") determine the intentional facts (e.g. the fact that "rabbits" refers to rabbits), but he does not perceive the unclarity of "determine." For his argument to go through, "determine" must mean no more than this: A-facts determine B-facts just in case B-facts are supervenient on A-facts.[17] Otherwise, the following is a non sequitur:

One could see Putnam as poised to adopt it [the view that there are non-reducible or "self-standing" semantic facts], since the drift of his work is to refuse to grant especial ontological privilege to any particular kind of fact, and that would include facts from the base totality. But there is a cost . . . the real difficulty is not epistemological, but ontological. For Quine appears to put into the base totality everything we could possibly want in order to determine reference and meaning. If we say he did not, then we are making an ontological claim. We are denying that semantics *supervenes* on the extensional facts about things [emphasis added].

In this passage, saying that facts in the base totality do not "determine" reference and meaning means denying supervenience. But when Moore – a philosopher Blackburn has thought about a great deal – denied that facts in the base totality determine moral facts he was not denying supervenience, and likewise when John McDowell and I both deny, from our respective points of view, that facts in the base totality determine semantic facts we are not denying supervenience. Our point is rather that, if you want to understand *why* semantic facts are supervenient on facts in the base totality – accepting, for the moment, this way of talking – you must, so to speak, look from above; you must look at the (allegedly)[18] "non–intentional" facts about how we use words (e.g. "We often assert 'There's a rabbit' when a rabbit is present, and not very often when there is no rabbit present, or when we don't see the rabbit") from the standpoint of your intentional notions, rather than trying to explain from below – trying to use physics, or behavior science, or computer science, or whatever, to explain why words refer. The negative part of this claim – the denial that intentional notions, such as reference and meaning, are reducible to physical–cum–computational notions – is something I argue at length in *Representation and Reality*. The analogy with ethics may be helpful here. If you want to know why two people who do the same things and think the same thoughts cannot differ in moral worth, you should ask a moralist, not a physicist. If you want to know why two people who causally interact with the same things (both directly and through the medium of their culture), think the same words, have the same dispositions, etc., cannot be referring to different things (apart from the trivial case of indexicals), you should ask a philosopher of language, not a physicist (or a computer scientist).

In particular, if you want to know why it does not make sense to imagine a world in which people use their words just as we do but in which the reference of all the words is systematically permuted is such a way that the truth conditions of whole sentences are unaffected – so that "cat" refers to cats*, etc.[19] – the answer is that using words in the way we do is what any good interpreter would *call* "Using 'cat' to refer to cats and not to cats*," etc. (Note that this answer employs the intentional notion of "calling something a so and so," i.e. referring. That is why this is an answer "from above" and not an answer "from below.")[20]

On one point I agree with Blackburn, however: this answer is also (formally) available to a metaphysical realist – but only, I would add, to a metaphysical realist who has given up the demand that the very possibility of semantical facts be explained from below, and thus one who is not a "naturalist" in what I described as the weird sense.

Thus, I agree with Blackburn that model-theoretic arguments cannot by themselves, as a matter of logic alone, "prove" that internal realism is correct, as opposed to metaphysical realism; but this is something I myself have repeatedly pointed out.[21] What model-theoretic arguments do, as Blackburn recognizes, is pose a problem – a problem with which, I claim, "naturalism" in either Quine's version or Blackburn's cannot deal. However, as I remarked in "A Defense of Internal Realism",[22] I do not think the metaphysical realist picture has any content today when it is divorced from the "naturalism" which leads philosophers like Blackburn (and perhaps Bernard Williams) to espouse it. The only form of metaphysical realism with "clout" in our time is (to call it by its proper name) materialism, and one cannot simultaneously agree that there are non-reducible semantic facts and honestly claim to be a materialist.

Miscellaneous

Let me make three remarks on other points in Blackburn's paper.

Re Blackburn's claim that Correspondence and Bivalence have "hygienic" interpretations: one must distinguish between "Correspondence" as a trivial claim which one can make once a language is in place – the claim that the sentences of that language have certain truth conditions, expressed in terms of the objects and relations which that language posits – and Correspondence as the metaphysical theory that there is a totality of All Objects (and All Properties, and All Relations, etc.) such that *every* language's universe of discourse (and every language's ideology, or selection of properties and relations) is just a subset of that totality (respectively, a subset of the totality of All Properties and Relations) and a Universal Correspondence Relation which assigns truth-conditions to an arbitrary sentence in an arbitrary language in terms of the totalities in question. This is the picture that informs metaphysical realism, and I believe it leads to both logical paradox[23] and philosophical confusion. (The denial that identity is ever conventional, discussed above, is an example of the confusion in question.) That "correspondence with facts" can be just a synonym for "true" is something I myself have pointed out (referring to William James, as Blackburn does), but when "true" is the word that does the work in explaining what "correspondence with facts" means, no Universal Ontology is presupposed.

Re the claim that Bivalence has a hygienic interpretation: Blackburn's formulation ("a determinate proposition is either true or false") is just not a statement of bivalence. Of course, a determinate proposition (one that is true or false) is either true or false; the question is whether a complete description of the world can be given using a language in which all propositions are determinate.[24]

Last but not least, Blackburn's claim that we cannot give up the idea of One Determinate Ontology (he calls giving this up "being cavalier about unification") "without treating our commitments not as beliefs at all but as instrumental acceptances of a different kind" depends on his claim that acknowledging conceptual relativity requires forswearing the ideal of unified knowledge, and this is a charge that I have already spoken to. The point of internal realism is not that there are perspectives[25] that you cannot conjoin, as Blackburn seems to think, but that there is no one privileged "ontology" in terms of which reality is to be described. Even unified knowledge can have a plurality of forms.

2   Reply to George Boolos

George Boolos raises some very deep questions about just where, if anywhere, one should "draw the line" between logic and mathematics. I want to defend the suggestion Boolos reports me as making, the suggestion that we count as logical truths only certain of the true sentences of second-order logic, namely those which are universal quantifications of valid first-order formulas.

Boolos examines the costs and benefits of my suggestion in a deep and searching way; it is now for me to examine his examination. A benefit of my suggestion, as I argued in *Philosophy of Logic*, is that the statement that a first-order sentence is valid will count as a truth of logic, as it intuitively should. But a difficulty that has been pointed out by several authors concerns the status of the second-order quantifiers; does second-order logic presuppose an "ontology" of sets? If it does, then the first-order variables do not really range over all objects, and in that case the universal quantification of a first-order formula does not really succeed in saying that that first-order formula is true no matter what the objects in the range of the first-order quantifiers are. The intuitive notion of validity is still not captured.

A way out of this difficulty has been proposed by Boolos himself (he summarizes it in the present chapter), and I know of no better. Boolos proposes that we think of a second-order (monadic) quantifier "($\exists F$)" as meaning not *there is a set F such that*, but rather *there are some things (call them F things) such that*.

One's reaction upon meeting Boolos's suggestion to, as it were, allow the existential quantifier to take a plural inflection may be that it is merely "cute," but, on the contrary, it seems to me to be extraordinarily deep, and the depth is brought out by just the way it resolves the previously intractable problem of explicating the intuitive notion of validity in any way at all. Taking these quantifiers as picking out individuals (in bunches), rather than "abstract entities" (sets of individuals), means that we can quantify over "all objects" in second-order logic without fearing that the very existence of our second-order quantifiers belies our claim that our first-order quantifiers do so range. And there is reason to want to able to do this even if one shares the view that I have expressed in many places, the view that there is no fixed totality of "all objects," and that "object" is an inherently extendable notion; for no matter how we extend the notion, we intend the laws of logic to remain good, and thus we may regard some principles as valid even if the notion of object they involve is an indeterminate one.

Boolos himself reports an objection to his suggestion (he ascribes it to Hartry Field) when the second-order quantifiers are diadic or polyadic: "the scheme provides no way to translate into natural language second-order dyadic or, more generally, polyadic quantification. In favorable cases, of course, pairing functions will be definable in the language and higher-degree second-order quantification reducible to monadic. But the availability of pairing functions cannot be considered to be guaranteed by logic."

Here there are two distinct problems. One is that finite domains are not closed under pairing functions. This does not affect the purpose for which I want to use second order logic (interpreted a la Boolos); to say a first-order formula is valid, I will quantify over all objects, whether the formula itself concerns all objects or not. (When relativization to a domain is desired, this can be explicitly indicated, e.g. by writing "for all domains D," or its symbolic equivalent, in front of the first-order formula and explicitly relativizing all its quantifiers to D.) Since the totality of all objects is certainly infinite, there is no difficulty in supposing that for any two objects in that totality there is another object which is their ordered pair.

The other problem is that, in so interpreting second-order quantifiers over dyadic, etc., relations I am using a *mathematical* notion (ordered pair); and is this not incompatible with counting even these second-order formulas (universal quantifications of valid first-order formulas) as *logical* truths? To this, my answer is that I am not claiming that either second-order quantifiers or pairing functions are logical notions; I am quite willing to regard some statements which contain "mathematical" notions as logical truths.

Boolos's own solution to these problems is quite different. His solution to the first I do not understand; while I agree that translatability into a language we already understand is not *necessary* for understanding in all cases, the fact is that I do not see any way of understanding quantification over dyadic (or higher-adic) relations on the lines of the "plural quantification" strategy he suggests (and which, as I have already indicated, I find a brilliant idea) without talking about ordered pairs of individuals; for the analogue of saying "there are some things, call them F-things" (this is the Boolosian way of handling an existential quantifier over sets) in the case of an existential quantifier over dyadic relations is surely to say "there are some pairs of things, call them R-pairs." Of course, we could just not interpret the existential quantifier over dyadic relations at all; we could just say "knowing how to use it is understanding it," but this is compatible with any account of its metaphysical status.

The fact is, however, that neither a desire to avoid some metaphysical problem (e.g. "ontological commitment") nor a desire to avoid "mathematical" as opposed to "purely logical" notions is behind my not wanting to class full second-order logic as logic. My reason is rather the fact that full second-order logic is not completely axiomatizable; this means that it does not correspond to a definite doctrine of deduction. It seems to me desirable to so define "logic" that it can be viewed as a canon of deduction (since that is what the subject originally started out to be). This is compatible with accepting the fragment of second-order logic which consists of universal quantifications of valid first-order formulas as logical truths, but not with accepting the whole of second-order logic. But in truth, I do not attach any profound significance to just where one "draws the line."

With respect to the historical part of Boolos's paper, let me simply say "Bravo!"

3   Michael Dummett on Realism and Idealism

I have learned enormously from Dummett's work, and I find his call for a more moderate realism and a more moderate idealism, and his suggestion that they may coincide, of great interest. If I focus in what follows on points in Dummett's chapter that occasioned some discomfort, that is because I value the opportunity to continue our discussions through the years.

The central theme in Dummett's writing on realism, early and late, is that truth can never be totally recognition-transcendent. My own picture of truth from *Reason, Truth and History* to *Representation and Reality*, the "internal realist" picture, was an attempt to show the compatibility of this idea with commonsense realism. Today I no longer accept that picture of truth; I shall not discuss my reasons for giving it up in this reply, but I shall discuss Dummett's reasons for thinking that even internal realism is too close to metaphysical realism.

It was when I read the description of internal realism late in the chapter that I became uneasy. When Dummett writes, "Putnam's moderate internalist notion of truth invokes both the ideal and the subjunctive conditional," I do not disagree, although, as I pointed out in my comments on Blackburn's chapter, in my internal realist writings I avoided reference to "ideal" epistemic conditions after I saw the misunderstandings that that term provoked in the early 1980s; what I spoke of were *sufficiently good* conditions.[26] But Dummett continues his exposition of my view, "truth is what we should eventually arrive at were we to commit nothing that was a mistake by our own lights." Here two things bother me: the "eventually" makes it sound as if, in the internal realist picture, truth depends on what we could verify in the future, even when the statement is about the past, and to speak of *nothing* that is a mistake by our own lights reinforces the impression that I was a Peircean; that is, that I envisaged convergence to a situation in which we "make no mistakes" about anything.

Nevertheless, I hope that this is not what Dummett means. As I wrote in another connection,[27]

> Is it incumbent, then, to go back to the Peirce–James view, that "truth" (as distinct from "warranted assertibility") is to be identified with the tremendously Utopian idea of "the final opinion," the theory to be reached (and to become coercive) at the end of *indefinitely continued investigation?* Not necessarily . . . Suppose, for the moment, that what is right in pragmatism is the idea that truth is an *idealization* – a useful and necessary idealization – of warranted assertibility. The idealization need not involve the Utopian fantasy of a theory satisfying all the requirements that the idealists placed on the "ultimate coherent account" (an account which, they argued, could only be known by the Absolute, that is, God). The idealists' ultimate coherent account had to contain the truth about every single question – it had to be what a contemporary logician would call a "complete and consistent theory" of everything. It is perhaps understandable that James and Peirce would accept the ideal of One Complete and Coherent Theory of Everything, since they were influenced by the very philosophy they were combatting. Yet James' own pluralism eventually led him to reject the idea that all truth must cohere in one final system. If a statement can withstand all the criticism that is appropriate given its context, perhaps that is truth enough. This general idea – the idea of truth as, in some way (not in Peirce's way, but a more humanly accessible, modest way), an idealization of the notion of warranted assertability – has recently been revived in writings by Michael Dummett, Nelson Goodman, and myself.

But it may well be that I am being overly sensitive. In any case, my purpose in quoting all this is to set the stage for considering Dummett's next remarks:

> By the nature of the matter, this ["what we should do were we to make no mistakes"] is something that we cannot in all cases know: what justifies us in assuming that there is some specific thing that we should in those ideal circumstances do? Indeed, to put the question in this epistemological form is to make it too weak; it should be a metaphysical question, namely: if there *is* some specific thing that we should do, *what makes it the case that we should do that*, even though we cannot be sure what it is?

Consider the proposition, "Caesar had someone shave him on the day he crossed the Rubicon." I believe that this proposition has a determinate truth-value.[28] "Ideal circumstances for determining that truth-value" are not hard to describe; for example, to have been with Caesar the entire day, observed him closely, and paid particular attention to whether or not he had someone shave him. Now "if there *is* some specific thing that we should do" (say, assert that Caesar did have someone shave him), "*what makes it the case that we should do that*, even though we cannot [now, two thousand years later] be sure what it is?"

If this is a "metaphysical question," it seems to me that it has a decidedly non-metaphysical answer. If what we should say in the envisaged "ideal" (sufficiently good) situation is that Caesar had someone shave him, what "makes it the case that we should do that" is that we would, were we in that situation, hear Caesar tell a slave, as it might be, to shave him, and see Caesar being shaved and see Caesar cross the Rubicon on that same day, etc.; and given our competence with the English language, we are quite sure that this would license us to assert "Caesar had someone shave him on the day he crossed the Rubicon." And if what we should say in the "ideal" situation is that Caesar did not have anyone shave him, the fact that we could testify to this would "make it the case" that we should say "Caesar did not have anybody shave him on the day he crossed the Rubicon." If this is not the answer to the "what makes it the case" question, nothing is.

But with respect to other kinds of judgement, e.g. judgements of rationality, and moral judgements, this may seem unsatisfactory. Here, after all there is frequently dispute as to what would constitute a sufficiently good epistemic situation for determining the truth of the judgement, and as to what would license making the judgement even in a well-described situation. But if one does believe that such a judgement is true, then one will typically have convictions about both of these matters, and one will have arguments for those convictions – methodological arguments, if the dispute is a methodological one, or moral arguments, if it is a moral dispute, or whatever sort of argument is appropriate to the judgement; and it is by means of such arguments that one should answer the "what makes it the case" question and not by appeal to a metaphysical answer to a metaphysical question.

If this sounds "Wittgensteinian," that is because it is the sort of answer Wittgenstein gives (I do not read Wittgenstein as a "radical internalist" as Michael Dummett does; on this, more below). Wittgenstein considers[29] cases in which there is dispute about the inner life of another person (for example, is he or she feigning a feeling he or she does not have?). And he says (I have rectified the translation):

> Is there such a thing as "expert judgement" about the genuineness of expressions of feeling – Even here there are those whose judgement is "better" and those whose judgement is "worse."
>
> Prognoses that are more correct will generally issue from the judgements of those who understand people better [*des besseren Menschenkenners*].
>
> Can one learn this knowledge? Yes; some can. Not, however, by taking a course in it, but through "*experience.*" – Can another be one's teacher in this? Certainly. From time to time he gives him the right *tip*. This is what "learning" and "teaching" are like here. – What one acquires is not a technique; one learns correct judgements. There are also rules, but they do not form a system, and only experienced people can apply them right. Unlike calculating rules.

So Wittgenstein's answer to what makes judgements "correct" is in terms of notions like "understanding people" (*Menschenkenntnis*), "experience," and even (ibid., 228) "imponderable evidence." And these are just the sorts of answer we ordinarily give; they are not metaphysical answers.

I think I know what will bother Dummett about this response (both mine and Wittgenstein's). Given the remarkable and beautiful architecture of his chapter, I would expect him to point out that this response is "banal," and say that a banal response cannot meet the question raised by the "radical internalist." "Of course we *say* that either Caesar had someone shave him or he did not have anybody shave him on that day," the radical internalist will respond, "but that does not mean that one of the disjuncts is determinately true. The whole disjunction is true, because it is what we say; but you begged the question by assuming that one of the disjuncts is determinately true. You have not shown that there is an admissible notion of truth other than being accepted as true."

The dialectical position of this "radical internalist" is not a comfortable one, however. For one thing, he or she cannot literally mean that we are to accept the schema:

"p" is true iff p is accepted as true

because this scheme does not satisfy Frege's Equivalence Principle (i.e. the disquotation schema). We do not accept:

> "Caesar was shaved the day he crossed the Rubicon" is accepted as true iff Caesar was shaved the day he crossed the Rubicon,

after all.

And it will do the "radical internalist" no good to just *think* that the notion of truth is identical with the notion of being accepted as true but not to *say* it; for, as Dummett rightly remarks, if the radical internalist cannot say it, he or she cannot think it either.

A better move for the radical internalist to make would be to say that *true* is just a device for disquotation, and not the name of a significant property that the proposition "Caesar had someone shave him the day he crossed the Rubicon" determinately does or does not have. Of course, this will not work either if "True is the name of a significant property that the proposition 'Caesar had someone shave him the day he crossed the Rubicon' determinately does or does not have" is something we "accept as true." It is not quite clear that there is such a (coherent) position as radical internalism. But the best move for the radical internalist is to join forces with Rorty, who recently says, "Let's try some new ways of thinking! We might like them. Our interests and values – both old familiar interests and values and some new ones which we may not yet be quite conscious of having – may turn out to be better served by these new ways."[30]

But if the radical internalist position is to be conceived of in this way, as just a proposal for a new way of talking, Dummett has mounted what seems to me the best possible argument against it by pointing out that the consequences would be disastrous. The heart of pragmatism is the idea that notions that are indispensable to our best practice, are justified by that very fact; and in this respect, I am a pragmatist.

It may be, however, that Dummett's metaphysical question, "namely: if there *is* some specific thing that we should do, *what makes it the case that we should do that*, even though we cannot be sure what it is?" is a question about my use of counter-factuals. Perhaps the question is this: what makes it the case that one of the two counter-factuals – (1) if we were in the "ideal" situation we would say that Caesar had someone shave him on the day he crossed the Rubicon; (2) if we were in the "ideal" situation we would say that Caesar did not have anybody shave him on the day he crossed the Rubicon – is determinately true, even though we cannot, now and perhaps even in the future, be sure which of the counter-factuals is true? But again, the answer – the only answer – is "banal." If (1) is true, what "makes it true" is that Caesar did have someone shave him on the day he crossed the

Rubicon, together with the fact that this is the sort of thing that a person who is with another person, and paying attention, can observe and record. And if (2) is true, what "makes it true" is that Caesar did not have someone shave him on the day he crossed the Rubicon, together with the fact that this is the sort of thing that a person who is with another person, and paying attention, can observe and record. "But this assumes what is at issue – that Caesar did or did not have someone shave him on the day he crossed the Rubicon, even if we cannot now or in the future justify an answer." Of course. What are we supposed to do, "refute" *skepticism?*

Dummett is perfectly right in thinking that if one is what he calls a "moderate constructivist," then one's explanation of the sense in which the notion of truth is not "recognition-transcendent" will involve counter-factuals. And at times Dummett himself has been attracted to a more extreme constructivism (or internalism), which may be why he equates regarding (any) unverified counter-factuals as having truth-values with "taking an externalist attitude towards counter-factuals." But regarding some statements (e.g. some counter-factuals) as having determinate truth-values even though we will never know what they are is only *radical* externalism when those statements are supposed to be such that we could not have recognized their truth or falsity, even if we had been well placed.

But is even radical externalism always mistaken? To be sure, there is a form of externalism that leads directly to skepticism: the form that insists we might all be "brains in a vat," which Crispin Wright discusses in his chapter in this volume. And our practice does, I believe, presuppose that that form of externalism is wrong, that truth is not, in a vast majority of cases, recognition-transcendent. But is it really *never* "recognition-transcendent"? Suppose I say,

> Even if there happen to be intelligent extraterrestials, we may never be able to verify that there are.

The antecedent of this conditional certainly presupposes that it is possible that

> There do not happen to be any intelligent extraterrestrials

(otherwise why the conditional?). But if is true that there do not happen to be any intelligent extraterrestials, could we verify it, even in principle? And if we cannot now say how we could, must we decide that, after all, we do not know what we mean when we say this might be true? I shall not discuss this question here, but I think we must ask whether it is obvious that commitment to the idea that truth is sometimes recognition-transcendent does really amount to "metaphysical realism."[31]

Wittgenstein

Dummett cites textual evidence that Wittgenstein held what he and I would both regard an untenable position with respect to mathematical necessity, counter-factuals, etc. I will not enter into an argument as to whether the passages Dummett cites must be read in the way he reads them. But I will say the following: (a) this is not material Wittgenstein *published* (Heaven forfend that anyone should publish as *my* views some of the ideas I have entertained, and even tried out in my courses); (b) by and large, Wittgenstein only discusses positions that he himself has been at one time or another strongly attracted to – one cannot infer that he continued to hold them; (c) I have been working on, and plan to publish, a number of studies arguing that Wittgenstein provides us with the basis for a sane realism.

Even if my interpretation of Wittgenstein is right, it does not follow that Dummett's is flatly wrong. There may, after all, be more than one "line" that one can extract from Wittgenstein's protracted philosophical reflections. But I would insist that the radical internalist line, if it ever was Wittgenstein's, should not be read into the later work.

Even in the unpublished works one can find quite different attitudes from the one Michael Dummett finds. I should like to close with two examples. In the unpublished "Lectures on Religious Belief," Wittgenstein says that the religious person is "using a picture."[32] But, at the end of the last lecture, he himself offers what Dummett would call a "banal" reading of this remark. And he adds, "If I wished to say anything more I was merely being philosophically arrogant."

Elsewhere Wittgenstein himself writes, "It is true that we can compare a picture that is firmly rooted in us to a superstition; but it is equally true that we *always* eventually have to reach some firm ground, either a picture or something else, so that a picture which is at the root of all our thinking is to be respected and not treated as a superstition."[33] That being true is not the same as merely being accepted as true is a picture that is firmly rooted in us if anything is, and it is at the root of all of our thinking, as Dummett very well reminds us. We can, from within our thinking and our lives, refuse to treat it as a superstition without thinking that we must provide the guarantee from outside that metaphysical realism seeks. And this is what I think Wittgenstein was trying to tell us.

4   Michael Hallett on Model Theory and Realism

Michael Hallett has written a profound survey of model-theoretic arguments bearing on realism issues, beginning with my own and working his way back to the beginning of the century, with instructive detours into questions of absoluteness in set theory, predicativity and impredicativity, etc. This is a rich chapter, and "must" reading for all future researchers into these topics.

In addition, from the very beginning of his chapter Hallett raises a deep and interesting question. It is this: to what extent can a metaphysical realist (about non-mathematical entities) evade the model-theoretic arguments I deployed by taking a strongly non-realist line about sets, etc.? "Models" are, after all, set-theoretic entities (sequences, some of whose elements are typically of sets of complicated sorts). If sets are not theory-independent entities, then can the use of permutations of individuals, the Downward and Upward Skolem–Löwenheim theorems, etc., all be rejected as having to do only with entities that are admittedly theory-dependent, and not showing anything about the theory-independent world?

My response will have three parts. First of all, the model-theoretic argument (either in "Realism and Reason"[34] or in *Reason, Truth and History*) does not depend on saying that THE WORLD *is* a "model" for the language in question. THE WORLD (i.e. the theory-independent world of metaphysical realism) is simply supposed to be something which has an intrinsic, built-in, division into "objects" (or "pieces," in the language of "Realism and Reason"). Even a metaphysical realist who happens to be a nominalist believes in THE WORLD in this sense. What I wrote (in "Realism and Reason") was that, in the standard (post-symbolic logic) realist semantics, "there is a relation between each term in the language, and a piece of the world (or a *kind* of piece, if the term is a general term)." This does not imply that the world itself is a sequence whose first member is the set of all "pieces" of THE WORLD, and whose subsequent members are individuals and sets of individuals and sets of ordered pairs of individuals – corresponding to the individual constants, one-place predicates, two-place predicates – of the language (i.e. a "model" in the technical set-theoretic sense). It simply implies that extensions can be assigned to the terms of the language in the standard way.

But perhaps even the notion that the extension of a general term like "cat" is a set of pieces of THE WORLD is supposed to be objectionable? This brings me to the second part of my response.

This will have the form of a dilemma. First horn: I assume that Hallett is imagining a metaphysical realist who does not disallow reference to mathematical entities; he simply does not have a realistic attitude towards them. (Simon Blackburn, when he wrote *Spreading the Word*, was such a metaphysical realist.) For such a thinker, talk of mathematical entities is all right as long as such talk does not claim to "correspond to some independent mathematical realm existing prior to it and therefore [to be] defective if it fails to pin this realm down." So why should I not be able to formulate my model-theoretic argument[35] for his behalf as follows?

> Let us define a permutation, call it Perm(x), which leaves observable macro-objects invariant and permutes at least some of the unobservables, in any physically possible world. (If the metaphysical realist allows me enough mathematics to do physics, such permutations can actually be defined.) Now, you do believe that there is a reference *predicate*, REF, even if you do not believe there exists (theory-independently, at any rate) a relation (an abstract entity) corresponding to it, and you are willing to say that for each hydrogen atom[36] X, and for each token of the term "hydrogen atom" in the language, that token of "hydrogen atom" REFS X. Now the point of the model-theoretic argument is that your behavior would be exactly the same, and the truth-values of all your sentences would be exactly the same, on the hypothesis that you are mistaken about the reference of your terms and each token of an arbitrary term (e.g. "hydrogen atom") really REFS not the things in what you take to be its extension (the hydrogen atoms) but their Perm-images (e.g. for each hydrogen atom X, "hydrogen atom" really REFS Perm(X), not X). Even if there is not, theory-independently, such an object as Perm, still, the *predicate* "x REFS Perm(y)" would seem to be a perfectly good predicate, just as "x's height is three times y's height" is a perfectly good predicate, even though (according to you) there is not, theory-independently, such an object as three.

Second horn: if the metaphysical realist in question does not allow *any* reference to mathematical entities, he or she faces the familiar questions as to how he or she is going to do science.[37]

Last part of my response: as my response to the second horn suggested, the statements we make about the world in modern physics quantify over mathematical entities as well as over physical ones (and sometimes it is indeterminate whether an entity is mathematical or physical, as I pointed out in my comments on Blackburn's chapter). But this means that the very notion of conceiving mathematical entities as theory-dependent and physical entities as theory-independent is unclear. What would it mean, for example, to think of a (classical) particle as theory-independent and its energy-momentum 4-vector as theory-dependent?

On the Notion of "Theory-dependence"

In "Realism and Reason" I rejected the idea that there is a "theory-independent fact of the matter" about reference, but I did not explain what the alternative view was (except for a reference to "verificationist semantics" which I now find embarrassing). And my Hegelian metaphor in *Reason, Truth and History* ("mind and the world jointly *make up* mind and the world") certainly did nothing to help matters (although I still like the metaphor). In a recent publication,[38] I explained the metaphor, and I would like to repeat the explanation here.

First of all, I do not believe that (most) objects are causally dependent on language users. There would still have been stars even if language users had not evolved, and oak leaves would have been green even if language users had not evolved. But there would not have been any sentences if language users had not evolved. There would have been a world, all right, but there would not have been any truths about the world.[39]

For a metaphysical realist this is not important, because for metaphysical realists, "discovering the truth" means discovering the truth that is waiting to be written down. In my view, there is no one metaphysically privileged description that is waiting to be written down. We invent better and worse ways of using words, none of which is THE WORLD's own way. But in spite of the fact that no way of using words is THE WORLD's own way, some of our sentences state facts, and the truth of a true factual sentence is not something we make up. We do not make the world, but we help to define it. The rich and ever-growing collection of truths about the world is the joint product of the world and language users. Or better, it is the product of the world, with language users playing a creative role in the process of production.

It seems to me that denying that there is a world (THE WORLD) which dictates a unique description to us (as the Fundamentalist's God was supposed to have dictated the bible to Moses) is not denying anything that is right in "realism." Giving up the idea of a "theory-independent world" is not denying that there is a world.

5 Michael Redhead on Quantum Logic

Michael Redhead has devoted a great deal of care and attention to a close reading and analysis of my successive views on the interpretation of quantum mechanics. I am grateful for his attention, as well as for the clarity of his exposition, and in these comments I want to explain why I no longer hold those views. His comments have been enormously valuable in forcing me to think carefully through and formulate explicitly a number of my own objections to my previous views that I have been brooding about and discussing with friends for some years now.[40] In addition, I want to reply to the charge of non sequitur that Redhead makes in connection with one of my arguments and to point out an important respect in which Redhead's account gets my earlier views wrong.

The Perspectival Interpretation of Quantum Mechanics

Redhead devotes nearly half of his paper to my 1978 "Quantum Mechanics and the Observer." He is quite right in thinking that that paper was very important for the development of my views, and, for that reason, I want to review some of its principal themes.

Although I say one or two things about quantum logic at the end of "Quantum Mechanics and the Observer," the bulk of that paper was devoted to presenting and defending an interpretation of von Neumann's views on quantum mechanics.[41] (Although von Neumann's interpretation of quantum mechanics does not presuppose quantum logic, the idea of using quantum logic to interpret quantum mechanics originated with von Neumann and is suggested, although not very clearly or persuasively, in the same book.[42] These two ideas – von Neumann's "perspectival" interpretation of quantum mechanics and quantum logic – are what I want to focus on in what follows.)

I call von Neumann's interpretation "perspectival" because its most striking feature is that the so-called "collapse" of the ψ-function upon measurement is alleged to depend on what I called the "perspective" of the observer, and this perspective appears to be one that the observer can choose, albeit within narrow limits. For example, von Neumann insists that we do not have to think of the collapse as taking place whenever a macro-observable is involved; I can, if I wish, take a perspective in which the collapse takes place only when a scientist reads the result of the measurement, say by looking at a dial, or takes place only when the nerve impulse from the eye reaches the scientist's visual cortex, etc. I can even adopt the perspective that the collapse takes place only when I myself (and not another human being) register (or my "consciousness" registers) the result of the measurement. This view has quite striking implications for the celebrated "Schrödinger's cat" paradox.

Schrödinger, the reader will recall, imagined a cat in an isolated system (today we might imagine a satellite in orbit). At a predetermined time t_0, one particle is emitted by an apparatus and strikes a half-silvered mirror. If the particle passes through the mirror (an event whose quantum-mechanical probability is $\frac{1}{2}$) the particle will strike a detector which will activate equipment which will electrocute the cat; if the particle is reflected (quantum-

mechanical probability $\frac{1}{2}$) the cat will survive. In what follows, I shall imagine that the apparatus tickles the cat rather than electrocuting it, not only
for humane reasons, but so that the "cat" (who may be a human scientist,
if we wish) can remember the outcome, no matter which it may be. If we let
$| \psi_{\text{tickled cat}} \rangle$ be the quantum mechanical state that the cat will be in if it is
tickled, and $| \psi_{\text{not tickled cat}} \rangle$ be the state that the cat will be in if it is not ticked,
then, the Schrödinger equation implies that after the time t_0 the cat will be
in the (unimaginable) state of being in a superposition of being dead and
alive, or in our case, of having been tickled and not having been tickled, i.e.
$\frac{1}{\sqrt{2}}(| \psi_{\text{tickled cat}} \rangle + | \psi_{\text{not tickled cat}} \rangle)$. Schrödinger's own resolution to the paradox, which was to say that the ψ-function does not give a "complete
description," and so some sort of hidden variable theory is needed, has not
proved successful; more recently, two main approaches have been pursued.

One approach is to say that the ψ-function "collapses" whenever a
superposition of the anomalous kind envisaged by Schrödinger would
otherwise result – a quantum state in which some *macro*-observable would
have an indefinite value, or rather a superposition of different definite
values. On this approach, the cat itself makes a "measurement," as it were
(even it is electrocuted, and so does not know the result of the measurement); and this measurement "throws" the cat from the state ψ into one
of the two states $| \psi_{\text{tickled cat}} \rangle$ or $| \psi_{\text{not tickled cat}} \rangle$. The other approach is to say
that the ψ-function never really "collapses" at all; the best-known version of
this approach is the "many worlds" interpretation of quantum mechanics
according to which, in the Schrödinger cat case, there are two, so to speak,
parallel worlds or parallel realities, one of which corresponds to the part of
the ψ-function (the "relative state") in which the cat is tickled and one of
which corresponds to the part of the ψ-function (the "relative state") in which
the cat is not tickled.

Von Neumann's interpretation, as I read it, differs from both of these
approaches. On von Neumann's view, I can adopt the perspective that the
ψ-function collapses at the time t_0, by saying that the cat makes a measurement at that time; but I can also adopt the perspective that the ψ-function
does not collapse until an external observer looks to see what happened.
And there is no fact of the matter as to which account is correct; operation-
ally, they lead to the same predictions, as von Neumann attempts to show
by means of an example.

In order to formalize this account, von Neumann introduces an idealized
picture of measurement. In this picture, a measurement always involves two
distinct systems and two observables. Let the system being measured by S
and the system doing the measuring be M. The purpose of the measurement is, let us say, to determine the value of an observable R, defined in the
system S. For simplicity, let us assume R has a discrete spectrum of possible

values r_i. In this case the measuring observable, call it U, which is assumed to be something (e.g. the position of a dial) which can be treated according to classical physics, must also have a discrete spectrum of values, u_i, corresponding to the values r_i of R. The vague requirement that the observable U be "classical" is an essential part of the von Neumann account, and, indeed, in of all versions of the "Copenhagen Interpretation." In practice, what it usually comes to is that we choose U to be a macro–observable.

Von Neumann's idealization consists in requiring that at the end of the interaction between M and S, the state[43] $|\psi\rangle$ of the combined system M+S can be written as a weighted sum[44] of tensor products: $|\psi\rangle = \Sigma\, c_i |\varphi_i\rangle |\psi_i\rangle$, where the $|\varphi_i\rangle$ lie in the Hilbert space of M and the $|\psi_i\rangle$ lie in the Hilbert space of S, and (for $i = 1, 2, 3, \ldots$) $\varphi_i\rangle$ is a state in which the observable U has the definite value u_i and $|\psi_i\rangle$ is a state in which the observable R has the definite value r_i. The different "perspectives" referred to above (e.g. in which M is a human being, or a particular human being, or a person's eye, or a person's visual cortex) correspond to different ways of (1) determining what counts as the total system involved in the measurement; and (2) dividing the total system into an M and an S (and specifying what U and R are). As long as M and S (and U and R) are so chosen that the state[2] at some suitable time can be written in the form indicated, the perspective is admissible. What it means to adopt the perspective is this: one is to predict that at the time in question the state will "collapse" from ψ to one of the states $|\varphi_i\rangle |\psi_i\rangle$, with a probability proportional to the square of the absolute value of the complex coefficient c_i. Thus if one adopts the perspective, one will *expect* the value r_i with a probability proportional to $|c_i|$, and the way one will *tell* if the value r_i has been obtained in S is by looking at M and seeing if the value of U is u_i.

One respect in which von Neumann's account of measurement is idealized is this: the assumption that after the measurement (including the "collapse") the system is in a state of the form $|\varphi_i\rangle |\psi_i\rangle$ can only be true if at the end of the measurement all interaction between S and M has ceased. But very often this is not the case; for example, in the two–slit experiment, the particle is absorbed by M, not removed to a non–interacting position. In "Quantum Mechanics and the Observer," I proposed to generalize von Neumann's criterion (as, I believe, it is generalized in practice by working physicists) by requiring instead that at the end of the measurement the state $|\psi\rangle$ of the combined system M+S must be able to be written as a sum (which need not be a sum of tensor products): $|\psi\rangle = \Sigma c_i\, |\Phi_i\rangle$, where the $|\Phi_i\rangle$ lie in the Hilbert space of M+S, and (for $i = 1, 2, 3, \ldots$) $|\Phi_i\rangle$ is a state in which the observable U in the Hilbert space of M has the definite value u_i *and* the observable R in the Hilbert space of S has the definite value r_i.

The argument that Redhead criticizes, for the possibility of knowing some observable that do not commute, offered in "Quantum Mechanics and the Observer" used as premises not merely the modification in the von Neumann requirements for a measurement just described,[45] but also the perspectival interpretation of the "collapse" that I attributed to von Neumann himself.[46] Given those two premises, the argument I offered follows straightforwardly. But I agree with Redheads that it was not satisfactory; not, however for the reason Redhead gives: the problem was not that my argument was invalid, but that, as I shall show in a later section, the premises were not true.

In the case I described in "Quantum Mechanics and the Observer," the state of the total system consisting of the particle and the emulsion at the time *just before the "collapse"* – that is, the state after the particle has had time to hit the emulsion, but before we have looked to see if it hit and where it hit – can be written in the from

$$|\psi\rangle = (\Sigma c_i |\psi^i_{\text{out}}\rangle) + c_{\text{in}} |\psi_{\text{in}}\rangle.$$

Each $|\psi^i_{\text{out}}\rangle$ is a definite state of the "classical" observables U, pertaining to just the measuring apparatus, whose value is i if and only if the detector in the ith region of the emulsion[47] fired (in my paper, I imagined looking at the emulsion and finding a spot in the ith region instead of having detectors wired to the regions), and $|\psi_{\text{in}}\rangle$ is also a definite state of U, corresponding to the negative result that none of the detectors fired. Simultaneously, each $|\psi^i_{\text{out}}\rangle$ is a definite state of the observable R, pertaining to just the particle, whose value is i if and only if the particle ended in the ith region of the emulsion, and $|\psi_{\text{in}}\rangle$ is also a definite state of R, corresponding to the negative result that the particle stayed inside the box. From the premise of perspectivalism, it follows that it is admissible to say that at the time of the measurement the state "collapses" either into one of the $|\psi^i_{\text{out}}\rangle$ or else into $|\psi_{\text{in}}\rangle$, with probabilities proportional to the squares of the absolute values of the various coefficients (i.e. the c_i and c_{in}). This corresponds to predicting that the particle will hit the ith region of the emulsion with the probability so calculated (and then telling whether the particle did hit one of the regions or failed to hit the emulsion at all by seeing which detector fired or if no detector fired). This is the conventional way of applying von Neumann's analysis to this measurement.

But (I pointed out) there is another admissible perspective in this situation. One can define a different "classical" observable U′, pertaining to just the measuring apparatus, whose value is 1 if and only if at least one detector fired (in my paper, I imagined finding a spot somewhere on the emulsion – it is immaterial whether one observed which region). I argued that the state

$$|\psi_{out}\rangle = (\Sigma c_i \ |\psi_{out}^i\rangle$$

is a definite state of the classical observable U' corresponding to the value U' = 1 (a hit is detected on the emulsion), and simultaneously a definite state of the quantum observable R' (particle in/out of the box), corresponding to the value R' = 1 (particle out of the box). Similarly, the state $|\psi_{in}\rangle$ is a definite state of the observable U' corresponding to the value U' = 0 (no hit is detected), and simultaneously a definite state of the observable R' corresponding to the value R' = 0 (particle remains in the box). Now the (unnormalized) state at the time of the measurement is $\psi = k_1|\psi_{out}\rangle + k_2|\psi_{in}\rangle$, where $k_1 =$ 1 and $k_2 = c_{in}$. It at once follows that it is admissible to say that the state "collapses" either into the state $|\psi_{out}\rangle$ or else into $|\psi_{in}\rangle$, with probabilities proportional to the squares of the absolute values of k_1 and k_2. This corresponds to predicting that the probability that the particle will hit the the emulsion is $|k_1|^2/(|k_1|^2 + |k_2|^2)$ (and then telling whether the particle did hit the emulsion or failed to hit the emulsion by seeing if a detector fired or if no detector fired). This is an unconventional way of applying von Neumann's analysis to this measurement, and it leads to a determination of whether the particle left/did not lead the box (a quantum mechanical "retrodiction").

By employing the first perspective, we say that there was a measurement which determined that the particle hit the emulsion in, say, the seventeenth region; by employing the other perspective, we can say that the particle is in, say, the state $|\psi_{out}\rangle$. But the inference is *not* the one Redhead criticizes:[48] "U = k (i.e. the kth detector fired), *therefore* the state is $|\psi_{out}\rangle$." Rather, the inference is: "U' = 1 (i.e. at least one detector fired, or there is a spot on the plate – since U' and not U is the observable we are interested in, it is immaterial whether one uses detectors attached to the regions at all, since one can perfectly well observe that the particle hit the plate somewhere without observing which region) – therefore, given the choice of U' and R' as the observables with respect to which the collapse takes place, the state after the collapse is $|\psi_{out}\rangle$)." The point is that two *different* "collapses" are involved, corresponding to two different "perspectives."[49] Redhead correctly observes that the inference can also be validated using quantum logic (via the derivation of Lüders's rule that Michael Friedman and I gave);[50] this is an instance of the general fact that perspectivalism and quantum logic give exactly the same results; each conditionalization using quantum logical probability corresponds to the choice of a perspective and a "collapse" in the perspectival interpretation. That my argument does not have to be accepted if one does not accept perspectivalism is also obvious, since in the first of the two non-perspectival approaches to measurement that I described earlier, there is a fact of the matter as to when and how the "collapse" takes place (so the whole idea of "putting" the collapse one place or another makes no sense), while in the second (the many worlds approach, and its relatives) there is no "collapse" at all, but only the need to distinguish between the state of the total system and the various "relative states" after the measurement.

One last point about von Neumann's account: it is also explicitly assumed that *every* projection operator corresponds to a meaningful quantum mechanical proposition (one to the effect that a system has/does not have a property). What has led me to retract my allegiance to the perspectival account and to quantum logic is the discovery, described below, that these assumptions cannot be jointly maintained.

Complicating the Life of Schrödinger's Cat

Philosophers writing about this problem[51] have added another wrinkle to Schrödinger's thought experiment. If it were possible to prepare a cat in the state $\psi = \frac{1}{\sqrt{2}} (\,|\,\psi_{\text{tickled cat}}\rangle + |\,\psi_{\text{not tickled cat}}\rangle)$, then that whole system would be in a definite state with respect to the property B corresponding to the projection operator P_ψ. Now, if the "collapse" occasioned by measurement took place at the time t_0 (the time when the cat was tickled/not tickled), and instead of staying in the state B, the cat was "thrown into" one of the two possible states of being tickled ($\,|\,\psi_{\text{tickled cat}}\rangle$) or being not tickled ($\,|\,\psi_{\text{not tickled cat}}\rangle$) by the "measurement," as the proponents of the first of the three approaches to measurement we mentioned maintain, then the quantity B did not have a definite value after time t_0, because the two-valued observable, call it T, such that $T = 1$ if the cat is tickled and $T = 0$ if the cat is not tickled and B do not commute. It follows that if we were able to figure out a way of measuring B (and, as mentioned above, it is one of von Neumann's assumptions that every projection operator corresponds to something which is measurable in principle), then we would be able to test the claim that the collapse always takes place at the time t_0 (when the cat is tickled or not tickled). We could not, of course, test this by making a T measurement, because if we look to see if the cat is tickled or not tickled, then we will see either a tickled cat $|\,\psi_{\text{tickled cat}}\rangle$) or a not tickled cat)$|\,\psi_{\text{not tickled cat}}\rangle$). But if, instead of looking to see whether the cat is tickled or not tickled, we measure the observable B, then if the cat remains in the superposition, the strange state $|\,\psi\rangle$, after t_0 (as long as no outside observer disturbs the system before the B measurement) we will find that $B = 1$ every time. If, on the other hand, collapse does take place even if no outside observer comes and looks to see whether the cat is tickled or not tickled, as the first approach maintains, then if we repeat this experiment a large number of times we will get the result B = 1 about half the time[52] and the result B = 0 the other half of the time. If we repeat the experiment a very large number of times and we get the result B = 1 every time, then the chance that the probability of the result B = 1 is really $\frac{1}{2}$ and our result is a statistical fluke will be virtually zero. So we could be as sure as you like that superpositions of the form $\frac{1}{\sqrt{2}}(|\psi_{\text{tickled cat}}\rangle + |\psi_{\text{not tickled cat}}\rangle)$ really occur, or as sure as you like that such superpositions never occur, and that collapse *always* takes place when the cat is tickled/not tickled, if that is the correct story, by performing this experiment a sufficiently large number of times.

This is not yet fatal for von Neumann's perspectivalism, but it does place constraints on how it can be understood, If we go back to the two approaches we described earlier, that is (1) the approach according to which the collapse always takes place (non-perspectively) when a state like ψ in which macro–observables are "superimposed" would otherwise occur, and (2) the many worlds interpretation, then we see that these approaches lead to different predictions in this highly complex case. The approaches are not empirically equivalent. If the first approach is correct, then B = 0 will be observed half of the time, on the average. If the many worlds interpretation is correct, then the external observer who measures B will always obtain B = 1. So both approaches cannot be empirically adequate. What about von Neumann's approach?

On von Neumann's approach, the perspective according to which the ψ-function does not collapse until I perform a measurement is admissible.[53] If the measurement I perform is a T measurement (looking to see if the cat is tickled or not tickled), then it will make no difference to my predictions whether I adopt the perspective according to which the collapse does not take place until t_1 (when I look) or instead adopt the perspective according to which the "cat" made a T measurement at t_0 and my looking to learn the result of that (earlier) measurement is a "classical" affair which does not call for quantum mechanical treatment. (I just learn what is already fixed and definite.) This, indeed, is what von Neumann argues. But if my measurement at t_1 is a B-measurement, what should I expect? To expect that I might see B = 0 would just be to assume that the ψ-function collapsed earlier, which is contrary to the perspective I adopted. So I must join the many worlders and predict that I will always observe B = 1. In short, this is not a case in which I am free to put the "cut" between the observer and the system wherever I like, because different predictions will result.

So far, we have the result that if von Neumann's perspectivalism is correct, then from the point of view of an external B-measurer the cat must stay in the superposition $\frac{1}{\sqrt{2}}(|\psi_{\text{tickled cat}}\rangle + |\psi_{\text{not tickled cat}}\rangle)$ until the B-measurement, even though from the cat's own point of view[54] the cat went into one of the two states $|\psi_{\text{tickled cat}}\rangle$ or $|\psi_{\text{not tickled cat}}\rangle$ at the earlier time t_0.

For the external observer, the cat's perspective is not admissible, unless the external observer's measurement commutes with the cat's tickled/not tickled "measurement," and a B-measurement does not. In the next section, I shall show that even restricting the B-measurer's perspectives in this way does not avoid inconsistencies.

Why Not Just Deny that B is Really Measurable?

It might seem easy for (a latter-day) von Neumann to avoid this whole problem by denying that observables like B are really measurable. But it is not clear that von Neumann can really do this without abandoning the claim that it is up to the external observer to decide if the cut was reduced before he or she made a measurement. And this claim is the heart of what I am calling von Neumann's perspectivalism.

In the first place, mere technical possibility of measurement is not at issue. Even if it is impossible to measure B for technical reasons (too much energy would be required, or whatever), this would only show that we cannot in practice choose between these different approaches to measurement on empirical grounds. In principle, they would still lead to different predictions; predictions which it would be physically possible to test, even if the test is not technically possible. At the very least, one would need an argument that physical law prevents the measurement of observables like B.

Recently, Jeffrey Bub[55] has begun to develop such an approach. In Bub's new interpretation, macro-observables are never superimposed at all; thus observables like B *cannot* have determinate values. They cannot be measured, because they have no determinate values to be discovered. But this approach is incompatible with von Neumann's, since it is von Neumann's position (in the case that the measurement by the external observer at t_1 is a T measurement) that there is no fact of the matter as to whether T took on a definite value at t_0 or at t_1. What von Neumann would need would be a physical law that prohibited B measurement (and not just because of "contingent" human limitations) without prohibiting states in which B = 1. In short, it would not be easy for (a latter-day) von Neumann to give up the idea that all projection operators correspond to "observables" without giving up precisely his most characteristic ideas about measurement.

The Inconsistency of Perspectivalism

Earlier I promised to show that von Neumann's several assumptions cannot be jointly maintained. The first hint of such a difficulty was raised by Nancy

Cartwright.[56] Cartwright was addressing my version of the quantum logical interpretation rather than von Neumann's perspectivalism, but, as I remarked above, these two approaches are empirically equivalent. Commenting on my thought experiment of replacing Schrödinger's cat by a scientist who is either "tickled" or "not tickled" (or observes some other macro-observable) at time t_0 when the photon passes through/is reflected by the half-silvered mirror, she asked whether the "cat's" predictions and the predictions of the external scientist would be consistent.

At first blush, they are not (but I still thought there was a way out).[57] The "cat," using Lüders's Rule (or the quantum logical conditionalization Michael Friedman and I described in "Quantum Logic, Conditional Probability and Interference," which gives the same results as Lüders's Rule) will assign a probability of $\frac{1}{2}$ to B = 1, if it assumes there is going to be a B measurement at t_1. The external observer will assign a probability of 1 to B = 1, if he or she is going to measure B at t_1. Given the "cat's" calculated expectation value, the "cat" would be irrational not to bet that B = 0 if it is offered odds better than 50:50 against; but if it does it will lose money every time! For, if on any occasion it did not lose money, then that would be an occasion on which the external observer would observe B = 0;[58] but if perspectivalism (or, alternatively, quantum logic) is right, there will never be such an occasion. Indeed, even if the "cat" is informed of the result of all its previous (unsuccessful) bets,[59] it will still never learn from this experience; for the information it possesses (that it is in the state $|\psi_{\text{tickled cat}}\rangle$, respectively $|\psi_{\text{not tickled cat}}\rangle$) is maximal information, and there is no way to calculate a probability from maximal information in perspectivalism except to use Lüders's Rule (i.e. von Neumann's "Projection Postulate," in its correct form).[60]

My answer to Nancy Cartwright depended essentially on quantum logic, and not just on perspectivalism. The answer was that the cat should be thought of as knowing *two* pieces of information which the quantum logic does not allow it to conjoint. (Redhead rightly points out the importance of the idea that we can know certain "unconjoinable" facts to my later version of the quantum logical approach, and he rightly points out that one of the aims of "Quantum Mechanics and the Observer" was to give an independent argument for that conclusion – but not, however, an argument independent of perspectivalism.) The "cat" knows[61] that it was originally in the state $|\psi\rangle$ corresponding to B = 1. Arguing that it has now observed that T = 1 (respectively, T = 0, and using Lüders's Rule, it concludes that it is now in the state $|\psi_{\text{tickled cat}}\rangle$ (respectively $|\psi_{\text{not tickled cat}}\rangle$), and this is perfectly legitimate (in both von Neumann's approach and the quantum-logical approach of "Quantum Logic, Conditional Probability and Interference"). But if it uses only this information, it is ignoring something else it knows;

namely, that it *was* in the state $|\psi\rangle$ and that that state has not been physically disturbed in any way. Hence, it may legitimately conclude that it is still in the state $|\psi\rangle$ (adopt a perspective in which no collapse took place at t_0). Note that in the quantum-logical interpretation, it cannot conjoint these two pieces of information, but it can follow the following rule: believe anything that follows deductively (in quantum logic) from either piece of information (or from compatible consequences of both pieces of information). So, if it is asked "What will be the result of a B measurement?" it should answer "B = 1," since that follows (in quantum logic) from its knowledge (in one perspective) that it is still in the state $|\psi\rangle$, and nothing contrary follows from its other piece of information (its other "perspective"). Probability (quantum-logical conditionalization, or Lüders's Rule) should only be used when no part of one's knowledge settles the given question with certainty.

The problem with this answer (as David Albert pointed out to me several years later) is that it applies only to *ideal* B measurement. If the B measurement is not ideal (or, alternatively, if we make a measurement of an observable B′ very close to B) then neither the information (from one perspective) that the "cat" is still in the state $|\psi\rangle$ nor the information (from the other perspective) that it is now in the state $|\psi_{\text{tickled cat}}\rangle$ (respectively $|\psi_{\text{not tickled cat}}\rangle$)) settles the question "What will be the result of the non-ideal B measurement (respectively, B′ measurement)?" deductively.

But the problem is still worse. For consider an ordinary laboratory measurement – a real measurement, not a thought experiment like the ones we have been imagining. To apply von Neumann's approach at all (with or without quantum logic) we have to idealize by pretending that we know the state of the system S+M, where M can perfectly well include the observer. Using the Schrödinger equation, we arrive at a predicted pre-collapse state of the form $|\psi\rangle = \Sigma\, c_i|\varphi_i\rangle|\psi_i\rangle$ as described above. Applying the projection postulate (Lüders's Rule), we get a post-collapse state of the form $|\varphi_i\rangle|\psi_i\rangle$ (and we look at the value of U to see which one, say, $|\varphi_{17}\rangle|\psi_{17}\rangle$). But, if we accepted the argument I made in my reply to Nancy Cartwright, we could *always* argue (as I had the "cat" argue) that the original state $|\psi\rangle = \Sigma\, c_i|\varphi_i\rangle|\psi_i\rangle$ has not been disturbed in any way (since the "collapse" is not a real physical process). And since any measurement we are interested in making in the future is imperfect (ideal measurements do not exist), we would always be in the position of having two "perspectives" (the one in which the state of the whole system is $|\varphi_{17}\rangle|\psi_{17}\rangle$, and the one in which the state of the whole system is $|\psi\rangle$) which yield different probabilities for the outcome of the measurement we are going to perform next.

The difficulty is that if we are to use von Neumann's procedures in the way we actually do, we must ignore the pre-collapse state $|\psi\rangle = \Sigma\, c_i|\varphi_i\rangle$

$|\psi_i\rangle$ after we have applied Lüders's Rule (which is why the transition from $|\psi\rangle$ to $|\varphi_{17}\rangle$ $|\psi_{17}\rangle$ appears as a *collapse*: the pre-collapse state loses all significance). But this blocks my answer to Nancy Cartwright. In sum, quantum logic does not repair the difficulty that perspectivalism faces, that the different perspectives do not in all cases correspond to compatible predictions. It is not consistent to predict that something will sometimes be observed if one knows that there is even one perspective from which it will never be observed.

Quantum Logic, Realism, and the Admissibility Criterion

Michael Redhead surveys my successive papers on the interpretation of quantum mechanics, focusing on the technical issues. In particular, Redhead points out the error in my treatment of the two-slit experiment in "Is Logic Empirical?," and describes the way in which Michael Friedman and I repaired the error in "Quantum Logic, Conditional Probability and Interference." Incidentally, the argument he summarizes shows that the "transition probability" – given by Lüders's Rule for the probability that F will now be observed upon a suitable measurement if (1) the given state was $|\Phi\rangle$; and (2) a non-maximal measurement found that P – is the only possible generalization of the classical notion of conditional probability with the properties that $P_{|\Phi\rangle}$ (F | P) is a generalized probability measure (defined for *all* F, P, maximal or non-maximal, commuting or non-commuting) in the sense appropriate to quantum logic, and $P_{|\Phi\rangle}$ (F | P) reduces to classical conditional probability whenever F and P commute. Referring to $P_{|\Phi\rangle}$ (F | P) as a "transition probability" as I just did, and as Redhead does, may give the impression that it is to be thought of as the probability of a physical change, but Friedman and I thought of it rather as an epistemic probability; the probability one should assign to F if one starts with the knowledge that the state is $|\Phi\rangle$ and one obtains (whether through physical measurement, clairvoyance, a lucky guess, or whatever) the additional information that P.

"Is Logic Empirical?" was written from the stance of a strong metaphysical realist. Thus, Redhead's claim that "However, says Putnam, [the disjunction $q_1 \vee q_2 \vee q_3 \ldots q_N$] does not mean that there is some specifiable j for which q_j is true" is correct, in a sense, for my interpretation of quantum logic in "Quantum Mechanics and the Observer,"[62] but it is wrong as a description of the position in "Is Logic Empirical?" As the title suggests, the idea of "Is Logic Empirical?" was that the world could be such that classical logic just fails to apply to it and a different logic is the "true" one. In particular, I held that quantum logic disjunction *was* selective: the disjunction $q_1 \vee q_2 \vee q_3 \ldots q_N$ *did* mean that there is some j for which q_j is true;

although what Redhead writes is not literally wrong, since the *j* in question might indeed be beyond the powers of human beings to "specify." But even if we could not specify the *j*, from a "god's-eye view" there was supposed to be such a *j*.

Redhead disposes of the very possibility of such a "realist" interpretation of quantum logic briskly, saying that "for a proper realist semantics we would like to impose the admissibility criterion" that to count as an admissible valuation Val has to be "a truth valuation mapping propositions . . . on to the two-element Boolean algebra of truth values, 0 and 1." While the impossibility of such a valuation was known to me when I proposed quantum logic as a *realist* interpretation of quantum mechanics, this admissibility criterion did not seem right, and it takes a philosophical argument that Redhead does not supply to show that it is not question begging.

The reason this "admissibility criterion" seemed question begging to me is that the argument that a logic that fails to meet the criterion is not realist too much resembles the following "disproof" of Intuitionist logic. Let L be a language formalized in intuitionist logic. Define (in a suitable meta-language) "True in L" à la Tarski. Then for each sentence *S* of L, it will be provable (using principles acceptable to Intuitionists) that:

$$\text{``}S\text{''} \text{ is true} \equiv S,$$

and also provable that:

$$\text{``}S\text{''} \text{ is false} \equiv \neg S,$$

where " '*S*' is false" is defined as " '¬*S*' is true."

Now, using the *classical* principle $S \vee \neg S$, prove (?!) " '*S*' is true $\vee$ '*S*' is false," and conclude that the intuitionists are just wrong in rejecting *tertium non datur*! Clearly this proof just begs the philosophical question at issue, by assuming the very principle that is in dispute in the meta-language. For this reason, students of the foundations of mathematics (e.g. S.C. Kleene, or Kurt Gödel, or Georg Kreisel) are always careful to use only principles common to both intuitionist and classical logic in comparing the logical properties of the intuitionist and the classical systems.

Similarly, if L is a quantum-logical language and we construct an appropriate meta-language, then (using only principles common to both quantum logic and classical logic) we can define "True$_L$" in such a way that for each sentence *S* of L, it will be provable in the meta-language that:[63]

$$\text{True}_L(S) \equiv S,$$

But if we were now to assume that "$\text{True}_L(S)$" obeys the laws of classical (Boolean) logic, and in particular that it obeys the distributive laws, we would be able to prove that quantum logicians are wrong in rejecting the classical distributive laws. If we do not do this, however, and we define:

1   Val $(S)= 1 \equiv \text{True}_L(S)$, and
2   Val $(S)= 0 \equiv \text{True}_L(\neg S)$

then, I saw, we will be able to prove using principles common to classical logic and quantum logic that:

3   (For all sentences S of L) Val$(S) = 1 \lor$ Val$(S) = 0$, and
4   (For all sentences S, T of L) Val$(S \lor T) = 1 \equiv$ Val$(S) = 1 \lor$ Val$(T) = 1$,

and (the quantum logician can say) this shows that the valuation is "realist"!

Of course, this "proof" will no more convince an opponent of quantum logic than the first proof will convince an intuitionist. The opponent of quantum logic will want Val to have the further property

5   Val$(S) = 1$&(Val$(T) = 1 \lor$ Val$(U) = 1) \cdot \equiv \cdot$ (Val$(S) = 1$&(Val(T) $= 1 \cdot \lor \cdot$ (Val$(S) = 1$&(Val$(U) = 1$)

i.e. he or she will want the classical distributive law to hold in the meta-language. And this seems to beg the question.

But to require (as Redhead does here) that to count as an "admissible valuation" Val has to be "a truth valuation mapping propositions . . . on to the two-element Boolean algebra of truth values, 0 and 1" is just to require that the meta-language in which Val is defined be Boolean and not quantum-logical. And this "proof" should not convince any proponent of quantum logic – or so I thought.

Nor was I immediately convinced by the following argument: suppose that for some particular S, T, U, I maintain the truth of S&$(T \lor U)$, but I deny that S and T can be conjoined (and a fortiori, I deny that they have a true conjunction) and I deny that S and U can be conjoined)and a fortiori, I deny that they have a true conjunction).[64] "Now," (Michael Dummett once said to me), "since you maintain that $T \lor U$ is true – and (as a 'realist') you say that that means that at least one of the disjuncts is true from a god's-eye view, even if you cannot *tell* which one is true without disturbing the truth-value of S – it should not be absurd to suppose that you might *guess* which one is true, and guessing will not disturb S. But if you guess, as it might be, T, then, since you still believe S, which you asserted to begin with when you asserted S&$(T \lor U)$, you will be committed to S&T, and if you guess

U, then you will be committed to *S&U*." As it stands, this argument is question begging, because it assumes the classical law of conjunction introduction, if ⊢ *S* and ⊢ *T*, then ⊢ *S&T*, which was given up in the form of quantum logic which I was using by then, as Redhead explains.

But the notion of "guessing" behind Dummett's question was quite important. The idea behind "Is Logic Empirical?" was that logic is empirical in the way that geometry has turned out to be empirical. Now, going over to a non-Euclidean geometry in physics does not require us to forswear the possibility of describing what is going on, although we have had to learn to think in new ways and to learn new mathematical languages. If the analogy is really right, then going over to quantum logic should not require us to forswear the possibility of describing what is going on in a quantum-logical world, although we may again have to learn to think in new ways and to learn a new mathematical language.

In the case described by Dummett, there is not necessarily a problem: I can maintain that *S* is true *and* guess that *T* is true, and simply refuse to conjoin them (as we saw above, the idea that one may possess pieces of information that cannot be conjoined was crucial to my answer to Nancy Cartwright). But can I always do this? That is to say, could I – by incredible luck, perhaps, or with divine assistance – guess correctly the truth-value of every quantum-mechanical proposition? What constraints would my guesses have to obey?

Well, since I am interpreting disjunction "realistically," whenever I guess that a disjunction is true, I must guess that a disjunct – a *specified* disjunct – is true. Whenever I guess that a statement is true, I must guess that its negation is false. If I guess that a conjunction is true, I must guess that every conjunct is true, and if I guess that two compatible propositions are true, I must guess that their conjunction is true. And, since *S* ∨ ¬*S* is a tautology in quantum logic, I must guess that one of each pair of propositions of the form *S*, ¬*S* is true. But now, even if the world somehow does not obey Boolean logic, my guesses will certainly do so. A complete system of guesses of the kind just described would precisely be a "a truth valuation mapping propositions . . . on to the two–element Boolean algebra of truth values, 0 and 1."

Of course, I am agreeing with Michael Redhead here. The point of this discussion is to make clear why he is right in imposing the "admissibility criterion" that he does. A realist who rejected the admissibility criterion would have to maintain that although every quantum-mechanical proposition does have a determinate truth-value, it is impossible for us to even guess what those truth-values might be. But this would be to admit that we cannot describe what goes on in a "quantum-logical world" in the way in which we can describe what goes on in a non-Euclidean world[65].

My Interpretation in "Quantum Mechanics and the Observer"

By the time I wrote "Quantum Mechanics and the Observer," I had come to see that a completely "realist" interpretation of quantum mechanics could not be achieved with the aid of quantum logic. Indeed, even an interpretation which is "realist" in the sense of the "internal realism" I had adopted as my stance towards the "realism/anti-realism" debate after 1976 is beyond my powers to provide. For the "internal realist" account of truth presupposes the legitimacy of counter-factuals like "if we were to make a sufficiently good measurement of R, we would get the value 1" – presupposes that such counter-factuals can have truth-values even if no R-measurement is actually carried out. But, as is well known, there is no satisfactory way of assigning truth-values to such counter-factuals in present-day quantum mechanics. Certainly one cannot assume that quantum-mechanical measurements simply discover values that are there already. (My attempt to support that point of view by changing the logic had collapsed, as we saw.)

What I tried to do in the closing pages of "Quantum Mechanics and the Observer" was to mix realism and anti-realism in a complex way, by combining perspectivalism with quantum logic. One was to take a "realist" attitude towards the observables corresponding to the "perspective" one adopted. I can illustrate the idea thus: if I verify $S\&(T \lor U)$, then, according to the proposal I advanced, whether I say that the disjunction $T \lor U$ is selective (i.e. take the attitude that one of the disjuncts is determinately true) or non-selective will depend on whether I choose to make an S measurement or a T, U measurement. If I choose to make an S measurement, then I must take a "realist" attitude toward S and a non-realist attitude towards T, U (interpret the disjunction as non-selective); but if I choose to measure the two compatible observables T and U, then I must take a "realist" attitude towards them, and "retrodict" the value I find in the way I described in "Quantum Mechanics and the Observer." Of course, the question as to which, if any, of these incompatible "realist" perspectives is right from a god's-eye-view was rejected. Today this idea seems unacceptable to me for more than one reason; in the present comments I have focused on the inconsistency of the perspectivalism which it presupposes.

6   Thomas Ricketts on Carnap

Thomas Ricketts's close reading of Carnap's *Logical Syntax of Language* is certainly a contribution to our understanding of that work, and I have learned much from it. I certainly agree that the notions of language-independent "fact," of things that "make true" the sentences of a language L, indeed, any substantive notion of *truth*, are absent from that work and are not presupposed by Carnap's argument. Yet I am not ready to admit that my criticisms of Carnap were based on misreadings, or that my charges of conventionalism and empiricism were completely unfounded. Ricketts's Carnap, the Carnap who holds no doctrines but only asks for "clarification," without any substantive position on what clarification consists of,[66] is just not the Carnap I knew and loved.

Re Carnap's empiricism: the fact is that Carnap wrote *Der Logische Aufbau der Welt*. And while readings of that work which resemble Ricketts's reading of the *Logical Syntax* have been offered, they depend on playing down both the massiveness of the construction presented in that work – if Carnap just wanted to give an example of the possibility of alternative, equally correct "bases" for the reconstruction of the language of science, it is striking that he choose to work so hard to provide a phenomenalistic, indeed a solipsistic, reconstruction – and the explicit statement in that work that the solipsistic (*Eigenpsychisch*) basis is epistemologically primary.

Re Carnap's conventionalism: Ricketts himself does attribute one quite substantive ambition to Carnap – "coordinating definitions that specify the linguistic behavior that would make individuals the speakers of a language with a given syntax." We have an idea of what Carnap had in mind from a late paper proposing a behavioral criterion for synonymy and analyticity in natural languages.[67] What corresponds behaviorally to analyticity, according to that paper, is the subject's refusal to say he or she would give up a statement, even in counter-factual circumstances that the investigator instructs the subject to consider. Thus our (counter-factual) unwillingness to give them up does make statements analytic; and it also makes them true in the only sense of "true" that Carnap recognized, a Tarskian disquotational sense. That it make them true in a metaphysical realist sense of "true" is not a position that I ever attributed to Carnap. (My other criticisms of Carnap's conventionalism turn on the later introduction of the semantic notion of "consequence" in Carnap's writing, and Ricketts makes it clear that he is not discussing that period in Carnap's thought.)

7 Reply to David Wiggins

I am very grateful to David Wiggins for his generous and penetrating paper. Because I am substantially in agreement with what he writes, I shall only comment on a few points.

On the History of Hydrosemantics

Recently Dan Warren has pointed out to me a striking anticipation of my doctrines in Kant's *Critique of Pure Reason*. I cannot resist quoting the passage (from A 728) in full:

> To define, as the word itself indicates, really only means to present the complete, original conception of a thing within the limits of its concept. If this be our standard, an empirical concept cannot be defined at all but only made *explicit*. For since we find in it only a few characteristics of a certain species of sensible object, it is never certain that we are not using the word, in denoting one and the same object, sometimes so as to stand for more, and sometimes for fewer characteristics. Thus in the concept of *gold* one man may think, in addition to its weight, colour, malleability, also of its property of resisting rust, while another will perhaps know nothing of this quality. We make use of certain characteristics only so long as they are adequate for the purpose of making distinctions; new observations remove some properties and add others; and thus the limits of the concept are never assured. And indeed what useful purpose would be served by defining an empirical concept, such as, for instance, that of water? When we speak of water and its properties, we do not stop short at what is thought in the word, water, but procede to experiments. The word, with the few characteristics which we attach to it [the stereotype?] *is more properly to be regarded as a designation than as a concept of the thing.*

Ah well . . . Kant keeps stealing my ideas!

Frege and Semantic Externalism

The view I defended in "The Meaning of 'Meaning' " has come to be known as *semantic externalism*, because it holds that the "external world" contributes to the fixing of reference. (The term is unfortunate, because it contrasts what is "inside the mind" with the "external" world; I would prefer to think of the mind as itself a system of object-and-quality-involving abilities. On this conception it is not only true that meanings are not in our heads, as I put it in "The Meaning of 'Meaning'," but – as John McDowell has long put it – it is also true that our minds are not in our heads.) Most of Wiggins's paper is devoted to showing how a broadly Fregean scheme should be modified to accommodate semantic externalism, and I find his discussion extremely valuable in this regard. Whether Frege would have accepted Wiggins's suggestions is a difficult textual question. Two reasons for possible doubt occur to me:

1 Concepts which are partly fixed by things and qualities of things in the way in which *acid, uranium, water,* and *horse* are may (and usually do) have vague boundaries. (Is U235 uranium? Are hydrogen ions an acid? Is heavy water water? Was there a "first horse"?) Given Frege's well-known hatred of fuzz, could he have accepted such a way of fixing concepts?

2 Are such concepts "transparent" to reason, as Frege insisted concepts by nature are?

But I will not attempt to decide this historical issue. In any case, even if Frege would not have accepted Wiggins's amendments and adjustments, he should have.

Note, by the way, that Wiggins's interesting distinction between a concept and a conception of that concept seems also to be anticipated by Kant's talk of concepts and characteristics we attach to them.

The Possibility of Experts

Wiggins does make two small criticisms, to both of which I can reply very quickly.

1 He holds that, since I notoriously cannot tell elms from beeches, there is something I don't know about the *meaning* of "elm" and "beech." I still resist this way of speaking; but I agree that to possess the concept of gold I have to have the beginnings of an identificatory ability. And I do; I have an identificatory ability because I know to defer to experts (and I can find an expert if I need one).

2 The criticism in the last line of Wiggins's paper ("the necessity of experts") baffles me. Not only did I never say that experts are "necessary" in connection with words like "horse" and "water", but I explicitly said "'Water' did not exhibit it [the division of linguistic labor] at all prior to the rise of chemistry."[68] This does not mean that "Water" changed its extension when experts (physicists and chemists) appeared on the scene: the contrary is the whole point of semantic externalism.

Again, I wish to repeat that, like all of Wiggins's work, this is a profound discussion, and will repay repeated reading.

8 Crispin Wright on the Brain-in-a-Vat Argument

I felt a great deal of pleasure on hearing, and later on reading, Crispin Wright's careful and insightful study on "Putnam's Proof that We Are Not

Brains in a Vat." Wright formulates very clearly – more clearly than I myself did, in fact – the premises and the deductive steps involved in my argument, and he is admirably sensitive to the aims of the argument. Only with Wright's concluding section do we come into disagreement.

Wright claims that "it is quite clear" that "this line of criticism" [of metaphysical realism] will fail. Thus the existence of a disagreement is clear, but the exact nature of the disagreement may not be so clear.

Skepticism, Internal and Infinitely Regressive

One way of exploring this question is to consider various ways in which one may be a skeptic. One sort of skeptic – a very uninteresting sort – may raise a skeptical doubt only so that, no matter what premises one may rely on in answering the doubt, he or she can respond, "and how do you know *that*?" Obviously, this sort of skepticism – call it infinitely regressive skepticism – is "unanswerable," but equally obviously the existence of infinitely regressive skepticism shows only that justification must end somewhere. My argument was obviously not meant to refute infinitely regressive skepticism.

A more interesting form of skepticism – the form all interesting skepticism has taken from Sextus Empiricus to David Hume and beyond – works from within (for this reason, we may call it internal skepticism). The aim of the internal skeptic is to convince us, on the basis of assumptions we ourselves hold, that all or a large part of our claims about the empirical world cannot amount to knowledge.[69] Of course, even if the internal skeptic succeeds, we may not agree to become skeptics; we may decide to revise some of our beliefs instead. But the possibility that the internal skeptic may force us to do this is precisely the great value of internal skepticism. A successful internal skeptical challenge must at the very least confront us with an antinomy, and one always learns from an antinomy. It was against internal skepticism that my brain-in-a-vat argument was directed.

The internal skeptic I imagined argues that on the basis of our own beliefs about the brain, etc., it follows that we might all be brains in a vat. My reply has the following form. (1) I argue that many of us – perhaps most of us, nowadays – believe that there are causal constraints upon reference. Those constraints have roughly the following form: to refer to an object in the physical world, or to a physical property or relation, one must either have an appropriate kind of causal connection[70] to the object, property, or relation (where part of the "appropriateness" of the connection lies in its being a differential, or "information-carrying" connection; e.g. my causal connection to cats is such that whether I apply the word "cat," on occasions when I am using the word in what I intend to be a case of demonstrative reference, normally depends on the presence or absence of particular cats; my casual connection to the property of being *charged* is such that whether I apply the word, on occasions of the same kind, depends on whether the object I am demonstratively referring to is charged, etc.), or be able to describe what it is one intends to refer to in terms of objects, properties, and relations to which one does have such an appropriate causal connection. (For the purposes of the brain-in-a-vat argument, the weaker assumption that such constraints are satisfied when the word is originally acquired is sufficient.) (2) If we do accept this much about the nature of reference, then the internal skeptic cannot, in fact, show on the basis of premises we accept that we may be brains in a vat. (The details are well described by Wright, and I shall not repeat them here.)

Two further comments: first, what my argument shows is that this form of internal skepticism works against a certain kind of metaphysical realist, but it does not work against my sort of realism. Second, the key premise – that there are causal constraints on reference – is one which is accepted by a good many realists, including some of the most severe critics of my own "internal realism".[71]

Now, the skeptic may grant that I have given a valid argument from premises we accept, and reply by challenging our belief that there are causal constraints on reference. Perhaps we are wrong, and transcendent reference is possible, the skeptic might argue. But at this point my skeptical opponent has ceased to be an internal skeptic and has become an infinitely regressive skeptic. And of course one cannot "refute" infinitely regressive skepticism; but that was never my aim.

What is puzzling about the concluding section of Wright's paper is that it seems to waver between pointing out that infinitely regressive skepticism has still not been refuted, and attempting a reply on behalf of an internal skeptic. But if the latter is Wright's intention, it is not clear what the reply is.

Skepticism "in the Presence of a Plausible Externalism"

Still, Wright claims that the skeptical doubt he describes is one that one can still hold "in the presence of a plausible semantic externalism." Since "semantic externalism" is current philosophy-of-language jargon for the idea that meaning and reference are subject to causal constraints, it does seem that Wright wishes his doubt to be one that makes sense compatibly with the acceptance of the sorts of causal constraint on reference that I outlined above. But does it?

We cannot, of course, ask Wright to describe exactly what the envisaged state of affairs is supposed to be, for the whole point of the doubt that is described not being "akin to Ω-inconsistency" (although superficially resembling Ω-inconsistency) is that the envisaged state of affairs is supposed to be such that, if we are in it, then we cannot conceive of its exact nature. However, if we are supposed to be able to think that we are in some state of affairs of a very general kind – a "certain type of situation" – we have to be able to say *what* type of situation that is, even if "any instance of the type that we can conceptualize can be demonstrated not to obtain."

Wright's description of the type is this: "they are debarred from arriving at the concepts necessary to capture the most fundamental features of their world and their place in it." They lack any assurance that "[they] are on to the right categories in terms of which to depict the most general features of the world and [their] place in it." They are not able to "form concepts which reflect the real kinds that there are." How is this talk of "fundamental features of the world," "right categories," "real kinds," etc., to be cashed out?

One way might be this: we could consider the hypothesis that there are physical magnitudes such that, if we knew of the laws connecting those magnitudes with one another and familiar phenomena, we would say that we were as badly deceived as the brain-people in the brain-in-a-vat story. Obviously this will not do, because, if "semantic externalism" is accepted, we will not be able to conceive of the laws connecting these magnitudes with one another and with familiar phenomena if the hypothesis is true; but, following Wright's lead, we might reword the hypothesis thus: we are so situated that we are unable to conceive of the true laws governing the most fundamental physical magnitudes. Does this work?

I think it is quite clear that it will fail. Of course, it does not fail if it is intended as expressing a mere worry about the limits of human science; so understood, the hypothesis may well be true, but does not imply any radical skepticism. (Perhaps Martians could carry physics all the way to the most fundamental laws, but human cannot.) But to understand the hypothesis as a skeptical doubt, let us return to the brain-in-a-vat story, and see what goes wrong if the brain in a vat tries forming, not the hypothesis that it is a brain in a vat, but the vaguer hypothesis just described. The difficulty is that the notion of a "physical magnitude" is the notion of a magnitude that applies to bodies distributed in space,[72] one which governs the time evolution of their positions, momenta, energies, etc., according to causal laws. But the brains in a vat cannot refer to "space" (i.e. to spatial relations, such as being "in" a vat) as those relations are understood by the unenvatted. The unenvatted notion of "space" and the unenvatted notion of a "physical" magnitude are no more available to brains in a vat than are the specific notions "in" and "vat." On the other hand, in their sense of "physical," the brains in a vat are not disbarred from discovering what "physical" magnitudes there are and what laws they obey. And if we are in a position fully analogous to that of brains in a vat (even if we are unable to conceive of what that position specifically is), neither can we be assumed to have available a transcendental notion of a "physical" magnitude; for to assume that we do is just to assume that the property of being "physical" is not subject to the causal constraints which constitute semantic externalism. Of course, the skeptic *may* doubt semantic externalism; but then the skeptic is not playing the internalist game any longer.

Nor will it help to just drop the reference to physical laws and magnitudes. Even the hypothesis that "we are not able to conceive of the most fundamental causal laws" is subject to the same difficulty. For just as brains in a vat refer to something quite different than unenvatted beings when they use such a word as "physical," so do they refer to something quite different when they use such a word as "cause." Consider a paradigm case of causation in the brain-in-a-vat world; say a "fire" (involving, say "wood") "producing" "smoke." Even if we follow Davidson's sensible suggestion[73] (in line with "semantic externalism") and say that the brains in a vat are, unbeknownst to themselves, referring to processes, data, etc., in the computer when they employ vat English, still the relation between whatever in the computer corresponds to a brain's perceiving "fire" and what corresponds to the subsequent "smoke" need not be that the former causes the latter. Rather, we may plausibly imagine that the entire sequence is programmed to occur in that order when a Brain emits the appropriate electrical impulses. There is, indeed, a counter-factual supporting relation between "fires" (of certain "substances") and "smoke" in the brain-in-a-vat world; a relation that may be relied on, used to justify inference licences, etc., just as the relation of causation is relied on, used to justify inference licences, etc., among the unenvatted, but it is not the same relation. Brains in a vat can no more refer to what the unenvatted call "causation" than they can to what the unenvatted call "fire," for semantic externalists[74] insist that the causal constraints that apply to our reference to any physical relation apply to reference to causation itself. And if we are in a position fully analogous to that of brains in a vat (even if we are unable to conceive of what that position specifically is), we cannot be assumed to have available a transcendental notion of "causation;" for to assume that we do is just to assume that the relation of causation is not subject to the causal constraints which constitute semantic externalism. Again, the skeptic *may* doubt semantic externalism; but then the skeptic is not playing the internalist game any longer. (It is, perhaps, the vagueness of terms like "fundamental categories," "real kinds," etc., that conceals from Wright the fact that he is tacitly assuming conceptual access to such general notions as "physical" and "causation." But I take it that what we mean by "fundamental categories" and "real kinds" is kinds and categories that play a fundamental role in the description of physical things and their causal relations; if not, then I will ask Wright to give me an account *compatible with externalism* of how a being whose position is analogous to that of a brain in a vat could refer to the property of being "fundamental.")

In sum, Wright's ingenious attempt to formulate a skeptical hypothesis which (1) reinstates the "contingency" of the relation between a theory's meeting our highest cognitive standards and its being correct, which is the most prominent feature of metaphysical realism, and (2) can be held by an internal skeptic, is not successful. Just making the terms used in stating the doubt more abstract will not exempt them for the externalist constraints on which my brain-in-a-vat argument turns.

More on Metaphysical Realism

There is, however, another way of seeing the significance of the brain-in-a-vat argument for the argument against metaphysical realism.[75] If we grant that, as they understand the terms, the brains in a vat *can* describe "the fundamental physical laws," the "basic causal relations," etc., even though, if we were present in the same world, and interacted with the computer, the brains, etc., in our normal unenvatted way, we would give a very different description of the same events – say, describe them as sequences of data processes in a computer – then we are led to the thought that the notion of *how things are* makes no sense apart from the way in which we interact with those things. As John Dewey urged in *Experience and Nature* and elsewhere, all reference is transactional. We are not led to say, with Richard Rorty, that there is no such thing as correct description or truth, except in an emotive sense (truth is a "compliment" we pay to certain sentences, according to Rorty), but we are led to agree with Rorty that the idea of the mirror of nature – the language that is nature's own language, intrinsically, the language that is "correct" for reasons which have nothing to do with how we interact with nature, apart from how we are embedded in nature – makes no sense. And if (as I believe Dewey did) we succeed in remaining realists while giving up the idea of the Mirror of Nature, we will have become what I call "internal realists."

Notes

1　Cf., in particular, *Reason, Truth and History*; the Introduction and chs 11 and 12 in *Realism and Reason; Philosophical Papers*, vol. 3; the last chapter of

Representation and Reality; *The Many Faces of Realism*; and "Model Theory and the 'Factuality' of Semantics," in Alex George (ed.), *Reflections on Chomsky*.

2 For a history of this term, see the intellectual autobiography included in the first three of my replies in *The Philosophy of Hilary Putnam: Philosophical Topics*, (1992), vol. 20, Fayetteville, AR: University of Arkansas Press.

3 My reasons for giving it up are briefly stated in the replies cited in n. 2; a fuller account will appear in my forthcoming Dewey Lectures (to be published in *The Journal of Philosophy*, after they are given in the spring of 1994).

4 When I presented this view in *Reason, Truth and History*, I employed the fiction of "ideal epistemic conditions," but in spite of my warning that this was a fiction, many readers took it literally. For this reason, from then on I have used the notion of "sufficiently good" epistemic conditions, as above. Cf., for example, *Realism and Reason*, pp. xiii–xviii; and see n. 26 below.

5 An example whose truth, if it is true, may be totally recognition-transcendent (I would now say) is: "There do not happen to be any intelligent extraterrestials."

6 This conception of use, which is represented by Dumett's program for "meaning theory," by Rorty's references to normal discourse as governed by "criteria" and "algorithms," and, in a different way, by my former "functionalism," is criticized in detail in *Representation and Reality*. Not only is truth not always recognizable by using anything that could be called a decision procedure, even under the best epistemic conditions; it is obvious that, in the case of empirical statements, decisions as to truth are generally defeasable (and so are decisions as to whether one's epistemic position is good enough to decide on the truth of a statement).

7 The relation between the two claims is this: if truth depends on use, and the world does not dictate how we are to use our words (although it constrains our choices), then the possibility of the sort of "conceptually relativity" that is asserted by the second claim opens up.

8 This example is used both in *The Many Faces of Realism* (pp. 18–20), and in *Realism with a Human Face* (ch. 6, pp. 96–104).

9 I discuss the nature of such equivalence in "Equivalence" (ch. 2) of *Realism and Reason*.

10 This paragraph and the two that precede it are virtually identical with three paragraphs in my reply to a similar argument offered by Bill Throop and Catherine Doran (1991), "Putnam's Realism and Relativity; An Uneasy Balance," *Erkenntnis*, 34, 3, 357–70. See my "Replies and Comments," *Erkenntnis*, 34, 3, 401–24.

11 That these sorts of statement are normally not translated when we have a case of two equivalent descriptions which are "extensionally isomorphic" was first pointed out by Nelson Goodman (1951), *The Structure of Appearance*, Cambridge, MA: Harvard University Press.

12 As I put this point in *Representation and Reality* (pp. 112–13), "It is known since *Principia Mathematica* that we can identify points with sets of convergent spheres and all geometric facts will be correctly represented. We know that we can also take points as primitive, and identify spheres with sets of points. So

any answer to this question ['Is a point identical with a set of spheres that converge to it?'] is . . . conventional, in the sense that one is free to do either. But what Quine pointed out (as applied to this case) is that when I say 'We are free to do either,' I am assuming a diffuse background of empirical facts. Fundamental changes in the way we do physical geometry could alter the whole picture. The fact that a truth is towards the 'conventional' end of the convention–fact continuum does not mean that it is *absolutely* conventional – a truth by stipulation, free of every element of fact. And, on the other hand, when we see such a 'reality' as a tree, the possibility of the perception is dependent on a whole conceptual scheme in place (one which may or may not legislate an answer to such questions as 'Is the tree identical with the space–time region that contains it?' . . .) What is factual and what is conventional is a matter of degree."

13   What Blackburn means by saying that arithmetic is "not concerned with numbers at all" is that – in a reconstruction first proposed by Paul Benacerraf and, I take it, endorsed by Blackburn here – we can construe the statements of pure arithmetic as statements about infinite sequences ("ω-sequences"). A statement of applied mathematics, e.g. "The Jewish Patriarchs are four," is then reconstrued as asserting a relation between the set in question (the set of Jewish Patriarchs) and members of each ω-sequence. Cf. Paul Benacerraf, "What Numbers Could Not Be," in P. Benacerraf and H. Putnam (eds) (1983), *Philosophy of Mathematics; Selected Readings*, Cambridge: Cambridge University Press pp. 272–94.

14   (1984), Oxford: Clarendon Press.

15   Ibid., pp. 208–9.

16   I discuss the relation between Quine's model-theoretic arguments and my own model-theoretic arguments in "Model Theory and the 'Factuality' of Semantics."

17   This is a rather unhappy sense of "determine," even in physics, by the way, since, given general relativity, it is the case that electromagnetic facts are supervenient on gravitational facts – no change in the electromagnetic facts without a change in gravitational facts – without its being the case that the electromagnetic facts are explained by the gravitational facts.

18   I say "allegedly" non-intentional facts because I myself believe that the notion of seeing something is an intentional notion. Quine's often-criticized notion of "stimulus meaning" is, of course, an attempt to dodge this very issue. If facts about "seeing" are not included in the base totality, then it is unclear why Blackburn wants to claim that "Quine appears to put into the base totality everything we could possibly want in order to determine reference and meaning." A quite different reason why one might wonder about whether the facts in the base totality really are "non-intentional" is that the most fundamental physical theory we have – quantum mechanics – employs the intentional notion of *registration of information* in a way which no one has to date succeeded in eliminating.

19   Cf. *Reason, Truth and History*, pp. 34–5.

20 Thus I would now reject the claim that I made in *Realism and Reason* (p. 225) that intentional relations are not "in the world." ("If the materialist cannot define reference, he can, of course, just take it as *primitive*. But reference, like causality, is a flexible, interest-dependent notion: what we count as referring to something depends on background knowledge and our willingness to be charitable in interpretation. To read a relation so deeply human and so pervasively intentional into the world and to call the resulting metaphysical picture satisfactory (never mind whether or not it is 'materialist') is absurd.") Today I would say that the interest relativity of ascriptions of reference (and causality) shows that there are alternative right descriptions of the world with respect to reference (and causality), but not that reference (and causality) are "not in the world." What is absurd is absolutizing any one of the alternative right descriptions.

21 E.g. in "A Defense of Internal Realism" (reprinted in *Realism with a Human Face*, pp. 30–42) and "Model Theory and the 'Factuality' of Semantics." Note that as far back as *Realism and Reason*, I wrote (p. ix), "[The model-theoretic argument] is not an attempt to *solve* this problem (how the 'correspondence') is fixed) but rather a verification that the problem really exists."

22 P. 37.

23 Cf. pp. 3–17 of the title essay of *Realism with a Human Face*.

24 On this, see "Vagueness and Alternative Logic." Notice also the enormous weight given to examples of vagueness ("Stand roughly here") in the early sections of Wittgenstein's *Investigations*. Note that it is not trivial, from *any* point of view, to argue that vague language is "dispensable" in the description of reality.

25 The metaphor of "perspectives" is, of course, Blackburn's, not mine, and it begs just the points at issue. There are ways of describing a physical object other than describing its appearance from a visual perspective; referring to alternative conceptual schemes as "perspectives," of course, makes it sound as if there must be ways of describing the world as it is apart from the descriptions. This is just the disastrous Kantian error that we need to avoid.

26 By an "ideal," or better, a sufficiently good, epistemic situation I meant something like this: if I say "There is a chair in my study," the ideal epistemic situation would be for me to be in my study, with the lights on or with daylight streaming in through the windows, with nothing wrong with my eyesight, with an unconfused mind, without having taken drugs or being subjected to hypnosis, etc., and look to see if there is a chair there. Being at or near the end of "completed science" tens of thousands (billions?) of years in the future would not help; indeed, by that time, no one will know that I existed, or that there was a study there.

27 "William James Ideas" (with Ruth Anna Putnam) reprinted in my *Realism with a Human Face*, pp. 222–3.

28 I am, of course, aware that there are cases in which it is indeterminate whether or not someone was shaved, but such cases are sufficiently rare to justify the belief that there is a fact of the matter in the case of Caesar on the day in

question. (I am by no means wedded to universal bivalence – on that question, see my "Vaguesness and Alternative Logics," in *Philosophical Papers*, vol. 3; *Realism and Reason.*)

29   *Philosophical Investigations*, IIxi, 227–8.

30   I am quoting from Richard Rorty's "Putnam and the Relativist Menace," unpublished.

31   I shall discuss this issue (and defend the view that truth is sometimes recognition transcendent) in my forthcoming Dewey Lectures (to be published in *The Journal of Philosophy*, after they are given in the spring of 1994).

32   In my forthcoming *Renewing Philosophy; The Gifford Lectures, 1990*, Cambridge, MA: Harvard University Press, I argue that Wittgenstein is *not* proposing a "non-cognitivist" account of religious belief in those lectures.

33   *Culture and Value*, p. 83.

34   In my (1978) *Meaning and the Moral Sciences*. Boston, London and Henley: Routledge and Kegan Paul, pp. 123–40.

35   For simplicity, I consider only the permutation of individuals argument; a similar reformulation can be constructed for at least some of the other model-theoretic arguments, I believe.

36   I have reformulated REF so that a general term bears REF to each *member* of its extension, not to the extension – the set – itself. The reason, of course, is that this metaphysical realist does not believe sets theory-independently exist. To be careful, one should also construe general terms as tokens, not types, in this argument.

37   Hartry Field (1980), *Science Without Numbers*, Oxford: Blackwell, and Princeton NJ: Princeton Unversity Press, does not solve this problem because, for one thing, it does not show how to eliminate quantification over functions and other mathematical objects in quantum mechanics – and the problem has nothing to do with the difficulty of interpreting quantum mechanics; it is just as bad for any of the hidden variable theories which have been proposed, and some of these have unproblematic interpretations.

38   (1991), "Replies and Comments," in the Special Issue on Putnam's Philosophy of *Erkenntnis*, 34, 3, 122–3.

39   I am aware that we sometimes identify sentences with abstract entities, e.g. their Gödel numbers. But to take this seriously as metaphysics is nonsense.

40   I want to acknowledge the stimulation that I have received from David Albert, with whom I have been discussing these questions since 1987; he is, of course, not in any way responsible for the present document. More recent discussions with Greg Jaeger, who still wishes to defend some form of perspectivalism, have also been extremely valuable, even if we have been unable to convince each other!

41   J. von Neumann, (1955), *Mathematical Foundations of Quantum Mechanics*. Princeton, NJ: Princeton University Press.

42   See also G. Birkhoff, and J. von Neumann, (1936), "The Logic of Quantum Mechanics," *Annals of Mathematics*, 37, 823–43.

43   That is, the state predicted by the Schrödinger equation, ignoring any possible collapse of the ψ-function.

44 In the continuous case, the summation would, of course, be replaced by an integral.

45 Cf. "Quantum Mechanics and the Observer," 253–5.

46 Let me say that I recognize that there will be those who interpret von Neumann differently. However, I do not see any possible way of making sense of the notion that the cut between the observer and the system, and the collapse of the wave packet, can be put in a number of different places other than a perspectival one unless one supposes (1) that von Neumann was just making an epistemic point (we cannot tell where the cut "really" is, but there is a fact of the matter); or (2) that von Neumann thought it was really consciousness that causes the collapse, and that we need to put the "cut" elsewhere because we cannot handle consciousness in physics. Neither of these interpretations seems to me to fit the text as well as the one I propose.

47 In my paper I divided only the emulsion, not the whole space, into regions, since the only two possibilities at t_1 are (1) the particle has hit the emulsion somewhere; and (2) the particle stayed in the box. It is easy to rewrite the above argument using cells which partition the whole (finite) region of space involved, as Redhead does.

48 "Putnam now claims that *in virtue* of knowing P_k^{out} [knowing the particle hit the kth region] we also know that the particle is outside the box and this (says Putnam) means knowing the value of

$$P \mid \psi_{out} \rangle$$

[the system is in the state $\mid \psi_{out} \rangle$] which of course does not commute with P_k^{out}."

49 Redhead's claim that "Putnam's mistake [*sic*] boils down to claiming:

$$P_k^{out} \to P \mid \psi_{out} \rangle"$$

(claiming, that is, that the proposition P_k^{out} *entails* the proposition

$$P \mid \psi_{out} \rangle$$

– "$\to$" is Redhead's symbol for entailment) is thus quite unwarranted; Redhead fails to see that what is involved is an unconventional (but admissible) *collapse* of the ψ-function from the state $\psi = k_1 \mid \psi_{out} \rangle + k_2 \mid \psi_{in} \rangle$ to the state $\mid \psi_{out} \rangle$ after the measurement of $U' = 1$. The "mistaken assumption that one can equate

$$P \mid \psi_{out} \rangle = P(\Sigma P_{out}^i > \mid \psi \rangle$$

with

$$\Sigma P_i^{out}"$$

(i.e. equate the proposition

$$P \mid \psi_{out} \rangle$$

with the disjunctive proposition "$|\psi_{out}^1\rangle$ *or* $|\psi_{out}^2\rangle$ *or* $|\psi_{out}^3\rangle$ *or* ...") was certainly *not* made.

50 Cf. M. Friedman and H. Putnam (1978), "Quantum Logic, Conditional Probability and Interference," *Dialectica*, 32, 305–15.

51 See, for example, my (1981), "Answer to a Question from Nancy Cartwright," *Erkenntnis*, 16, 3, 407–10, and David Albert (1982), "On Quantum Mechanical Automata," *Physics Letters*, 98A, 249–52, and (1987), "A Quantum Mechanical Automaton," *Philosophy of Science*, 54, 577–85.

52 Since, if we let $|\psi_{B+}\rangle = \frac{1}{\sqrt{2}}(|\psi_{tickled\ cat}\rangle + |\psi_{not\ tickled\ cat}\rangle)$ and $|\psi_{B-}\rangle = \frac{1}{\sqrt{2}}(|\psi_{tickled\ cat}\rangle - |\psi_{not\ tickled\ cat}\rangle)$, we can write $|\psi_{tickled\ cat}\rangle = \frac{1}{\sqrt{2}}(|\psi_{B+}\rangle + |\psi_{B-}\rangle)$. Since $|\psi_{B+}\rangle$ is the eigenstate of B corresponding to the eigenvalue B = 1 and $\rangle$ $|\psi_{B-}\rangle$ is the eigenstate of B corresponding to the eigenvalue B = 0, it follows that the probability with which B = 1 will be observed if a B measurement is performed on a system in the state $|\psi_{stickled\ cat}\rangle$ is $\frac{1}{2}$. (A similar argument shows that the probability is also $\frac{1}{2}$ in the state $|\psi_{not\ tickled\ cat}\rangle$.)

53 At one time Wigner, who was influenced by von Neumann, argued that a variant of this perspective, in which it is always a consciousness that reduces the wave packet, is not just admissible, but is *the* metaphysically correct account.

54 If the "cat" is a human scientist, then if at the preset time *t* he or she registers the information that he or she has not been tickled (or else feels the tickle), he or she must treat a "measurement" as having taken place, since otherwise the "cat's" description would not include a fact he or she knows.

55 J. Bub, (forthcoming), "A Quantum Logical Solution to the Measurement Problem of Quantum Mechanics," in *Proceedings of "Quantum Logics: Gdansk '90,"* a conference on quantum logics held in Gdansk, Poland, September 1990.

56 Cartwright raised this difficulty at a conference; I summarize the difficulty and attempt to answer it in the paper cited in n. 57.

57 Cf. my "Answer to a Question from Nancy Cartwright."

58 Unless we can suppose that "cats" sometimes observe external observers observing B = 0 even though no external observer does observe B = 0. But if we can suppose this, so can the cat; and then the cat is plainly supposing something contradictory.

59 David Albert has pointed out that such information can be communicated to the "cat" without preventing the possibility of a repeat of essentially the same experiment. David Albert and I will go into the details in a forthcoming paper.

60 G. Lüders, (1951), "Über die Zustandsänderung durch den Messprozess," *Annalen der Physik*, 8, 322–8.

61 Possibly on the basis of previous B measurements, whose results have been fed back to it (cf. n. 56).

62 I briefly recapitulate the view of that paper in the closing section of the present part of this chapter.

63 From here on, I do not distinguish in the notation between *S* and its name.

64 This will happen if *p* is not quantum-mechanically "compatible" with either *q* or *r*.

65 Indeed, the Kochen and Specker proof of the non-existence of a valuation

satisfying the admissibility criterion (cf. their (1967) "The Problem of Hidden Variables in Quantum Mechanics," *Journal of Mathematics and Mechanics*, 17, 549–87) gives an example of 117 quantum-mechanical propositions about a specific quantum-mechanical system such that if one explicitly guesses the truth-value of each one in any way at all, then one will falsify a statement which is true on the quantum-logical interpretation. If one sticks to the "realist" quantum-logical interpretation of "Is Logic Empirical?" one will have to say, "Well, our guesses – and the corresponding processes in our brains – form a Boolean subalgebra, and a being whose brain is Boolean in this way cannot hope to visualize a non-Boolean world." But this is to admit that even in this completely finite case we cannot – even in our imagination – give a complete description of what is going on, if we accept the quantum-logical interpretation. And this is *disanalogous* to what happens when we go from Euclidean to non-Euclidean geometry.

66 "Carnap is open to considering *whatever is offered* by way of clarification," Ricketts writes (emphasis added).

67 (1955), "Meaning and Synonymy in Natural Languages," *Philosophical Studies*, 6, 33–47.

68 "The Meaning of 'Meaning'," reprinted in my *Mind, Language and Reality*, p. 228.

69 Obviously internal skeptics may be, and traditionally have been, skeptics about other sorts of knowledge as well, but I speak only of knowledge about the empirical world here, because that is the only kind of knowledge that my brain-in-a-vat argument concerns.

70 Note that I do *not* claim that the notion of an appropriate kind of causal connection can be spelled out without employing the notion of reference and other intentional notions. Thus the position that there are causal constraints on reference does not imply that reference can be reduced to causality.

71 Cf. my reply to Blackburn for an account of "internal realism." Among the critics of my position who accept the existence of causal constraints on reference are Richard Boyd, Michael Devitt, Clark Glymour, and, perhaps, Blackburn himself.

72 To be sure the space may be a more general space than ordinary 3-space; e.g. Hilbert space, or the space of supergravitation theory; but these more general spaces are explained by relating them to ordinary space.

73 In (1986), "A Coherence Theory of Truth and Knowledge," in E. Lepore (ed.), *Truth and Interpretation*, Oxford: Basil Blackwell, pp. 307–19.

74 Indeed, this doctrine of externalism has often been thought (mistakenly in my view) to be a way of refuting my own "model-theoretic" arguments against metaphysical realism. Michael Devitt, Clark Glymour, and Richard Boyd have all repeatedly insisted that the words "causal connection" are "attached to causal connection by causal connection," and that that is what makes it possible for us to refer to causal connection. I am not here making an ad hoc extension of externalism for dialectical purposes, but appealing to a feature which opponents as well as proponents of internal realism recognize to be characteristic of "semantic externalism."

75 I owe thanks to Garry Ebbs for pointing this out to me.

Select Bibliography of the Publications of Hilary Putnam

(1954a): "Synonymity and the analysis of belief sentences," *Analysis*, 14, pp. 114–22.

(1954b): "A definition of degree of confirmation for very rich languages," *Philosophy of Science*, 23, pp. 58–62.

(1957): "Decidability and essential undecidability," *Journal of Symbolic Logic*, 22, pp. 39–54.

(1957b): "Psychological concepts, explication and ordinary language", *The Journal of Philosophy*, 54, pp. 94–9.

(1957c): "Three-valued logic," *Philosophical Studies*, 8, pp. 73–80.

(1958): (with Martin Davies): "Reductions of Hilbert's tenth problem", *Journal of Symbolic Logic*, 23, pp. 183–7.

(1960a): "An unsolvable problem in number theory," *Journal of Symbolic Logic*, 25, pp. 220–32.

(1960b): "Minds and machines," in Sidney Hook (ed) *Dimensions of Mind* (SUNY Press, New York), pp. 362–85.

(1961a): (with Martin Davis and Julia Robinson): "The decision problem for exponential Diophantine equations," *Annals of Mathematics*, 74, pp. 425–36.

(1961b): "Comments on the paper of David Sharp: the Einstein–Podolsky–Rosen Paradox re-examined," *Philosophy of Science*, 28, pp. 234–9.

(1962a): "Dreaming and 'depth grammar'," in R.J. Butler (ed) *Analytical Philosophy* (Basil Blackwell, Oxford), pp. 304–24.

(1962b): "It ain't necessarily so," *Journal of Philosophy*, 59, pp. 658–70.

(1962c): "What theories are not" in E. Nagel, P. Suppes and A. Tarski (eds) *Logic, Methodology and Philosophy of Science* (Stanford University Press, Stanford), pp. 215–27.

(1963a): "A note on constructible sets of integers," *Notre Dame Journal of Formal Logic*, 4, pp. 270–3.

(1963b): "An examination of Grünbaum's philosophy of space and time," in B. Baumrin (ed) *Delaware Seminar in the Philosophy of Science*, 2, (Interscience, New York) pp. 93–129.

(1963c): " 'Degree of confirmation' and inductive logic," in P.A. Schilpp (ed) *The Philosophy of Rudolf Carnap* (Open Court, LaSalle), pp. 270–92.

(1964a): "Robots: machines or artificially created life?," *Journal of Philosophy*, 61, pp. 668–91.

(1964b): (with Paul Benacerraf) (eds): *Philosophy of Mathematics, Selected Readings* (Prentice Hall, New Jersey).

(1965a): "A philosopher looks at quantum mechanics," in Robert G. Goldony (ed) *Beyond the Edge of Certainty: Essays in Contemporary Science and Philosophy* (Prentice Hall, New Jersey), pp. 130–58.

(1965b): "Craig's theorem," *The Journal of Philosophy*, 62, pp. 251–9.

(1965c): "Trial and error predicates and the solution to a problem of Mostowski," *Journal of Symbolic Logic*, 30, pp. 49–57.

(1965d): (with Gustav Hensel) "On the notational independence of various hierarchies of degrees of unsolvability," *Journal of Symbolic Logic*, 30, pp. 69–86.

(1965e): (with J.S. Ullian) "More about 'about'," *The Journal of Philosophy*, 62, pp. 305–10.

(1967a): "Mathematics without foundations," *The Journal of Philosophy*, 64, pp. 5–22.

(1967b): "The thesis that mathematics is logic," in R. Schoeman (ed) *Bertrand Russell, Philosopher of the Century* (Allen & Unwin, London).

(1967c): "Time and physical geometry," *The Journal of Philosophy*, 64, pp. 240–7.

(1967d): (with Burton Dreben) "The Craig interpolation lemma," *Notre Dame Journal of Formal Logic*, 8, pp. 229–33.

(1968): "Is logic empirical?," in R. Cohen & M. Wartowski (eds) *Boston Studies in the Philosophy of Science*, vol. 5 (D. Reidel, Dordrecht).

(1969a): "On properties" in N. Rescher (ed) *Essays in Honor of Carl Hempel* (D. Reidel, Dordrecht).

(1969b): (with H.B. Enderton): "A note on the hyperarithmetical hierarchy," *Journal of Symbolic Logic*, 35, pp. 429–30.

(1971): *Philosophy of Logic* (Harper & Row, New York).

(1973): "Meaning and reference," *Journal of Philosophy*, 70, pp. 699–711.

(1974a): "How to think quantum logically," *Synthese*, 29, pp. 55–61.

(1974b): "The 'corroboration' of theories," in P.A. Schilpp (ed) *The Philosophy of Karl Popper*, vol. 2 (Open Court, La Salle).

(1974c): "The refutation of conventionalism," *Nous*, 8, pp. 25–40.

(1974d): (with Joan Lukas): "Systems of notations and the ramified analytical hierarchy," *Journal of Symbolic Logic*, 39, pp. 243–53.

(1975a): *Mathematics, Matter and Method: Philosophical Papers, Volume I* (Cambridge University Press, Cambridge and New York).

(1975b): *Mind, Language and Reality: Philosophical Papers, Volume II* (Cambridge University Press, Cambridge and New York).

(1975c): "The meaning of 'meaning'," in K. Gunderson (ed) *Language, Mind and Knowledge, Minnesota Studies in the Philosophy of Science, Volume VII* (University of Minnesota Press, Minneapolis).

(1975d): "What is 'Realism'?," *Proceedings of the Aristotelian Society*, 76, pp. 177–94.

(1976): "Two dogmas revisited," in G. Ryle (ed) *Contemporary Aspects of Philosophy* (Oriel Press, London), pp. 202–13.

(1977a): "A Note on 'progress' ," *Erkenntnis*, 11, pp. 1–4.

(1977b): "Realism and reason," *Proceedings of the American Philosophical Association*, 50, pp. 483–98.

(1978a): *Meaning and the Moral Sciences* (Routledge & Kegan Paul, London & Boston).

(1978b): "There is at least one 'a priori' truth," *Erkenntnis*, 13, pp. 153–70.

(1978c): (with Michael Friedman): "Quantum logic, conditional probability and interference," *Dialectica*, 32, pp. 305–15.

(1979a): "Analyticity and apriority: beyond Wittgenstein and Quine," in P. French (ed) *Midwest Studies in Philosophy*, 4, pp. 423–41.

(1979b): "Empirical realism and other minds," *Philosophical Investigations*, 2, pp. 71–2.

(1979c): "Reflections on Goodman's *Ways of Worldmaking*," *The Journal of Philosophy*, 76, pp. 603–18.

(1979d): "The place of facts in a world of values," in D. Huff and O. Prewett (eds) *The Nature of the Physical Universe: 1976 Nobel Conference* (John Wiley & Sons, New York).

(1980): "Models and reality," *Journal of Symbolic Logic*, 45, pp. 464–82.

(1981a): *Reason, Truth and History* (Cambridge University Press, Cambridge and New York).

(1981b): "Quantum mechanics and the observer," *Erkenntnis*, 16, pp. 193–219.

(1982a): "Peirce the logician," *Historica Mathematics*, 9, pp. 290–331.

(1982b): "Three kinds of scientific realism," *The Philosophical Quarterly*, 32, pp. 195–200.

(1982c): "Why reason can't be naturalised," *Synthese*, 52, pp. 3–24.

(1982d): "Why there isn't a ready-made world," *Synthese*, 51, pp. 141–68.

(1983a): (with Paul Benacerraf) (eds) *Philosophy of Mathematics: Selected Readings* (Cambridge University Press, Cambridge & New York).

(1983b): *Realism and Reason, Philosophical Papers, Volume III* (Cambridge University Press, Cambridge & New York).

(1983c): "On truth," in S. Cauman (ed) *How Many Questions: Essays in Honor of Sidney Morgenhesser* (Hackett, Indianapolis) pp. 35–56.

(1984): "Is the causal structure of the physical itself something physical?," in A. French, T.E. Uehling & H.K. Wettstein (eds) *Midwest Studies in Philosophy*, 9, pp. 3–16.

(1985a): (with W.K. Essler and W. Stegmüller) *Epistemology, Methodology and Philosophy of Science: Essays in Honor of C.G. Hempel on the Occasion of his 80th Birthday* (Reidel, Dordrecht).

(1985b): "A quick read is a wrong wright," *Analysis*, 45, p. 203.

(1985c): "After empiricism," in J. Rajchman and C. West (eds) *Post Analytic Philosophy* (Columbia University Press, New York), pp. 20–30.

(1985d): "Reflective reflections," *Erkenntnis*, 22, pp. 143–54.

(1986a):　"Computational psychology and interpretation theory", in S. Pylyshyn and W. Demopoulos (eds) *Meaning and Cognitive Structure: Issues in the Computational Theory of Mind* (Ablex, New Jersey) pp. 101–16.

(1986b):　"Information and the mental," in B. Lepore and J. Leplin (eds) *Truth and Interpretation: Perspectives on the Philosophy of Donald Davidson* (Basil Blackwell, Oxford).

(1986c):　"Meaning and our mental life," in E. Ullman-Margalit (ed) *The Kaleidoscope of Science* (D. Reidel, Dordrecht), pp. 17–32.

(1986d):　"Meaning holism," in L. Hahn and P.A. Schilpp (eds) *The Philosophy of W.V. Quine* (Open Court, La Salle), pp. 405–31.

(1987):　*The Many Faces of Realism (The Paul Carus Lectures, 1985)* (Open Court, La Salle).

(1988):　*Representation and Reality* (MIT Press, Cambridge and London).

(1989a):　"Model theory and the 'factuality' of semantics," in A. George (ed) *Reflections on Chomsky* (Oxford University Press, Oxford), pp. 213–32.

(1989b):　(with Ruth-Anna Putnam) "William James's ideas," *Raritan*, 8, pp. 17–44.

(1990a):　*The Meaning of the Concept of Probability in Application to Finite Sequences*, Ph.D. thesis, University of California, Los Angeles, 1951. (Garland, New York and London).

(1990b):　*Realism with a Human Face* (edited by James Conant) (Harvard University Press, Cambridge and London).

(1990c):　(with Ruth-Anna Putnam) "Dewey's logic: epistemology as hypothesis," Transactions of the C.S. Pierce Society, 26, pp. 407–34.

(1991a):　"Does the disquotational theory really solve all philosophical problems?," *Metaphilosophy*, 22, pp. 1–13.

(1991b):　"Logical positivism and intentionality," *Philosophy*, 30, pp. 105–16.

(1991c):　"Philosophical reminiscences with reflections on Firth's work," *Philosophy and Phenomenological Research*, vol. 51, pp. 143–7.

(1991d):　"Reichenbach's metaphysical picture," *Erkenntnis*, 35, pp. 61–75.

(1992a):　*Renewing Philosophy* (The Gifford Lectures in the University of St Andrews) (Harvard University Press, Cambridge and London).

(1992b):　"Replies to 'The Philosophy of Hilary Putnam'," *Philosophical Topics*, 20, pp. 347–408.

(1994):　*Words and Life* (Harvard University Press, Cambridge and London).

Index of Names

Note: because reference to Hilary Putnam occurs so frequently throughout the volume there is no listing for him in this index.

Feyerabend, P.K., 144
Field, H., 36, 255, 292
Frege, G., 3, 4, 10, 31, 41, 45, 46, 61,
182–4, 187, 206, 207, 209, 282
Friedman, M., 9, 168, 174, 175, 197,
270, 276, 294

Gardner, M., 167
Geach, P., 202
Gentzen, G., 91
George, A., 289
Gibbard, A., 221, 222, 223, 241
Gibbins, P., 168
Gifford, Lord, 11
Glymour, C., vi, 7, 98, 147, 295
Gödel, K., 9, 76, 80, 84, 88, 91, 128,
179, 180, 192, 193, 277, 292
Gold, M., 7, 113, 117
Goldfarb, W., 94, 197
Goodman, N., 204, 257, 289
Gross, S., 197

Hale, R., 1, 11, 241
Hallett, M., vii, 5, 6, 66, 262–5
Hamilton, W.R., 48
Hanson, R., 137, 148
Hilbert, D., 3, 89, 90, 91, 92, 186, 193
Husserl, E., 206, 209

James, W., 253, 257
Juhl, C., vii, 7, 98

Kant, I., 12, 13, 62, 133, 134, 146, 177,
183, 184, 250, 282
Kelly, K., vii, 7, 98, 147
Kemeny, J., 104
Kleene, S.C., 117, 277
Kochen, S., 168, 294, 295
Kreisel, G., 277
Kripke, S., 13, 22, 26, 30, 214, 250
Kuhn, T., 136, 137, 139, 140, 148
Kunen, K., 93

Leibniz, W., 213, 217
Lewis, D., 28, 30, 36, 93, 250
Locke, J., 201

Löwenheim, L., 69, 73
Luders, G., 274, 294

McDowell, J., 26, 214, 252, 282
McGinn, C., 26
Machover, M., 93
Makkai, M., 92
Marx, K., 135, 137
Matiyasevich, Y., 3
Mill, J.S., 201
Minar, E., 197

Neurath, O., 189
Noether, E., 93

Paris, J., 152
Parsons, C., 31, 36
Pearson, D., 168
Peirce, C.S., 3, 33, 39, 40, 124, 125,
126, 257
Plato, 113, 117
Poincaré, H., 85, 86, 87, 88, 93, 193
Popper, K.R., 116
Putnam, R.A., 291

Quine, W.V.O., 3, 13, 21–7, 30, 31, 38,
39, 51, 81, 136, 139, 140, 148, 205,
247, 248, 250, 251, 290

Redhead, M., vii, 8, 161, 164, 166,
266–80, 293
Reichenbach, H., 110, 163, 206
Richard, J., 86
Ricketts, T., viii, 8, 9, 176, 280–1, 295
Robinson, J., 3
Rorty, R., 150, 289
Russell, B., 82, 83, 85, 86, 88, 93, 177,
185

Schlick, M., 177
Schrödinger, E., 266, 271
Searle, J., 26
Sebestik, J., 48
Seidenfeld, T., 152, 156
Seig, W., 152, 156
Sisyphus, 149, 150